Praise for *Across Black Spaces*

Across Black Spaces is a path-breaking volume of essays and interviews by one of the top African American philosophers. It is a masterful work, full of vivid writing, definitive analyses, and sharp critiques of domination. Yancy is clearly the leading philosopher and critic of race and racism in the nation. I predict that this highly learned work with its wit and genius will transform our perception of what is possible in a racialized society. Yancy's work is magnificent and in some places truly revolutionary.

—**Molefi Kete Asante**, professor and chair,
Department of Africology, Temple University,
author of *The History of Africa*

Across Black Spaces is an opportunity for both those who know George Yancy's vast opus and new readers to encounter a distillation of his leading themes and reflections. Yancy is now one of our great public intellectuals and this collection of essays and interviews is an inspiring introduction to the realities of black experience in the United States.

—**Naomi Zack**, professor of philosophy,
Lehman College, CUNY

This collection features George Yancy at his best. Yancy is fearless in his quest to ground philosophy in lived experience that is both fully human and Black.

—**Shannon Sullivan**, author of *Good White People:
The Problem of Middle-Class White Anti-Racism*

By revealing Yancy's own experiences as a Black man, *Across Black Spaces* offers us a mirror in which to see our own. This is an essential resource in helping us do so.

—**Todd May**, Class of 1941 Memorial
Professor of the Humanities, Clemson University

With a keen eye looking beyond the academy, George Yancy provides a treasure trove of deep insights into white-racist realities from his own and others' Black experience. A leading global philosopher whose honest critical-racism writings have led to white death threats, he offers a panoply of life-hardened understandings for building a truly democratic America and, indeed, planet earth.

—**Joe Feagin**, Distinguished Professor, Texas A&M
University, and author of *Racist America*

In *Across Black Spaces* George Yancy speaks his powerful and righteous truth on the life and death question of what it means to be Black in the USA of 2020. The most powerful philosophical work illuminates everyday experience and Yancy brilliantly grounds his analysis in realities of contemporary Black experience. Fired by a consciousness of the limits to our time on earth, Yancy has no time to display philosophical erudition for its own sake. His work will disturb, provoke, and move you.

—**Stephen Brookfield**, John Ireland Endowed
Chair, University of St. Thomas, Minneapolis–St. Paul

Bold, brave, and bracing. This welcome compilation of George Yancy's widely published work forcefully weaves together indictments of white supremacy, tributes to courageous builders of resistance to its violence, and reflections on the role of Black philosophy in deepening our understanding of what philosophy is and does. Exploring with many interlocutors the rich cultural spaces African Americans have created and sustained in the face of the terrors of white supremacy, Yancy helps us see just how African American philosophy, and by extension, the activity of philosophy more generally, arise out of the complex lived spaces to which they are a response.

—**Elizabeth V. Spelman**, Smith College

For years, George Yancy has been a truth-telling voice of courage, wisdom, and attempted reconciliation in the racially polarized public sphere. At a time when racial issues have become more central than in decades to the national conversation, his philosophical insight is needed more than ever before. This invaluable collection of articles, interviews, sketches of pioneering black thinkers, and autobiographical reflections, will provide, for those who do not yet know him, a wonderful introduction to his work.

—**Charles W. Mills**, Distinguished Professor of
Philosophy, The Graduate Center, CUNY

Speaking one's truth has been indicative of many efforts to transgress the dehumanizing epistemic and existential boundaries imposed on black being by virtue of various vicious construals of black embodiment as somehow bereft of the sensitivities and sensibilities of full human subjectivity. Here in *Across Black Spaces*, George Yancy splendidly joins, converses with, and commends a chorus of black figures who traverse the borders of disciplinary domains and genres in ways that exemplify and bear witness to the expansive terrain of critical black thought.

—**A. Todd Franklin**, Christian A. Johnson
Professor of Philosophy and Africana Studies, Hamilton College

Across Black Spaces

Across Black Spaces

Essays and Interviews from an American Philosopher

George Yancy

ROWMAN & LITTLEFIELD
Lanham • Boulder • New York • London

Published by Rowman & Littlefield

An imprint of The Rowman & Littlefield Publishing Group, Inc.
4501 Forbes Boulevard, Suite 200, Lanham, Maryland 20706
www.rowman.com
6 Tinworth Street, London SE11 5AL, United Kingdom

British Library Cataloguing in Publication Information Available

Library of Congress Cataloging-in-Publication Data
Library of Congress Control Number: 2019956636

ISBN: 978-1-5381-3161-9 (cloth : alk. paper)
ISBN: 978-1-5381-3162-6 (pbk. : alk. paper)
ISBN: 978-1-5381-3163-3 (electronic)

™
∞ The paper used in this publication meets the minimum requirements of American National Standard for Information Sciences—Permanence of Paper for Printed Library Materials, ANSI/NISO Z39.48-1992.

Dedicated to all people who dwell lovingly within
Black Spaces

Contents

Acknowledgments

I would like to thank Natalie Mandziuk, my editor at Rowman & Littlefield, for her sustained enthusiasm for publishing my philosophical work. She is a superb editor to work with. To another brilliant editor of mine, Emma Clements, thanks for being so flexible with my schedule. And thanks for your thoroughness when it comes to looking over my work. I'm so thankful for your incredible editorial oversight on this book and others. Thanks to Rose Oliveira, Linda Lear Special Collections Librarian at Connecticut College, for bringing to my attention an important letter written by Joyce Mitchell Cook. I would also like to thank the scholars who engaged with me in the conversational pieces that appear within this book. It is through your engaging questions that my thoughts are called forth. In this regard, I would like to thank H. A. Nethery, Azuka Nzegwu, Maria del Guadalupe Davidson, Brad Evans, Alex Blasdel, and Scott Jaschik. Thanks for creating a fecund dialogical space where two souls are able to meet and take part in the magic of shared language. Within this context, I would like to thank Anita Allen for her continued support. Anita is not only a brilliant philosopher, but an enviable, diligent, and outstanding academic administrator. I am honored to be her friend and colleague. She has always been there when I needed her. I'm indebted. I would also like to thank Simon Critchley and Peter Catapano. Both Simon and Peter are thanked for amplifying so many voices that engage the timely and timeless issues within philosophy. They have effectively integrated philosophy within the context of a critical demos. Thanks to both of them for making philosophy relevant without sacrificing rigor and conceptual complexity. And, Peter, well, your editorial brilliance is bountiful. Thanks for shaping my voice. Connected with Simon and Peter, I would like to thank hundreds of readers who have personally written to me to thank me for engaging an idea or shedding light on some concept or for moving them to tears. I'm encouraged by your responses. Also, thanks to all of those who don't agree with me. Respectful and healthy disagreements speak to a functioning and vigorous democracy.

Special thanks to Susan Hadley who continues to read just about everything I've written. Your attention to detail is appreciated, especially the sheer amount of time that you take to read over often elaborate and at times cumbersome sentences. I find it hard to take an objective stand on my work. It's difficult to recognize sentential and conceptual lacunae. There are times when I read a word into a sentence that doesn't even exist. So, thanks for being my second pair of eyes. More importantly, thanks for helping me to rethink ways of being more receptive and vulnerable to helpful suggestions. It is amazing how working so intimately with another person calls so many complex parts of the self to the fore. So, thanks for a shared trust, a dimension of love that says—I'm there for you, supporting you, even if you aren't aware.

To the Yancy children: I'll love you forever!

Finally, earlier versions of each chapter have appeared as published articles which I have revised/expanded for this book. I am very thankful to all of the following publishers who granted permission to reprint this material. Chapter 1 is a modified version of "The Ugly Truth of Being a Black Professor in America" that appeared in *The Chronicle of Higher Education* (*The Chronicle Review*), April 29, 2018. Chapter 2 is a modified version of "Backlash" that appeared in *Inside Higher Ed*, April 24, 2018. Chapter 3 is a modified version of "Is White America Ready to Confront Its Racism? Philosopher George Yancy Says We Need a 'Crisis'" that appeared in *The Guardian*, April 24, 2018. Chapter 4 is a modified version of "Walking While Black in the White Gaze" that appeared in "The Stone," *The New York Times*, September 1, 2013. Chapter 5 is a modified version of "It Feels like Being on Death Row" that appeared in *CounterPunch*, May 10, 2018. Chapter 6 is a modified version of "Why White People Need Blackface" that appeared in "The Stone," *The New York Times*, March 4, 2019. Chapter 7 is a modified version of "It's Black History Month. Look in the Mirror" that appeared in "The Stone," *The New York Times*, February 9, 2017. Chapter 8 is a modified version of "Will America Choose King's Dream or Trump's Nightmare?" that appeared in "The Stone," *The New York Times*, January 15, 2018. Chapter 9 is a modified version of "Is Your God Dead?" that appeared in "The Stone," *The New York Times*, June 19, 2017. Chapter 10 is a modified version of "I Am a Dangerous Professor" that appeared in "The Stone," *The New York Times*, November 30, 2016. Chapter 11 is a modified version of "Philosophy as a Practice of Suffering: An Interview with George Yancy" that appears in *Philosophia Africana* (19:1, 2020). With courtesy of the Africa Knowledge Project, chapter 12 is a modified version of the article "Interview with Professor George Yancy," which was originally published in *The Journal* on *African Philosophy*, Issue 16, 2017: 66–84. The *Journal on African Philosophy* can be accessed online at https://www.africaknowledgeproject.org/index.php/jap/. Chapter 13 is a modified version of "Thinking about Race, History, and Identity: An Interview with George Yancy" that appeared in *The Western Journal of Black Studies*, Vol. 40, No. 1, 2016: 3–13. Chapter 14 is a modified version of "African-American Philosophy: Through the Lens of Socio-Existential Struggle" that appeared in *Philosophy & Social Criticism*, Vol. 37, No. 5, 2011: 551–74. Chapter 15 is a modified version of "On the Power of Black Aesthetic Ideals: Thomas Nelson Baker as Preacher and Philosopher" that appeared in *AME Church Review*, Vol. CXVII, No. 384, 2001: 50–67. Chapter 16 is a modified version of "In the Spirit of the AME Church: Gilbert Haven Jones as an Early Black Philosopher and Educator" that appeared in *AME Church Review*, Vol. CXVIII, No. 388, 2002: 43–57. Chapter 17 is a modified version of "Joyce Mitchell Cook: Autobiographical and Philosophical Fragments" that appeared in *The Western Journal of Black Studies*, Vol. 41, No. 3–4, 2017. I would also like to thank the Lear Center for Special Collections and Archives at Connecticut College for permission to use a letter written by Joyce Mitchell Cook to the editor of *Satyagraha* that appeared in Vol. 53, No. 25, March 10, 1970: 105–118. Chapter 18 is a modified version of "The Pain and Promise of Black Women in Philosophy" that appeared in "The Stone," *The New York Times*, June 18, 2018. Chapter 19 is a modified version of "The Perils of Being a Black Philosopher" that appeared in "The Stone," *The New York Times*, April 18, 2016. Chapter 20 is a modified version of "The Scholar Who Coined the Term Ebonics: A Conversation with Dr. Robert L. Williams" that appeared in the *Journal of Language, Identity, and Education*, Vol. 10, No. 1, 2011: 41–51. Chapter 21 is a modified version of "Geneva Smitherman: The Social Ontology of African-American Language, the Power of *Nommo* and the Hermeneutics of Linguistic Combat and Identity" that appeared in the *Journal of Speculative Philosophy*, Vol. 18, No. 4, 2004: 273–99. Chapter 22 is a modified version of "Socially Grounded Ontology and Epistemological Agency: James G. Spady's Search for the Marvelous/Imaginative within the Expansive and Expressive Domain of Rap Music and Hip Hop Self-Consciousness" that appeared in *The Western Journal of Black Studies*, Vol. 37, No. 2, 2013: 66–79.

and conceptual trajectory of Black philosophical thought. Indeed, there are conceptual and lived historical family resemblances, especially within the context of the United States, that shape the philosophical thrust of Black philosophy. There are lived connective sociohistorical forces that impact the morphology of philosophical questions posed, dilemmas faced, philosophical aims sought, and the ways in which theory isn't fetishized as an end in itself. Within this book, Black spaces are profoundly relational, dynamically *lived* phenomena. And while whiteness cannot be completely removed from the integument of these relationships, Black spaces are by no means reduced to whiteness or to its logics.

As I pen modifications to this introduction, it is late August 2019. I am reminded that 400 years ago in August of 1619, "20 and odd" Africans were brought to British North America in Virginia either as enslaved or as indentured servants or some combination of both. And while it is true that Spain and Portugal had engaged in the enslavement of Black bodies as early as the 1400s, these "20 and odd" Africans were brought here and exchanged, a process that would be the beginning of that brutal history of white American terrorism against Black bodies.

Hence, these three epigraphs are apropos. Joy James points to the crucible of actual concrete struggle through which Black freedom was/is sought. Within the context of fighting for the value of one's life where the history of anti-Black racism violently rejects the value of one's life, unless on terms defined by whiteness, one faces the phenomenon of freedom not as a conceptual abstraction, but as a struggle against those who would seek to secure one's constant state of unfreedom and captivity. This is Hegel's master–slave dialectic *grounded* within a specifically *racialized* Manichean binary where Black social death and physical death was/is certain, where Black bodies were beaten, abused, and flayed. The battle doesn't seem to be centered around the "master's" desire for recognition. Rather, front and center is the denigration and negation of Black humanity, the attempt to denude Black embodiment of spirit, subjectivity, and perspective.

Charles Mills points to the fact that Black bodies were always already historically defined according to a partitioned social ontology in terms of which their humanity was questioned, rendered suspect, where Black people were considered and treated as "sub-persons." On this score, the human qua human is "white." Hence, white philosophers, sociologists, and anthropologists were engaged in theory building that valorized whiteness and conferred "superiority" upon whiteness and white people; they assisted in constructing the normativity of whiteness or whiteness as the transcendental norm. Hence, Black philosophy—as an attempt to conceptualize what it means *to be*, to be human, to be free, to have dignity, to be treated equally, to have incontrovertible value, to be racialized as Black and to rethink the meaning of one's

Blackness—will begin with questions that are socially, politically, histori- cally, and existentially urgent. Black philosophy, then, not only cuts through ideal theory, but finds its conceptual home, its resistant vitality, within the sphere of nonideal theory, where the racist shit has long since hit the pro- verbial fan, where, not to put too fine a point on it, *Black people are dying*.

Frederick Douglass shifts the medium of philosophical performance, com- menting on the sonic expression of Black lived experience under slavery in North America. The sorrow songs or African-American spirituals are them- selves descriptions and expressions of existential embodied malaise, deep mourning, and profound lament under white supremacy, under conditions where Black bodies are exempt from being included within abstract concep- tual frameworks of white personhood. Douglass also brings attention to the fact that the sorrow songs were more persuasive than volumes of philosophy vis-à-vis the terror of slavery endured by Black people. Douglass power- fully points to the indispensability of the interiority and powerful sensibility of Black embodied life. His is a powerful argument for the importance of Black forms of symbolic representation, endurance, hope, shared intersubjec- tive community formation, that were saturated with and activated by Black *affectivity* and that communicated and explicated more effectively Black enslaved life than did traditional "philosophical discourse." These voiced performances were pregnant with coeval pain and suffering. They didn't just symbolically represent that pain and suffering, but functioned to transmute pain into flesh; they were words made flesh. So, all of the aforementioned quotes begin within the context of historically configured Black space. They don't exhaust the complexity or nuance of Black spaces, but each one points to what I would deem important Black meta-philosophical assumptions, ones that communicate a vital conceptual and lived historical horizon in terms of which this book constitutes an engaged process of thinking across various Black spaces.

In *Across Black Spaces*, I engage a panoply of Black discursive, concep- tual, philosophical, autobiographical, historical, and cultural spaces. The motif of moving *across* speaks to the fact that the text is organized according to a multidisciplinary framework. I can't imagine doing philosophy in any other way. The motif also suggests the sense of moving *through* a panoply of spaces. Books are not to be written for ourselves, though they often function as gifts that we would like to see make an important generative impact on shaping the thoughts, relationships, and lives of people who read them. I am especially excited about this book as it pulls from a broad range of important historical and contemporary topical issues (some of which are deeply painful) that I've written about, but published within different venues. A few of the topical pieces published here have garnered an incredibly sizable readership that I had not anticipated. The readership has grown especially with respect to my public intellectual work at *The New York Times* philosophy column, "The Stone." Writing for "The Stone" has allowed me to materialize what I had always thought was what philosophy and philosophers needed to do—to move beyond the walls of the academy and engage in forms of risk or high-stakes philosophy and a more democratic exploration of ideas within the space of the demos. This process of writing beyond the academy creates different forms of relationality to one's own writing and to those for whom one is writing. As such, one's responsibility is more complexified. I find myself rethinking the impact of my writing, especially in terms of a different temporal register. That is, the impact of the writing is more immediate and the responses come more quickly and, as many readers of some of my work will know, are often profoundly threatening.

Across Black Spaces pulls from a diverse range of longer articles and interviews from professional journals, and shorter articles and interviews in such important critically engaging venues as *The New York Times*, *The Chronicle of Higher Education*, *Inside Higher Ed*, *The Guardian*, and *CounterPunch*. All of the pieces included within this book have been revised, with most also having been expanded. I did this for purposes of both clarification and conceptual elaboration. In many places I felt the need to say more. In some pieces where I had previously been required to adhere to a certain word count, I included those parts that were left out. Because of these changes, each piece has been made stronger and more engaging. Hence, collectively, the entire book is richer for it.

I think of these chapters as introductory, though deeply engaging and generative of critically engaged discussion and debate. They engage material, topics, and philosophical figures that have been undertheorized. Their introductory character is partly defined by opening a dialogical space, for many, regarding a diverse range of philosophical topics that are framed through the lens of Black philosophy. Through this lens, one's historical, philosophical, and ethical imagination is expanded, especially as Black philosophy contests hardened assumptions within traditional (read: white) philosophy.

The book is divided into four sections. "Writing While Black: Bearing the Weight of Public Witnessing" engages very serious contemporary issues that must be addressed with profound urgency or a sense of moral outrage. That section comes first as the issues addressed there are about death and dying, and the important project of learning how to live in a world that is so ethically cowardice and indifferent. "Untying Odysseus: Traversing Black Philosophical Fragments" invites the reader into three conversations about a range of issues autobiographical, historical, and philosophical. While there is no doubt some measure of overlap, each chapter constitutes a separate dialogical space that is engaging, nuanced, and speaks to the importance of risk and vulnerability. Of course, any attempt to specify or nail down with absolute clarity one's identity and one's ideas will fail as the self is always far too opaque and deferred, and one's ideas are always subject to revision. Moreover, each exposure is accompanied by concealment. Yet, each conversation is rich in detail and revelatory. My hope is that the conversations invoke more fruitful and challenging questions. I am honored to have been mutually and respectfully present to my interlocutors. "Doing Philosophy in Black: Foundational Traces and the Weight of the Present" provides a framework for thinking about Black philosophy or African-American philosophy or Africana philosophy. There is so much more work that needs to be done when it comes to exploring the work of early Black philosophers. To my knowledge, many professional philosophers don't engage the archive. I'm especially delighted to have done archival research on philosophers Gilbert Haven Jones, Thomas Nelson Baker, Sr., and Joyce Mitchell Cook. Out of the three, I knew Cook personally. She was a dear friend who is the first U.S. Black woman to receive the PhD in philosophy in 1965. It is because she left me with all of her books and many of her published and unpublished writings, and because of the many engaged conversations that we shared, that I was able to produce the unprecedented chapter on her life and work within this book. Lastly, the two interviews that end this section refuse to mince words about what it means to be racialized and gendered as a Black philosopher. The last section, "Meaning-Making and the Generative Space of Black Performative Discourse," situates the reader within that sonic space to which Douglass brings attention. As human beings, we are all engaged in processes of meaning-making—through various symbolic means. This last section opens a conversation about language and the ways in which different linguistic forms of expression communicate different ways of engaging, changing, transacting, and coping with each other and the world. Robert L. Williams, who coined the term Ebonics, sets the stage for rethinking the importance of language, meaning-making, and resistance. Next, I play with the idea of what it would look like to engage in philosophical reflection through the use of African-American language. I invite readers to engage with this section as I'm optimistic about the potential of Black vernacular speech as a mode of expression that is capable of communicating lived Black experiences in ways that are unique. The last chapter in this section engages another site of Black expressive discursivity as it manifests within the context of rap and Hip Hop. Hence, the last chapter, paying tribute to the diverse discursive and performative communities of rap and Hip Hop, and especially to the work of James G. Spady, places us, as with the previous two chapters, within the space of dynamic quotidian Black life. I often envy the parrhesiastic boldness of rap artists and the robust expressive agency and experimental audacity within Hip Hop culture. There are times when I think that whole volumes of philosophy come up short. For me, philosophy is a living process; it is intense

Part 1

WRITING WHILE BLACK: BEARING THE WEIGHT OF PUBLIC WITNESSING

Deploying one's voice outside of academia proper comes with its risks, fears, and joys. And some of us who do this work may sometimes forget the sheer magnitude of responsibility that comes with speaking to so many readers. Others may even forget the material conditions and the labor of others that have made speaking publicly possible. I try to remember both. For me, that means writing with a hesitant hand or typing with reluctant fingers—even a heavy heart. It also means, for me, being thankful for opportunities created by those who didn't have to give a damn, but they did. Each critically and conceptually generative site—*The Chronicle of Higher Education*, *Inside Higher Ed*, *The Guardian*, *CounterPunch*, and *The New York Times* philosophy column "The Stone"—has functioned as an indispensable opportunity to engage with a much broader community of readers who are invested in the democratic importance of critical intelligence. In fact, some of the pieces within this section generated a level of attention and acclaim that I had not anticipated. Yet, through these venues, I have learned a deep lesson about the importance of humility and responsibility.

Once I began to receive hundreds of messages and responses to my public intellectual work, it then hit me greater than ever that readers are powerfully moved by what we write, by our commitments, our metaphors, our arguments, and our expressed and articulated passions. I guess that the first time that I really felt the weight of this sense of responsibility was when I began to teach. These are real lives. These are human beings who are being influenced by me. I know that this sounds trite, but once we really take seriously the idea that in our classes students are there to be transformed, to be critically engaged, to learn just how complex, beautiful, and horrible our world is, the gravity hits, at least for me, with a mighty blow that makes me feel incredibly vulnerable and humble. That there is so little time to live, which is how I frame my pedagogical and intellectual work, I feel seized by a sense of overwhelming impossibility: What can I possibly do to make a radical difference in the lives of my students given not only the short amount of time that we spend in classrooms together, but the deeply precarious and short time that we are alive between birth and the grave? So, this existentially rich and weighty sense of shared reality, which at times feels more like existential dread, finds its way into my pedagogy and my writing. This is not to say that my classrooms or my writings permeate with nihilism or pessimism, but both are saturated with the reality of our facticity, our finitude, our ineluctable demise. Once my students are feeling all cozy and safe, as the classroom is filled with abstract discussions and intellectual stimulation, once we have reached that predictable routine of performing our roles as "students" and "professor," I make a point of disrupting that space, of fissuring it, of reminding my students that *all of us* will, at some point, sooner or later, become rotting corpses. That, I explain, is the great equalizer. No matter how smart, brilliant, wealthy, beautiful, fit you are, no matter your MCAT scores, your LSAT scores, or your GPA, we will all perish—perhaps for the whole of eternity. The universe might forever continue to redshift or it might, eventually, blueshift. I explain that I am not certain. But that lack of certainty regarding the cosmos feels so abstract, so distant when compared to the immediacy and certainty of the reality that *we* will die.

After hearing this, students will often become completely silent. I must admit that this silence is very awkward and yet profoundly beautiful. I can see their faces; they see mine. There is this sudden recognition that something has been haunting our pedagogical joy, our unquestioned and collective happiness, our sense of "permanence." It is palpable. No matter how many times I've decided to remove that veil, the sting of our collective finitude continues to hit me, along with the reality of bodily decomposition and putrefaction. Opening the door to the unspoken that is the haunting background of our practices shakes my body; I mourn for me and my students, and humanity. As stated, though, there is also a profound beauty. Despite the rush of affective overload, there is a sense of clarity that emerges. We see each other differently, perhaps for the very first time. Our discussions going forward will carry the trace of what we have collectively faced—our inevitable death. I would like to think that our perceptual practices have changed, that we have begun to see the impermanence, the ephemerality that now accompanies our being-together, our discussions, our next meeting, our shared laughs, and our shared pain. The beauty is in that transformation. We are no longer simply students and professor, but fragile creatures and mysterious beings who have been dying from the moment that we were born in a universe with no *self-evident* ultimate meaning. Ironically, that makes our time together even more joyful, even more precious. There are times when at the conclusion of my classes for the semester, students collectively applaud. I would like to think that part of the applause signifies an abundance of joy, a returned gift, a realization about how pedagogical spaces can function to disturb and shake our entire being, forcing us to new heights of bravery, honesty, passion, and love.

But why open this section on public intellectual work in this way? Well, it is one way of saying that the chapters within this section involve my attempt to communicate something about our fragile condition, something about *my* pain and suffering, something about how many of us experience profound levels of racial injustice, something about why I *must* do what I do, and something about a collective and yet personal invitation *to you*. All of these chapters were originally written for venues that are designed to reach a broad public audience, ones designed to encourage us to think, to rethink, and think yet again within the context of the public sphere, a space where the demos ought to be affectively vital and exuberant, not atomized and motivated by perfunctory forms of social interaction, and insipid forms of social greeting. Each chapter is written with a certain urgency. And while we may never see eye to eye, or literally find ourselves face to face, these chapters are meant to encourage dialogue, not forms of hate, not vitriol, not violence. They are meant to reach across time and space to a receptive interlocutor; perhaps even a potential friend. As you'll see, though, I've been the recipient of hate, vitriol, and violence. It is also for these reasons that I write with a hesitant hand or type with reluctant fingers. I have loved ones who would rather that I not write within the public intellectual sphere. The assumption, of course, is that "academic" writing is safer. I find the "academic" versus "public intellectual" distinction problematic. It is certainly problematic for me. I hope that my practices within my profession (philosophy), which I see as an existential calling, bear this out.

As you read this section, the reasons for my reluctance and hesitancy to engage the public sphere will be apparent. Yet, the chapters within this section that cover a range of socially, politically, and existentially pressing themes—such as being the object of death threats, being placed on surveillance lists, being Black and male within a white America which has yet to deliver on its promises, warnings of our country's democratic atrophy under neofascist leadership, and demanding that white people see themselves *as they are* and acknowledge their perpetuation of systemic forms of racism, and challenging our (for those of us who believe) theologies that ostracize our neighbors as opposed to our dwelling near them—are written from a place that refuses to be silent. How can I refuse to be silent? There is so much to give back to those who have made my voice possible, the greatest of whom are my Black parents, and especially my Black mother, who were denied real possibilities of even seeing themselves as public intellectuals. And then there is truth-telling to be done, the sort that requires epistemic humility. So,

Chapter 1

The Ugly Truth of Being a Black Professor in America

N

"Dear Nigger Professor." That was the beginning of a message that was sent to me. There is nothing to be cherished here, despite the salutation. Years ago, Malcolm X asked, "What does a white man call a black man with a PhD?" He answered, "A nigger with a PhD."[1] In other words, having the PhD doesn't modify my status of being thought of or perceived as a "nigger" vis-à-vis the white gaze. Through the white gaze, my status as a "nigger" subtends any qualifier that might be said to contradict the racist codification of my being a "nigger." In short, the term "nigger," within the context of white hegemony and white racist mythopoetic constructions, is not falsifiable. There are no exceptions. In this sense, its use is predicated on a *perverse* and deeply problematic sense of white "religious" dogmatic fanaticism.

The message came in response to an op-ed I published in *The New York Times* in December 2015. I'd spent much of that year conducting a series of interviews with philosophers about race. This was an unprecedented series of interviews conducted for *The New York Times*, "The Stone." I wanted to hold a disagreeable mirror up to white readers and ask that they take a long, hard look without fleeing, without seeking shelter. My article, "Dear White America," took the form of a letter asking readers to accept the truth of what it means to be white in a society created for white people. I asked them to tarry with the ways in which they perpetuate a racist society, the ways in which they are racist. In return, I asked for understanding and even love—love in the sense that James Baldwin used the term: "Love takes off the masks that we fear we cannot live without and know we cannot live within."[2] This kind of love is not about sentimentality, but courage, growth, and maturity. Indeed, this kind of love is about experienced loss, a way of relinquishing those lies that help to structure what it means to be white. It is a species of symbolic death that is hard to undergo.

Instead, I received hundreds of emails, phone messages, and letters, an overwhelming number of which were filled with white racist vitriol. My university did its important and necessary part—top administrators assured me that my academic freedom was protected. Yet my predicament was not easy. Campus police had to monitor my office and classrooms. Departmental instructions were clear: no one was to provide any strangers with my office hours. I needed police presence at my invited talks at other universities. It all felt surreal—and dangerous. When I became a "professional philosopher," being escorted to class by campus police is not something that I had in mind. The entire experience raised important questions for me. What had I done wrong? Or, more importantly, what had I done right?

This is what it's like to be the target of racist hatred:

Another uppity Nigger. Calling a Nigger a professor is like calling White Black and Wet Dry.

Even the most sophisticated nigger will revert back to their jungle bunny behavior when excited.

You can dress a Nigger up in a suit and tie and they'll still be Niggers.

This belief that niggers even reason is blatant pseudo-intellectualism.

For these writers, "nigger professor" is an oxymoron. A nigger is a nigger, incapable of reason. Kant, Hegel, and Jefferson all made similar claims about Black people being bereft of rationality. Perhaps I'm just parroting (as Hume said of Black people)[3] what I've already heard. I'm just a nigger who dared to reason, only to discover that reason is white. I had been the quintessential idiot; I had been the victim of a cosmic hoax.

The concept of there being an intellectual Negro is a joke.

Perhaps this person had spoken to the woman who left the following on my university answering machine:

Dear professor, I am a white American citizen. You are the one who is the racist against white people, evidently. A professor—I bet you got it [your PhD] through a mail order.

On a white racist website, one writer has apparently seen through my game:

This coon is a philosopher in the same way Martin King was a PHD and the same way that Jesse Jackson and Al Sharpton are "Reverends": Just another jive assed nigger with a new way to pimp.

Some of my students of color have asked me, "Why talk about race with white people when at the end of the day everything remains the same—that is, their racism continues?" "Why teach courses on race and whiteness?" "Do you really think that such courses will make a difference?" I find these questions haunting; they pull at my conscience.

Indeed, there are times when I ask myself, "Why do I do this?" After all, I don't write about whiteness because it is a new fad in philosophy. And I'm certainly not a masochist. There is no pleasure to be had in being the object of hatred. I'm sure that a few of my Black colleagues and colleagues of color think that I've lost my sanity. Perhaps they think that I've asked for all of this and that had I remained silent I would have been fine. The reality, of course, is that they too are seen as niggers. Silence will not help.

In 2015, I was invited to be a plenary speaker at a well-established philosophy conference. I was excited. After all, I was there to deliver my talk within the company of kindred philosophical spirits, those who knew something about feminism, disability, aesthetics, and race. There was one other Black philosopher in attendance, though he was older, taller, heavier, and very gray. As I recall, all the other attendees were white.

The day after I gave my talk, the other Black philosopher told me that several white attendees had, with no apparent hesitation, complimented him on *my* talk: "That was a very important talk that you gave yesterday." "Wow, great talk!" "Inspiring." No less than seven congratulatory gestures were made.

Had there been only one or two, perhaps it could have been brushed off. But seven times? This was the manifestation of an all-too-familiar mode of being white—a habit of perception that sees Black people as all the same, through a fixed imago. This was white racism. My colleague, the Black philosopher who had *not* given the talk, somehow "became" me, and I him. We became a mass, indistinguishable.

In that sophisticated and philosophically progressive white space, I could hear a strange and profoundly irritating echo of the little white child whom Frantz Fanon encountered on a train: "Look, a Negro!"[4] There was a familiar sense of being fixed, static. The two of us became one Black man; any Black man; every Black man. We were flattened, rendered one-dimensional, indistinct, and repeatable.

Hey Georgie boy. You're the fucking racist, asshole. You wouldn't have a job if it wasn't for affirmative action. Somebody needs to put a boot up your ass and knock your fucking head off your shoulders you stupid fucking goddamn racist son of a bitch. You fucking race baiting son[s] of bitches. Man, you're just asking to get your fucking asses kicked. You need your fucking asses kicked. You stupid motherfucker. Quit fucking race baiting, asshole.

It is probably true that I would not have my job were it not for affirmative action. Many white women wouldn't have jobs either! And of course, white men have benefited from white supremacy for years. In fact, their whiteness has always *affirmed* them, allowed them to enter certain spaces, provided them with a sense of glorified history and superiority. Also, no matter how poor, they would always rest at night knowing that a nigger is a nigger, an exemption that would compensate for any sense of lack. But affirmative action is not white supremacy in reverse; it is not anti-white, but pro-justice. It was created so that with my PhD, which I earned with distinction, I would actually be able to teach at a university. Affirmative action, in the case of Black people, is a response to systemic racist disadvantages. It's important to get that history right—not twisted.

I felt particularly sickened by the letters—there were quite a few—sent to me through regular postal mail, handwritten and signed. These are even more disturbing than emails, given the level of industry expended (writing, printing, stamping, mailing). The opening of one such letter read, "I'm a racist? How dare you call me that! You are a racist and, hey, since Blacks call each other 'nigga' I'm taking the liberty of doing the same. Either the word is offensive and taboo or it isn't."

Personally, I'm not buying it. I once had two white male students attempt to argue that they should be allowed to use the n-word whenever they wanted, and that it is discriminatory to say that they can't. Any response at all felt too generous. I have often heard white people express the feeling of being somehow left out from Black spaces, which are necessary for Black sanity precisely because of white racism. Desired Black spaces are not anti-white spaces. Given the history of white colonial usurpation, Black spaces function to communicate to white people that such spaces are hands-off. And given the logics of whiteness, there is no need to waste my time telling me that white people also have the legitimate need for white spaces, spaces that are not anti-Black. Just think about it. You can't have self-defined white student unions or a nationally recognized white history month. How does one even begin to disentangle such academic organizations and national recognitions from white supremacy? And what would white student unions discuss? "We need more of a white presence on campus!" What about white history month? "Let's honor this month by reading more works by William Shakespeare or learning more about the underrepresented study of European and Greek philosophy!"

It is as if white people are driven by a colonial desire to possess everything. DuBois asked, "But what on earth is whiteness that one should so desire it?" He answered, "Whiteness is the ownership of the earth forever and ever, Amen!"[5] These two white students spoke with arrogance and the desire for total white ownership. It was not so much that they were deprived of historical knowledge, as that rather, this knowledge meant nothing when it came to their sense of loss of power. What they did not possess, they felt forced to take. Perhaps it is not unreasonable to say that whiteness respects no boundaries unless, of course, those boundaries have been designed through the logics of whiteness to exclude, to enslave, to intern, to incarcerate, to redline.

To read white racist vitriol can be traumatic. To *hear* white racist vitriol intensifies the impact. One listens to the inflection of the voice, its volume, its nervousness and hatred, its terror. I registered the wounds physiologically. Mood swings. Irritability. Trepidation. Disgust. Anger. Nausea. Words do things. They carry the vestiges of the bloody and brutal contexts which gave them birth. One might think that being called a nigger so many times might decrease its impact. It doesn't.

"All black people in the United States, irrespective of their class status or politics," according to bell hooks, "live with the possibility that they will be terrorized by whiteness."[6] The many responses of white people to "Dear White America" were just that—twenty-first-century white terror. That terror can come in many forms. Perhaps a Black man screams "I can't breathe!" eleven times, but no one cares (Eric Garner). Or perhaps, after he has been shot by "accident," he musters enough strength to say aloud that he's losing his breath (Eric Harris), only to hear a white police officer respond, "Fuck your breath!" Perhaps his spine gets severed (Freddie Gray). Perhaps he is a teenager and is shot sixteen times (Laquan McDonald). Pulling out a wallet can lead to getting shot at forty-one times and hit with nineteen bullets (Amadou Diallo). Perhaps he is a mental health therapist (Charles Kinsey) whose job is to ensure the safety of an autistic client who has wandered off when suddenly, despite the fact that he is the therapist, he is shot by a SWAT officer. Or perhaps he is a security guard (Jemel Roberson) who effectively apprehended an "active shooter" and when the police arrive, he, Roberson, is shot dead. Perhaps she is an innocent seven-year-old Black child (Aiyana Stanley-Jones) and is killed by police during a raid. Just as was true for Emmett Till over sixty years ago, there is no place that one can call safe in America for Black bodies. Such cases of state violence instill overwhelming terror and trepidation as I drive by a white police officer sitting in his/her car or as I walk into a store as the white police officer stands at the counter. Within such contexts, I feel the weight of a deep existential precariousness. At any moment, I may lose my life because I'm Black. Or, more accurately, I may lose my life because he/she constructs something that is not me, a doppelgänger that whites have created and to which they react with deadly force. And while there was no *deadly* violence that resulted within the conference space where I delivered my 2015 philosophy plenary talk, white violence was nevertheless present.

By recounting, in explicit language, the white backlash that I encountered after writing "Dear White America," those violent and dehumanizing racist modes of address, I risk becoming retraumatized. The retelling is imperative, though. For too long, I have had Black students say to me that they feel unsafe at predominantly white institutions (PWIs). I must believe them. And while they may not have been called a nigger to their faces, such white spaces position them as inconsequential, deny their Blackness through superficial concerns for "diversity," and take their complaints as instances of individual problems of institutional adjustment. I insist on bearing witness to Black pain and suffering at PWIs because the deniers are out there. We are told that what we know in our very bodies to be true isn't credible. This is a different kind of violence, the epistemic kind. I'm here to say, "Your fears and anger are not unfounded."

On November 11, 2017, I received a letter in my university mailbox. It was handwritten on both sides in black ink on a sheet of paper torn from a yellow legal pad. There was no return address. Every time I've touched it, as I've done for purposes of writing it down word-for-word, I wash my hands afterward.

Dear Mr. Yancy, I am writing to you to voice my displeasure with what you said about WHITE PEOPLE. You claim that all white people are Racists! Really now? You, sir are one to talk!! You sound just like the following Racists. Here is a list of who I mean. They're Al Sharpton, Oprah Winfrey, Whoopi Goldberg, Spike Lee, Samuel L. Jackson, Bill Cosby, Danny Glover, Harry Belafonte, Movie Director John Singleton, Shannon Sharpe, Scottie Pippen (former NBA player), Rappers Ice Cube, Chuck D., Flavor Flav, DMX, and Snoop Dogg; former MLB players Carl Everett, Ray Durham and Hall of Famer Hank Aaron! When I read what you said about white people, I was like this guy is a total lowlife Racist piece of shit! It's so true! You are an asshole! You deserve to be punished with several fists to your face! You're nothing but a troublemaker! You need to really "Get a life!" I've had enough of your Racist talk! You'd better watch what you say and to whom you say it! You may just end up in the hospital with several injuries or maybe on a cold slab in the local morgue! I wouldn't be surprised if you've gotten several Death Threats! You're inviting trouble when you accuse the entire White Race of being Racists! You've got a big mouth that needs to be slammed shut permanently! I'm not going to give you the opportunity to find out who I am. Good luck with that! By the way, this letter I'm sending you is certainly not a Death Threat! I could've done that, but that's not me! I'm tired of your Racist kind!

Please tarry with these words. My life has just been threatened. The writer belies their intention by denying that the letter is a death threat. Notice the need to communicate to me that "I could've done that."

The writer does communicate something quite revealing, though. They imply that they could be someone I see every day, someone I walk by, greet, or even teach. All the smiles, the eye contact, and the social spaces of interaction—and yet there I am, just a "nigger" to you. Here again there is that experienced weight of a deep existential precariousness.

After receiving the letter, I decided to share it with my graduate philosophy seminar. We had been discussing race and embodiment. I think that I wanted my students to help carry some of what I was feeling. I read it aloud. I had not anticipated my emotional response. As I finished, my eyes watered, my body became stilted, I felt a rush of unspeakable anger. "I can't take this shit anymore," I said. "I need a few minutes outside of class." Silence pervaded the classroom. Looking back, I wish that I had said, "Fuck it all! It is not worth it. White people will never value my humanity. So, let's end this class session on that."

Instead, I came back into the room, where everyone was still silent. My students' faces, for the most part, were turned down. I know what they had felt, Black students, students of color, and white students alike. They bore witness to my vulnerability, my suffering. And they saw the impact that white racism could have within an otherwise safe academic space. A few moments passed, I apologized, and resumed teaching. But the classroom was not the same. We had witnessed something together. That space will never be the same.

Chapter 2

Discussing the Backlash to "Dear White America" with Scott Jaschik at *Inside Higher Ed*

Scott Jaschik: How bad were the attacks you received after your piece in the *Times* was published? How fearful were you for your safety?

George Yancy: The attacks were horrible, despicable, and vile. It wasn't enough that many white readers completely distorted the message of "Dear White America," which was one of love and vulnerability, they also pulled from an ugly history of white racist epithets and white racist imagery. I was called a "hoodrat" and a "pavement ape," which pulled from the ways in which Black people have been denigrated as subhuman animals. I was also called a "nigger" more times than I can recall. So, they pulled from that ugliest of racist terms. One white reader said that his only regret was that he didn't call me a "nigger" to my face and then beat me until I was half dead. Other white readers also fantasized about "beheading me ISIS style," of putting a meat hook in my body, of knocking my head off my shoulders, of leaving me on a cold slab, and shutting my mouth permanently. Others expressed that I should go back to Africa. It was as if I (or my ancestors) came to North America on my own initiative. To suggest that I go back to Africa bespeaks a profound sense of white arrogance. After all, the reality of white presence here is because of earlier colonial settlers from Europe. So, they are on land stolen by those who look like them. One white writer suggested, "There are two ways you can return to Africa: On a passenger ship, or in a coffin freighter. Choose quickly." Notice the urgency of that warning, the implied threat to my life. You see, for many white Americans, I am disposable. For others, I'm more beast than human. "This ignorant monkey has no audience but other ignorant monkeys." Or, "Colored monkeys are like stalker chicks who just won't leave you alone." Or, "This monkey isn't talking to me." Or, "As I see it, the only people whose racism is a problem is colored monkeys. They don't want to live without White people. They CAN'T live without White people."

I was very fearful for my safety. White racism, after all, is a form of fanaticism. And I'm afraid of fanatics. We all should be. Fanaticism is predicated on a lack of criticality or no need for critical thinking at all. I'll leave unaddressed whether one can be a fanatic when it comes to promoting justice or love or peace. We should keep in mind, though, that many atrocities have been committed in the name of "justice," "love," and "peace." However, whiteness is a form of perverse collective obsessiveness and self-absorption that is structurally anti-Black and that attempts to destroy anything that stands in its colonial path, its explicit and implicit historical mission, and its ontological supremacy. I would argue that whiteness as a form of fanaticism is indicative of what Simone de Beauvoir calls the "serious world," a world where things are believed to be, as it were, preestablished. The serious person, as she argues, subordinates his/her freedom to that which is considered ahistorical or unconditioned.[1] So, as a "hoodrat" and a "pavement ape," it is believed that *I am* ontologically those horrible things. Think here of how the Jews were depicted as "vermin." This is more than racist biology, but a racist metaphysical way of construing the *being* of Jews.

I was instructed to send the ugly messages that I received directly to Emory Police, which I did. Many students were completely unaware of why campus police were walking me to class. My students showed a look of awkward concern. I too experienced the escorts as awkward, but necessary. After all, as a professor, we just assume that we are safe. Well, I certainly did prior to this. My fear became exacerbated, though, by the fact that white racism has become so unabashedly threatening due to the moral equivocation regarding racism that plays out from the highest office in this nation, which indicates a form of moral forfeiture and moral ineptness. With a white nationalist in the Oval Office, white racism on the proverbial ground acquires deep sustenance, support, and "justification."

Jaschik: Were you surprised by the depth of the backlash?

Yancy: Yes, I was. I knew that there would be white people who would disagree with "Dear White America" and those few, or so I thought, who might express anger. What I didn't expect was the pervasiveness of the negative responses and the fact that the anger took the form of such raw and nasty hatred directed at me. It was as if I was guilty of some ethically atrocious deed committed against white people. Then it occurred to me. The reality was that so many white people began to feel hatred toward me and threaten acts of violence against me because they were asked to examine their own white racism. They had exclusively reserved the term "racism" for the Ku Klux Klan. So, for many white people, they can't be said to be racist because they apparently don't hold outward and explicit racist beliefs against Black people or people of color. Yet, "Dear White America" was designed to disrupt any clear demarcation between "good whites" and "bad whites," where that distinction obfuscates the various ways in which white people, pure and simple, have internalized white racist ideas, emotions, images, and the ways in which they are embedded within a white systemic racist structure and are thereby complicit in the process of perpetuating racialized injustice. In other words, for me, there is no white innocence. So, the hatred was projected onto me because I had put my finger on the pulse of their denied racism. I had touched something that they didn't want to be identified. Such an experience, of course, can be frightening. So, they denied what I pointed out and called me, among so many other things, a racist.

What I found especially strange about these responses is that they were so incredibly nasty despite the fact that I engaged in self-critique as a way of building a bridge between us. My aim was to be vulnerable, to open myself to be wounded. One might say that I revealed wounds that pointed to ways in which I'm a sexist and the impact that my sexism has on women. All of that un-suturing, all of that opening myself to be seen, was met by white suturing, a concealed whiteness that hunkered down and refused to risk self-exposure. To fantasize about the use of meat hooks, to desire to see me on a cold slab, to want my mouth shut permanently, to accuse me of writing "Dear White America" because my aim was to get white women to perform oral sex on me, well, these were forms of backlash that were unleashed from the depths of a white psyche that I had not anticipated. I know about the history of white brutality and bloodlust, but that letter was just too much for white readers to consume. So, white people choked and vomited their hatred onto me.

As I've said earlier, I was surprised by the degree of backlash. In addition to all of the white racist virulence, there were other ways in which I experienced backlash. For example, a trusted white colleague said to me, after I began to receive such nasty white racist responses, that I was being disingenuous about being surprised by the backlash. She suggested that I must have known prior to writing "Dear White America" that I would receive such responses. Yet, I said to my white colleague that I had *not* expected that degree of white racist vitriol. To say that I underestimated the response is different from accusing me of being disingenuous. The latter charges me with being deceitful. This added insult to injury. Having been bombarded with such extreme white hatred wasn't enough, I had to hear my white colleague imply that I lied. It was as if she was saying that I somehow asked for what happened to me. It is perhaps easy for some white people to interpret this incident with my white colleague as one of those "less racist" incidents. However, I don't need white people or my colleague to speak *for me*. I can speak for myself. In this case, not only was I targeted by white readers who I'm assuming I didn't know, but I was the *target* of my colleague's white authoritarian denial of my epistemic integrity. This phenomenon is not uncommon. White people presume to know Black people better then Black people know themselves. As such, it is imperative that I get to define my reality, my frustration, my sense of injustice. Indeed, it is imperative that I name my colleague's response. It was racist!

Jaschik: *Inside Higher Ed* has reported on a number of scholars who have been attacked in similar ways—many of them Black professors who write about white racism/white privilege, etc. Why has writing about white racism become so controversial?

Yancy: Writing about white racism has always been controversial, especially for Black people and people of color. Historically, whether intentionally marking whiteness or not, we have been targets of white racism. Explicitly revealing its toxic insides, however, compounds the problem. Not all writing, of course, about racism is controversial, especially within our contemporary moment where the view is that racism has become a fringe phenomenon, or something committed by a few white "extremists," that is, those white people on the margins. For those of us, however, who reject the illusion, really the lie, of a "post-racial" America, and who are unafraid to tell the truth about the everyday micro-racism and macro-racism that Black people and people of color continue to experience, we are subjected to backlash, threats, and reprimand. Here is the problem. Many white people believe that they are "innocent" of racist crimes against Black people and people of color. They see themselves as neoliberal subjects, socially detached, and isolated. Yet, that self-conception is part of how white privilege operates. Whiteness provides a false narrative of meritocracy and individualism, which distorts profound forms of social connectedness. Many white people, I think, believe that after the Civil Rights Movement ended, the problem of systemic racism and its insidious manifestation also ended. But this is so untrue. It is a distortion of reality and a denial of Black phenomenological and existential reality. So, when some of us hold up a disagreeable mirror to the face of white America, there is deep defensiveness, denial, and failure to take responsibility for the continued existence of white racism. After all, there is comfort in narratives that lie. Well, I refuse to lie. And if I refuse to lie about my sexism, which isn't to say that there are not profound layers of opacity regarding my sexism, then I damn sure refuse to lie about whiteness.

Jaschik: Would you change anything about your original essay in light of the backlash? Are there ways scholars can reach those who seem to ignore your points?

Yancy: I don't think so, though I wish that I had not undergone so much white racist vitriol. It came daily. In fact, the horrible experiences, in many ways, made it clearer to me just how white racism is alive and apparently ineradicable in terms of being in the social DNA of white America. Regarding your other question, I'm not very optimistic at all. Many white people would rather live with a lie than to admit the ways in which their implicit racist biases impact Black people and people of color or the ways in which they continue to benefit from white privilege relative to the disadvantages of Black people and people of color. In fact, white privilege is parasitic upon the disadvantages of Black people and people of color. I understand that there are poor white people in America, but they are still white. I want white people to understand how being poor *and* Black expands and complicates forms of racialized suffering. There will be some white people who will prefer to go to their graves than to admit to their racism. And, then, there are other white people who seem to get it, who are prepared to undergo processes of loss, of learning how to become an ethically different human being. But even as there are whites who seem to get it, they will often fail to understand just how much work is involved in daily confronting their racism. There are lots of white people, those who are smart, those who have benefited from higher education, those who are professional academics, who believe that they've arrived, that they are uncomplicated allies. They still fail to understand just how difficult the journey is, how grappling with whiteness is a life project. Reading a few books on whiteness or critical philosophy of race will never be enough. One's whiteness is not a conceptual puzzle. Rather, it is a site of terror, complicity, and violence. That is not something that is a puzzle. I'm talking about people of color who are dying because of the ontology of whiteness, its institutional framework, its habituated forms of comportment, its embeddedness within social and discursive forces that are haptic and toxic. So much more work needs to be done and to be done with urgency. I think that we need to create small risk-taking spaces where scholars like myself can engage with white people who are ready to listen and who are willing to augment their capacities to listen and to tell the truth about their racism and to share it with others, as bell hooks might say. In this way, white people can do the lion's share of teaching other white people about racism. After all, racism is a white problem. So, in the end, there is nothing about the original essay that I would change in light of the backlash.

Jaschik: What should colleges and universities do to protect the academic freedom of scholars who speak out as you did?

Yancy: My university was very supportive of my academic freedom and very much concerned for my safety. Colleges and universities must become spaces where students risk their dogmatism, risk being touched and transformed by ideas that encourage freedom, mutual respect, and profound forms of love, where that love, as James Baldwin says, "takes off the masks that we fear we cannot live without and know we cannot live within."[2] Colleges and universities must be encouraged to engage in critical dialogue, mutual passion or shared suffering, and recognition and respect of our differences. We need a profound form of *Bildung*, of cultivating generative affective modes of being and practice. It is not about universities and colleges adopting a left political ethos or a right political ethos. No. It is about our institutions of higher learning creating spaces where students engage each other through the love of ideas, the love of learning, and the love of each other. I'm sure that to some ears that sounds like idealism on steroids. Then again, there are many who really don't give a damn if there is a shared and collective love within the classroom. However, this is not about romanticism. It is a form of love that dares to think beyond forms of normativity that perpetuate violence, that distort mutual understanding, and reject necessary forms of mutual vulnerability. I know that this sounds impossible, but we must insist upon the impossible in a world that is on the brink of utter moral, ecological, and possibly nuclear catastrophe. And yet, the deep frustration is there. As civil rights heroin Fannie Lou Hamer once said, "I'm Sick and Tired of Being Sick and Tired."[3] And yet she continued to fight.

Chapter 3

Is White America Ready to Confront Its Racism and Be in Crisis? With Alex Blasdel at *The Guardian*

Alex Blasdel: What was the message of "Dear White America" and why do you think it proved so provocative?

George Yancy: "Dear White America" was a letter of love. We don't talk much about love within our current public discourse. Indeed, the language of love deployed as a means of radical transformation and mutual respect seems to have no place within our public discourse. So, by a letter of love I meant that it was a letter that was an invitation for white people to engage honestly with their racism, to be vulnerable, and to let go of or at least begin to question their "white innocence." Think of the letter as a site of hospitality, a welcoming, an attempt to dwell near, which is a profound act of risk. Think of the letter as an intervention that was partly designed to disrupt political chatter and one-upmanship.

After conducting nineteen interviews with philosophers and public intellectuals at "The Stone," *The New York Times*, the objective was to write a piece that functioned to sum up what I learned. The aim was to write a piece that would frame in a nice coherent and concluding way some of the conceptual similarities and differences that resulted after conducting the interviews. However, I wanted to do something different. I felt compelled to make an appeal, to speak from the heart. I knew that I had to write a letter that was direct and candid. In short, there was no room for bullshit. I tried to create a mutually vulnerable space where white people could confront the ways in which they harbor racist assumptions, emotions, and embodied habits. Perhaps I was asking for the impossible. But who says that we cannot ask for the "impossible"?

So, I also invited white people to explore (or certainly try to explore) the very problematic ways in which they are complicit with white systemic and institutional power and privilege. It doesn't follow from this that all white people are members of the Ku Klux Klan or that white people are born rac- ists. That would be ridiculous. Yet, that is what many white people assumed that I meant.

I think that the anger partly resulted from a defensive posture, one that is linked to a failure of nerve and honesty that is needed for white people to confront courageously the truth about how racism is insidious and constitutes structural, embodied, and habitual comings and goings of white America. The very idea that I would suggest that there is something there to see, that there is something there to be exposed and is worth exploring, was enough to trigger the incendiary responses. Who wants to see their own moral fail- ures, their own perpetrated violence? Whites are afraid to look. And fear can breed anger. James Baldwin reminds us that people who insist upon their "innocence long after that innocence is dead" turn themselves into monsters.[1] White America has long lost its innocence. Given its horrendous treatment of the indigenous peoples of this land, there was never any innocence. There were monsters, though. Land takers. Brutal dispossession. And then body snatchers and the selling and buying of Black flesh. To be haunted while asleep has its advantages, because one will awake. But to be haunted while awake by a teratological structural whiteness is far more frightening.

I didn't want monsters. I wanted a courageous white America, one pre- pared to de-mask, to confront aspects of its self-deception, and to love in return. Even as I write those lines, I feel the weight of a white history that belies any such return. More powerfully, painfully, and tragically, I hear the sounds of Black cries, voiced terror, screams of pain and suffering that force a realistic and no-nonsense self-critique: "How dare you ask this of a people who would lynch us without a cause, murder us for no reason at all, dismem- ber our Black bodies before white mobs seeking white revenge for shit for which they themselves are guilty and for which they bear collective respon- sibility?" It is hard to argue with history. And I certainly have my doubts about white radical transformation. One white writer was unequivocal: "You deserve to be punished with several fists to your face! You're nothing but a troublemaker! I've had enough of your Racist talk! You'd better watch what you say and to whom you say it!"

Blasdel: This is an important segue. What sorts of response did you get to the piece?

Yancy: The majority of the white responses were vile, despicable, and uncon- scionable. I was told to commit suicide immediately. I was called a "mon- key," "boy," and referred to as excrement. There seemed to be this obsession with identifying me with dirt. Hence, quite a few times I was called "a piece of shit." This pulls from some deep white psychological motifs. After all, whiteness is "pure," "clean," and "virtuous." Blackness, within this racial Manichaean divide, is "impure," "dirty," "immoral," and "evil." Of course, I was also called by that most horrible, dehumanizing, and insulting of words, "nigger." I couldn't even keep count of the number of times the n-word was used. One white person's response to the letter consisted of a series of the n-word—nigger, nigger, nigger, nigger, nigger. I've questioned why the overkill. Perhaps he/she had to reassure themselves of my "subhumanity." The more it is iterated, the more convincing.

White racism dripped from their lips. The responses pulled from old white racist imagery that depicted Black people as bestial and animalistic. What became clear to me are the deep ways in which that discourse, those assumptions, and imagery are still quite palpable within the white American psyche.

So much of white America is unprepared and unwilling to have a courageous conversation about racism. They would rather avoid the conversation, blame me, call me a "race baiter." This is, I assume, like playing the race card. Race and racism are not games. Race is determinative of life and death; it has deep necro-political implications. So, the "race baiter" charge was just a way of dismissing me, of avoiding discussion. It is easy to blame me; it is much harder to look at one's white self within a disagreeable mirror, one that refuses to lie.

Given the racist insults, one might argue that many of the points that I was trying to make were confirmed. I did receive a few very powerful and beautiful responses from white readers who said to me that they accepted the gift that I offered and that they would critically and honestly engage their racism even as they knew that the challenge would be difficult and required serious work. "Thanks Professor Yancy for your thoughts," one woman wrote. "The system is racist. As a white woman, I am responsible for dismantling that system as well as the attitudes in me that growing up in the system created. I am responsible for speaking out when I hear racist comments." Another person wrote, "Beautiful words, thoughtful words, and words that needed to be said. Thank you for holding up a mirror to my inner hate." A shared understanding of the complexity of white racism was staring back at me. "Thank you. I am a white liberal/ardent backer of civil rights, but as you say, also a racist. Godspeed, and thank you for helping to keep me honest." Or, "I have been living this past year with the growing understanding that my white privilege is toxic." Or, "I would like to offer you a gift in return: A commitment to fully accept the racism (and sexism) that is embedded in me, acknowledge the privilege that comes with having been born a white American, try my best to be educated about the suffering my racism and privilege causes others." While I was humbled, I had to remind myself that these were words. The actual work still had to be done. I believe that these white people understand that. After so much vitriol, it was important, though, to hear white people call their racism out. Nevertheless, after so many insults, I have come to have profoundly less hope in white America. And, yet, I continue to write about and to white America. With a private wink to my dear Black poet friend and colleague, perhaps I, too, will soon stop talking to whiteness. Given the backlash that I experienced by the sheer act of writing a letter to white America, a letter that asked for love in return, I don't think that it is unreasonable for me to step aside. The problem, here, of course, is that there is nowhere to step where whiteness has not already inhabited that space—that aside.

Blasdel: How does *Backlash* take up that response, and take forward the argument of "Dear White America"?

Yancy: My authored book, *Backlash*, is a continuation of the letter of love that began with "Dear White America." I make no effort in the book to avoid sharing the racist vile responses that I received. I also engage my own personal trauma experienced as the result of so much white racism. And I engaged this with as much clarity and vulnerability as possible. I think that vulnerability is an important site for engaging questions of race and racism. I especially think that white people must become vulnerable. When I perform vulnerability through my writing, it's my way of refusing to remain silent. Also, my aim is not only to challenge a specific modality of *writing* philosophically, but a mode of *being* philosophically. Because I have come to think about the practice of philosophy as a site of suffering, it shows in my work.

White America, all Americans, must witness the vileness of white backlash. My book inundates its white readers with unmitigated reality and asks white readers to dwell within a space of Black trauma. By "dwell within," I mean to be touched by, to be moved by Black trauma. And it asks the white reader to linger, to touch the truth about their whiteness and its complicity with collective Black trauma. So, it dares to ask "good whites" to explore their racism, their hated, their white racist microaggressions and complicity with white racist macroaggressions. The book is an outgrowth of a post-racial America that was always a lie. And it asks white readers, in the words of James Baldwin, to use it as a "disagreeable mirror"[2] to look at themselves. The book asks white people to become disoriented; to allow themselves to dwell within a space of confusion about what and who they are through understanding a different way of being. I argue that whites must come to see themselves as situated within a social ontology of no edges, to come to understand and *to feel* what it means for their white embodiment as constitutive of violence vis-à-vis Black bodies. Think of the potential seismic moral implications of this new understanding and mode of being.

Blasdel: You compare white racism to sexism. What do you mean by that?

Yancy: I am a sexist. I don't say this with pride. It is not a confession. And it is certainly not an act of self-flagellation. I have better things to do. And I don't say it in order to receive praise. I am not a hero for being honest. I don't think that any of us men, raised within a culture that promotes pornography, the degrading sexual objectification of women, the fragmentation of women's bodies, and the perpetuation of rigid gender roles, escape such problematic forms of masculine "normalization." Let's admit it. Patriarchy is powerful. It shapes men's habits, perceptions, conceptions of romance, authority, pleasure, emotions, body comportment, conception of rights, control over space and the space of others, you name it. Of course, this doesn't mean that we are incapable of resisting. We certainly can resist, and we must.

In "Dear White America," my aim was to model for white people, to demonstrate what courageous speech looks like expressed publicly, what public vulnerability looked like. That was my aim. For the most part, it was a missed opportunity for so many white people. They became so obsessed and defensive that they failed or refused to bear witness to the ethical thrust of my public disclosure. So many of them were obsessed with "proving" their white "innocence" that my attempt to enact vulnerability as a desired end was overlooked. Then again, the kind of vulnerability for which I desired contradicted precisely any sense of illusory white innocence.

Blasdel: When you talk about "whiteness" in the letter and book, what do you mean?

Yancy: Whiteness is a structural, ideological, embodied, epistemological, and phenomenological mode of being—and it is predicated upon its distance from and negation of Blackness. This is what so many white people forget or refuse to see: their being racialized as white and socially and psychologically marked as privileged has problematic implications for my being Black.

Whiteness is what I call the "transcendental norm," which means that whiteness goes unmarked. As unmarked, white people are able to live their identities as unraced, as simply human, as persons. And this obfuscates the ways in which their lives depend upon various *affordances* that Black people and people of color don't possess. In fact, the white body is itself an affordance; it makes things happen. It is an affordance because the social world complements the white body. This is because the social world has already been sedimented with white values, modes of being, feeling, walking, aspiring, etc. Whiteness is the background in terms of which white people move and have their being, where they move through the world with racialized effortless grace. *It is hard to see the very being that one is; to see that which the act of seeing is often complicit in not seeing.*

White racism is a continuum, one that includes the Ku Klux Klan, the loving white Christian and the anti-racist white. Even good, moral white people, those who have Black friends, friends of color, married to people of color, fight for racial justice, and so on, don't escape white racist injustice against Black people and people of color; they all continue to be implicated within structures of white privilege and to embody, whether they realize it or not, society's racist sensibilities. White people possess white privilege or white immunity from racial disease. And because of this, others of us, Black people and people of color, reap the social, political, and existential pains of that racialized social skin.

Blasdel: Are you hopeful about your gift being accepted?

Yancy: As intimated above, I would say that I'm torn. I am by no means optimistic. History, however, is not closed and time is open-ended. Yet, there is nothing about time that guarantees the end to white supremacy. White supremacy is capable of conceding some things and yet preserving its core values and sustaining, as Joel Olson would say, a place for Black people that no white person will ever inhabit, no matter how poor that white person.[3] The logic of the Thirteenth Amendment to the U.S. Constitution made involuntary servitude unconstitutional and yet white power was preserved through the criminalization of Black people. In this way, white power continued to hold sway. Critical race theorist Derrick Bell is correct where he argues that any "victories" gained by Black people within America are episodic "peaks of progress,"[4] where lapses and regressions return. White supremacy is able to bend without breaking. It is able to eat and swallow oppositionality and resistance to its hegemony. In fact, it can even create necessary spaces for anti-white resistance while still being able to function, to survive. The point here is that whiteness is consumptive. Our objective should be to starve it.

White America needs to engage in a form of what I have come to term *crisis*. This process of crisis needs to occur at the center of whiteness, white identity. When we generally think of something being in a state of crisis, we see it as something that should be controlled, perhaps medicated, made stable. For me, being in crisis means that white people lose their way, they begin to experience forms of instability, of breakdown, of metanoia. This crisis is linked to white people grappling seriously with why they needed to project their vileness onto Black people and people of color in the first place. That crisis moment, I would think, is linked to the realization of the emptiness of whiteness, its vacuity. The gift contained in *Backlash* offers an embodied way of rethinking, re-feeling, and re-positioning what it means to be white. It is a gift that offers loss, which is so counterintuitive.

Today is white America's time to weep, to become vulnerable, and un-suture itself, which means, for me, a process of suffering oneself to be seen, of remaining wounded. The gift of *Backlash* is a radical call to white America to tarry with its own racist vomit, and to linger with the stench of the racist catastrophe of which it is responsible, before any talk of "reconciliation" is even possible.

At the end of the day, though, I often feel that I am facing a dilemma. Do I give up on white people, on white America, or do I continue to fight for a better white America, despite the fact that my efforts continue to lead to forms of unspeakable white racist backlash? At this point in my life, especially after so much *personal* white racist backlash, I am convinced that America suffers from a pervasively malignant and malicious systemic illness—white racism. There is also an appalling sense of indifference in our country that helps to sustain it. That indifference is itself a cruel reality, a reality that often makes me want to scream at the top of my lungs until I fall flat on my face from exhaustion. That indifference makes me sick to my stomach.

Chapter 4

Walking While Black in the White Gaze

Long before "Dear White America" and being the target of white backlash, I had known from an early age what it means, what it feels like, to be embodied as Black in North America. In short, early on, my young Black body registered the truth about the terror and dangers of whiteness.

"Man, I almost blew you away!"

Those were the terrifying words of a white police officer—one of those who policed Black bodies in low-income areas in North Philadelphia in the late 1970s—who caught sight of me carrying the new telescope my mother had just purchased for me.

"I thought you had a weapon," he said.

The words made me tremble and pause; I felt the sort of bodily stress and deep existential anguish that no teenager should have to endure. There are times when I think about just how close to death I came. My heart beats faster and I feel the precariousness of my finitude. During those times, my children disappear one by one. They cease to exist, because I would have died on that tragic night. The words that you're reading now would be nonexistent. It is really a chilling experience. There are times when I imagine the bullet entering in my fragile Black body, piecing my flesh. In the stench of that low-income housing hallway, a stench that was so familiar, I would be there dying, taking my last breath, while the white police officer was convinced that he saw a gun, that I was "dangerous," that I looked "suspicious." This would have been a pre–Trayvon Martin killing, a murder, leaving Black parents to mourn the death of their innocent Black child.

This officer had already inherited those poisonous assumptions and bodily perceptual practices that make up what I call the "white gaze." He had already come to "see" the Black male body as different, deviant, ersatz. He failed to conceive, or perhaps could not conceive that a Black teenage boy living in the Richard Allen Project Homes for very low-income families would own a telescope and enjoyed looking at the moons of Jupiter and the rings of Saturn.

A Black boy carrying a telescope wasn't conceivable—unless he had stolen it—given the white racist horizon within which my Black body was policed as dangerous. To the white police officer, I was something (not some-*one*) patently foolish, perhaps monstrous or even fictional. My telescope, for him, *was* a weapon.

In retrospect, I can see the headlines: "Black boy shot and killed while searching the cosmos."

President Obama, in his now much-quoted White House briefing not long after the verdict in the trial of George Zimmerman, expressed his awareness of the ever-present danger of death for those who inhabit Black bodies. "You know, when Trayvon Martin was first shot I said that this could have been my son," he said. "Another way of saying that is Trayvon Martin could have been me 35 years ago."[1] Personally, I wait for the day when a white president will say, "There is no way that I could have experienced what Trayvon Martin did (and other Black people do) because I'm white and through white privilege I am immune to systemic racial profiling." That is the type of truth-telling that is necessary. It is that kind of white truth-telling and honesty that could instigate its own potentially pervasive white crisis.

Obama also talked about how Black men in this country know what it is like to be followed while shopping and how Black men have had the experience of "walking across the street and hearing the locks click on the doors of cars."[2] I have had this experience on many occasions as whites catch sight of me walking past their cars: *click, click, click, click.* Those clicks can be deafening. There are times when I want to become their bogeyman. I want to pull open the car door and shout: "Surprise! You've just been car-jacked by a fantasy of your own creation. Now, get out of the car." Of course, this form of protest would only "confirm" what white people have always thought: Black bodies are out of control, dangerous, and violent.

The president's words, perhaps consigned to a long-ago news cycle now, remain powerful: they validate experiences that Black people have undergone in their everyday lives. Obama's voice resonates with those philosophical voices (Audre Lorde, Frantz Fanon, and James Baldwin, for example) that have long attempted to describe the lived interiority of racial and racist experiences caused by white people and within white contexts. He has also deployed the power of narrative autobiography, which is a significant conceptual tool used insightfully by critical race theorists to discern the clarity and existential and social gravity of what it means to experience white racism. As a Black president, he has given voice to the epistemic violence that Black people often face as they are stereotyped and profiled within the context of quotidian social spaces, where they are defined outside of their own epistemic integrity. So, Obama, at least in this case, reinforces a collective Black epistemic understanding that Black people have of their lives and how whiteness attempts to place those lives under social and existential erasure.

David Hume claimed that to be Black was to be "like a parrot who speaks a few words plainly."[3] And Immanuel Kant maintained that to be "black from head to foot" was "clear proof" that what *any* black person says is stupid.[4] In his Notes on the State of Virginia, Thomas Jefferson wrote, "In imagination they [Negroes] are dull, tasteless and anomalous," and inferior.[5] In the first American Edition of the *Encyclopedia Britannica* (1798), the term "Negro" was defined as someone who is cruel, impudent, revengeful, treacherous, nasty, idle, dishonest, a liar, and given to stealing.

My point here is to say that the white gaze is global and historically mobile. And its origins, while from Europe, are deeply seated in the making of America. So, the white gaze is integral to white world-making.

Black bodies in America continue to be reduced to their surfaces and to stereotypes that are constricting and false, that often force those Black bodies to move through social spaces in ways that put white people at ease. As such, we often don't move with effortless grace, but with caution. We know that our Black bodies incite an accusation vis-à-vis whiteness. We move in ways that help us to survive the procrustean gazes of white people.

The white gaze is also hegemonic, historically grounded in material relations of white power: it was deemed disrespectful for a Black person to violate the white gaze by looking directly into the eyes of someone white. The white gaze is also ethically solipsistic: within it only whites have the capacity of making valid moral judgments.

Even with the unprecedented White House briefing, our national discourse regarding Trayvon Martin and questions of race have failed to produce a critical and historically conscious discourse that sheds light on what it means to be Black in an anti-Black America. If historical precedent says anything, this failure will only continue. Trayvon Martin, like so many Black boys and men, was under surveillance (etymologically, "to keep watch"). Little did he know that on February 26, 2012, he would enter a space of social control and bodily policing, a kind of Benthamian panoptic nightmare that would truncate his being as suspicious—a space where he was, paradoxically, both invisible and yet hyper-visible. "Man, I almost blew you away!" That is the icy warning that grows out of the dynamics of white panoptic racialized policing. The "almost," though, is so often skipped. The Black body is simply blown away.

As Ralph Ellison says, "I am invisible, understand, simply because people [in this case white people] refuse to see me."[6] Trayvon was invisible to Zimmerman; he was not seen as the Black child that he was, trying to make it back home with Skittles and an iced tea. He was not seen as having done nothing wrong, as one who dreams and hopes.

As Black, Trayvon was already "known" and rendered invisible. His childhood and humanity were already criminalized as part of a white racist narrative about Black male bodies. Trayvon needed no introduction: "Look, the Black; the criminal!"

Many have argued that the site of violence occurred upon the confrontation between Trayvon and Zimmerman. Yet, from my perspective, the violence began with Zimmerman's nonemergency dispatch call, a call that was racially assaultive in its discourse, one that deployed the tropes of anti-Black racism. Trayvon Martin's parents, Sybrina Fulton and Tracy Martin, have decided to refer to George Zimmerman as "the killer." I follow suit here. Hence, the killer says, "There's a real suspicious guy." He also says, "This guy looks like he's up to no good or he's on drugs or something." When asked by the dispatcher, he says, within seconds, that "he looks Black." Asked what he is wearing, the killer says, "A dark hoodie, like a gray hoodie." Later, the killer says that "now he's coming toward me. He's got his hands in his waist band." And then, "And he's a Black male."[7] But what does it mean to be "a real suspicious guy"? What does it mean to look like one is "up to no good"? The killer does not give any details, nothing to buttress the validity of his narration. Keep in mind that the killer is in his vehicle as he provides his narration to the dispatcher. As "the looker," it is *not* the killer who is in danger; rather, it is Trayvon Martin, "the looked at," who is the target of suspicion and possible violence.

After all, it is Trayvon Martin who is wearing the hoodie, a piece of racialized attire that apparently signifies Black criminality. The killer later says, "Something's wrong with him. Yep, he's coming to check me out," and "He's got something in his hands." The killer also says, "I don't know what his deal is." A Black young male with "something" in his hands, wearing a hoodie, looking suspicious, and perhaps on drugs, and there being "something wrong with him," is a racist narrative of fear and frenzy. The history of white supremacy underwrites this interpretation. Within this context of *discursive violence*, the killer was guilty of an act of aggression against Trayvon Martin, even before the trigger was pulled. Prior to his physical death, Trayvon Martin was rendered "socially dead" under the weight of the killer's racist stereotypes. The killer's aggression was enacted through his gaze, through the act of profiling, through his discourse and through his warped reconstruction of an innocent Black boy that instigates white fear.

What does it say about North America when to be Black is the ontological crime, a crime of simply being?

Perhaps religious studies scholar Bill Hart is correct: "To be a black man is to be marked for death."[8] Or as political philosopher Joy James and race theorist João Costa Vargas argue, "Blackness as evil [is] destined for eradication."[9] Perhaps this is why when writing about the death of his young Black son, the social theorist W. E. B. DuBois said, "All that day and all that night there sat an awful gladness in my heart—nay, blame me not if I see the world thus darkly through the Veil—and my soul whispers ever to me saying, 'Not dead, not dead, but escaped; not bond, but free.' "[10]

Trayvon Martin was killed walking while Black. As the protector of all things "gated," of all things standing on the precipice of being endangered by Black male bodies, the killer created the conditions upon which he *had no grounds to stand on.* Indeed, through his racist stereotypes, and his pursuit of Trayvon, he created the conditions that belied the applicability of the stand your ground law, and created a situation where Trayvon was killed. This is the narrative that ought to have been told by the attorneys for the family of Trayvon Martin. It is part of the narrative that Obama brilliantly told, one of Black bodies being racially policed and having suffered an all too familiar repeated history of racist vitriol and racist deadly stereotypification in this country.

Yet, it is a narrative that is too late, one already rendered mute and inconsequential by the verdict of "not guilty." Trayvon dies; the killer walks free.

Chapter 5

It Feels like Being on Death Row

That familiar and painful feeling of being helpless in the face of innocent Black bodies gunned down in the streets of North America by the state and proxies of the state continues to grow. After hearing about the two Sacramento police officers who tragically shot and killed twenty-two-year-old unarmed Black male Stephon Clark because they thought that he had a gun when in fact he had a cell phone, I was seized by that feeling. Once again, I find myself trying to make sense of what it means to be Black in contemporary white America, an America that has always spelled out in unambiguous and brutal terms that Black bodies are disposable, especially when compared to white bodies, white life. There was that profound sense of grieving yet again for a Black body, a Black life, killed in the belly of this beast called white America. There was that sudden flood of outrage and deep melancholia as I was inundated with recent memories. After hearing the 911 audio tape of the killing of unarmed seventeen-year-old Black male Trayvon Martin, I wept. After hearing the "I can't breathe" cries of forty-two-year-old Black male Eric Garner, who eventually died of what the coroner described as a choke hold from a white police officer, my body felt constricted. His cries were existential entreaties that fell on opaque ears and hearts. One wonders if they could in fact hear him at all. After the racial profiling of twenty-eight-year-old Sandra Bland and the subsequent treatment of her (having been thrown to the ground) by a white police officer, I felt as if I should have been there to show her the respect and love that she deserved. I felt that familiar anger that arises from knowing that Black women have historically experienced (and continue to undergo) forms of intersectional violence and violation partly because they don't measure up to the myth of white female "fragility," "purity," and "innocence." I began to visualize past photos of lynched Black bodies as white men, women, and children looked with curious and excited white gazes. When I think about that mixed space of white terror and white desire, even a perverse sexual desire, there is that distinct feeling of disgust, physical and moral.

Stephon Clark's case reminded me of the tragedy of twenty-three-year-old Amadou Diallo, who was a Black man from Guinea, and how he was shot at forty-one times and hit with no less than nineteen bullets on February 4, 1999. Like Clark, Diallo was said to have a gun in his hand. As we know, a police officer yelled out, "Gun!" Yet, there was no gun, only a wallet. He had reached and grabbed his wallet. The urgent existential question is this: What is it about a Black man or Black teenager holding an innocuous object such as a wallet and yet white police officers see weapons? Recall my telescope ordeal: "Man, I almost blew you away!" Even toy guns become real guns in the hands of young Black boys. Ask twelve-year-old Tamir Rice. He was shot in roughly two seconds after white police officers arrived on the scene. There was no hesitation; there was no second thought, no un-suturing, no benefit of the doubt. The white racist logic goes like this: he is Black and therefore guilty. To be Black in America, according to white racist logic, which is undergirded by white myth-making, is to be *born* guilty, violent, criminal, dangerous. According to such myth-making, Black bodies must be stopped dead before they contaminate the white body politic, before they unleash their "inherent violence." Truth be told, if you are Black, you might find yourself lost in a white neighborhood, searching for help and be shot dead because you were believed to be a "threat." Recall that it was nineteen-year-old Renisha McBride who, while seeking help after being in a car accident, was shot dead by white male Theodore Wafer as she was heard by him "banging" on his front door. Then again, as briefly mentioned in chapter 1, Black bodies can literally find themselves on the ground with their hands raised, as in the case of forty-seven-year-old Black male Charles Kinsey, and still be shot. On July 18, 2016, Kinsey clearly stated to police officers that his client, who had wandered away from a mental health facility, had a toy truck and that they should not shoot. Kinsey was concerned that his client would appear, by the police officers, as if he had a weapon. Yet, a police officer on the scene fired three shots, one of which hit Kinsey in the leg. According to Kinsey, when he asked why he was shot, the police officer replied, "I don't know." James Baldwin writes, "But it is not permissible that the authors of devastation should be innocent."[1] In short, there is no innocence here. "I don't know, on my view," explains the deep and indelible racist assumptions that many white Americans have of Black bodies, assumptions that are embedded in the form of embodied and psychic racist dispositions or habits that are etched into the white psyche, a psyche that imagines guns where there are wallets or cell phones, or telescopes. This isn't just a question about white police officers possessing false beliefs. Rather, within such contexts, it speaks powerfully to the ways in which many white police officers *don't see* innocent Black bodies, unarmed Black bodies, or Black lives that matter. It has to do with forms of embodied white racist rigidity that often operate beyond the radar of cognitive reflection, resulting in a reflexive "common sense" that leaves Black bodies dead. This is why wallets and cell phones in the hands of Black people become guns, toy guns become real guns, Black bodies on the ground with their hands raised become threatening bodies, and Black bodies in search of help become criminal bodies trying to break into a white man's home, to steal from white spaces, and why Black men (Donte Robinson and Rashon Nelson) innocently sitting in a Starbucks are deemed "suspicious," and why an eight-year-old Black girl (Jordan Rodgers) selling water has the police called on her by a white woman, and why a Black female graduate student (Lolade Siyonbola) at Yale University who is having a nap in her dorm's common room is deemed cause for a white female student to call the police on her. The reality is that to be Black in white America is to be suspicious, a problem to be dealt with, an "anti-citizen" whose "rights" no white person is bound to respect.

Stephon Clark's tragic death came two weeks after I shared with my university students that I try never to pull out my cell phone when just casually walking down the street. My white students often look with credulity. Perhaps silently they say to themselves: "What in the hell is he talking about?" I let them know that the history of white America's fear of the Black body (my Black body) forces me to abandon ordinary activities like reaching for my wallet in the presence of white police officers, running down the street for a bus in the presence of white police officers, or holding my cell phone in the presence of white police officers. In fact, I try not to do these things in the presence of white people, more generally, especially as they also see with distorted white gazes and where they can very easily function as proxies of the state and thereby enforce law and order. Like George Zimmerman, the killer, they will police in advance my Black body as "suspicious." In fact, my fear is so great that neither white police officers nor white civilians need be immediately present. The historical madness of white gratuitous violence from white people experienced by Black people forces me, for my own survival, to monitor my own actions even in their absence, especially as they might appear suddenly. I don't seem to get a break to be simply human or a person, to walk with effortless grace in white America. And while I have no desire to be white, my humanity *must* be respected. I want to be free in my everyday body comportment. I want to be free in my embodied movements, in the movement of my hands, walking down the street, sitting in a restaurant, taking a nap, driving in my car, abiding by the law. "What in the hell is he talking about?" The question itself bespeaks the safety of whiteness, its ignorance and its indifference.

If I had the opportunity to speak with Stephon Clark before his death, I would have warned him of something that I would be at great pains to share. Theo Shaw, who in 2006 was a member of the "Jena Six," in Jena, Louisiana, once wrote to ask me a deeply moving and disturbing question: "Is to be Black and male in America like being on death row?" It was hard for me to answer the question, especially as I didn't want to negatively impact Theo Shaw's aspirations. Yet, I refused to lie to him as I would have refused to lie to Stephon Clark. *Yes!* To be a Black male in white America, with its white state violence, and its history of white supremacy, is like being on death row. There is that sense of just waiting to die, just waiting for one's own death, one's execution, put to death by white authority, judged already guilty, in virtue of being Black. There is that sense of being confined within a space where it feels hard to breathe, hard to move one's body without the constant reality of surveillance, of constantly having one's privacy invaded and one's rights violated and removed.

Now, Theo Shaw is obviously aware that not all Black males are imprisoned waiting for gubernatorial clemency. Yet, he asks the question. The weight of the question and my answer to it speaks to the *lived* experiences of so many Black males in America. After all, according to what we have witnessed, a white police officer will still shoot you as you're on the ground with your hands raised. Or, you can be shot and killed as your cell phone or your wallet becomes a phantasmatic gun. Out of love, I would have said this to Stephon. I would have reminded him that, for the most part, white America has never loved him, and that it was never meant for him to be human in white America. As Toni Morrison tells readers in *Beloved*, I would have also said to Stephon that he must love his body because the history of white America says that it is better that it swings from a tree, incarcerated or dead. Love in this case, Black love, is a radical act of existential and political resistance. Morrison writes, "In this here place, we flesh; flesh that weeps, laughs; flesh that dances on bare feet in grass. Love it. Love it hard. Yonder they do not love your flesh. They despise it. They don't love your eyes; they'd just as soon pick em out. No more do they love the skin on your back. Yonder they flay it."[2] And I would have told him never to forget this. When we forget that Black bodies are deemed ontologically antithetical to white conceptions of "purity" and "safety," it is then that we live under a false veil of neoliberalism. And just when you think that you have been accepted as an individual, you discover that the meaning of your Black body has always already been confiscated and instead of a lethal injection, your body is blown away—gone, forever unrepeatable—because some white police officer felt that their life was in danger. It was not an individual that was seen, but a stereotype, a myth, a racist construction. The you that you are wasn't present, but an old and frozen racist imago was present, which means that you have been tethered to a temporal zone that is stuck in the past. The white police officer doesn't interact with you in your robust presence. The encounter isn't coeval. This is why un-suturing not only ruptures the white police officer's mode of sutured embodiment, but the un-suturing fissures temporality, fracturing the projected past and allowing for the flood of the present, the flood of your Black presence, one that is not ontologically fixed by their white violent practice of suturing, of remaining in the past and thereby foreclosing the present and the future.

As we are rarely ever granted innocence in white America, we are, in the main, a "guilty people," Black, disposable, tragically stained from birth. The disposability, the tragedy, and the stain are significant. It isn't simply about the death of the Black body. Something more insidious is at stake. Perhaps what we are witnessing is the necessarily continuous policing of the Black body as a site of extreme existential precarity, a constant restriction of the Black body to that of the "walking dead" so that white people can maintain their sense of existential assurance (perhaps even insurance) that they are not one of us.

Chapter 6

Blackface: What Does It Say about White America?

Trayvon Martin, Stephon Clark, Eric Garner, Amadou Diallo, Tamir Rice, Renisha McBride, and so many others were all targeted because they were Black. That is the enduring reality and tragic narrative of being Black in North America, which is a bastion of white racist supremacy. White America must be prepared to exercise a form of unforeseen courage and painful honesty to look deep enough to face the reason why they have found it necessary to position Black bodies as *their* targets, as objects of their projections. I have not seen that white America; not yet. It would require a process of un-suturing that would bespeak both white vulnerability and a form of white forthrightness to admit to the white racist toxicity to which they have given birth and have nurtured. But is white America really prepared to reveal and to *confront* its entrails? Unlike for Odysseus, there is life on the side of letting go, of un-suturing, of unplugging one's ears and throwing away the mast.

In *Black Boy*, Black literary figure Richard Wright discusses how he is dismayed that white America will continue to fail to understand what it means to be Black in America because it "will take a bigger and tougher America than any we have yet known."[1] I share Wright's dismay as I have not seen any evidence of such a bigger and tougher white America when it comes to seriously interrogating, collectively, white racism in this country. White America suffers from a moral weakness and spinelessness when it comes to the level of honesty and exposure that is required to seriously tackle the problem of white racism. Think here of the recent inundation that we have had of instances of whites donning blackface. There isn't much dispute regarding the racist history and the racist nature of blackface. While Virginia governor Ralph Northam denies that he is the student in blackface next to another white person wearing KKK "regalia" in his 1984 medical school yearbook, he has admitted to darkening his face to look like Michael Jackson when he went to a

41

dance party. There is also Florida State representative Anthony Sabatini who, while a sophomore in high school, donned blackface, replete with a do-rag, gold chains, sunglasses, and a New York Yankees cap. And then there were the two University of Oklahoma white students in a video where one of them was putting on blackface and where she apparently says, "I am a Nigger." As of this writing, both Sabatini and Northam have refused to resign from their political offices. The white students in the video, however, have withdrawn from the university. In each of these cases, the damage had already been done. Black bodies had already been targeted.

There are many ways to frame these blackface incidents: very infrequent so no real need to worry; just a few proverbial bad apples; a few cases of white ignorance that should be called out; or, some otherwise good white people who were simply naïve. What I have witnessed in real time are white pundits and white commentators who demonize these *individual cases* and white persons and thereby distance themselves as far as possible from them. Make no mistake about it, these cases are abhorrent and unacceptable. What I find even more unacceptable, though, is white America's collective failure to treat blackface as a teachable moment about the ingrained nature of white American racism. So, what we really need to do now is the courageous work necessary to look deep into the soul of white America. These cases of blackface will come and go, but Black pain and suffering will remain a constant unless white supremacy, white privilege, and white power are *completely* dismantled.

Let's face blackface head-on, which means let's address the structure of whiteness that drives the performance of using burnt cork or shoe polish by white people to darken their faces. So as not to mince words, blackface is historically grounded in white supremacy and as such is an act of epistemological and ontological terror. In other words, blackface is a form of "white knowing," which is really a form of white unknowing, a form of white projection, which, etymologically, means to "throw forth." Blackface is also a form of stipulating (manifested in the mode of performance) what it means *to be* Black through lies about what it means *to be* white. Whites in blackface perform "Blackness," ergo Blacks exist as thereby performed. On this score, Black bodies are scripted, consumed, and re-performed as problem bodies. As such, they are and have been the targets of the white toxic imaginary. Blackface is indicative of a long history of whiteness and its attempt to make sense of itself through both the consumption and the negation of Black humanity. Blackface speaks to the parasitic nature of whiteness and its need to "feed." After all, whiteness, in its colonial logics, must consume and yet paradoxically exclude that which is other, that which is Black. For whites, as Mary Elizabeth Hobgood would argue, Blackness is both "fascination and repulsion."[2] This suggests something quite profound. What if blackface reveals something that is far too threatening for white America to discuss, to admit, something far too weighty for white America to tarry with, something that would require a bigger and tougher America? What if blackface is clear evidence of the emptiness of whiteness, the hollowness of its being as an identity marker? If this is true, and I have no reason to believe that it isn't, then calling blackface out, whether in the past or the present, reveals an important aspect of the larger structure and social ontological character of American whiteness.

In fact, revealing blackface in this way can function as an important step toward starving whiteness of its need for the other, its need to be what it is not, its need to masquerade, its need to vomit its lies onto the Black body and pretend as if the Black body has always been the embodiment of something putrid and smelly. Yes, vomit! That is a powerful and yet descriptively robust and accurately grotesque metaphor to deploy when it comes to describing blackface. After all, blackface describes the pain and suffering felt by Black people whose bodies and identities underwent processes of transmogrification, where they were rendered grotesque and bizarre, covered with white ugly and rank myths. Blackface was not a Black problem, but a white problem. And it continues to this day to be a white problem. To be clear, we know that servant-performers existed before the racist grotesquery of white American blackface minstrelsy. As noted in Kwame Anthony Appiah's and Henry Louis Gates' edited book, *Africana: The Encyclopedia of the African and African-American Experience*, "During the Middle Ages minstrels were servant-performers who entertained their patrons by playing music, singing, telling stories, juggling, or performing comic antics and buffoonery."[3]

Within the white American antebellum context and after, however, anti-Blackness was at the very heart of white blackface minstrelsy. The Black body functioned as *the* repulsive and revolting object in terms of which white people unleased their disgust toward Black bodies. White American blackface performers engaged in exaggerated and distorted gestures, warped dialect, and racist clowning that reflected the larger anti-Black white American imaginary vis-à-vis the Black body. As white performers blackened their faces with burnt cork, re-presented the Black body in caricatured, silly, ersatz, inferior, horrible, and damnable ways, they were able to mark Black bodies publicly as appallingly stupid and subhuman. Within this racist construction, though, white bodies remained "normative," "intelligent," "civil," "nonthreatening," engaging in "mere entertainment." Within the context of this process of white normative framing, however, whites implicitly and explicitly reinforced deeply problematic and false "racial differences" between Black and white bodies. As Ronald L. Jackson, II argues, "The darkened face, created from the moistened debris of burnt and crushed champagned corks, insolently signified that Whites did not want to see Blacks for who they really were culturally, but, instead, . . . an iconographic image, a scripted racial body inscribed with meanings and messages Whites enjoyed seeing, ones that were self-affirming and insular."[4]

On this score, American whiteness embodied and embodies an episte-mological and ontological divide that it takes as "normative," as "common sense." And it tells a history (philosophical, aesthetic, ethical, religious) that is about itself, a self-redeeming and self-congratulatory history. This domi-nant self-narrative is itself indicative of white power and privilege. As Peggy McIntosh writes, "When I am told about national heritage or about 'civiliza-tion,' I am shown that people of my [white] race made it what it is."[5] At the base of this narrative history are lies and distortions; indeed, more broadly, there is an entire underside of white modernity that consists of enslaved and dehumanized Black bodies and often forgotten indigenous bodies across the Americas that were brutally deracinated, brutalized, and decimated. The point that I'm making here is that "racialized others" are part of a larger white supremacist global history. In short, the Black body and bodies of color are the delectable delights of white consumption. To use Vincent Woodard's relevant discourse, blackface in particular can be described as a site of "con-sumption rituals" and "consumption practices."[6]

Richard Dyer is keenly aware of the racialized and racist bifurcation that blackface played within North American culture. He writes, "One function of the exaggerations of blackface, and the film stereotypes of African-Americans in large measure drawn from it, was to make very clear and sharp the difference between black and white races."[7] While I agree with Joe R. Feagin and Hernán Vera that "white-on-black racism is thus a—if not *the*—crucial paradigmatic case of racism historically and in the present,"[8] it is also important to note what Christy Mag Uidhir calls "race mismatching," which also applied to people of color, more broadly. He writes, "Even the most cursory of glances through the history of cinema reveals the practice of race-mismatching—whether as *cinematic blackface* or one of its racially other-colored cinematic kin (*yellowface, redface, brownface*)—present not only in cinema's infancy but also through its Golden Age all the way to the contemporary Hollywood era."[9] Similarly, tracing the expanding practice of racial caricature and race-mismatching, Hernán Vera and Andrew M. Gordon note, "Blackface minstrelsy carried over from the music hall stage into silent movies, as in *The Birth of a Nation* (1915), and into sound movies as well, beginning with the first talkie, *The Jazz Singer* (1927). White actors also performed onstage in the nineteenth century as Asians, Asian Americans (the tradition of 'yellowface'), or Native Americans and continued to do so in silent films and even into American movies of the 1960s and beyond."[10] In its expansionist desire to consume, the point here is that whiteness thrived and thrives through a racist framing of non-Europeans as problematic and distorted, which are falsehoods and fictions that buttress the "superiority" of whiteness. Feagin and Vera write, "Constructed and incorporated in a centuries old racist framework, they [non-European immigrants] have often become 'Chinks,' 'Japs,' 'gooks,' and 'greasers.'"[11]

Blackface is predicated upon whites making a sharp difference between themselves and Black people and that therefore whites had to engage in a profound act of prestidigitation, as it were, a magical trick that involved a massive form of self-deception. This trickery is consistent with the trappings of ideology. Whiteness, as a species of ideology, deems as "natural" (say the Black body as a "brute" or "hyper-sexual" or "lazy") that which it has *socially* generated, and then it conveniently forgets this fact. In doing so, the Black body is reified as possessing such characteristics as "brutishness" or "hyper-sexuality" or "laziness." In short, such features are redefined as natural or biologically intrinsic to the Black body. Of course, institutions and discursive and material forces support such a problematic conception of the Black body.

Whites in blackface took themselves to be mirroring Black bodies *as such*. Within white theatrical spaces of blackface performance, such spaces were forged to "confirm" the "truth" that white gazes beheld. White people gathered within such spaces to have their worldview proven beyond doubt. White audiences, through their attendance and their laughter, helped to "validate" the white racist distortions as true. After all, they laughed at those who were deemed fundamentally different from themselves, and that laugher helped to sustain the necessary distance even as Southern whites no doubt longed for the return of the "slavish" and "happy" Black body. As Grace Elizabeth Hale writes, "Minstrelsy entertained not just through ridicule but also through nostalgia."[12] Whites came in large numbers to see what they refused to admit were *their* creations, *their* myths. They came to see "Black darky reality" depicted through blackface, through representations created by an arrogant white race who would dare to assume that they knew Black people better than Black people knew themselves. Yet, the entire white *mise en scène* was emblematic of white world-making, the construction of fictions into facts and lies into truths. Like a white mob lynching of a Black body, white people came to see what they themselves had already projected well in advance unto the brutally beaten and burned Black body.

During performances of blackface, imagine the ease with which whites gazed upon what they took to be "God's creation." After all, there was a great deal of European "discovered facts" to support this assumption. German naturalist Johann F. Blumenbach claimed that Adam and Eve were white. And it was Carl Linnaeus, known as "the father" of taxonomy who was fond of saying, "God created, Linnaeus organized." Linnaeus also stated that Black people, unlike whites who were ruled by law, were ruled by caprice, which meant that they were naturally unpredictable.[13] What more proof is needed? So, the white audiences looked on with perceptual ease, certain of what they saw before them: Black dim-witted, and easily frightened buffoons. As Ronald L. Jackson, II notes, "White theatergoers could leave the stage play feeling assured that they were behaving respectfully in the eyes of God and that the playwright was simply portraying Black and white lives exactly as they existed with a slight exaggeration of Black facial features just for fun."[14] And they watched and left with little or no conscience at all.

Returning to the act of vomiting as a metaphor for thinking about blackface minstrelsy, imagine whites in blackface on the stage. The actor vomits up all of the lies and distortions onto the Black body. Here is where the combined performance displays its full grotesquery. The whites in the audience, metaphorically, begin to eat the vomit. After all, they accept the putrid lies as digestible truths; the lies fill them with self-certainty about their "superior" status. Imagine the stench. The smell of mendacity. So, here one feels the full weight of the metaphor. So, as the Black body, I am treated as the "happy darky," the "ludicrous Black figure," "the Black idiot," the "Black simpleton," the "inferior 'nigger.'" Yet, whites deny that they have created these assumptions. The denial sustains their white "purity" and "innocence." However, as Black people, we are the targets of such violent depictions. More accurately, who and what we are constitute an apparent isomorphic relationship to those depictions. *We are those happy darkies.* And since we are those "happy darkies," whites, even newly arrived whites to the American shore, were able to partake of the festive meal of white lies. Joe R. Feagin writes, "The shows were very popular with white workers, including new European immigrants then seeking to be defined as 'white.' They were also eagerly attended by members of the elite, including presidents John Tyler (even at his inauguration) and Abraham Lincoln, as well as prominent novelists like Mark Twain."[15] Blackface was an equalizer among whites—immigrant, poor, wealthy.

Historically, blackface exists because white supremacy exists. Blackface is a cruel practice; one might even say an odd and twisted economy of white perverse desire. Blackface is also a weapon and Black people are its target. We are not the horrible and derogatory racist myths that so many white people have said and continue to say that we are, whether through blackface or some other horrible white American pastime. I know who I am. Blackface tells me absolutely nothing about myself, but it does tell me about your whiteness, your grotesque vomit. So, clean it up. You must do the lions share, because blackface is your problem, your burden, not ours.

Chapter 7

Look in the Disagreeable Mirror: Rethinking Black History for White People

For those who take Black History Month (BHM) seriously, we must raise our voices especially now given America's contemporary unabashed mendacity, hypocrisy, and white nativism intensified in the age of Trump. While it is a month in which African-Americans celebrate our achievements, ones that were gained against nearly impossible economic, social, and political odds, we must remind white America of the deep existential brutality that African-Americans faced as we struggled to live under white supremacy, a system that rendered us "sub-persons." And even as we fought to make America "our home," a home that we must recognize was already brutally taken from Native Americans by white invading and colonial settlers, our Black bodies faced unconscionable white enslavement, brutality, and oppression; we lived through forms of carnage, mutilation, rape, castration, white terror, and injustice that will forever mark the profound ethical failure of this country.

Yet, as a people, we forced America to look deep into its soul and to see the moral bankruptcy that lay there. We demonstrated that the American experiment had failed Black people and people of color. By doing so, we embodied far more of the spirit of freedom and justice than those who withheld America's promise. After all, even America's founding fathers *owned* Black people, sold us and reduced us to tools to be wielded according to their perverse white desires. It is that brutal and contradictory history from which America cannot wash the blood from its hands. And just as Jews refuse to forget Hitler's Germany, we refuse to forget the racist, often unspeakable, atrocities that we endured here in America. More specifically, it is this resistance to forgetting that must be nurtured as we find ourselves within the midst of a dangerous form of anti-globalism, white nativism and xenophobia under President Trump's vision for making America "great again," a vision closer to D. W. Griffith's 1915 *The Birth of a Nation*, a film predicated upon white fear and denigration of Black bodies.

On the one hand, America stood for freedom and liberty. Yet, Black people were denied these. White people lived in a profound form of Sartrean bad faith. Speaking to this, white social critic Lillian Smith, who was raised as a child in the Deep South, and who authored *Killers of the Dream*, observed, "I had learned that God so loved the world that He gave His only begotten Son so that we might have segregated churches."[1] She also noted, "I learned it is possible to be a Christian and a white southerner simultaneously . . . to pray at night and ride Jim Crow car the next morning and to feel comfortable in doing both."[2] It is this bad faith, this ethical perversity, that haunts the history of white America. And as Frederick Douglass notes, "Between the Christianity of this land and the Christianity of Christ, I recognize the widest possible difference."[3] And in his speech "What to the Slave is the Fourth of July," Douglass said to white America, "The Fourth of July is yours, not *mine*. You may rejoice, *I* must mourn."[4]

As I listened to President Trump's BHM remarks on February 1, 2017, it was painfully obvious that he didn't bear witness to *that* Douglass. It is convenient for him not to know that Douglass. In this nightmare of Trumpism, we mustn't forget Douglass' words, just as we mustn't forget the dejection felt by the Chinese people who America excluded for racial reasons by the Chinese Exclusion Act of 1882. We mustn't forget about the anti-Japanese internment camps during World War II. These actions contradicted America's alleged identity as a nation whose arms are open to the stranger, the outcast; a nation that, in theory, does not discriminate based upon race and national origin.

In our current morally catastrophic moment, it is important to critically consider Trump's signing of an executive order that temporarily blocks both immigrants and nonimmigrants from such Muslim countries as Syria, Iraq, Iran, Libya, Somalia, Sudan, and Yemen. This has implications beyond questions of constitutional legitimacy. This ban, along with the plan to build a wall along the U.S. border with Mexico, is indicative of deeper issues regarding American white nativism, and the fact that so many Americans have become seduced by a neoliberal malaise of individual hopelessness and trepidation that they are willing to overlook concerns of constitutionality and their own moral conscience. Trump's divisiveness is not only xenophobic, but anti-theological according to his own professed Christianity.

At this moment, we are symbolically walking from Jerusalem to Jericho and Trump is telling us it is "better," "safer," not to attend to the wounds and sorrows of the "stranger." This is America's crucible. The Judaic concept of *Tikkun Olam* ("repairing the world") is bastardized under Trump's executive order. We are instead in the midst of a dangerous form of idolatry that praises unmitigated power, valorizes American white nativism, and borders on neofascism. Martin Luther King, Jr. has been quoted widely as saying, "Without love, there is no reason to know anyone, for love will in the end connect us to our neighbors, our children and our hearts."[5] And just who are our neighbors? They are undocumented immigrants who seek to be with their families in the United States; they are refugees and "strangers" with whom we share a common humanity and who flee war torn countries. As we fight against draconian orders that would make us turn our backs on those in need, we must also collectively fight against an Orwellian nightmare that would have us believe that $2 + 2 = 5$.

As Americans across race celebrate BHM, it is important to tarry with unimaginable and *systemic forms* of marginalization, pain, and suffering that Black people had to endure at the hands of a country that has failed to live up to its ideals of freedom and equality for all. Then again, perhaps "failed" is too generous. Perhaps it is more appropriate to say that this country, for the most part, didn't give a damn if it lived up to its ideals or not vis-à-vis Black people and people of color. We must face white America's sins unequivocally and collectively. Hence, celebrating BHM, inter alia, is about facing a nonideal historical and existential situation. It is about collective grieving and mourning for Black people who were, as suggested, never meant to be included within the ideal norms of American democracy, and yet who forced themselves to dream as they faced nightmares, who forced themselves to continue breathing as they were suffocating from the stench of Black bodies lynched and burned alive, and who forced themselves to stay alive when suicide would have been easier.

BHM also asks of white people something far more than just having white students read a poem by some Black poet. BHM is about you, white people, too. It is not simply about what happened and continues to happen to us as Black people, but about the racist historical conditions that were established that allowed you freedom of mobility, freedom of being, and a sense of personhood. I know that white people also had to work hard, and some were poor and were confined to the role of indentured servants, but they were *not* Black. So, if you are white, take this month and grieve. Find a private and sacred place to weep, to grieve for those whose dark skin marked them for subpersonhood. Acknowledge that whiteness saved those who looked like you from the vicious barbarity visited upon Black people. And in that moment, I want you to lament a country that continues to privilege whiteness, that continues to fall far short of what is written on parchment.

White people ought to use BHM to engage in a shared form of vulnerability and mourning, a collective recognition, with a courageous countenance, of how white racist complicity and Black suffering were historically linked and are currently intertwined. Such a courageous act of vulnerability is not about white guilt, but white responsibility. There is a specific wound that is necessary for white people; it is a kind of wound that will un-suture forms of trapped and concealed lies. King compared racism to "a boil that can never be cured as long as it is covered up but must be opened with all its pus-flowing ugliness."[6] To cover up, within this context, is what I call white suturing.

BHM can function as an important instigation for white people to unmask their white privilege, especially for those working-class whites in the Rust Belt. Personally, I empathize with your economic pain and suffering. I understand your lack of economic growth, but are you prepared to understand that we not only suffer economically, but we suffer because of white racism, because we are Black? Judith Butler says, "Let's face it. We're undone by each other. And if we're not, we're missing something."[7] If I am to be undone by your economic pain and plight, then you must be willing to be undone by the economic *and* white systemic and prejudicial racist pain that we, as Black people and people of color, feel and continue to endure.

Now, if you think that I'm playing the race card, then I ask you to perform this small task. Look at your white face in the mirror. Allow your economic plight to anger you. And just as you do this, try to imagine your face encased in dark skin. And as you look in the mirror seeing a dark face look back, be honest with yourself. Isn't it better to be white and to struggle economically than to struggle economically *and to be Black* under the same circumstances? My guess is that you would rather the former. Whiteness continues to provide comfort and a sense of self-worth within a context of white supremacy. Blackness, within the same context, materializes into another struggle with which we must contend. Our struggle is not only economic, but profoundly ontological. Butler also warns us that "we make a mistake when we take 'self-preservation' to be the essence of the human."[8] There is something indeed inhuman about insulating ourselves from the touch of the other, willfully ignoring the pain and suffering of the other. We are headed into an ethical abyss beyond which there may be no return. BHM has much to teach. For example, before he was murdered on April 4, 1968, King had planned to deliver a sermon that was entitled "Why America May Go to Hell." While King did not give that sermon, we should heed his prophetic warning.

Chapter 8

King's Dream or Trump's Nightmare?

No need to equivocate. Let's come clean: President Trump is a white racist! That needs repeating: *President Trump is a white racist!* Why repeat it? Because many have been under the grand illusion that America is a "post-racial" nation, a beautiful melting pot where racism is only sporadic, infrequent, and expressed by those on the margins of an otherwise mainstream and "decent" America. That's a lie; a blatant one at that. We must face a very horrible truth. And America is so cowardly when it comes to facing awful truths about itself.

So, the disjunction is a clear one, especially as we must face the fact that we are at a moral crossroad. Will America courageously live out Martin Luther King, Jr.'s dream or will it cowardly go down the road of bigotry, racist vitriol, militarism, xenophobia, hatred, and divisiveness, preferring to live out Trump's nightmare instead of King's dream? King says, "The way of acquiesce leads to moral and spiritual suicide."[1] For those of us who defiantly desire to live, and to live out King's dream, to make it a reality, we mustn't acquiesce at a time when King's prophetic warning faces us head on: "Why America may Go to Hell." We desperately need each other at this moment of moral crisis and malicious racist divisiveness. Will we raise our collective voices against Trump's white racism and those who make excuses for it or submit and thereby self-destructively kill any chance of fully becoming our better selves? Personally, I can't remain silent. While many civil rights leaders were critical of King's political, ethical, and religious resistance to the Vietnam War, he adopted the position that "there comes a time when silence is betrayal."[2] To honor King, we mustn't remain silent, we mustn't betray his legacy, we mustn't betray our critical intelligence and conscience when they inform us that we are clearly witnessing (and to our own national and international detriment) draconian, antidemocratic, neofascist proclivities.

So many Americans suffer from the obsessive need to claim "innocence," that is, to lie to ourselves. Yet, such a lie is part of our moral undoing. While many will deny, continue to lie, and claim our national "innocence," I come bearing deeply troubling, but not surprising, news. White racism is now comfortably located within the Oval Office itself, right there at 1600 Pennsylvania Avenue, embodied in our forty-fifth president, one who is—and I think many would agree, *must agree*, without any hesitation—an unabashed white racist. There are many who will resist this characterization, but Trump has desecrated the symbolic aspirations of America, exhumed forms of white supremacist discourse that so many would assume is spewed only by the Ku Klux Klan or Neo-Nazis.

Trump doesn't need to march in Charlottesville, VA, carrying a tiki torch. He doesn't need to shout the Nazi slogan, "Blood and Soil." He doesn't need to wear KKK regalia. He doesn't need to publicly call some of us "niggers." We already have enough evidence. The question is: are we looking at the same Emperor? Like the little child in Hans Christian Andersen's tale, I refuse to lie and have no space for pretense: Trump is naked!

On January 11, Trump, perturbed with lawmakers who suggested that America commit to restoring protections for immigrants from places like Haiti, El Salvador, and African countries, is said to have asked, "Why are we having all these people from shithole countries come here?" According to some present, Trump went on to suggest that the United States should consider bringing more people from places like Norway. Assuming that all of this is true, and as of this writing I have no reason to doubt it, we can't run from this one. There is no spin that can obfuscate this. White House press secretary Sarah Huckabee Sanders will probably do just that, obfuscate the truth, or avoid the issue, or simply lie.

Trump's base will become even more emboldened, taken by Trump's penchant to "speak his mind." I can imagine leaders in the Republican Party who, rather than acting based upon ethical duty and instead following party loyalty, may very well treat this as a "matter of the heart" ("We don't know Trump's heart"), "poor phrasing," or "taken out of context." The problem with lying, obfuscation, and making excuses, though, is that one is often forced to tell more lies, cloud the truth even further, make more excuses. These words from Trump are a blight on this nation, a dagger in the very heart of what we claim to be "noble" about America, a verbal drone fired at our fragile democratic experiment. And if we are honest, we will agree that the national and international damage done by Trump's white racist virulence is a heavy moral price to pay; a profound moral tragedy. And for those who remain silent, you also stand accused.

With such a continuous display of unabashed white racist sensibilities, Trump has pulled deeply from the white racist imagination. The last that

I checked, a "shithole" refers either to a toilet or the anus. Then again, in Trump's mouth, it could mean both. So, according to Trump's alleged logic, let's get this right. We are to believe that places like Haiti, El Salvador, and African countries are indicative of places where feces are deposited or places from which feces are expelled. Either way, Haitians, Salvadorians, and Africans function, in Trump's white racist imaginary, as "dirt," "crap," that which "stinks," is "foul" and "nasty," that which causes us typically to recoil. These are the people who bring with them "contamination," which functions as a trope for uncleanness, pollution, corruption. This supports Trump's white nativist narrative regarding making America great again; it is to make America white, "pure," "clean," "unsullied," and "moral" again. It is not by accident that those who are preferred are from Norway. After all, for Trump, they are "pure," "clean," and "moral," which are tropes for whiteness.

Trump could have taken this from a Nazi handbook. Nazi ideology embraced Nordicism, which held that whites in northern Europe were "superior," *Übermenschen*. Clearly, Trump, like Hitler, has a preference for Nordic types. Of course, regardless of race, Trump has this penchant for dictatorial male figures. This isn't just ignorance on Trump's part; this is moral catastrophe, moral ineptness of the highest order, antidemocratic aspirations, and racist vitriol that certainly has no place in the Oval Office. Well, unless the Oval Office speaks for America, and America supports Nordicism. Then again, philosophically, Trump is not far off from the anthropological "genius" of Immanuel Kant who, in "On the Different Races of Man," held that the first race, which was obviously white, was "very blond (northern Europe), of damp cold."[3] Unsurprisingly, Kant held that Black people, because they are Black, are stupid. These are the same Black people who Trump characterized by saying: "You live in your poverty, your schools are no good. You have no jobs. What the hell do you have to lose?"[4] The answer is clear: our souls to a racist.

Strange, isn't it? From the "shithole" of Africa, the beauty, profundity, and complicity of human life evolved. I guess Trump knew this, though. After all, he is "a very stable genius."

Joel Kovel writes that "aversion is the cardinal manifestation of modern American racism."[5] This is why we had de jure segregation. White people didn't want to be "contaminated" by Black bodies, by mixing with "bad blood." White people expressed an aversion toward those of us who were racialized as Black. We were considered "dirt"—stuff that needed to be removed, kept in its place. Like a shithole, our presence should be flushed away, kept at a distance. Like feces, white people refused to touch Black people unless it was on their own white perverse terms. Like feces, we were expelled from white spaces, we were deemed "uncivilized" (meaning, not white). Kovel writes, "Recall that dirt is at symbolic root anything that can pass *out* of the body, and that hence should not pass back *into* the body, nor even touch it."[6] He also writes, "Of all prejudiced-against people, none have suffered the appellation of filthiness so much as Negroes."[7] Tragically enough, Kant, our towering philosopher of the Enlightenment, also held that "all Negroes stink."[8] As Jan Nederveen Pieterse notes, "It is no wonder then that soap became both a symbol and yardstick of civilization."[9] Dove advertisers *should* have known this history.

I fear for America; I fear for the soul of America. If this was the 1930s, I firmly believe that Adolf Hitler and his Nazi regime would approve of Trump's white racist divisiveness and racist discourse. This is not pure speculation, especially as Nazi propaganda at the time, as argued by Stefan Kühl, defended the horrible treatment of Jews by critiquing white America's hypocrisy regarding its racist treatment of Black people.[10] The point here is that white America was caught facing a moral quandary. The Nazis were saying that, white America, in many ways, is like them. Hence, undergirding this critique of America is the implication that the Nazis approved of white America's racist treatment of Black people—you know, the ones taken from that "shithole" known as Africa, the "unclean" ones, the "vermin." They are the ones who should never be allowed in or the ones who should "go back." Within this context, think about how American citizenship itself has been defined vis-à-vis Trump's despicable words telling four Democratic congresswomen of color (Rashida Tlaib, Alexandria Ocasio-Cortez, Ayanna Pressley, and Ilhan Omar) to "go back."[11] This white supremacist logic bespeaks "white purity," the evils of ethnic cleansing, and takes us back to the American Naturalization Act of 1790 that limited immigration to free white persons who were said should be of "good character." It doesn't take much to see the pattern. Kühl writes, "The American Immigration Restriction Act of 1924 was applauded by German racial hygienists."[12] He continues, "One other important German figure, in a famous book from 1924, was full of praise for the fact the Immigration Restriction Act excluded 'undesirables' on the basis of hereditary illness and race. His name was Adolf Hitler; the book was *Mein Kampf.*"[13] Trump's deployment of white racist ideology is filled with tropes of "racial disease." Trump described Congressman Elijah Cummings' Baltimore district as a "disgusting, rat and rodent infected mess."[14] Lest we forget, it is important to remember that Jews were referred to as "rats" that carried "contagious diseases." Such vile characteristics are the steps taken before "the final solution," where Jewish humanity was no longer recognized. In his racist attack against Cummings' district, Trump added that "no human being would want to live there."[15] The problem with this characterization of the denial of the humanity of Black people is that *Black people* already *live* there!

If Americans are courageous enough, ethical enough, have a strong enough conscience, a broad sense of history, and refuse to play a dangerous and stupid game of selling their souls for party loyalty, then perhaps we are pre-pared to accept the truth that America is losing (if it has not already lost) any moral standing that it once presumably possessed. We are certainly not "the light of the world." We are not "that city that is set on a hill [that] cannot be hidden." If Trump's white supremacist behavior in the White House doesn't get collectively called out, condemned, and stopped, then America needs to hide its face, run away in shame, and declare national and international moral forfeiture. What more do the American people need, to scream at the top of their voices: "We refuse evil, we refuse white supremacy!" America has made a Faustian deal, that many politicians are too weak-willed and gutless to confront when it comes to holding America to a higher standard than those held by Trump.

Trump continues to embolden white supremacists and unabashedly com-municates (and other times dog whistles) to them that it is fine to be who they are. After all, he stated that there is an "egregious display of hatred, bigotry, and violence on many sides," and that "there's blame on both sides"[16] follow-ing the white racist violence in Charlottesville, Virginia. Following Trump's logic, there was blame on both sides when America fought against German fascism; there was blame on both sides when the American North fought against the American South; there was blame on both sides when America fought for its independence from Great Britain, when Black people rebelled against American slavery, when Native Americans fought against their colonial decimation, when women fight against their attackers. Along these skewed lines, I'm sure that I, too, will be blamed for calling Trump a racist. Where do we draw the line? I have waning faith that many of us know where, but that Trump has no idea. And that should worry the hell out of us all.

Chapter 9

Is Your God Dead? A Question from the Underground

Why this question? Why now? And why from the underground? The question is posed for those of us who claim to be believers, but who are perhaps looking in the wrong direction. And why now? Well, now is always urgent, always pregnant with possibilities. Now speaks to the seemingly unbearable weight of the present. And the reason this question is posed from the underground is that it comes from beneath the surface level, deeper than the perfunctory, surface practices of contemporary religiosity. So, is your God dead? That is the question that I'm positing *right now*. Like Blaise Pascal, I don't mean the God of the philosophers or the scholars, but, as he said, the "God of Abraham, God of Isaac, God of Jacob."[1] With no disrespect, my hope is that the question comes as a jolt. And without being outraged, angered, and quick to throw around self-righteous accusations of my "blasphemy," know, too, that I am a hopeful monotheist. I might even be called a Christian, only I continue, every day of my life, to fail. Friedrich Nietzsche's observation weighs heavily on my Christian identity: "There was only one Christian and he died on the cross."[2] So, call me a failed and broken Christian, but a Christian nevertheless—forever striving, failing, striving, and failing again.

Have you buried God in the majestic, ornamental tombs of your churches, synagogues, and mosques? Perhaps prosperity theology, boisterous, formalistic and mechanical prayer rituals, and skillful oratory, have hastened the need for the eulogy. The prophetic voice of Rabbi Abraham Joshua Heschel, who was an activist and close friend of Martin Luther King, Jr. and a student of philosopher Martin Buber in Germany, can help us to answer this question and to do so in a way that sheds light on what I see as contemporary expressions of theological and religious shallowness. As Heschel writes, "We worry more about the purity of dogma than about the integrity of love."[3] By remaining in your "holy" places, you have sacrificed looking in the face of your neighbor on the street. You know the one; the one that "smells" because she hasn't bathed in days; the one who carries her home on her body; the one who begs. Surely, you've seen that "unholy" face. She is the one that you prefer to "love" from a distance. And I'm sure that you've driven through economically oppressed configured Black spaces where you've double-checked that you have locked your car doors from the "monstrous others." You know the sound. I certainly know it—*click, click, click*. That lock is an extension of a failure for greater intimacy; the failure to unlock your heart, to un-suture your soul, to radically undo your gaze. The deeper question is: what do you fear the most, and are you able to identify the motivation and the emotion that moves your index finger to lock yourself in?

I've seen your eyes suddenly look away, making sure not to make eye contact with the "unclean." After all, it's prayer time and you're running late for holy communion, the Eucharist. And, yet, we are already touching her. Despite what you may think, our bodies don't have edges; there are no outside limits. In your refusal to stop, to linger, to stay, to look into her eyes, your body that you think has edges has already done its damage, has already left its mark in its absence, in its fleeing the scene. The socially marginalized state of the woman continues, only now compounded by "the touch" that was/is your absence. As religious scholar Elisabeth T. Vasko writes, "To be human is to be a person in relation."[4] And it is that social and existential relationality that ties you to, and implicates you in, the life of that economically destitute woman. Heschel writes, "How dare we come before God with our prayers when we commit atrocities against the one image we have of the divine: human beings?"[5] If there is a shred of life left in *your* God, full resuscitation might begin with remaining in the presence of the suffering face of that woman. If your God is dead, perhaps the possibility for a resurrection is to be found in attending to the pain and sorrow of that one image of the divine there on the street.

My hands are also dirty; I'm guilty of missing (or perhaps even rejecting) the opportunity to recognize something of the divine in the face of the "Other" on the street. I'm pretty sure the other day I looked away when I caught a glimpse of a homeless man approaching. Partly, this failure is because our churches, synagogues, and mosques have become idols. Heschel asks, "What is an idol?" He answers, "Any god who is mine but not yours, any god concerned with me but not with you, is an idol."[6] And when we're reminded of the bloodshed that has been spilled in the name of the God that we claim as our own, the idolatry is foregrounded. You have all heard the underpinning: "God Bless America," which I see as the words of a bankrupt neoliberal theology. In fact, there is something profane in that statement. James Baldwin speaks to this idolatry where he writes, "We humans now have the power to exterminate ourselves; this seems to be the entire sum of our achievement. We have taken this journey and arrived at this place in God's name."[7] So much horror has been committed in the name of God. If there are any blessings to be had, the request, surely, mustn't be partisan. After all, at least for Christianity, Judaism, and Islam, it is believed that human beings were created in the image of God (the *Imago Dei*). This means, then, that all non-Christians were created in the image of God; Arabs and Jews were created in the image of God. Syrian refugees, those who our current Trumpian administration have deemed "threats," were created in the image of God. Furthermore, Kim Jong-un, Vladimir Putin, members of the Ku Klux Klan, and Bashar al-Assad were all created in the image of God. So, even as we ask God to Bless America, surely, we must ask God to bless those who we have deemed "threats" or "enemies." As a young boy, the idea of exempting no one from redemption tested my mother, who was a Baptist. One night I asked my mother if I could pray for the devil. Strange, I admit. She didn't respond immediately. My mother eventually said, yes. So, there I was on my knees,

> Now I lay me down to sleep,
> I pray the Lord my soul to keep,
> If I should die before I wake,
> I pray the Lord my soul to take.
> God bless my mother, my sister, and my friends. *And God bless the devil.*

My older son recently brought to my attention a Mark Twain quote where Twain asks, "Who in eighteen centuries, has had the common humanity to pray for the one sinner that needed it most?"[8] Well, there I was, in Richard Allen Project Homes, as a little Black boy, doing just that. While theologically rich, I no longer pray for the devil. The more important point here is that we need a paradigm shift in how we lay claim to our religious identities, our religious practices. Why not lay claim to religious identities and practices that are suffused with compassion, a shared reality of suffering together, where *your* pain is *my* pain? Indeed, King says, "Injustice anywhere is a threat to injustice everywhere."[9] Heschel suggests that we should be mortified by the inadequacy and superficiality of our anguish when it comes to the suffering of others; the sort of anguish that forces us to weep until our eyes are red and swollen, where we suffer from sleepless nights and agonizing days. He writes, "We are a generation that has lost the capacity for outrage."[10] Personally, I have not witnessed forms of religious and theological outrage against national and global poverty, white racism, sexism, homophobia, bullying, building walls, "alternative facts," visa/immigration bans, and xenophobia. I await the day, perhaps soon, when those who believe in the "God of Abraham, God of Isaac, God of Jacob," will lock arms and march on Washington, will refuse any longer to live under the weight of poverty, militarism, violence, white neofascism, dogmatic party lines, injustice, and mendacity. Heschel reminds us that when we establish a way of life predicated upon a lie, "the world can turn into a nightmare."[11] He makes it clear that the Holocaust did not emerge suddenly. "It was in the making for several generations. It had its origin in a lie: that the Jew was responsible for all social ills, for all personal frustrations. Decimate the Jews and all problems would be solved."[12] The signs are here in the current administration. The children of Jewish parents who faced Hitler's tyranny tell them that authoritarianism under Donald Trump's administration feels too eerily familiar. "Make America Great Again" is a call for law and order, one buttressed by a white nativist ideology. The lie on which the Holocaust began is still with us. Anti-Semitism is on the rise as well as the belief that Black pathology is eroding America from within. Black people are told that we live in poverty (as if passively). That our schools are no good (as if we don't know how racist power structures operate and how money is unfairly distributed). And we have no jobs (no thanks for the reminder). In addition, so this divisive logic goes, if we just build a wall our problems will dissipate. After all, as we were told, it is Mexicans who are bringing drugs, crimes, and rapists. And yet recently, Trump, at Liberty University, said to a graduating class of future evangelical leaders, "In America, we do not worship government, we worship God." The students applauded and cheered. If what Trump said is true, then why didn't the students turn their backs to him, to protest the contradiction between the poisonous effects of his white nativism, extreme divisiveness, and his "theology"? Unless, of course, Liberty University's God is clad in a profane theological whiteness. Heschel writes, "We have trifled with the name of God."[13] The graduating students at Liberty University should have been told that "the age of moral mediocrity and complacency has run out. This is a time for radical commitment, for radical action."[14] When applauding Trump, the students were not applauding a prophetic visionary; they were applauding someone with a dangerous Pharaonic mentality, one who is intemperate, self-indulgent, power hungry, unpredictable, and narcissistic. Remember that the applause was for someone who refuses to take the nuclear option off the table; who said that global warming is a hoax and who has now pulled out of the Paris Agreement; one who said of ISIS that he would "bomb the shit out of 'em." Heschel reminds us that "Pharaoh is not ready to capitulate. The exodus began but it is far from having been completed."[15] That exodus, originating with Moses and the emancipation of the Jews, as Heschel suggests, is eternal, and signifies the march toward not just an outward physical emancipation, but a spiritual one—one that demands fierce self-reflection. I take it that, for Heschel, all of the oppressed of the world are in need of an exodus. Heschel wrote in a later work, "One's integrity must constantly be examined."[16] Musician Bob Marley, in his song "Exodus," says that we must open our eyes and look within ourselves. And he asks if we are satisfied with the life we're living. Some voices refuse to let us sleep. King had such a voice, Marley had such a voice, and so did Socrates.

Heschel writes, "The prophet's word is a scream in the night."[17] I wait to be awakened by that scream. I have not yet heard it. It is that scream, that deep existential lament, that will awaken us to the ways in which we are all guilty of claiming to "love God" while forgetting the poor, refusing the refugee, building walls, banning the stranger, praying and worshipping in insular and segregated "scared" spaces, the ones filled with racism, sexism, patriarchy, xenophobia, homophobia, and indifference. I am pretty sure that no contemporary Christians have seen God. No contemporary religious Jews have seen Yahweh. And no contemporary Muslims have seen Allah—certainly not face to face. Yet, all of us have seen the aftermath of murdered innocent children from war torn countries, their fragile innocent bodies covered with blood. I am haunted by the little body of three-year-old Aylan Kurdi who lay dead and face-down in 2015 on a Turkish beach after his family attempted to flee violence in Syria. I continue to be haunted by the murder of an unarmed Trayvon Martin in 2012. Hundreds of thousands of children from around the world are suffering. We all have known about the cruel and despicable violence toward transgender individuals. We know about the magnitude of human trafficking, the enormity of poverty, and the sickness of hatred. Vasko writes, "Through lamentation, voice is given to pain."[18] Yet, our lamenting, our mourning for those who suffer, is far too short-lived. And our charity given to those who wail and suffer in the night only temporarily eases their pain. According to Heschel, "One may be decent and sinister, pious and sinful."[19] We can so easily deceive ourselves. I certainly do it. After all, look how "ethical" I am as I address readers to face their failures? I hope that my irony isn't lost on the reader. The fact of the matter is that I continue to fail. We easily forget the sheer weight of human suffering, the agony. Heschel asks, "If all agony were kept alive in memory, if all turmoil were told, who could endure tranquility?"[20] Heschel and Vasko help to remind us that we ought to be suspicious of our tranquility. In fact, I would ask, what if that tranquility, that "peace of mind," rests on the stench of rotting corpses that are, as it were, beneath our feet? What if as we pray and rejoice in our churches, synagogues, mosques, we are throwing handfuls of dirt on God's casket? After all, prayer and rejoicing can also function as forms of narcissism, as ways of drowning out the screams of the poor, the oppressed. Finding it impossible to pray during the Vietnam War, but instead finding it necessary to demonstrate, Heschel confided in a journalist, "Whenever I open my prayerbook, I see before me images of children burning from napalm."[21]

Perhaps it is time for collective demonstration, to delay going to the Western Wall in Jerusalem, to leave the pews in the church, and perhaps pray one less time a day. None of us is innocent. Heschel reminds us, "Above all, the prophets remind us of the moral state of a people: Few are guilty, but all are responsible."[22] Yet, we have failed to deepen our collective responsibility. Some of us will never do so. What would the world look like if believers from every major religion in every country, state, city, and village, shut down the entire world for just a day, only twenty-four hours, and did everything they could in the name of an "awareness of the monstrosity of injustice"? What would America look like, on that one day, if we who call ourselves believers, decided to shut down our cities and weep together, hold hands together, commit together to eradicate injustice? Perhaps then, for the first time in American history, we will unlock our sacred doors, take a real and measured step beyond our sanctimoniousness, and see each other face to face. Heschel asks "Where does God dwell in America today?"[23] I can't say. He also asks, "Where does moral religious leadership in America come from today?"[24] I have not seen it. Perhaps like Diogenes the Cynic, you'll find me carrying a lamp in the daytime. But instead of looking for an honest man, I will be looking through the catacombs of your own making, asking, "Is your God dead?"

Chapter 10

Being a Dangerous Professor and Refusing to Be Adjusted

For those familiar with George Orwell's *1984*, you will recall that "Newspeak was designed not to extend but to *diminish* the range of thought."[1] I felt the weight of our Orwellian ethos as many of my concerned students emailed me to inform me, perhaps warn me, that my name appears on the Professor Watchlist, which was created by the conservative group known as Turning Point USA. I could sense the gravity of the warning in their email messages; there was that sense of relaying what is to come. The Professor Watchlist's mission, among other things, is to sound the alarm that there are some of us within academia who "advance leftist propaganda in the classroom." For the record, I have never called myself a "leftist," nor a "liberal," nor a "progressive." The Watchlist appears to be consistent with a nostalgic desire "to make America great again" and to oppose and expose those voices within academia that are anti-Republican or express anti-Republican values. It is the goal of "outing" that is so deeply problematic. In my philosophy classrooms, I have never had anything to hide. So, the act of "outing" itself helps to create the veneer of something secretly subversive. In fact, the outing is reminiscent of a certain homoerotic fear, a form of exposure that is designed to mark, to embarrass, to censor, to silence, to expose. And for many of us, making America "great again" is frightening and threatening, especially as the "return" speaks to me, as an embodied Black male, of a more explicit and unapologetic racial dystopia. Dreaming of yesterday, for many of us, is not a privilege, not a desire, but a nightmare. There is no desire to return. There is no "great again" for which we anticipate.

So, when I first heard from one of my students and then actually confirmed her concerns, I was engulfed by a feeling of righteous indignation, even anger. Yet, I was reminded of literary figure Toni Morrison, in *The Bluest Eye*, who says that "anger is better. There is a sense of being in anger. A reality and presence. An awareness of worth."[2] And while, on the surface, there doesn't seem to be a connection between anger and the erotic, I was also reminded of cultural theorist Audre Lorde where she explores the erotic within the context of constructing bookcases, writing a poetic verse or critically examining an idea. She notes that such activities are "a measure of joy which I know myself to be capable of feeling."[3] So, for me, the anger that I experienced is "a reminder of my capacity for feeling," and it is that feeling that is disruptive of the Orwellian gestures embedded within the Professor Watchlist. Its devotees would rather I become numb, afraid, and silent. However, it is the anger that I feel that functions as a saving grace, a place of being.

The Watchlist would rather that we run in shame after having been called out. In fact, if we are not careful, such a Watchlist can have the impact of philosopher Jeremy Bentham's Panopticon, which was a prison designed to create a form of self-censorship among those imprisoned. The Watchlist is not simply designed to get others to spy on us, to out us, but to install forms of psychological self-policing to eliminate any and all unconventional thoughts, critical pedagogical approaches, and theoretical orientations that are subversive of the rigidity of the status quo, its oppressive tendencies and marginalizing efforts. The new Professor Watchlist functions as a species of 1940s and 1950s McCarthyism, especially in terms of its overtones of "disloyalty" to the American Republic. And it is reminiscent of a semblance of COINTELPRO (CounterIntelligence Program), which was operative in the 1960s and designed to surveil political organizations within America. After all, the Watchlist *watches*, scrutinizes, inspects, guards.

I had already thought that I had been marked enough. After all, as Black I am marked as "bestial," "criminal," and "inferior." I have always known of the existence of that *racialized* scarlet letter; it marks me as I enter stores. The white security guard never fails "to see" it. The stigma identifies me at predominantly white American Philosophical Association conferences. I feel the burden of that "difference" within that space because the conference space is filled with whiteness. That mark follows me as white police officers pull me over for no other reason than because I'm Black. As Frantz Fanon writes, "I am overdetermined from without."[4] But now I feel the multiple markings; I am now the "un-American" because of my ideas, my desires and passions to undo injustice where I see it, my engagement in a form of pedagogy that leaves my students angry because of their newfound awareness of the magnitude of suffering that exists in the world. Yet, I reject being marked by the new Professor Watchlist, because I refuse to be philosophically and pedagogically adjusted.

To be "philosophically adjusted" is to belie what I see as one major aim of philosophy, which is to speak to the multiple ways in which we suffer, to be a voice through which suffering might speak and be heard, and to offer a gift to my students that will leave them maladjusted and profoundly unhappy with the world as it is. Having them to tarry in that state is what I call doing "high-stakes philosophy." It is a form of practicing philosophy that refuses to ignore the horrible realities of people who suffer, and that rejects ideal theory which functions to obfuscate such realities. It is a form of philosophizing that refuses to be seduced by what Friedrich Nietzsche called "conceptual mummies." Nietzsche notes that for many philosophers "nothing actual has escaped from their hands alive."[5] In my courses, the ones that the Professor Watchlist would like to flag as "un-American," and as "leftist propaganda," I refuse to entertain my students with mummified ideas, and abstract forms of philosophical self-stimulation. What leaves their hands is always philosophically alive, vibrant, and filled with urgency. There are times within the classroom when there is a pervasive silence that indicates the weight of the loving work to be done or the reality of the suffering that we've come to uncover within the classroom through critical conversation. I want my students to engage in the process of freeing ideas, freeing their philosophical imaginations, not clipping the wings of their imaginations. I want them to lose sleep over the pain and suffering of so many lives that many of us deem disposable. I want them to become conceptually unhinged, to leave my classes discontented and maladjusted. I agree with Martin Luther King, Jr. where he said: "I never did intend to adjust to the evils of segregation and discrimination. I never did intend to become adjusted to religious bigotry. I never did intend to adjust myself to economic conditions that will take necessities from the many to give luxuries to the few. I never did intend to adjust myself to the madness of militarism, and the self-defeating effects of physical violence."[6]

If it is that form of maladjustment that the new Professor Watchlist wants to place under surveillance and intimidation, then my classrooms and my pedagogy have no use for such intimidation tactics. Socrates knew of these and said, "As long as I draw breath and am able, I shall not cease to practice philosophy."[7] And by that Socrates meant that he will not cease to exhort Athenians to care more for justice than they did for wealth or reputation.

So, in my own defense, and in my classrooms, I refuse to remain silent in the face of racism, its subtle and systemic structure. My white students will continue to make an effort to become allies of people of color (even as allyship is such a complex relational process) and mark and remark their white privilege across various social spaces. I refuse to remain silent in the face of patriarchal and sexist hegemony and the denigration of women's bodies. I refuse to remain silent about the ways in which women have internalized our (male) assumptions of how they should look and what they should feel and desire. I refuse to be silent about forms of militarism where innocent civilians are murdered, and where such lives are lost in the name of "democracy." I refuse to remain silent when it comes to acknowledging the existential and psychic dread and chaos experienced by those who are targets of xenophobia and homophobia. I refuse to remain silent when it comes to transgender women and men who are beaten to death by those who refuse to create conditions of hospitality. I refuse to remain silent in a world that is divisive and broken. I refuse to remain silent in a world where children become targets of sexual violence, and where unarmed Black bodies are shot dead by the state and its proxies, where those with disabilities are mocked and still rendered "monstrous," and where the earth suffers because some of us refuse to hear its suffering, where my ideas are marked as "un-American," and apparently "dangerous." Well, if it is dangerous to teach my students to love their neighbors, to rethink constructively and ethically who their neighbors are, and how they have been taught to see themselves as disconnected and neoliberal subjects, then, yes, I am dangerous and I refuse to be adjusted.

Yet, the surveillance continues. Just this year, 2019, I discovered a new site for marking my "dangerous body," my "disruptive discourse," my desire that students think freely, critically, and passionately. Rate My Racist Professor is now live and running. Perhaps someone read "Dear White America" and once again failed to understand the love that motivated it. Well, that would not be the first or the last time. So, once again, I must have gotten under somebody's skin. I'm fine with that. Isn't this what I aim to do? After all, as white, you certainly have *skin in the game*. For far too long you have benefitted from that white skin and claimed your "innocence." Well, my aim is to irritate that ease with which you are encased in your whiteness, that integument that you wield as if your body is discreet, with discontinuous edges. The fact of the matter is that your whiteness, your white skin, has always already been in the game—the historical, social, political, aesthetic, metaphysical, and economic game. And there is no clear exit, but there is a space for disruption, a place where danger is another word for love.

Part 2

UNTYING ODYSSEUS: TRAVERSING BLACK PHILOSOPHICAL FRAGMENTS

I have always found interview conversations to be fulfilling. I like the back-and-forth dynamism, the unpredictable element, the possibility for range. I believe that these features are in my first book, *African-American Philosophers, 17 Conversations*, which has influenced so many young burgeoning Black philosophers. That book dared to explore the complexity that exists at the intersections between one's meta-philosophical assumptions and one's *lived* experiences, one's self-understanding, one's intuitions, one's political frustrations, one's personal challenges, one's symbolic world, and one's overall conceptual repertoire which might, at the time of the interview, involve important lacunae. Before the interviews, I had a somewhat inchoate view of all of this, but the meta-philosophical and biographical yield was phenomenal and unanticipated. Part of the success of the book is that this kind of approach had never been taken before with a critical cadre of Black professional philosophers. What was also behind its success was the uncovering of what it means to be a Black philosopher in the twentieth century—the pain of it, the risks involved, the oppressive state of the profession, the conflicts over philosophy's relevance to the real world, the sexism, the elitism, the racism, the curricular and canonical challenges, the personal challenges, and so much more. The diversity of conceptual trajectories and philosophical insights were of the highest caliber. This book was published in 1998. I had left Yale already with my MA. It was the kind of book that I desperately needed while at Yale, a place which, for me, at that time, was partly alienating and partly insensitive. The philosophical brilliance and personal tenacity conveyed in that book was the balm that I needed, but, unfortunately, didn't have. It wasn't just what they said that moved me, but the actual conversations (etymologically, "to turn with or together"), the coming together, that was transformative. *Engaging* with them is what was so powerful. It was the exchange, the give-and-take risk, the mutual vulnerability, the frankness, the patience, and the honesty.

I am under no illusions that much of what we reveal, we are also conceal-ing. The interviews were not religious confessions. There are limits. And yet, interlocutors can indeed strive for important moments of transparency, of parrhesia, exposure, and courageous speech. While I was not as clear then as I am now about this, it's what I had in mind when conducting the interviews for *African-American Philosophers, 17 Conversations*. It is also what I had in mind when conducting interviews on the topic of race with philosophers and public intellectuals for my book, *On Race: 34 Conversations in a Time of Crisis* (2017).

Entirely conversational, this section of *Across Black Spaces* pulls from what I see as one of the indispensable facets of practicing philosophy—*dialogue*. In this section, I do just that. I dialogue with three important inter-locutors: Harry A. Nethery, who teaches in the Department of Philosophy at Florida Southern College; Azuka Nzegwu, who is managing editor of Africa Knowledge Project, which promotes critical African studies; and Maria del Guadalupe Davidson, who teaches in the Women's and Gender Studies Department at The University of Oklahoma. Each scholar *turned with* me in the mode of conversing and the mode of incomplete knowing, which allowed me to think more deeply, broadly, and in ways nuanced and experimental.

The metaphor of untying Odysseus within the context of this section is meant to express a form of practice that involves a process of cultivating ways of letting go of assumptions that occlude a certain capacity for open-ness within the dialogue. I'm not sure if we can ever be completely "untied," certainly not regarding the complexity and opacity of the self and its attempt to understand itself. Furthermore, the process of untying is complicated by the fact that there are many different contexts that possess their own norma-tive assumptions and constraints that make this kind of openness challenging. In contexts that are politically, socially, existentially, and interpersonally momentous, untying Odysseus is necessary. In these contexts, we must be open to respond to the Sirens, to risk un-suturing, to risk being addressed from outside of ourselves, to risk placing oneself on the verge of being transformed because one dares to place one's assumptions in abeyance. The process of untying has to begin with some level of trust or openness, no mat-ter how miniscule. The hope is that the trust will increase as the exchange continues, where two or more people risk being mutually vulnerable.

I like the metaphor of untying Odysseus within this section because, as we know from the tale, Odysseus tied himself to the mast of a ship and plugged the ears of his men with beeswax. So, this was a case where the option of being "fully" engaged and reciprocally present was foreclosed from the beginning. We cannot completely blame Odysseus. After all, the Sirens were known to ensnare sailors to their deaths. However, there are forms of symbolic death that are necessary, especially within a world in which there is so much mendacity, so much misunderstanding, distrust, self-centeredness, disinformation, balkanization, and cowardice. Unlike Odysseus, we need those who are willing to un-suture, to risk, to venture to listen, to dare to hold themselves and their interlocutors to a higher standard of what it means to de-mask and possibly create a context where we are present-to-each-other. Hence, undergirding my understanding of the metaphor of untying Odysseus is a gesture toward the human as fundamentally relational, that we are inextricably tied to each other, and where the challenge is to recognize this ontological connection and derive from it a form of *active* ethical human praxis that understands our individual and mutual fragility. Fearless listening, which is by no means easy, accompanied by fearless speech, helps to contain that fragility. By "contain," I don't mean to control or to confine, but to provide the necessary support, the nurturing and fecund care that will help to elicit the risk and to safeguard the space within which one is being fragile or where one actually *breaks*. In classrooms where conversations transcend the dyadic, where multiple voices are involved, and where honesty and un-suturing feels far more public, I have tried and been successful, though not always, to sustain that sense of providing a safeguard. In such situations, one must be willing and prepared for the unexpected deluge of affect, even tears—*I've got you, we've got you!*

I am humbled by the dialogic conversations within this section of the book. I am honored to have been invited into a space of giving and sharing. The conversations are expansive, and, I hope, for the reader, engaging and encouraging of un-suturing. What I especially like about them is the challenge that each one presents. From questions related to my article "Dear White America," care of the self, suffering, parrhesia, whiteness, my personal identity, what brought me to philosophy, to questions about how I understand Black philosophy, Blackness, Malcolm X, and history, I had to dig deep. This is partly what conversations of this sort ought to do. They ought to send us on an interpersonal search, where what we reveal isn't always known to us in advance. These dialogues do just that. They are encouraging, they help me to remember, synthesize concepts, but also to create in real time, on the spot. They help to unconceal to me those areas that need to be explored in greater detail. They reveal a profile that demonstrates not only the little that I know, but the more that I desire to know, the self that is always in process, protean, humble, fragile.

Chapter 11

Philosophy as a Practice of Suffering
with H. A. Nethery

H. A. Nethery: It seems to me that *Backlash: What Happens When We Talk Honestly about Racism in America* is one of the most important books of our last decade. Can you tell us how the book project came about, and what you hoped to accomplish with it?[1]

George Yancy: Thanks for the accolades regarding *Backlash*. Essentially, I was motivated to write the book after I received tons of white racist vitriol in response to an article that I wrote for *The New York Times* philosophy series, "The Stone." The article is entitled, "Dear White America" and was published on December 24, 2015. Within days of its publication, it went viral. I received death threats and was called horrible racist epithets. Since the publication of that article, I have been called the n-word so many times that I've lost count. I was instructed to kill myself and threatened that my mouth needs to be shut permanently. I was told that I might find myself on a cold slab and told that I should go back to Africa even if that meant on a coffin freighter. There was so much more. These vile messages were left on my university answering machine and communicated through personal letters sent directly to me via my university postal address. White supremacist websites also deployed their full range of historically twisted, offensive and deeply troubling racist shibboleths and imagery. In short, I became the target of some of the most horrendous white racist hatred that I've ever experienced. All of this hatred led to the need for me to have university police escorts to class at my home university and police presence at some of the universities where I was invited to give talks. It was a very surreal experience. There was often an ominous feeling, a feeling of danger lurking in spaces that I had come to engage as safe, ordinary. Suddenly, such spaces became hard to traverse without hyper-vigilance. Within such a context, the sound of footsteps took on a different meaning. One might say that I began to feel a general manifestation of de-familiarization, where my perception of sounds and my proximity to other bodies became a problem, a potential conflict or confrontation to be dealt with.

The irony is that I intended "Dear White America" as a letter of love to white people. My desire was to encourage white people to examine the ways in which white racism subtly functions in their quotidian lives, how it constitutes the formation of their identity, and how it renders them complicit with forms of structural and systemic racism that adversely impact Black people and other people of color. The article dared to hold up a disagreeable mirror to white America; to enable white people to see themselves as they are, as they had failed or refused to see. Love functioned as a site of uncovering, a gift that dared to unveil. Yet, we know how dangerous such a process can become. After all, masks, as James Baldwin knew all too well, help to conceal aspects of ourselves that we don't want to see.[2] Imagine being told that the moral and ethical self that you "know" yourself to be is structured by a narrative, a vocabulary, that is undergirded by white racialized and racist logics that occlude or militate against seeing the deeper truth about yourself, a self that is inextricably linked to and responsible for the pain and suffering of others. That can be terrifying. And, yet, there is a certain necessary "terror" when it comes to growth, awareness, the cultivation of radically new ways of rethinking and re-feeling what it means to-be-in-the-world, to rethink and re-feel one's embedded social ontology and the reality of one's epistemic and affective opacity vis-à-vis the suffering of others.

Backlash not only traces the white racist vitriol, but it functions as an extension of the original letter of love; it continues the necessary project of uncovering the myth of white innocence. You see, for me, the conceptualization of "white innocence" is part of the vocabulary of whiteness itself. So, the stories that white people tell themselves, the world-making activities that they perform, are based upon lies. Within those stories, I am the "race baiter," the "racist," the "troublemaker" who would dare to instigate a critique of whiteness within a "post-racial" North America. *Backlash* refuses such lies, myths, acts of bad faith, and epistemology of ignorance. So, what I hoped to accomplish through writing *Backlash* is what I intended with the original article—to trouble the lives of white people, to unsettle their sense of existential, social, and ethical comfort. I want them to tarry with the ways in which they continue to be racist even as they check their proverbial lists of racial dos and don'ts. The hands can't clean dirt from the body while the hands remain covered in dirt. The dirt of white racism must be exposed and confronted.

Your question also raises the issue of origins. The more that I think about the origin of *Backlash*, I think that it is helpful to think about different moments of an extended temporality. So, even as "Dear White America" was published in 2015 and *Backlash* in 2018, the forceful anti-racist content of both extend beyond their historical emergence. Hence, *Backlash*, on this score, is the manifestation of past enslaved Black bodies as they screamed in anguish and fought for their freedom under the horrors of North American slavery. *Backlash* is the painful and yet liberating voices of Frederick Douglass and Harriet Jacobs as they diligently fought against the traumatic horrors of slavery. *Backlash* is Malcolm X's fortitude displayed as he fought to speak truth to white supremacy. As we know, each of them, in their own way, experienced forms of anti-Black recoil and aggression as they dared to play the role of the parrhesiastes, the one who speaks parrhesia or courageous speech. My point here is that *Backlash* is a text that carries the trace of historical Black righteous indignation in the face of white supremacy, white power, white hubris, and white privilege. So, the hope remains the same: the overthrow of white supremacy, and the articulation of a radical social ontology that reveals what it means for us as human beings to be fundamentally connected, interconnected, inter-corporeal, especially as these concepts bear on the *lived* reality of race. I refer to this fundamental connection as an ontology of no edges, one which implicates an ethics of no edges. Of course, this would involve a fundamental rethinking and rejection of a philosophical anthropology rooted in neoliberal logics. An ethics of no edges will also force us to rethink the ways in which what constitutes the ethical or the unethical isn't delimited to rational autonomy. Rather, the ways in which we are shaped, constituted, and installed by historical, discursive, and structural heteronomous forces must be brought to bear on how we are defined ethically. After all, within this context, and I especially had white people in mind as I theorized this view, there are forms of violent touch according to which one is forced to rethink a very limited conception of what it means to be responsible.

Nethery: One element of *Backlash*, and an element of all of your work, is that you bring a sense of humanity to your work. Your texts are written by a human who feels pain, misery, and joy, which is different (to say the least) from most contemporary philosophy as it is written today. Your work, I think, is in line with the early Socrates, who argued that philosophy is the practice of taking care of oneself and others. How do you see the relationship between the self and one's work? Is it possible to radically distance oneself from one's work? What do you think are the consequences of doing philosophy in such a manner?

Yancy: Yes. And that sense of humanity is what I never want to forget. For me, practicing philosophy is not simply about wonder; it is a site of suffering. I understand this suffering in at least two ways. First, as you suggest, there is the suffering that comes with a dimension of philosophical practice that takes the form of being a Socratic gadfly. On this score, philosophical practice engages various public spaces and isn't a practice confined to the academy. It involves engaging in forms of critical discourse that refuse to allow various manifestations of social injustice to go unmarked. For me, philosophy is the embodiment of a commitment that one makes to end the deep social and political horror that people undergo, that they experience daily.

Within this context, I see philosophical practice as a dangerous practice. It is dangerous because one attempts to raise one's voice outside of the stove-heated room of Cartesian reflection, a form of reflection that is emblematic of a species of philosophical monasticism that engages philosophical practice at the level of pure abstraction. For me, there are forms of abstraction that falsely attempt to purify philosophy of its Socratic impulse to speak on the proverbial streets, to engage the demos in critical self-reflection toward the goal of radical self-transformation, care of the self. This is what "Dear White America" was about.

The letter of love aimed to speak to white America about its failure to care for itself, to know itself. Care, within this context, is being deployed as a form of striving, which, etymologically, means "to quarrel" or "to resist." So, care of the self involves, for me, modes of quarreling, modes of resisting, and modes of attempting to undo forms of institutional and historical interpellation that have shaped the white self, brought the white self into social and political being, and that have shaped larger racist and thereby toxic forms of sociality. So, to "know thyself," within this context, is to encourage white people, as James Baldwin would say, to engage in historical battle with themselves,[3] to battle against the maintenance of a white self that doesn't know its racist limits, a white self that is opaque to itself. Hence, to know thyself, knowing one's embodied white self, is a continuous process, not one of arrival, where one achieves some pure state of anti-racism. As a contemporary gadfly, that is my message, inter alia, to white America. Whiteness is an historical project that requires white people to engage in a continuous counter-project of undoing whiteness, a counter-project of looking at themselves courageously within the disagreeable mirror of the Black counter-gaze.

Yet, there is a price to be paid and that is the suffering that I began with. I have no desire to be forced to drink hemlock as in the case of Socrates. However, when one refuses to sanitize or deodorize philosophy, as Cornel West would say, where one engages in critical forms of discourse that challenge the messy social and political status quo, and the stench of ethical ineptitude, there will be the inevitable backlash, the hatred, the threats.[4] So, for me, the love of wisdom is a calling that refuses to be silent in the face of horrendous forms of suffering caused by greed, indifference, hegemony, and hatred.

I reject forms of philosophical practice that attempt to detach themselves from history. I understand philosophy as a vocation. For me, it is a calling *to speak along with* the downtrodden and *to speak out* for the least of these. I also support meta-philosophical assumptions that reject forms of philosophical practice that embark upon their points of inquiry as if from *nowhere*. This is why African-American philosophy, and Africana philosophy, more generally, are areas that I'm philosophically at home with. They embody modes of philosophizing that take social and political struggle seriously, and that begin from a *locus philosophicus* that self-consciously grounds themselves within the muck and mire of historical facticity, political turmoil, existential resistance and travail. I demonstrate this in my first book, *African-American Philosophers, 17 Conversations*, which was published in 1998. That book is the first of its kind in American philosophical scholarship to engage in critical conversations with prominent African-American philosophers in a single volume, to engage their work at the intersection between their lived social and political experiences and how they understand themselves as philosophers, especially as African-American philosophers. The book was unprecedented. Yet, as early as 1998, I had already begun to articulate certain meta-philosophical assumptions about how I understood what it meant to practice philosophy and the structure of that practice. I also theorized a similar conceptual understanding of philosophy with the publication of my book, *The Philosophical I: Personal Reflections on Life in Philosophy* in 2002. Again, the objective was to gather together a critical cadre of internationally known philosophers to engage the relationship between their philosophical views and how those views are shaped and inextricably linked to their autobiographies. And the objective was to get a broad range of philosophers working within various areas of philosophy—from pragmatism and social and political philosophy to feminist philosophy and philosophy of science.

So, for me, philosophy always begins from *somewhere*. You know, Descartes is famous for his search for epistemological foundations and how, for him, that search involved the bracketing of the lived space of sociality. For me, I'm also interested in Descartes the human being, the father who suffered and how that suffering impacted his philosophizing, his philosophical identity. As you know, Descartes' daughter, Francine, died when she was five years old. That was tragic. She died of scarlet fever. I'm concerned about what that was like for Descartes, which raises the unpredictable, the precarious nature of our finitude and how that reality impacts our philosophical intuitions and imaginations. That is the space within which philosophizing *dwells* for me. It is also the social space through which we become who and what we are through the existence of others. This is why I'm philosophically enthralled by John Mbiti's anti-Cartesian idea that the existential and social "I" that I am is predicated upon a collective "we."[5] By the way, I think that it is important that we never forget that Western philosophy is not philosophy qua philosophy. Mbiti's point forces us (or certainly ought to) to rethink Western philosophical arrogance. Western philosophy has no a priori authority regarding what it means *to be*. Being is larger than any one framework of intelligibility.

And this brings me to the second way in which I understand the practice of philosophy as a site of suffering. As a young boy, I had an intense affective way of being-in-the-world. I was obsessed with the fact of human death, the fact that our existential facticity is profoundly mysterious and that the cosmos is so silent about why we are here at all. But it wasn't just about the fact that *we will die* someday; it was (and is) about the fact *I will die* any day. The use of "any day" within this context speaks to the fact that not a single moment is guaranteed. Along with this sense of death, I felt a deep sense of existential dread that we are thrown into existence without any clear sense of why we're here, whether or not God exists, whether or not the cosmos has any meaning beyond what we give it, whether or not we have immortal souls, if there is any meaning to be acquired after death or if death is the final absurd moment of our being here. Loving wisdom is also about grappling passionately with such haunting questions and, for me, I suffer, I agonize, I grieve over the fact that there are no easy answers. I have compared this suffering to that of an orphan, to an agonizing feeling of forlornness. That is how I often feel; there is a sense of being abandoned within a careless and cold cosmos for which there may be no answer other than the fact of complete chance that we exist. Yet, even as I suffer, there is the absolute beauty of what I call the gift of being. And even if our individual existential duration is less than the blink of an eye relative to cosmic time, there is profound meaning in that, something even beautiful.

So, it is not only the pain and suffering that are experienced as deep hostility within the context of an anti-Black America that I bring to philosophizing, it is the pain and suffering, the fear and trembling that comes with this profound feeling of being abandoned. Hence, both forms of suffering mediate my writing. My friend, philosopher Tim Golden, provides a very helpful language for me to formulate what it is that I'm doing when I write philosophically. I've come to see my writing as moving from an abstract space exemplified by the term *logos* (word or reason) to a concrete space exemplified by the term *sarx* (flesh). That is what I do. I engage philosophical ideas within the flesh, which may sound like a truism. However, being around so many philosophers with a penchant for philosophical abstraction, one is led to believe that they think of themselves as residing in a pristine mental bubble, one removed from anything as "cumbersome" as being embodied. Then again, perhaps what I have in mind is closer to the process of giving flesh to reasoned and agonizing ideas, or, more accurately, where reasoned and agonizing ideas are always already enfleshed. After all, I'm always already situated within the all too human reality of dread, suffering, pain, and death. These are all lived experiences in-the-flesh. So, through the process of writing, I bring my full and "impure" humanity and embodied self to the writing, which troubles and mediates *logos* through the reality of *sarx*. Then again, is *logos* ever separated from *sarx*? Philosophers who treat philosophy as an ahistorical practice, one removed and untouched by the embodied social selves that they are, elide the embodied human face of ideas and thereby attempt to play the role of gods only to deliver philosophical idols, lifeless, and barren. But, unlike Athena, who was born fully whole from the head of Zeus, we are born from the messiness and beauty of interlocking, collective human flesh—fragile, precarious, porous.

Nethery: The idea of philosophy as a practice of suffering seems to connect with the concept of parrhesia, which you discuss in much of your work. Can you please elaborate on this concept? When did you first start working with this idea, and how does it fit into the framework of your philosophical work today? How do you see the connection between parrhesia and philosophy as a practice of suffering?

Yancy: Let me first say that the idea of philosophy as a practice of suffering has absolutely nothing to do with self-flagellation; there is no desire to engage in punishing oneself as a means toward "religious" healing or sanctification. There is no obsession with "purification." Moreover, practicing philosophy, within the context of this connection, is not self-indulgently masochistic. On the contrary, to get a richer sense of what I have in mind think about Dr. Martin Luther King, Jr. and his social activism. As a social philosopher, he understood what it meant to practice a form of philosophical engagement that involved suffering. In other words, he knew what it meant to practice philosophy in the mode of a gadfly, which involved stinging the conscience of white America. In fact, in his powerful "Letter from Birmingham City Jail," King understands his prophetic work as shaped by the Socratic impulse. He importantly references Socrates as someone who engaged in parrhesia; he sees Socrates as someone who created mental tension in the minds of those who would rather not examine their lives, who would rather remain asleep.[6] Yet, King argues that tension is necessary for our growth, our social, political, and ethical maturity. King also understood what Socrates faced as a result of creating such tension. This necessary tension is linked to unmasking the ways in which we live according to falsehoods and how, once those falsehoods are revealed, deep anger results. In his letter, King says that he is not afraid of the word tension.[7] He knew that white racism had to be challenged. He knew that a necessary tension was needed to create a *crisis* within the stagnant social order and the habitually rigid embodied psyches of white people. Yet, there was also the recognition, the painful awareness, that philosophy as courageous speech, as parrhesia, is tied to forms of vile counterattack. He knew that there was a price to be paid. This does not mean that King wanted to die. *He wanted to live.* In the last speech that he gave on April 3, 1968, the day before he was assassinated, King talked about this openly. He talked about how, like anybody else, he would like to live a long life. He said that longevity has its place in our lives.[8] Yet, there was this understanding that speaking courageously would not be subordinated to the fears of vicious acts of retaliation. And even Socrates said (as he stood before his accusers) that as long as he could draw breath he would *not stop* practicing philosophy, that he would continue to create that necessary mental tension. So, there is a link here between philosophy, parrhesia, and suffering or certainly modes of suffering that result from showing people what they refuse to see. Now, obviously, my conceptualization of philosophy as a practice of suffering isn't given a priori, but I ground that conceptualization within various historical instances of that practice; hence, the importance of Socrates and King, and an entire tradition of African-American prophetic discursivity and embodied praxis. But this isn't just about the modes of suffering that result from hate, retaliation, fear of seeing the truth, and the refusal to commit to justice and its application to all.

I want to ask here: How can the practice of philosophy as a site of loving wisdom, where wisdom is imbued with a powerful and relentless intolerance for human suffering caused by various actors—whether individuals or states—not involve suffering? Indeed, one is bound to suffer if one opens one's heart to the hard realities of poverty, violence, racism, sexism, sex trafficking, femicide, domestic violence, mass shootings, homophobia, war, drone strikes that kill civilians, the death of refugees, the death of immigrants, the senseless killing of children, the murder of unarmed Black bodies, the separation of innocent children from their parents, the criminal justice system, violently occupied territories, and so on. You see, I also see a connection between practicing philosophy, parrhesia, and the suffering that comes with profound love. King certainly understood this. The horrors named previously are hauntingly present and overwhelming realities. For me, my body is moved with emotional chills and tears can often overflow. That is what philosophy is for me. Loving wisdom produces a powerful form of expressive love. It dares to look suffering in the face without flinching, without fleeing. Even as I write this next sentence, I'm impacted by my relative privilege. I think of the twenty-nine children who were violently killed, their body parts severed, by the Saudi coalition airstrike in Yemen on August 9, 2018, and I feel sick to my stomach; I feel as if my body will implode with rage and sorrow. I also feel a terrible defeat, a nagging feeling that the love that I have for those children, children who I never knew, would not have made a difference. Of course, I don't need to go overseas. As I've said many times before in writing and while giving talks, I wept when I heard the gunshot that took the life of seventeen-year-old Trayvon Martin on February 26, 2012. As you will recall, his life was brutally taken by George Zimmerman, the man who, in my opinion, pursued Martin. I've personally spoken to Martin's parents, Sybrina Fulton and Tracy Martin, who shared with me that they refer to Zimmerman simply as "the killer," refusing to speak his name. You see, words matter; naming practices can empower. I also agree that the appellation—*the killer*—is apropos.

Your question has forced me to think about all of this in ways that I have not done heretofore. So, there seems to be three ways of thinking about how I see philosophy, parrhesia, and suffering. Asking courageous questions about our being, our conscious existence, here at this moment in cosmic history, carries the weight of suffering for me. Look, I don't know *why* we are here. The cosmos is apparently silent, and painfully so for me, on that question. And if there is a God, and I am a hopeful theist, why is coming to know such a fact so obscured? After all, the universe doesn't provide us with the answer in a way that is indubitable. It is with deep uncertainty and anxiety that I continue to hope. Speaking truth, trying to speak courageously, to hegemonic systems and violent and unjust social practices often leads to reactionary forms of unjust and cruel acts of pain, dirty name-calling, threats of death or even actual death; that is another form of suffering. And then there is the suffering that comes with being vulnerable, with an open heart that dares to love those who have been deemed "ersatz," "the wretched," the "disposable." So, for me, practicing philosophy is a form of love that goes beyond *the love of wisdom*; it is a *daily* practice of having one's heart open (and opened), of being emotionally exposed vis-à-vis others, to feel one's body as a form of stretched social skin that touches the lives of so many others. These things capture, for me, the meaning of suffering, which etymologically means "from below," or "to bear." Imagine teaching undergraduate and graduate philosophy students that philosophy is about bearing so much pain and sorrow—that it is a practice of suffering. As strange as this will sound, I came to this understanding of philosophy before I knew that there was a field called philosophy. It may have been inchoate, but it was there, infusing my affect. It was only later in my life that I came to practice philosophy in this way self-consciously. These ways of thinking about suffering are linked to the reason that I write on the themes that I do, and why I write in the style that I do. I can't imagine doing otherwise. And even though in some abstract sense I can obviously imagine doing otherwise, I nevertheless *refuse* to do otherwise.

Nethery: How can we cultivate this sense of philosophy as a site of suffering within our undergraduate students in an ethical and responsible manner, that both cares for and cultivates the student? In your work, you stress a connection between suffering and vulnerability. Is it possible to make this connection part of the practice and practical benefit of philosophy? What might an undergraduate philosophy curriculum that undertook such a task look like?

Yancy: I think that it begins with us, those of us who take it as our vocation, our calling, to teach philosophy, to demonstrate within our classrooms what is at stake in our lives philosophically. So, to cultivate that sense of philosophy as a site of suffering vis-à-vis our undergraduate students, I think that we need to exemplify, to perform, and to instantiate, our humility and frail humanity. So, right there before our students, perhaps even on the first day of class, I think that we need to speak to our students about how all of us will, at some point, die. This is not about spectacle or hyperbole. Also, I don't attempt to communicate this in some sociologically abstract fashion, but to communicate the hard reality that *you and I will die*. In fact, my aim is to communicate the fact that you and I have been dying from the moment we began to live. I engage in this truth-telling practice by asking my students to look at each other, to lock eyes. And while they are looking at each other, I ask them to come to terms with the reality that in one hundred years all of them (us) will be dead, rotting, stinking, corpses. This semester (spring 2019), I asked each of them to think about their nonexistence in 2119, a hundred years from now. The expression on many of their faces clearly communicated discomfort. And there was a giggle that always seems to hide some hard truth that they would rather not face. When they are looking at each other, before I mention death, I often hear slight laughter. This seems to happen regardless of the audience. I think that part of the reason for this is that we fail to look at each other, to really look at each other, to see each other. So, I know that it is a bit awkward. Yet, the moment that I state that none of us will be here in one hundred years, that none of us will be alive, I have seen in the faces of many of my students (and those who are not my students) a look that says, "I can't believe that he said that." It's as if I've taken away the fun of an in-class group activity. Of course, there are other times, after I've raised the issue of their mortality, that the laughter (that giggle that I mentioned) continues, which I see, again, as possibly a function of a form of denial or avoidance.

I think that this is what we need to do. So many of our students are so sure of themselves, but I want them to feel unsure, which, within this context, functions to get them both to appreciate the here and now differently, but also to get them to begin to carry the weight of both the joy *and* pain in life. We need to create dangerous classroom spaces. By dangerous, of course, I don't mean that there will be violence in the classroom, though I do mean a form of violation, a violation of their arrogance and narcissism, a violation of their sense of disconnection, a violation of their naivete. After all, they have been fed on a poor diet of neoliberalism; they see themselves as atomic. They have become fat on a diet of ideologically driven "happiness" and contentment. We need to help our students to understand, to feel, their sense of vulnerability and embodied connection. We need to get them to appreciate the value, the precariousness, of *this* moment—right now! That is part of taking the masks off, of refusing to bullshit them on the very first day of class. In doing so, I am conveying something about responsibility and ethics. To put the existentially uncomfortable fact about their death before them, I am asking for and encouraging a different response, a different way of being-in-the-world, of being-in-my-class, of being ethical. The aim is to communicate that within my classroom you will bear witness to an uncomfortable form of philosophical engagement and courage. On that first day, my aim is to unconceal the shadow of death. I communicate to them that they will need to bear the weight of what it means that they will die, that the fellow student next to them will die, and that all that they deeply love will someday die. I even mention the finitude of their parents. Bringing death so close to home, asking them to dwell within a space that will involve the death of their parents, elicits a profound look of sadness. And I assure you that this one is especially painfully hard for me. I, too, am vulnerable to that truth, that reality. We are in this together. So, I'm getting them to rethink what it means to be, to be alone. I'm getting them to feel differently about their parents, about their fellow classmates, to realize that the face of their parents or other embodied students sitting right next to them might disappear at any moment, taken and perhaps gone forever within the history of this vast cosmos. This practice actually interrogates the neoliberal, individualist assumptions that many of my students possess before taking my classes. Death is profoundly individual, nonfungible, noninterchangeable. No one can do it *for me* or *for you*. Yet, it is overwhelmingly and intensely *relational*. Your death will also impact me. I am pained by it—even devastated. It is that pain and devastation that reveals the lie that I am atomic. Your death shakes my core; it is an existential tremor that bespeaks not only our common fate, but what we mean to each other, what we are to each other, how we are inextricably linked to each other, how when "I have lost 'you' [I] discover that 'I' have gone missing as well."[9] As John Donne put this:

> And therefore never send to know for whom the bell tolls;
> It tolls for thee.[10]

This isn't about scare tactics; it is about love, the kind of love that, as Baldwin says within another context, forces us *to see ourselves as we are*. Your use of the term "cultivate" is important here. My aim is to cultivate, to foster, to nurture, a deeper sense of affectivity and attunement.

But you see, I must also be prepared to share aspects about myself, my vulnerability, my fears, and my faults with my students. This doesn't mean that one loses respect. In fact, I've found that my show of vulnerability will actually generate deeper mutual respect and that it enables students to reach beyond their fears and also become vulnerable, which means that it is important that all of us demonstrate mutual care. I say this because we are talking about genuine and potentially painful forms of suffering and vulnerability within the classroom.

So, yes, I do think that it is possible to make the link between suffering and vulnerability, and what these mean to the practice of philosophy. Philosophy isn't only about clarity of thought, logical argumentation, and being able to ask clever and smart questions. Philosophy is about undergoing powerful and transformative experiences that leave us humbled and productively angry. Philosophy ought to open us up to the cries of the "other," even aspects of the repressed "other" within ourselves that we have masked for far too long. When students leave my classroom, I want them to leave carrying the weight of the world, its pain and suffering. Unlike the mythical figure Atlas, who was punished by Zeus to carry the sky (or the heavens) on his shoulders, what I am asking my students to do isn't a consequence of them having been disobedient. Rather, I am saying that to carry that weight of human suffering, to face it, is in fact a form of disobedience against a social world that prefers ethical mediocrity, empty chatter, entrepreneurial self-aggrandizement, and evasion. What we need is a philosophical curriculum that doesn't stay on a fixed course, but *runs* in a radically different direction as the etymology of the term curriculum would suggest. We need affective dissonance vis-à-vis those patterns of philosophical practice that attempt to remain "pure." And even those philosophical approaches (pragmatism, Africana philosophy, feminist philosophy, Continental philosophy, critical phenomenology, critical philosophy of race) that attempt to see the world more effectively within nonideal terms, they too must do more; they too must face suffering with greater vulnerability, as they are not immune to philosophical calcification, fixed canonization, and the professionalization of philosophy that refuses interdisciplinary engagement and that produces hermetically sealed philosophers incapable of seeing beyond their own conceptual myopia. I want to see a form of philosophical practice that weeps, that cries in the academic corridors, because real life suffering *ought to* force a real crisis in our philosophical assumptions and practices. We need texts—ones that are written, visual, photographic, sonic, musical, filmic, performative, embodied—that refuse, as Frantz Fanon would say, to leave existence by the wayside.[11]

Nethery: I would like to move to a different, but closely related topic, in light of our discussion about suffering and vulnerability. In *Black Bodies, White Gazes*, especially the second edition, you are antagonistic, to say the least, to the notion of hope. In this same vein, a lot of your white interlocutors (at conferences or in interviews) seem to express frustration when you do not give them any concrete "solutions" to the problem of anti-Black racism. I am also skeptical of hope, as it seems to me that hope carries within it the risk of a kind of passivity. What is it about hope that you find problematic? How has your view on the idea of hope changed over the years?

Yancy: Yes, there are many who express frustration and a sense of perplexity when I open a talk with the words: "In this talk I may not leave you with much hope." I'm sure that it even seems counterintuitive, but for me it is an importantly fecund space to occupy. Why so? When it comes to white audiences, my sense is that many want me to cut to the chase and provide a neat and tidy solution to the problem of whiteness. But what I really want is for white listeners to learn how to tarry with a profound feeling of discontent and not to move too quickly to a "solution" to the problem of whiteness. The discourse of "solution" can also bypass the sheer complexity of whiteness. Sara Ahmed, who has produced a very important and a multidisciplinary engaging body of critical explorations on race, colonialism, and queer theory, has also engaged this point in very profound ways. Ahmed knows what it is like for white people to raise their hands immediately after she has given a talk on race, seeking a formulaic solution to the problem of white racism or wanting to know what they can do. The willingness to do something about whiteness is obviously politically and existentially important and necessary, but it is by no means sufficient. The gravity of the problem of whiteness is weighty in ways that so many white people have not even come to realize. Ahmed's point, and I agree with her, is that the question itself can transform the problem of white-ness into an "object" that stands apart from the white people who pose the question, where asking the question itself can easily function to obfuscate the ways in which, as white, they are the problem, they are complicit in perpetu-ating white racism.[12] The objective is not to move from that place of trauma, not to move away from that place of being unhinged regarding one's often new understanding that there is no place called "white innocence." Tarry. Remain. Linger in that space of painful awareness. This raises the issue of temporality. Hope presupposes temporality. So, there is a way in which hope, for white people, moves them too quickly into the future, away from the pres-ent, *the now* of white oppressive behaviors, habits and institutions and their problematic implications for Black people and people of color.

I also think that you are correct about hope and passivity. White people can remain passive in their active stance of remaining hopeful. It is sort of like Dr. King's critique of a conception of time that presupposes that time will make a positive difference if only we wait. If hope is about waiting and wait-ing presupposes that history will "naturally" move toward a positive outcome then we, as a nation, are in trouble. When I ask white people to remain in the present it is not to suggest passivity. Remaining in the present, tarrying, without the seduction of hope, points to a sort of realism, an active and critical engagement regarding the complicated ways in which whiteness is embedded within the fabric of our political, economic and social lives, and the ways in which whiteness is embedded within white psyches, which constitutes a site of collective and individual white opacity.

I also argue that forms of hope expressed by Black people can also function in problematic ways. Think about it this way. What if Black hope is a func-tion of perpetuating white privilege, power, and hegemony? What if Black hope can be accommodated? In this way, whiteness will remain structurally intact, because it makes room for Black hope, where Black people continue to express an aspirational future where Black humanity will finally be fully recognized. There is, as you know, a problem with the very idea of asking or even demanding white people to recognize Black humanity. Black people should not even need to ask white people to recognize their humanity. There is a way in which to make such a demand feels so incredibly unfair. After all, Black people *are human beings* and to feel the need to demand the recognition of this, from white people, feels like (or rather is) an additional injustice, an insult to injury.

But to return to the problem of Black hope, it is important to realize that, as a Black man, I'm "free" because of a tradition of on the ground Black resistance to white supremacy, a tradition that was suffused with hope. They looked over the horizon and saw a promised land. So, that kind of hope that has sustained Black people over centuries of white oppression is vital. Yet, what if there is a kind of hope that is always already limited and constrained by white self-interest such that the logics of that hope function to undermine something far more disruptive? This is a case where white power structures actually allow, provide a space for, Black people to hope because hope always looks forward, keeps us satiated for another day hoping for change. This is why in the new and expanded 2017 edition of *Black Bodies, White Gazes*, I suggest that perhaps we need what I call a post-hope moment, which would constitute a moment where Black people decide against a structurally constrained hope and engage in a post-hope form of praxis that says that the future is too far off, that we want complete transformation today, *now*. It is actually a different way of thinking about temporality and the demand for justice. It is a form of demand that the logics of white accommodation and white gradualism cannot withstand. To use a powerful metaphor here, I would like the system of white supremacy *to choke*, to discontinue eating Black bodies, consuming us, making use of us as we wait for the next "change for the better." But what do we really have, what have we really accomplished when the logics of "better" continue to exist alongside the hegemony of whiteness and its structural integrity? For me, that form of doing "better" is undergirded by an accommodated hope, one that is not only being exploited by white supremacy, but one that keeps Black people looking toward a future temporality whose "forward" movement is always already constrained by whiteness. So, in addition to finding problematic those white people who refuse to remain in the profound discomfort of the present, I also find an accommodated hope to be suspect and problematic. The Afro-nihilist work of Calvin Warren, who is a colleague of mine at Emory University, and the theorization of the concept of cruel optimism by Lauren Berlant, have impacted how I've come to rethink hope. However, the moment that I actually came to see the problem of hope vis-à-vis white supremacy was while discussing white racism and hope with a student of mine, Brian Klarman. He and I were discussing issues related to Afro-pessimism and on one particular day it hit me with great dismay that perhaps instead of hope as a process that eventually undoes white supremacy, perhaps Black hope is a function of white supremacy. I think that a post-hope moment rethinks temporality and really encourages a form of urgency that refuses another day of Black pain and suffering caused by white privilege, white normality, white power, and white hegemony. Post-hope speaks to the passionate cry of civil rights activist Fannie Lou Hamer where she said, "I'm Sick and Tired of Being Sick and Tired."[13] That statement, that meta-observation, that affective unrest, it seems to me, is a clarion call that under-girds the value of Black life in the present, *at this moment.*

Nethery: In your 2012 text *Look, a White!*, you call for the creation of "wide-awake dreamers," that is, young people who can dream of a new world while being wide awake to the problems of this world. The hope, then, is that the problems of this world are not reduplicated. However, I have not seen you deploy this concept in any of your texts after *LaW*. Is there a reason for this? What do you think about the idea of wide-awake dreamers now?

Yancy: Thanks for pointing this out. In that book, I discuss "wide-awake dreamers" in the chapter entitled, "Loving Wisdom and Playing with Dan-ger." I was influenced to write that chapter partly because of an experience that I had after giving an interview on the Chris Moore Show, KDKA 1020. I was invited on the show to discuss *Black Bodies, White Gazes*, the first edition, 2008. After the show, a white male listener decided to send one email message after the next to the president of Duquesne University, which is where I was teaching at the time, to a number of Duquesne philosophy graduate students, to the *Pittsburgh Post-Gazette*, and to the Archdiocese of Washington, DC. He thought that what I had to say about whiteness wasn't in keeping with a Catholic academic institution. His objective was to get me fired. Part of the reason that he wrote so many times is that no one responded. At one point, I had hoped that he would send a letter to Rome complaining about me. In retrospect, his letters were a foreshadowing of what was to come. Of course, after "Dear White America," the letters, voice messages, email messages, became far more threatening. In any event, his letter writing campaign didn't get any traction, though someone from Duquesne University did write to him to say that his problem was with me and that he should write directly to me. However, he never wrote to me, which is unfortunate because so much of what he said about me was so ill-conceived. For him, it was an opportunity missed. I say this because he and I could have had a potentially productive conversation, perhaps even a friendship. Stranger things have hap-pened. After "Dear White America," one white guy called me on my office phone. At the time I wasn't answering my phone because of so much harassment, but I momentarily forgot. On the other end of the line, this white guy insisted that I answer questions about what I said about white racism. I told him that I didn't have time, but he insisted. I spoke to him in a very calm voice. I'm pretty sure that we communicated by email a few times. Afterward, I received an email message from him that was apologetic. He also said in the letter, and I kid you not, "I love you Dr. Yancy." Strange? Yes. Unanticipated? Certainly. I'm still not sure what to make of it. I've often thought about that guy. My desire is that he meant what he said and that he realized that he had misunderstood the message of "Dear White America." My hope is that he came to realize that the letter to white people, which was intended as a letter of love, was asking for something far more daring and beautiful. You know, now that I've thought about it openly in this way, my sense is that he returned that love.

In the chapter, "Loving Wisdom and Playing with Danger," the concept of "playing with danger" was not meant to communicate something flippant. The idea of playing was designed to communicate the capacity to be daring and audacious. It also communicated the idea of *taking part in.* I already knew that to be Black in white America was already to take part in something dangerous. It was speaking courageously as Black that multiplied the danger. So, for me, the idea of loving wisdom in Black, as it were, revealed layers of the precarious. I wanted my white students to play with danger, to *take part in* thinking beyond the status quo, of reimagining the present, of refusing to accept that the present is fixed. That, for those who would rather we not think otherwise, is dangerous. So, I wanted my students to understand and to understand that loving wisdom isn't another name for some sort of romanticism. That love was about praxis and critical interrogation of the social world and one's own identity.

This idea was linked to the idea of dreamers. My objective was to contrast this with Plato's critique of the Athenians who he saw as wanting to sleep, to remain asleep, as a way of not facing their own ethical shortcomings. Hence, not any dreamers will do. Some dreamers are just asleep, comparable to the walking dead. Other dreamers have their eyes fixed on abstractions (perhaps idols) that have lost their smell of the earth, as Adrienne Rich would put it.[14] This is why I stressed "wide-awake dreamers." In this way, to dream is to think otherwise, not to sleep and not to be seduced by abstractions and lose sight of the horizontal, as it were, suffering that is right there on the proverbial ground. I was writing directly to my white students. To keep one's eyes open means that one must be prepared to see *what is there.* There are many whites whose eyes are physically open, but they don't see. So, I'm not just talking about eyes that are physically open, but about a form of seeing that reveals, that unconceals, a seeing in a way that the world appears with a new and complex intensity. This is why I quoted in the book the work of critical race theorist Charles R. Lawrence, where he talks about challenging established understandings,[15] meaning that there is something there to see, but it hasn't been probed or seen through. And the concept of "established," connotes that which is customary, conventional, commonsensical, coherent, and even "rational." So, there is an entire world that has been given as readymade, off the shelf of an unquestioned organized framework of intelligibility. This is why Lawrence emphasizes the introduction of new and unfamiliar challenging ideas and perspectives, ways and modes of seeing anew. He is referring to dreamers who are dangerous to the established order.[16] For me, I am seeking those white students who are ready, with the help of the Black gaze, to be reborn, to allow the scales to fall from their eyes, and to explore aspects of their white self-opacity. Historically, what is especially significant to note here is that Lawrence's work, as early as the 1980s, critically explores the white racist unconscious, the white opacity that I've argued white people possess. I think that it is important to keep in mind that many of the ideas that critical *philosophers* of race, and this includes me, explore, have been grappled with, and critically engaged, by earlier Black scholars for whom credit isn't given.

I'm not sure of why I have not deployed the concept of wide-awake dreamers in my other work, but the resonance of that concept stays with me. Given our contemporary moment of pervasive presidential deception, lies, moral equivocation, and neofascist and authoritarian proclivities, I think that we are in desperate need of wide-awake dreamers across racial divides and other identificatory markers. A figure like Trump, who seems to admire authoritarian right-wing figures, is keen to construct a world that is based upon disinformation and obscurantism. Lord Acton was right when he warned of absolute power corrupting absolutely. Yes, this is what Trump seems to want—some semblance of absolute power. So, in our contemporary moment, wide-awake dreamers must take part in being dangerous. By the way, as I talk about this, I am by no means optimistic. When I conceptualized wide-awake dreamers back in 2012, you couldn't have told me that we would get Trump in 2016. Yet, wide-awake dreamers must be tasked to do the impossible. And here I'm talking about *white* wide-awake dreamers. Black people have already demonstrated the ways in which the "impossible" is possible. I have to believe that white people are capable of seeing through the return of the repressed. Of course, for many of us, whiteness has never been repressed, but there is something, some evil, that has clearly been unleashed since 2012. So, in 2019, we are facing a deep existential crisis. My hope is that there are white people who are prepared to be engulfed by insomnolence and who will tarry through the storm and undo the chains of deception, denial, and indifference.

Chapter 12

Musings: On Autobiography and Africana Philosophy with Azuka Nzegwu

Azuka Nzegwu: In your words, tell us who you are, what you are about, and what you teach.

George Yancy: The question of identity is a complex one. We articulate who we are within the context of a discourse that has its limits. So, I would say that I am a self who is incapable of fully saying who I am as my being is both linked to a past, which is often too opaque to see with absolute clarity, and a future that is always not yet. So, I'm caught within these temporal poles and the limits of discourse. However, this doesn't and shouldn't generate absolute silence. After all, we can and do have the agency to rethink the meaning of the past and anticipate the future from a meaningfully pregnant and agential present. We must engage the question of who we are; it's both ontologically and ethically significant. Indeed, we are the kind of beings who are capable of raising the question of the meaning of our being. And it seems to be a unique capacity within the context of our expansive and perhaps lonely universe. One might say that we are the universe as self-conscious. Of course, on a significantly less cosmic register, through the lens of white racism, this capacity for self-consciousness, indeed, critical self-consciousness, is denied vis-à-vis Black people. On this score, Black people are denied *Geist* or spirit. We are more like inert matter, perhaps mere vegetable life. We are said to lack the capacity for self-determination, the sense of critically engaging in processes of world-making, where we construct forms of meaning and symbolization that are expressive of Black modes of being-in-the-world. The implication here is that white people must "give us" meaning. This is consistent with the idea of the "white-hero" figure, the "white paternal" figure, and notions of manifest destiny, where it is the "natural" teleological design for white people to rule the world, especially to rule over Black people and people of color. As we know, though, and as we must never forget, such is the nature of whiteness, which is a site of oppressive colonial desire and emblematic of a form of misanthropy. In other words, whiteness is a lie and it must be exposed as such. So, telling *my story* within the context of white supremacy, challenges white racist assumptions that I lack agency, that I lack a perspective on the world, that I lack subjectivity. In fact, the act of self-reflection, because I am Black, is an anti-Hegelian practice, especially as Hegel erroneously held that Africa has no *Geist*.

So, I would argue that your question functions as one of empowerment. It asks me, as an embodied Black person, to engage in the dynamic and self-validating process of self-naming. As we know, Frederick Douglass, Malcolm X, Audre Lorde, and so many other Black thinkers knew this to be true. Whiteness as a structure of policing is threatened by Black voices that speak their own names, construct their own realities, build their own worlds. So, in the spirit of speaking my own name, I am an ex-slave whose ancestors came to North America on some wretched slave ship. I was never meant to be free. I was never meant to be recognized as fully human or meant to be treated as fully human. I was meant to serve the needs and perverse desires of white people. I was meant to internalize the white gaze, to see myself according to their anti-Black logic. I was meant to live the life of a slave, a life "ordained" by a white anti-theology predicated on aspirations of world domination. Given this history, part of who I am, of who I must be, is based upon a refusal to placate whiteness. So, I understand my identity as one that is filled with resisting evil in all of its forms, though especially whiteness. This, by the way, is not to say that white people are evil because of some "inherent" ethical defect. That is *not* my position. Whiteness didn't have to emerge. There is no metaphysical force behind it. Yet, whiteness is a site of *social* metaphysics that has deep, powerful, and deadly implications for Black people and people of color. Hence, undergirding this claim is the proposition that whiteness, as a site of racialized hegemony, can be undone. Yet, even as whiteness continues to brutalize Black bodies and bodies of color, white people must come to realize that whiteness is a social disease that is also killing *them*, eradicating *their* capacity for a robust sense of being human.

One absolutely significant aim of mine, which is structurally linked to who I am, is to expose whiteness for the lie that it is, but I'm also deeply burdened by the massive suffering that we as human beings endure. I want to engage critically the causes of that suffering even as I might add to it. This means that I most remain vigilant of the ways in which I perpetuate forms of oppression (sexism and gender inequality, for example) of which I'm not always aware. This lack of awareness, however, does not free me from responsibility. After all, my being unaware doesn't eliminate the pain that others experience as a result of my ignorance. And just because I might be unaware of myself as the perpetrator, my actions have problematic effects on those who are vulnerable.

In short, I ought to be aware; I ought to engage epistemic claims and counter-perspectives that are capable of challenging and undoing my ignorance.

I also see myself as trying to live as fully as possible between birth and the grave, which has to do with appreciating beauty, of being thankful for the gift of being, of celebrating the fact that I exist and coming to terms with the fact that I must die. I am also a hopeful theist, which means that I have hope that there exists the divine, the reality of which I cannot *know*. Yet, hope persists. That is who I am. As I live my life in this way, I am surrounded by suffering. And I too suffer. How can I not? It is all around me, all around us, though we pretend it doesn't exist. This intensity of affect regarding suffering not only impacts how I teach, but what I teach. I teach my students how to die to their prejudices, their distortions, their hubris. This form of death can be very painful. Again, I continue to fail even as I continue to teach these things. So, the courses that I teach are ones that are not simply defined by a social justice thrust, but they are courses that require deep forms of radical reorientation. They are courses that are designed to get students to see the world in ways that they come to have compassion and a deep sense of anger that the world is so broken. That is what I do pedagogically. Within this context, anger is essential; it refuses to leave the world as found, as established, as uncaring, as ethically inept.

Nzegwu: Why did you choose philosophy? Was it love at first sight; if so, how did it develop?

Yancy: This is a question that I love answering. I was always a philosopher. As a young Black boy raised in Richard Allen Project Homes, which we can call the "ghetto," though it was always a place called home, I engaged in deep philosophical questions. I would wonder aloud to my mother if we can know for certain if God exists. I would question her about the truth of religious systems, the meaning of death, the meaning of why we are here. In short, early in my life, before I came across the actual term "philosophy," I was being philosophical, curious. In fact, I would say that I was suffering over questions that carried a profound melancholy for me. So, I would say that philosophy choose me as much as I choose it. But I would agree, it was love at first sight. The moment that I discovered philosophy's root meaning as the love of wisdom, I was sold. I was overwhelmed, profoundly moved that there was an area that posed questions that I had already been doing right there in the "ghetto," a place from which I was not supposed to come out alive. Discovering such a field was like discovering one's vocation, as in one's calling, one's voice, one's destiny, as it were. It was not, and has never been, simply about a profession, a job. Philosophy is about how I live. It is not simply about wonder, though it is that, but about tarrying with our finitude, the reality that we are here within this cosmic mystery and don't know why. For me, a strange feeling of suffering accompanies something like philosophical wonder. For me, our cosmos, our being here, is a painful enigma. This doesn't mean that we don't have theological narratives, poetic narratives, aesthetic narratives, and scientific narratives that attempt to give meaning to this mystery, this enigma. We have those. Yet, how can we claim to know the whole with certainty? We can't. This is partly why I am a hopeful theist. We can't have complete epistemological certainty regarding these issues. For me, my form of hopeful theism embodies a love that takes a leap where certainty comes to an end or where "certainty" is hegemonically defined within the context of a specific paradigmatic way of looking at the world. A narrow scientific naturalism would fit such a description. My hopeful theism is a profound love for what seems at times to be null and void. After all, the universe is so incredibly silent. It doesn't seem to speak its ultimate meaning. So, I envelop myself within this mystery and continue to hope, to risk loving that which I don't know for certain even exists.

Nzegwu: How do you personally define African and/or Africana philosophy? What makes this area of philosophy particularly distinct and exciting for you?

Yancy: Great question. Well, when I formally came to philosophy at the age of seventeen, the issue of philosophical diversity had not occurred to me. This was partly because I was introduced to white male philosophers in the set of encyclopedias that my mother bought. I recall that she had to pay a little bit each month on them. I am so thankful that she did this. The philosophers who I encountered within the encyclopedias—Socrates, Plato, Aristotle, Baruch Spinoza, David Hume, Immanuel Kant, Bertrand Russell, and others—constituted a monochromatic space of whiteness and maleness. At the time, I thought that I was the only Black philosopher alive. I'm serious. Absolutely none of my school teachers referred to any Black thinkers as philosophers. I certainly have no memory of this. But this is also very intriguing. I say this because that means that white ideological indoctrination had already begun early in my life. I came to believe that there was one form of philosophy in town—Western (white) philosophy. But it wasn't called that; it was simply called philosophy. That is one way that false universals are created; they are simply stipulated as universal and then they obfuscate their origins. The idea is to erase all forms of contingency and historical particularity. In this way, historical origins emerge as if *ex nihilo*.

After I came under the influence of the brilliant historian and cultural theorist James G. Spady, I was introduced to the critical field of what I would come to understand as African-American philosophy. This introduction was a game changer, an epistemological paradigm shift for me. Not only did I come to realize that I was not the only Black philosopher, but that philosophical thought by Black people had to be as old as humanity itself. Let's be real. Human beings began, and I'm pretty sure that most if not all recognized anthropologists and archeologists agree to this, in Africa. So, our first feelings of wonder, our sense of awe, perplexity, and symbolic representation of reality as human beings came out of that matrix, out of that geographical, embodied, womb of the continent of Africa. So, African philosophy, for me, would be those ways of *meditating* on the meaning of life, cosmology, concepts of the person, the divine, ethics, the good, the beautiful, space and time, music, and the organizational dynamics of social life, that originated within the complex context of different cultural life-worlds in Africa. That is where we must begin if we want to understand human beings and their first steps toward making (mediated) sense of the world and their place in it.

By the word meditating, I don't wish to make a false distinction between meditating and *thinking*. This has to be avoided lest we make the mistake of dogmatically holding the absurd position that "thinking" began in Greece, the so-called cradle of philosophy. This is a form of Eurocentrism that is poisonous. The pre-Socratic philosophers *meditated* on being, reflected on it. All human cultures engage in forms of meditation, deep reflection on what it means to be. And while there is rich conceptual and historical terrain to be plumbed regarding the "originality" of Greek thought, that is, for example, whether or not the Greeks borrowed (to put it nicely) certain African philosophical concepts without proper citation, I am a pluralist when it comes to philosophy. Hence, no culture has a monopoly on the meaning of philosophy. To do so is to commit a vicious conceptual circle. All cultures are philosophically vibrant, even if they didn't or don't use the Greek term, *philosophia*. For me, to be human is to engage the question of being; it is to perform a certain meditative stance to the world. This plurality is geographically located, which requires an analysis of how various forms of reflection emerge vis-à-vis that geographical location. This also means being attentive to the languages that are operative within those geographical spaces, and how those languages embody different metaphors and grammars that impact partly how the world emerges as meaningful at the level of the symbolic.

While Africana philosophy has come to denote philosophical diversity within the African diaspora, my main focus has been on African-American philosophy, the forms of philosophical meditation that engage what it means to be Black here in North America. I should note that I am very much interested in the ways in which Africana philosophy is said to embody shared philosophical assumptions, that is, assumptions that instantiate the reality of *Africana* philosophy itself. So, I'm fascinated by the synthetic work to be done and that has been done. African-American philosophy is historically grounded in resistance. The fact that *we do think*, a relatively new concept in the history of white America and Europe, is itself a phenomenon of resistance. We always knew that we could think. However, within a context of anti-Black racism, thinking is partly a site of countering the white mythos that we don't think or can't think. The context of anti-Black white racism creates the condition whereby what we do as a matter of being human becomes an act of resistance, a counter-anti-Black act. So, given the historical context within which Black people in North America found themselves and find themselves, a context where their very being is questioned, where they are deemed "inferior" and "subhuman," much of their philosophical meditation has been engaged toward the end of gaining freedom, justice, and equity. This is one reason that many African-American philosophers engage primarily in political philosophy, ethics, questions of social justice. Of course, it does not follow that *all* African-American philosophers engage these questions because they explicitly link them to the existential plight of Black people or to their own lives because they have experienced anti-Black racism. Being an African-American philosopher in North America who does ethics or political philosophy is not a tautology. We make choices. Yet, there is a connection between the fact that many African-American philosophers demand Anglo-American and European philosophy to transcend their hermetic closure to the importance of African-American experiences, and the recognition that our experiences have intrinsic philosophical value. Yet, it isn't just a demand, but an intervention. In short, African-American philosophers engage in serious meta-philosophical critiques of the ways in which white philosophers downplay (or even render irrelevant) the nonideal conditions under which African-American people suffer, forms of suffering that must be engaged philosophically. In this way, African-American philosophers not only expose the white racial limits of Anglo-American and European philosophy, they engage in the creative process of developing important philosophical tools for understanding what it means to be Black in North America. Needless to say, there is no single metaphysical way of being Black in North America, though there are profound shared modes of social being, situational facticity, and shared epistemological frames of reference, all of which speak to a complex identity. For me, not only are we not "post-Black," but it is not even clear that such a moment is desirable. Performing "post-Blackness" will neither save you from a white police officer's bullet nor free you from being called that most nasty of racist epithets—"nigger."

Within the context of Black identity, it is also important to be attentive to the ways in which African-American male philosophers participate in forms of erasure of philosophical issues pertinent to Black woman. This raises the importance and indispensability of African-American feminist philosophical thought. It is important that African-American male philosophers don't repeat the same androcentric assumptions operative in European and Anglo-American practices of gender exclusion (in or outside the field of philosophy), forms of epistemic violence, and patriarchy. Within this context, African-American women philosophers bring to bear upon our collective Africana philosophical practices an awareness that is neither tethered to white feminist epistemological productions nor African-American male epistemological productions.

Unlike the white philosophers encountered in the encyclopedia, African-American philosophical thought challenges white normative assumptions that render the content of my experiences as fit for sociology or psychology, but not philosophy. Hence, white philosophy can and does bespeak a certain kind of death vis-à-vis Black critical subjectivity. African-American philosophy and Africana philosophy excite and expand the philosophical imagination as they pry open the closed doors on the notion that "genuine" philosophical thought as it is articulated through white forms of embodiment is the *only* form of philosophical thought. So, African-American philosophical thought, as I see it, challenges the limits of thought itself, that is, thought as exclusively defined as a Greek project or as a European project.

You know, life is strange. As the young Black kid who thought that he was the only Black philosopher, I have been so incredibly proud to have, to my knowledge, published the first major essay on Thomas N. Baker. He was the first Black male to receive the PhD in philosophy in the United States from Yale in 1903. He was born enslaved in 1860. There are two enigmas here. How does a Black person born before Emancipation Proclamation (1863) eventually become the first to receive the PhD in philosophy, and from Yale of all places? And how does a Black kid raised in the "ghetto" become a professional philosopher and then write the first major article on Thomas N. Baker? But the mystery deepens. Joyce M. Cook was the first Black woman to receive the PhD in philosophy in the United States, which she also received from Yale, but in 1965. I had become very close to Cook, and it was her desire that all of her published and unpublished papers, and her library, would be left to me upon her death. Sadly, and with great remorse, Joyce M. Cook passed away in 2014. Cook's desire was honored. In fact, I have since, again to my knowledge, published the first major essay on Cook. When I think back and think about being that young Black kid, and then think about my essay on Baker and my relationship with Cook, I imagine that if our Black ancestors are indeed around watching us then I have been looked after with much love. I am deeply thankful.

Nzegwu: What specific topics of African and/or Africana philosophy resonate with you? What do you want to pass on to your students, as well as to the next generation of thinkers?

Yancy: As a Black philosopher, I am passionate about issues of racial embodiment. I'm interested in the ways in which Black bodies under racial duress do ontology, epistemology, ethics, metaethics, political theory, phenomenology. And while these questions are raised within a context of white anti-Black racism, it does not follow that my African-American philosophical interests fall exclusively within the context where whiteness is toxically present. Hence, what is the meaning of love, the good life, and beauty within Black spaces of being? In what ways do Black people imagine the world? In what ways do Black boys and girls value human existence, make meaning, and conceive of the cosmos, and their place within it? To bring this home in a very powerful way, what did Trayvon Martin, Tamir Rice, and Aiyana Stanley-Jones imagine as they walked the earth? What form did their conversations take as they dialogued with the divine just before they fell asleep at night? How did they understand love? How did they make sense of their beliefs? How did they experience the mystery of their own being?

Imaginative thinking that takes place within Black spaces needn't be resistant spaces, certainly not always resistant to whiteness. What is it like for Black bodies in North America to dream-in-Black? After all, we have been forced to dream in white. The semiotic content of our dream-world is so saturated with values, images, desires, and aspirations that are white, that have their origin within white spaces of meaning-making. So, the issue of African-American agency is crucial to the work that I do. What does it mean to be a free Black agent in the world? What does it mean to possess a healthy form of Black male masculinity? What does it mean to be a Black woman who loves and experiences love? What does it mean to be trans and Black in a world where you dream of love and relationality that don't fit the proverbial mold? What does it mean to create meaning, beauty, and love, outside of a white frame of reference? These questions are as much about African-American philosophy as is the question of freedom from white oppression. What I want my Black students to know is that who and what they are is a complex affair—one that is multilayered; to know that what they productively and creatively *think* and *feel* (not that these must be diametrically opposed) speak to genuine ways of engaging the world. I want them to know that they are infinitely valued and loved. For the next generation of thinkers, and I'm thinking here about white thinkers, I encourage the capacity to suffer, where suffering opens a space for care and deep longing for a sense of connection, a connection that challenges an ontology of edges. This point about no edges, is also a hope that transcends race. We all need to rethink inhuman forms of relational ontology. This point about rethinking a relational ontology is obviously a significant philosophical concept for me as it reappears throughout a few chapters within this book.

For my Black students, I want them to know that parrhesia or courageous speech is necessary. It is necessary especially as we find ourselves living under a Trump world of unabashed white racism, white nativism, xenophobia, homophobia, and transphobia. Indeed, we have arrived at a very dangerous place in human history, a place where we are living under a white solipsistic man who has fantasies of being a god. Historically, we have seen this before and his name was Adolf Hitler.

Nzegwu: What, if any, role does philosophy play in helping us understand the national, social, and economic issues of our time?

Yancy: Philosophy has everything to do this these issues. Philosophy, for me, has a Marxian strain to the extent that it should have aspirations to change the world, not to interpret it over and over again. Yet, that aspiration must be couched within a shared sense of care, mutual validation, and profound respect. Just any change will not work. After all, things could get worse. Philosophy must grapple with a world in which North Korea is made to feel safe, even as we would want its people not to suffer under a brutal dictatorship. And, yet, even here, we must be critically conscious of the ways in which we desire to impose North American ways of being onto those who are not American. Even national "good intentions" can carry forms of neocolonialism and often do. Indeed, humanism itself can insidiously force a nation to abandon what makes it already feel integral, culturally rich, and politically stable. This is especially so when humanism becomes just another name for white colonialism or when democracy is just another name for creating zero-sum logics that are embedded within a democratic capitalism that undermines democracy itself. The transportation of North American neo-liberalism to African nations will conflict with African cultural values that express robust forms of ontological mutuality. Philosophy must speak to climate change and the ways in which various notions of epistemology and ontology are bedfellows with forms of exploiting the earth, where we conceive of the earth as infinitely disposable. This is not just a question of capitalist greed, but one of philosophical anthropology, one that interrogates our most fundamental views about what it means to be human, to be good stewards of the earth. What we need is a conception of philosophy that dares to love, where love involves profound risk and calls upon new and radical forms of imagining what could be or what is not yet; and then muster the courage to take the necessary steps toward creating a community that is dear to us, that is beloved. As the Global South suffers, we thrive. That kind of dynamic presupposes a corrupt understanding of humanity on the part of those who thrive. Philosophy is useless if it does not speak with courage, if it does not attempt to move the world in the direction of a human community where if one of us suffers, then we all suffer. I also think that there is the necessity for philosophy to critically rethink its insular tendencies. It needs to rethink its conceptual terrain through interdisciplinarity. In this way, philosophy places itself in dialogue with those groundbreaking areas of investigation that are already doing important work at trying to engage complex national, social and economic issues. This will importantly impact the myopia of philosophical theorizing.

Nzegwu: Teaching is an important profession that makes a big difference. Why did you choose to be a professor? Or was that path inevitable?

Yancy: Yes. It makes a huge difference, a fundamental difference. For me, education is a form of self-cultivation, self-interrogation, and embodying the habits that encourage speaking courageously. So, teaching is about fundamental transformation. The classroom is an experimentally open space within which the teacher and the students learn not only mutually transmitted concepts, but how pedagogical trust might be rejuvenated within an unfortunate space where competition is often valorized; where zero-sum logics rule the academy. So, as a teacher, it is important that my students trust me and that I trust them. Without trust, there is no mutual vulnerability. Without trust students are reluctant or refuse to be honest, not only about what they fear they don't know, but also about what they do know and don't feel comfortable sharing. They must be made to feel safe that not knowing, discovering that one does not know, has its own touch of beauty. Not knowing brings attention to an opening, an opportunity, a space to grow. And what they do know, what they may have concealed for many years, requires a safe space within which to un-suture, to unburden, to become vulnerable. If my students don't feel as if they can speak the truth about themselves, even truths that are painful, then I have failed to create the kind of pedagogy that I most value. This doesn't mean that I want my classrooms to become sites of confession, but I do want my students to know that I too am fallen, imperfect, finite, troubled. I want them to know that education can also function as a site of suffering, suffering together, a space where they are not alone.

Recently, I had my students read about the many problematic issues regarding anti-Asian American racism vis-à-vis the model minority myth. Pedagogically, it was a collectively powerful experience. After reading the material, most of my Asian American students were silent. I don't think that they had ever been asked to explore anti-Asian American racism within the context of a classroom, especially within the context of a predominantly white academic institution. So, I waited, but there was no immediate response that indicated to me that very much was taken from the material. Suddenly, there was this incredible moment when a Chinese American female student spoke up by sharing her experiences of having men speak to her in racist and derogatory terms. She shared with us that one male approached her only to say that he had "Yellow fever" for her. Another male approached her and "praised" her for her ability to speak English. She also talked about how she was rendered "exotic" through the white racial frame. What was especially interesting about these cases is it was Black males who had said these things to her. So, we discussed the internalization of the white racial frame by Black people, in this case Black males. She went on to say that she was aware of how whiteness operates. She also mentioned that the material that we had read had articulated her experiences with greater clarity. She also mentioned that she had not taken any courses before where my way of directly confronting white racism was practiced. So, I asked her how all of this made her feel. Her voice cracked and she began to cry. It was a powerful moment. So, I shifted everything onto the students. I asked them to deal with this. No one said a word. By this time, she was wiping her tears. So, I moved slowly up the aisle and gestured and asked her to come to me. I hugged her and said that "we are here for you. We stand with you." This captured that sense of not being alone. Philosophy was never meant to make students weep, but there we were doing nonideal theory, which is such an embodied practice. My teaching assistant and I concluded that all of those who remained silent will now be able to question themselves, to interrogate why they refused to support or move to embrace their fellow classmate. My sense is that they didn't know what to do. This was a philosophy course. Prior to reading material on race and racism, we had read Plato and Descartes. There was nothing that prepared them for this act of vulnerability within the context of a classroom. The student, by the way, cried even more as I hugged her, and spoke those words of support and inclusivity. It was a surreal but incredibly generative pedagogical and ethical moment. So, yes, teaching can make a big difference.

By the way, my initial desire to become a professor was not grounded within what I now articulate as this deep sense of existential sociality. For me, it was the inevitable end of obtaining a doctorate in philosophy. I would not do this any differently, though. Teaching is a calling of sorts and it requires tremendous responsibility. I can assure you that this responsibility can at times be frightening, especially as we sometimes don't have the answers or thought that we did and discover that we don't. That, again has its own beauty. Teaching is an important lesson in epistemological humility and deep self-interrogation.

Nzegwu: Reflecting on philosophy and Africa, philosophy and Black life, philosophy and Black knowledge, how do we ensure those remain part of the epistemological framework of philosophy? How do we ensure that the progress we make does not die out? How do we preserve our legacies?

Yancy: We need to make sure that Black people are in positions of academic authority and influence. And we should bear in mind that not all Black people, because they are Black, are passionate about Black knowledge production and sustaining that production. So, we mustn't be seduced by a myopic view of how Black people think or what they value. Think about it. White academic colonization is a powerful and effective tool. Used effectively, Black academics will toxically desire to become white. That is pathological; a state of self-hatred. I think that it is important that we encourage deeper forms of Black self-love and a sense of love of cultural diversity that does not degenerate into some form of dogmatism or balkanization say, between Black people in North America and those in Africa. This divide-and-conquer tactic can be quite effective in splitting us. I think that we need to train young Black scholars and expose them to a multiplicity of philosophical perspectives, to encourage critical thinking about their deeper cultural and often hybrid origins. After all, not all Black people in North America came through the Middle Passage, but this does not negate forms of theorization and intersubjectivity that reveal our conceptual and affective family resemblance. It will also involve financial resources that will enable institutional building, that is, creating sites of Black knowledge cultivation and production. We need role models who are capable of embodying the best of what Black people have brought and bring to the epistemic community table. Black students throughout their education need to see Black bodies in positions of academic and administrative power, Black bodies that refuse to accept the "impossible." We need more journals like the *Journal on African Philosophy*, that are dedicated to the perpetuation, development, and cultivation of critical Black philosophical meditation. We need critical spaces where we get to negotiate our own identities and agendas as Black knowledge producers. I also think that there needs to be greater organic philosophical exchange between Black philosophers in North America and African philosophers from the continent and throughout the diaspora. This will ensure a consolidated effort to preserve Black philosophical legacies, ones that speak to forms of Black global knowledge production, and forms of production whose origins develop from different gendered social locations. Keeping our legacies alive is not simply about cultural longevity; it is a question of Black existence in a global space of white domination.

Nzegwu: Since philosophy is about ideas, can you speak on the idea of transformatory change in light of your local politics?

Yancy: This question is a complex one for me. I say this because I believe that we all have different forms of labor to perform, to bring about transformational change. It is my conviction that philosophy must play a public role. It cannot settle for forms of navel gazing as people suffer in front of one's face, right there within the everyday social spaces that we traverse. Loving wisdom must propel us forward to love humanity. This is what philosophy must do on the proverbial ground. In short, philosophy engages within the quotidian marketplace. Given this, my aim has been to speak to different publics. I do this through, for example, writing for *The New York Times* philosophy column, "The Stone." The essays that I have written have received national and international attention. I have contributed to shaping policy stances at the American Philosophical Association (APA). For example, the white supremacist backlash that I received after writing the article "Dear White America" led to an unprecedented public announcement by the APA against bullying. Had I not written that article, perhaps that change would not have happened as soon as it did. I also wrote an article entitled, "I Am a Dangerous Professor."[1] The article was written after I was placed on the conservative

"Professor Watchlist." It created a community of critical voices that supported my efforts. There were supportive messages that read, "I, Too, Am a Dangerous Professor." Some junior academics wrote to me thanking me for having written the article as they could not have done so because of not yet having received tenure. So, there is a way in which philosophical ideas engaged through different public media can have a national and even global reach at transforming lives and ideas. For example, I was so incredibly surprised and honored after I wrote the article, "Is Your God Dead?"[2] Soon after it was published, I learned that some ministers actually incorporated it into their Sunday sermons. I also learned that the venerable Bhikshuni Thubten Chodron, an American Tibetan Buddhist, delivered a two-part discussion of "Is Your God Dead?" on YouTube.[3] Imagine that. Imagine how that article was able to reach entire congregations, and religiously diverse communities. The article argued that we have failed to build a broader theological community predicated on recognizing the humanity of the *least of these*, those who suffer because of various forms of bias, violence, and marginalization. We pass by those suffering bodies right before our eyes. If philosophy is the love of wisdom, then we must be careful that our love for wisdom doesn't exclude our love for those who suffer.

Nzegwu: How does African and/or Africana philosophy build our knowledge? What epistemological concerns do we have to pay attention to?

Yancy: African and/or Africana philosophy helps to build our collective (human) knowledge by being part of a larger critical conversation that is open to multiple perspectives. But not just open to them; there must also be the openness to be changed by them. The process of building knowledge takes place through critically synthesizing and challenging multiple sites of knowledge production. Hence, where Black people are engaged in theory and praxis, where Black lives matter across the diaspora, we need the insights of anthropology, psychology, sociology, economics, political theory, genetics, and history to bear upon who we are and what we aspire to become. There is no need for disciplinary narcissism. So, we have to pay attention to our tendencies to create forms of "philosophical purity" that divide and render other epistemic communities as "ersatz" or intellectually inconsequential. This is something that haunts forms of knowledge production that are not critically self-reflexive. We can become obsessed with method, which can potentially militate against the dynamic flow of knowledge exchange and new forms of epistemic hybridity. Obsession with method can function as a form of epistemic idolatry and can actually inhibit the growth of knowledge. So, African and Africana philosophy must remain self-reflexively aware of toxic forms of epistemic totalization even as they must insist upon the audibility of their philosophical perspectives. These two things are not mutually exclusive. I think that it is also important that African and Africana philosophy remain true to the ways in which knowledge production should also reshape and continue to improve the conditions under which that production is made possible. In this way, there is a constant and dynamic epistemic, communal, and structural flow.

Nzegwu: There are lots of African concepts that speak to humanity and community. Within the global diaspora, to what extent should African derived values shape the philosophy and lives of people of African descent?

Yancy: That is a wonderful question. I think that has always happened. What do I mean? Well, coming through the Middle Passage, Black people of African descent brought with them their own ideas of beauty, aesthetics, ontology, spirituality, social organizational structures, concepts of what constitutes persons, the divine, and so on. This does not mean that such ideas remained static or should remain static. So, we never came to the so-called new world without having our own sense of the world. Of course, forced into a dangerous, deadly, dehumanizing, and maddening situation because of unethical and distorted white colonial desires, Black people had to develop a syncretic worldview, which points to metastability, one that creatively weaved together ideas foreign to them. But this is indicative of a people who are able to make profound adjustments to remain alive, a process involving both forms of preservation and modification through the cooperation of new material. That entire process incredibly embodies a Jazz motif. We are an improvisational people; and, a blues saturated people who refuse to die. We keep moving on. I particularly like the Ubuntu concept that says, "I am what I am because of who we all are." What if we instilled that concept within the political space of the global Black diaspora, and then practiced it? I would think that we would see a radically different form of global and collective Black consciousness. My point is that we have to challenge the ontology of the Western world, especially with the spread of neoliberalism. If what we are depends upon all of us, then think about how that ontology would shape how we rethink community, unity, and collective humanity within a context where Africa as a continent has been terrorized and divided. What if that ontology became the glue that transcended post-colonial divisions and those divisions resulting from the vicious legacy of the African Slave Trade? My sense is that the African world and its many scattered people might rise up to show the *white world* what it means to be human, to be mutually entangled spiritually and social ontologically. Now, that is not a panacea. It is certainly not about African hegemony. My point is that the voice of Africa, its political vision for humanity, is far too silent in the global village. New questions need to be posed about the ways in which white people have dictated how the rest of the world should live, should be, should exist. We need African countries to unite and hold a summit on what an African conception of world peace looks like, what an African conception of community looks like, what an African conception of love looks like, and what an African conception of spirituality looks like. This doesn't mean that African conceptual paradigms are monolithic. This is not to say that Africa has the solution to every global problem, but, let's be honest, Africa must not live in the shadow of a white world. We have seen for far too long how fundamental assumptions within their (white) metaphysics have failed us. Perhaps it is time for a battle for the souls of humanity, the precious lives of human beings. Perhaps it is time that we raised the unasked question: will humanity last under the metaphysics of white people, white cultures, white forms of world-making?

Nzegwu: Who has inspired and motivated you? Who has influenced your work?

Yancy: In a formal academic sense, that is an easy one. It would be James G. Spady. I say this because he was the one important Black scholar, historian, and critical cultural theorist who taught me how to engage with books, articles, music, and images in a deeply critical fashion. In terms of motivation, Spady functioned as a model, as an exemplar of what a free and intellectually audacious Black scholar looks like. And he influenced me very early on when I was still a teenager. Yet, he saw something in me. He saw the tremendous potential. This is so important in the lives of young Black people; they need to be able to witness what critical dialogue looks like, what it means to read across various intellectual fields. And they need to be recognized and validated. This is what Spady brought to bear on my intellectual proclivities. So, I was fortunate that we crossed paths when I was still in high school and had just come to experience myself as a philosopher in a formal sense, that is, having discovered the term itself. So, there was a clear and profound motivational impact; there was also the process of buttressing an insatiable desire to learn more, to read more, to articulate ideas with greater precision, rigor, and synthetic, conceptual pregnancy. So, Spady was the one who placed me squarely within important Black intellectual spaces. And when I say that I mean that he had me engaging important questions and themes within the Negritude Movement, the Harlem Renaissance, the Black Arts Movement, Afro-Surrealism, Dadaism, the Civil Rights Movement, Pan-Africanism, the organizational and historical importance of the Universal Negro Improvement Association (UNIA), the Nation of Islam, and engaging the lives, writings and ideas of such figures as Cheikh Anta Diop, Kwame Nkrumah, Nnamdi Azikiew, Ngũgĩ wa Thiong'o, Kamau Brathwaite, Martin Luther King, Jr., Elijah Muhammad, Malcolm X, George G. M. James, Elmer Imes, Marcus Garvey, bell hooks, Sonia Sanchez, Geneva Smitherman, Katherine Dunham, Paula Giddings, Ralph Bunche, W. E. B. DuBois, Grandmaster Caz, Sister Souljah, Eve, Kool Herc, Afrika Bambaataa, Tupac Shakur, and the entire panoply of cultural, racial, political, spatial, historical, musicological, sonic, and aesthetic elements within rap and Hip Hop culture and other forms of musical expression. In short, Spady is one of the leading cultural theorists in the world. And he does all of this deep exegetical work without asking for permission to do so. That is intellectual agency! That is one way of being a free Black intellectual.

Nzegwu: The movement #BlackLivesMatter was started by three Black women to address racism and racial injustice prevalent in the United States. The movement is quintessential in that it brings to us the issue of inequality that many Black people and people of color face in America, and other parts of the world. It does so in a way that disrupts from traditional protest hierarchy by forcing the nation and former community leaders to look at its past and at its promise. In what ways has the quest for equality and humanity been crucial to our identity and selves, both nationally and globally?

Yancy: Yes! Let's say their names: Alicia Garza, Patrisse Cullors, and Opal Tometi. And you know, this is not about disrespect for one's elders. It is about holding Black leaders accountable, Black leaders who don't seem to have any sense of what young Black people are experiencing, witnessing, imagining, and thinking within the contemporary context of North America anti-Black racism. It is also about Black women's agency and the power of young Black people, more generally, to theorize and conceptualize ways in which they must fight and mobilize within their own moment through history, a history that requires rethinking outdated modes of resistance and protest. The movement #BlackLivesMatter holds politicians accountable, they hold the police accountable, and they hold presidential candidates accountable; and they do this with a powerful sense of discard for forms of superficial respectability politics. Indeed, like many Black everyday people, grass roots people, in the past, they hold accountable the United States and its continued systemic nature of white supremacy. Yet, unlike over fifty years ago, they have technology at their political disposal, and they are technologically savvy. They've returned the Black gaze on the panoptic hegemony of the white gaze, and they record as much as they can of North America's cancerous injustice. That is a form of youth-led agency and political independence. Of course, the deep moral crisis in America is the fact that we are living within the twenty-first century and white America has to be told that we, Black people, matter, that we are not disposable. You know, Cornel West makes this point where he says that the humanity of Black people is a relatively new idea in the modern Western world. So, our quest for humanity is so central to our collective diasporic identities. Anti-Black white racism is a global phenomenon. The horrible treatment of people of color by processes of white empire building is a tragic legacy of Europe. When you are treated as the wretched of the earth, the subaltern, the voiceless, as surplus to be eradicated, your identity formation is often negatively impacted. Frantz Fanon talks about this in terms of how Black people have trouble with their body schema in an anti-Black world. Ralph Ellison talks about a powerful sense of being rendered invisible. W. E. B. DuBois talks about double consciousness. James Baldwin talks about how Black bodies are expected to make peace with mediocrity. And Toni Morrison talks about the need to love our flesh because the white world will burn it, flay it, lynch it, hate it. Black people have done the impossible. When faced with the white world, we have had to fight against extraordinary odds to define ourselves, resist like hell to deflect an entire system that said we were "inferior," "hyper-sexual," and "immoral." We have had to give our lives fighting for dignity and freedom. However, as Maya Angelou says to us—and yet still I, you, we rise.[4] That is Black tenacity within a *white* world that refuses to respect you, that refuses to value your life, that refuses your subjectivity, that refuses your humanity.

Nzegwu: How do you teach African and/or Africana philosophy? What politics do you face within your university or college?

Yancy: I don't face any overt political forms of resistance to teaching such courses if that is what you mean. But, let's be clear, to engage African or Africana philosophical systems or frames of reference on their own philosophical terms is already a deeply political act as one is challenging so many of the conscious and unconscious assumptions about what constitutes "real" philosophy. To be within a white monochromatic academic space, and to teach courses that call into question the very "universality" of whiteness is to inhabit the space of the political. In brief, one of my areas of focus is African-American philosophy. So, I make sure to include a range of thinkers. In fact, some of them are not professional philosophers, but they are doing philosophy. No question about it. So, it is not just about teaching those African-Americans who received doctorates in philosophy; it is about engaging a range of Black critical voices through different critical expressive registers (literary, musical, autobiographical, etc.) that are productive epistemically and affectively, that speak philosophically to the Black experience.

Nzegwu: What are you currently working on? Projects? Books?

Yancy: My book *On Race: 34 Conversations in a Time of Crisis* was published in 2017 by Oxford University Press. There is no book like this in which such a range of prominent philosophers and public intellectuals are engaged in conversation about race. I conducted all of the interviews. Nineteen of those interviews were originally conducted for a special series on race within *The New York Times* column "The Stone." My new authored book *Backlash: What*

Happens When We Talk Honestly about Racism in America was just published in 2018 by Rowman & Littlefield. I would say that this is one of the most candid and brutally honest discussions about white racism by a contemporary professional philosopher. That book was hard to write, emotionally draining. It critically engages much of the white hatred that I received after I published the controversial article, "Dear White America," which also appeared in "The Stone." Since its publication, I still receive white racist messages. In fact, in February 2019, I received a small envelope in my university mailbox. There was a short message written on a small piece of blue paper. The message was nasty and succinct: "Get out of my country you racist hypocritical overpaid piece of shit." Not too long ago, someone also wrote to me wishing for me to get "Stage 4 cancer." There is nothing new about these forms of white racist vitriol. They constitute the very heart of white racist America, though I will never get used to them. I also recently coedited a book with my colleague and friend Emily McRae, entitled *Buddhism and Whiteness: Critical Reflections.* The book consists of a critical collection of chapters from Buddhist scholars/ practitioners that engage the nature of whiteness and dismantling white racism. I also edited a book entitled *Educating for Critical Consciousness.* This book consists of a collection of chapters written by a critical cadre of thinkers who engage the question of pedagogical critical consciousness within the context of our Trump presidency. It is a necessary text that theorizes ways of sustaining critical thinking and combating anti-intellectualism, "alternative facts," and unabashed forms of xenophobia and white nationalism that are operative at the "highest office" in the United States. I will begin working on an authored book on sexism. The aim is to bring a similar call for honesty regarding forms of toxic masculinity that I asked of white people in "Dear White America." My hope is to explore aspects of my own toxic masculinity without turning the text into a problematic confessional voice. I also plan to begin thinking about writing a book on what I have theorized as the suturing and un-suturing of whiteness. Those two concepts will help to lay bare aspects of the structure of whiteness and explore its possibility of rupture and what that looks like.

Nzegwu: What are the challenges in teaching African and/or Africana philosophy in the United States and Africa?

Yancy: I think that one of the things that we should be aware of is the potential of teaching African-American or Africana philosophy within academic spaces where there is the assumption by one's white colleagues that such areas are really secondary to "real" philosophy—that is, the sort of philosophy done by the white canonical figures. In this way, within the United States, African-American philosophy or Africana philosophy are treated as possibly "exotic" areas of inquiry or as frames of reference that have sociological importance only, not real *philosophical* importance. By the way, I reject these kinds of intellectual rigid divisions. Sociologist Joe Feagin, for example, has done some incredibly powerful and influential work on race, work that overlaps with and critically informs what many of us are doing within the area of critical philosophy of race. Part of the challenge is getting students to understand that the nature of philosophy is not defined outside of history, but is an historical phenomenon. We have to also decolonize the minds of Black students who have come to think of Black forms of knowledge production as "inferior" to white forms of knowledge production. Again, this is partly because so many Black students have not seen Black people in positions of academic authority or intellectual authority at the college or university level. The lack of Black presence is especially true for Black philosophers given their continued paucity. I recall a Black prospective philosophy graduate student who shared with me that she feels deeply discouraged to apply to philosophy departments where there are embarrassingly low numbers of other Black graduate students in the department. This is a greater systemic problem that has to do with admissions committees, more robust fellowships that encourage Black students to apply to certain graduate schools, and the priorities of philosophy departments. In terms of Black faculty within philosophy, there are problems in terms of hiring practices, retention, creating welcoming spaces for Black faculty within predominantly white academic spaces, and rethinking the function of service, especially as Black faculty are often doing inordinate work taking care of the academic and emotional needs of students of color. I would also argue that as we think about Black students pursuing careers in philosophy, we must provide better quality education for Black children early on so that their imaginations can begin to soar in specific intellectual directions. How can we begin to raise the question of thinking about a career in philosophy when Black students have to deal with the racist ethos and practices that support the school-to-prison pipeline? How do we get them to think about what it means to be a critically engaged Black student and someday a critically engaged academic when most of their teachers are white women with so little seasoned training as teachers? These white women bring their own deeply racist assumptions to those Black and Brown spaces, spaces where these children, especially Black boys, are not even allowed to be boys. As you can tell, I think that your question has layers of complexity. Within the context of Africa, however, I do have one observation. I have been told by some of my African students that at some African universities, the "real" philosophy that takes center stage is European philosophy. I am sure that there are exceptions, but, if true, and I have no reason not to believe what I've been told, then this is a case of vicious post-colonialism.

Nzegwu: How do we increase the presence of Black students in African and/ or Africana philosophy?

Yancy: I sense that I've anticipated this question within the body of my previous response. So, it is a nice segue. Again, I think that we need to start early on. Teach Black students that there are Black philosophers. Let them know that philosophy matters to them. Let them know that they are doing philosophy even as they may not be aware of this. Encouraging Black students in this way is a deep philosophical anthropological project, because one is actually saying to Black students that they already critically engage the world. This means that despite what a white racist paradigm says, young Black students are always already imaginatively engaging the world. There isn't one magical strategy to use to increase the number of Black people within the field of philosophy, but it must begin with showing Black students that we, Black philosophers, actually exist. They need to see us. It is harder for them to see themselves in the faces of white men or white women, especially when they are *not* also being told that Black people around the world *do* philosophy. Indeed, they are often not even aware that Black philosophers actually teach at universities. I have had Black students say to me that they want to major in philosophy after taking courses with me. I am honored. Yet, it wasn't just seeing a Black body quote from Plato, but it was making philosophy relevant to their lives, to their experiences as Black. So, they need exposure to African philosophy and Africana philosophy, fields that speak to them in ways that are different from a course that moves them from the pre-Socratics to American (white) pragmatism or European (white) continental philosophy. This does not mean that *Western* philosophy is to be avoided. That would be silly and a form of intellectual myopia, perhaps even intellectually poisonous. I am not a purest in that sense. That is too dangerous. However, I am not being philosophically unfair here or putting down say, American pragmatism or continental philosophical thought. I greatly admire the work of William James on the ethics of belief and John Dewey on his critique of professional philosophy and his understanding of habits, and Martin Heidegger's and Merleau-Ponty's work on questions of embodiment and being-in-the-world. I also admire the neo-pragmatist work of Richard Rorty. When I first engaged philosophy, after finding out that there was such a term, I voraciously read Plato. The point is that white students see themselves reflected back to them in the works of these thinkers, while philosophy goes unmarked as white. We must let Black students know that there are various philosophical systems and various understandings of philosophy. And there are some that reflect their sense of themselves back to them in ways that others may not and were never meant to. This does not mean that Black students should be told *not* to study Kant or Hegel, or Sartre, or Simone de Beauvoir. Again, that would be ridiculous. Philosophical passions should never be policed in that way. But we should always make students cognizant of the complexity of how a philosopher's work and life speak to each other. So, while it is true that Hegel and Kant were racists, this should not occlude studying them or

Chapter 13

Thinking about Race, History, and Identity with Maria del Guadalupe Davidson

Maria del Guadalupe Davidson: Malcolm X once said that History is the most important of all disciplines. Do you agree that racism and other bigotries rely on ahistorical arguments that either vaguely or specifically conjure up biological myths, myths that are easily and quickly subverted by history?

George Yancy: Yes. For Malcolm X, history was especially important in terms of gaining access to a past that demonstrated the humanity of Black people and their contributions to world history. I think that this understanding of history and its importance to Black people no doubt structured the ethos of the Nation of Islam, more generally. One might say, and I realize that Malcolm didn't say it this way, that his conception of history was anti-Hegelian vis-à-vis the history of Black people, especially sub-Saharan African people. His deployment of history functioned to communicate to Black people living in Harlem and other Black inner-city enclaves that they are a proud people whose history is grounded in self-conscious reflection and civilizational complexity. I think that Malcolm saw the importance of using history critically on behalf of Black people as a corrective, a sort of epistemological corrective, to the multiple white racist myths formulated by European and Anglo-American thinkers. Indeed, there was an entire white supremacist worldview that had to be critiqued, rethought, and overthrown. So, in this sense, I do think that it is important to engage history as a tool to deconstruct white racist myths. In this way, history can be used as a weapon. And I think that Malcolm was correct. Malcolm understood history as a site for self-knowledge, self-definition, self-respect, self-empowerment, and self-preservation. This is why reading was such an important revolutionary act for Malcolm while he was in prison. Reading and learning about history were liberational. Like Frederick Douglass, Malcolm understood that reading was a powerful way of critiquing and countering one's enslaved mentality, of understanding the racist machinations that were/are established to keep one oppressed, uniformed, ignorant.

Without any doubt, the history of white supremacy continues to haunt Black people and people of color. Given the incredible, despicable, and violent resurgence of unabashed white racism, reading Malcolm X at this historical moment may very well function as a way of helping us to rethink the precarious nature of Black lives. It is his relevance that I find so amazing. Perhaps "amazing" connotes the wrong emotion that I'm trying to communicate. Perhaps the word that I'm looking for is mind-boggling or overwhelming. I can't believe that we are in this place where the detestable nature of white supremacy cannot be called out unambiguously by the person who occupies the "highest" office in the land. So, we need Malcolm's frankness, his courage.

You know, I was a voracious reader of Malcolm X. Earlier than that, my father had these recordings of Malcolm. I recall laying back on the floor listening to his voice, admiring his cadence, his vocabulary, and dreaming of speaking before large audiences. Reading so much by Malcolm and about Malcolm, though, I was more than ready to think critically about Spike Lee's 1992 movie, *Malcolm X*. After the movie I read everything I could get my hands on. It was a fascinating intellectual and deeply personal transformative experience. One thing led to another. I had this very exciting moment where I got to meet his wife, Betty Shabazz on February 20, 1991. She had come to Philly to give a talk. One wonderful thing about that encounter is that she autographed my copy of *The Autobiography of Malcolm X*. My sense was that some who were present during her talk desired that Betty's voice reflect the voice of Malcolm, but she had her own voice. I was also able to interview Robert Little, who was Malcolm's youngest brother, in 1993. It was a fascinating conversation. We discussed Malcolm's siblings, his life and mission, and his death. I'm pretty sure that it was all of this that led me to visit Malcolm's gravesite, which was such an emotionally moving experience. He's buried at Ferncliff Cemetery in New York. As I stood there, I remember feeling overwhelmed. I brushed away the few leaves that had gathered over his grave. I thought about much of what I had read about him. I then said a private prayer. I recall leaving with the words—*As-salamu alaykum*.

Davidson: Yes, history can be used for all sorts of ends. That comes from the fact that no historian, no matter how thorough, can ever produce a "true history"—after all, one simply can't put down everything that happened within a particular time span to a particular people or individual, not to mention all that we do not yet know, or will never know. So, given this, how would you narrate Malcolm's history-cum-epistemology? What is he emphasizing and what are the costs?

Yancy: It is important to note that the early Malcolm believed in a kind of mythopoetic worldview in the form of Yacub's history, which involved the story of an arrogant Black scientist who created white people. White people were believed to be a "demonic" race and were destined to rule the earth until Black people regained their ascendency. Of course, this is not to deny the sheer brutality and barbarity of white supremacy that Black people actually experienced or that Malcolm X (then Malcolm Little) and members of his family experienced. Given the actual history of white supremacy in North America, one can see how that history would have informed, and, indeed, have been used to support, the historical narrative of Yacub's history. By doing so, the central tenet of the historical narrative of Yacub's history, that is, that whites are a "demonic" race, would have been more plausible to Malcolm. In fact, one might argue that the hermeneutic framework of Yacub's history functioned as a site of Black self-empowerment. I wonder, though, whether this was a case of one myth replacing another. Then again, I would think that all grand historical narratives, to some extent, have embedded within them certain myths, where such myths function to provide people with a coherent and intelligible sense of who they are. Within this context, myths are not so much the opposite of historical facts, but play a constitutive role in collective self-understanding. Yet, I think that it is important to isolate, challenge, and overthrow those myths that are predicated upon the relegation of other human beings to the status of subhumanity or that target others as somehow onto-logically unfit to exist. What is interesting, though, is that as one view of his-tory is deployed, and at times dogmatically, other ways of deploying history are concealed. So, Yacub's history would have valorized Black people and "demonized" whites. The cost of this version of history could function to cre-ate a certain historical myopia on the part of Malcolm. What we really want, it seems to me, is a fuller and richer narrative of history that avoids myopia and is capable of capturing the complexity of history. Yacub's history, it seems to me, is a meta-narrative that the later Malcolm, after his pilgrimage to Mecca, would find problematic, especially within the context of his understanding of the nonuniversalization of *all* white people as "devils." I think, though, that more work needs to be done in exploring the meaning of Yacub's history. I say this because the Honorable Elijah Muhammad, while in Chicago, was aware of and interacted with phenotypically white Muslims. So again, we need greater exploration regarding Malcolm's views and how they differed from those of the Honorable Elijah Muhammad regarding the meaning of Yacub's history and how that historical narrative was deployed. My guess is that the Honorable Elijah Muhammad had in mind white people in North America and in Europe as they were problematically and characteristically malevolent given their treatment of Black people and other people of color. Hence, this would belie the assumption that the Honorable Elijah Muhammad ever taught the view that *all* phenotypically white people are "devils."

Regarding your other point, I'm not sure of what to say about Malcolm's "epistemology," but I do think that it is fair to say that Malcolm's thinking

grew as he became older. I think that Black nationalism would have functioned as the epistemic and social ontological horizon in terms of which he
thought about questions of Black identity, Black self-determination, political
group formation, Black empowerment, education, economics, land, liberation, and counter-violence.

Davidson: One can easily assert that all collectives define themselves—who
they are—through an historical narrative: when and where they have been,
and when and where they expect to go. As a result, it seems inevitable that
there will be, as you put it, "myth-making."

Yancy: Racism, for example, thrives on myths. Within the North American
context, Black people were deemed inferior, hyper-sexual, and bestial; they
were said to be the wretched or the damned of the earth. One can think here
of the Hamitic myth. It holds that Black people are descendants of Ham who
apparently looked upon his father, Noah, while the latter was nude. Noah is
said to have been in a drunken stupor. What Ham did exactly is somewhat
unclear, but one interpretation is that it involved something "sexual." As a
consequence, Noah is said to have cursed Ham's son, Canaan. Hence, as the
descendants of Ham/Canaan, Black people have inherited the curse of being
a "servant of servants." This narrative was used by white enslavers to support the enslavement of Black people, to "demonstrate" that Black people
were born to serve others because of their "servile" and "docile" nature. In
this way, their enslavement was buttressed through religious or Scriptural
authority. So, here we have a case where a particular interpretation of bibli-
cal history is used to support Black moral degeneracy, and to do so through
quasi-metaphysical assumptions. I say this because the Hamitic myth appears
to allow for a kind of indirect divine sanction, that God somehow "allowed"
the moral degeneracy of Black people to be passed on to Black people
through Ham's son. This, of course, raises the racist logic of Manichean symbolic thinking, where Black people are the dark pole and white people constitute the diametrically white, and, thereby, "morally superior," pole. Within
this context, Black people constitute the dark/evil pole of a narrative that has
broad cosmological implications. Frantz Fanon also wrote about this racial
and racist Manichean divide, how the Negro constitutes a phobogenic object
through the white, colonial superimposition of an oppressive image or imago
of the Negro as "evil," as the very essence of "sin."[1] One can also think here
of Dr. Samuel A. Cartwright. He was the nineteenth-century white Louisiana
physician who believed that Black people possessed certain diseases that
had certain character manifestations. For example, he held that Black people
suffer from the "Negro disease" or "mental illness" known as *Drapetomania*, which was a kind of "Negro mania" for running away.[2] Hence, when
Black people fled plantations, this was explained through the assumption of

a mythical disease. I think that *Drapetomania* can be said to constitute a biological myth masquerading as a "biological fact," which attempted to undercut the idea that Black people fled plantations because they desired to be free.

What is important is the problematic and false character of such explanations/myths. The explanations were used to obfuscate the reality of choice on the part of white enslavers. If Black people have been cursed or if they suffer from "Negro diseases," are biologically inferior, bestial, etc., then how white people treat them is "justified" by a mythical discourse that provides, as it were, a transcendent or objective cause grounded in nature to treat them as ersatz. In this way, white people attempt to elide their freedom through a myth that has the force of necessity. It is this same force of necessity that would establish North America as an essentially white *Herrenvolk* polity, one driven by manifest destiny. Yet, it isn't just the myths that oppress. Such an argument would reduce the forces of North American slavery to a species of philosophical idealism or ideational content only. It is important to keep in mind that it was the existence of white material power, physical brutality, and institutional frameworks through which those myths were enacted and enforced. I would argue that the myths and the material institutional forces of the enslavement of Black people are mutually implicative and interpenetrative. I would also argue that white racism is a site of disguise and historical obfuscation, which brings me back to Malcolm X. He thought that through a counter-historical narrative, and here it was also about getting one's facts right, not just about introducing one myth for another, Black people would be able to subvert the white racist mythical order of things. For Malcolm, as suggested previously, using history was done so in the service of Black people; it was about Black liberation, freeing Black people from the chains of historical ignorance; it involved a process of psychological decolonization through education (*educare*, "to lead out"). You know, I don't think that this process of being properly informed about one's history is sufficient for Black liberation, though I do think that it is necessary. I recall that Fanon remarks in *Black Skin, White Masks* how delighted he would be to know that a Negro philosopher carried on some form of correspondence with Plato. Yet, Fanon proceeds to wonder exactly how this historical discovery would mitigate the suffering of Black children living under physical oppression. But I think that Malcolm has a point. The process of *leading out* of ignorance is indispensable for Black liberation. On my view, I think of this historical effort as a process of ideology exposure. In other words, ideology exposure attempts to unveil the ways in which whiteness attempts to function as if it is beyond history— as the transcendental norm. Ideology exposure is a process of demystifying whiteness. Of course, ideology exposure can also function to demythologize "Blackness." After all, we can't have only one version of "Blackness." This point is related to your observation that rightly identifies how collectives define themselves. There are deeper historical forces, forms of collectivity based upon collective narratives and productive myths that impact how people, on their specific historical trajectories, define Blackness. Temporality, movement, and migration impact one's point of entry into the question regarding the nature and meaning of Blackness. I think that all human beings as collectives deploy narratives that consist of myths. It seems to me, though, that such a practice can lead to genocide once a particular collective embodies myths about its own status a "superior" and where that myth has built within it implications for the decimation of other collectivities that are deemed "inferior," "waste," "vermin," "surplus," disposable, and ungrievable.

Davidson: What first drew you to the field of philosophy? Did you find philosophy or did it find you? What do you see as the strengths and the weaknesses of this discipline's methodology and approach to discourses on race in the United States?

Yancy: This is a question that I'm frequently asked. In terms of me finding philosophy or philosophy finding me, I would argue that it was paradoxically both. When I was about sixteen or seventeen, living in Richard Allen Homes, which was a housing project for low-income families, I discovered the etymology of the word philosophy while reading through *The World Book Encyclopedia*. Upon coming across the word *philosophia*, which is transliterated from the Greek as "the love of wisdom," there was a powerful moment of self-recognition. At that moment, I felt that I was able to provide a name for what had always been there, which I would call a certain propensity and passion for asking profound and engaging questions. Yet, it wasn't just about the esoteric nature of the questions. There was a passion, by which I really mean a sense of suffering. As a young boy, I would ask my mother questions about religion and its truth-claims. I wondered aloud about why there were so many religions and how we could know with certainty that we had found *the one* true religion. I would also ask about death. Death was a deep mystery to me. Well, it still is. But as a boy, I just could not make sense of why I had to die, why I had to leave, why it is that someday I would no longer be. This is what philosopher Cornel West has called the "death shudder."[3] As I recall, I would spend a great deal of time just trying to imagine myself gone, no longer, which, of course, isn't possible as I'm still the one imagining myself gone. Yet, as a young boy, the inevitability of death was hard to bear, disturbingly so. In fact, the idea of someday not existing made we wish that I had never been. Strange, I realize, but there I was. I was elated by the process of being, of being alive, of loving my mother and my sister. Why all of this just to someday leave it all? It made no sense to me. So, I felt it as a cosmic slight. In retrospect, it also smacks of a pretty large ego. After all, here I was thinking that the universe personally had it in for me. Then again, I think that all of this was indicative of the burgeoning aspirations of a philosophical disposition. I was turning radically inward, possessed by an incredible intensity of being.

Back then, I guess that I reasoned that had I never been, I would not need to worry so much about someday not being. By the way, I would also struggle mightily, often with tears flowing, with the philosophical problem of God's existence. This was later when I was a teenager. The problem of the existence of God was another one of those philosophical conundrums that produced, for me, a deep sense of suffering. Why would God not reveal God's self *to me*? Of course, as with death, I would later think of this as a bit narcissistic. It was hard for me to understand why God, assuming (as I did and still do) that God really exists, would not appear to me so as to remove *all doubt*. Why make it so difficult to know, especially as this left the real option of discarding the idea of the existence of God altogether? You know, though, it wasn't just about removing doubt. I think that my desire to know God was like a child longing to know its absent parent, longing to touch the hand, as it were, of the *beloved*. And while I can now hear the Freudian overtones and the anthropomorphism, I don't think that it can be reduced to such terms. I needed to know, I desired to know, the ultimate reason for things. You know, "Why there is something as opposed to nothing?" It is the ultimate ontological question. I needed to know why I am at all, why anything is at all. And I was brought up to believe that the answer to such fundamental questions was God. I should confess that my passion remains when it comes to my philosophical concern regarding the truth-claims of religion, the inevitability of death, and the existence of God. These themes still bear a great deal of existential weight for me. That child still suffers, still hungers, still wants to know. And I don't feel as if it is like Job from the Bible. Look, we just don't *know*, though we have faith or hope. And I think that there are modes of longing that are expressed in ways that are not motivated by arrogance. This longing isn't simply about me; it implicates our entire human species. Let's face it, why are we here? Do you know for sure?

Of course, the race issue within philosophy had not occurred to me until later, though it was there at the very moment that I read the entire entry in *The World Book Encyclopedia*. All of the pictures of the philosophers were of white men. So, there was the race issue as well as the gender issue. At this stage in my intellectual development, I think that I just saw them as thinkers. In retrospect, though, whiteness was right there on the page speaking to me about what I couldn't be. In other words, those pictures functioned insidiously to exclude; placing me, as a young Black male, under erasure. So, there must have been some awareness of race, though inchoate. I say this because I came to believe that I must be the only Black philosopher because there were no pictures of any. Having read the entire entry in *The World Book*

Encyclopedia, I went on to read Bertrand Russell's *The History of Western Philosophy* and Will Durant's *The Story of Philosophy*. These texts also reinforced my conception of the philosopher as normatively white. It still had not dawned upon me in a critical fashion that these were *white* philosophers, where whiteness, within the field of philosophy, would later come to signify a site of epistemic hegemony and the exclusion of philosophical voices of color. It was not until after I *finished* my undergraduate training in philosophy at the University of Pittsburgh—which many claimed to be the best philosophy department in the country during that time—that I was specifically introduced to the work of Black philosophers. Fortunately, for me, the prominent Black scholar James G. Spady took me under his proverbial wing and introduced me to the works of a critical mass of Black philosophers. This shift away from white bodies as representative of what philosophers looked like was amazing and yet disconcerting. Why didn't I know that there were professional Black philosophers until the end of my undergraduate year? After all, I was at the very best philosophy department in the country. Moreover, I had gotten through high school with no knowledge of the existence of Black philosophers. I think that this returns us to Malcolm X. I had been deprived of a very significant part of our history. Indeed, in conversations with my friend and colleague Janine Jones, the process of excluding the history of Black people in philosophy functioned to support a myth not only about what philosophy is but who philosophers are.

To date, specifically within the field of philosophy, I have managed to author and edit the majority of books on the subject of whiteness. In terms of philosophers of color, there are three of us who have done the lion's share of this work. That would include me, Linda Alcoff, and Charles Mills. Also, back in 1996, and this was due to the influence of Spady and his methodological emphasis upon the importance of oral histories, I conceived of the idea of interviewing Black philosophers. The idea was to create a text that was not available for me when I most needed it. The text to which I'm referring is entitled *African-American Philosophers, 17 Conversations*. It was published in 1998 and has since become what I think might be called a philosophical triumph when it comes to the publication of philosophy texts, to say nothing of philosophy texts that deal with African-American philosophical themes. Within the context of dialogically engaging the theme of what it means to be a Black philosopher in North America, these seventeen philosophers discussed questions of Black philosophical identity formation, questions of canon formation, the meaning of African-American philosophy, and questions regarding how they became interested in pursuing philosophy in the first place. There was simply no book like it. Importantly, seven of the philosophers interviewed were Black women. Since its publication, I have had younger Black philosophers say to me that *17 Conversations* was the single book that helped them to make the decision to pursue a career in philosophy. Indeed, I was once told by a younger Black male that it was *17 Conversations* that saved him, that provided him with a conceptual space for seeing himself as a philosopher. So, I think of that book as doing so much in terms of encouraging young Black people to begin to see themselves as professional philosophers. I also edited *Cornel West: A Critical Reader* in 2001, which brought together for the first time in American history a book-length critical exploration of the ideas of a major living Black philosopher.

I think that the aforementioned autobiographical details are not divergent from what we have been discussing regarding how I see the strengths and the weaknesses of philosophy's approach to discourses on race in North America. The details speak to my efforts to shift the center of conversation. In the philosophy department at the University of Pittsburgh, to my knowledge, there was no philosophical discussion of race, though the expression of whiteness as privilege and as hegemonic was everywhere to be found. My sense is that the concept of race was simply not deemed a philosophically worthy topic of conceptual analysis. This should have been especially embarrassing given the history of racism in this country. How can philosophers talk about justice, equality, rights, and ethics and leave out of discussion the ways in which white racism infused all of these philosophical concepts? The profession was and continues to be in a state of bad faith, of lying to itself. How could so many white philosophers see themselves year after year at American Philosophical Association conferences and not stop and mark those spaces as problematically white, or male for that matter? So, I came to see that the love of wisdom is inflected by race; indeed, saturated with race, racism, and sexism. My sense is that philosophy is concerned with specific philosophical problems as these problems are related to certain *interests* and value assumptions about what constitutes philosophy and a philosophical problem. Of course, this is a pragmatist insight, but not all white pragmatists have seen or dared to explore how whiteness specifically shapes philosophical interests and intuitions. For me, much of philosophy is inflected by (one might even say infected by) whiteness. The point that I'm raising here is not that philosophy is *simply* a question of philosophical pluralism, where it is understood that different philosophers perform different philosophical labor. My argument is that race is a topic that is excluded from a certain conception of philosophy and that this is a problem that is situated at the heart of so much of European and Anglo-American philosophical practice.

Davidson: So, there are important meta-philosophical issues at stake?

Yancy: Yes. Given that the field of philosophy has been and continues to be dominated by white men, it is crucial that we theorize and demonstrate the reasons why it is that the concept of race is deemed philosophically nugatory.

What is it about philosophy's own self-understanding that prevents it from engaging the issue of race and, by extension, racism? Many white philosophers (and the history of the profession) see their task as engaging theory at the level of pure abstraction. At this level of engagement, the embodied nature of philosophy loses its relevance to human life, that is, it loses its capacity to face the quotidian, nonabstract world of suffering human beings. Philosophy also loses the importance of how context and how certain raced bodies, with specific configured experiences, impact the epistemic claims that we make. And even though white philosophers working within the continental tradition are certainly more open to examining the philosophical significance of the complexity of *lived* embodied experience and the importance of effective history and facticity, this does not mean that they are particularly attentive to theorizing ways in which whiteness/race inflects the contours of their philosophical worldviews or the ways in which their whiteness defines both their credibility as philosophers and the credibility of the content of their philosophical positions vis-à-vis philosophers of color. So, even as history, contingency, subjectivity, gender, facticity, and agency are valorized as philosophical topics worthy of philosophical reflection, many white philosophers within the continental tradition still leave the subject of race, and especially their own whiteness, unexamined. So, it has primarily been philosophers of color who have attempted to change the ways in which the field of philosophy sees itself in relationship to the question of race. One might say that Black philosophers and philosophers of color have vigorously called philosophy out on its bad faith regarding race and racism. Of course, there have also been white feminist philosophers who have been instrumental in this change, though many of them continue to critique the maleness of philosophy and leave unexamined the whiteness of those said male philosophers. Indeed, many of these feminist philosophers leave unexamined their *own* whiteness. I think that some of them, and I will *not* say more here, engage in power moves that belie their aspirations to become genuine allies of women of color in the field of philosophy. I think that we need to hear more from Black women philosophers and women of color in philosophy who are willing to call these white women out, those white women who hide under the banner of doing feminist philosophy. This, of course, can be potentially detrimental to one's career and psychological well-being. To address the issue of what white women philosophers think about whiteness and how it informs various philosophical themes (ethics, aesthetics, epistemology, political philosophy, etc.), I asked white women philosophers to examine the whiteness of philosophy in my edited book, *The Center Must Not Hold: White Women Philosophers on the Whiteness of Philosophy* (2010). I also asked a critical cadre of white scholars, many of whom were white women philosophers, to personally engage their whiteness in my edited book, *White Self-Criticality beyond Anti-racism: How Does it Feel to be a White Problem?* (2015).

What we now find at major philosophical conferences are sessions dedicated to questions of race, though I would suspect that there are still some white philosophers who deem such sessions as mere "sideshows." Keep in mind, though, that there are philosophers of color who are analytic in philosophical orientation who bring tremendously insightful analyses to bear upon the concept of race. And the profession is all the better for it. Of course, given my own existential phenomenological leanings, I think that the analytic approach fails to capture the density and complexity of race as *lived*. In fact, I might add that I think that abstract, conceptual approaches to race can function to obfuscate the complexities of the lived experience of race and how we are all actually implicated in processes of racialization. So, I want to describe the process of racialization, often in what sounds like a philosophical-cum-literary style. Philosopher and prominent literary figure Charles Johnson has mastered, and brilliantly so, that creative space for doing philosophy through a literary lens. My use of a certain writing style emerges within the context of lived experience and I do so for purposes of not only achieving more concrete, detailed description, but to expose the layers of racialized experience. It is as if philosophical logos remains too abstract, whereas for me, philosophical logos, and I mean this in a nontheological way, must be made *flesh*. To be fair, though, even those philosophers working within the analytic tradition vis-à-vis the philosophy of race or critical philosophy of race are cognizant of the fruits to be gotten from alternative approaches to race other than analytic.

I guess that I am Fanonian in this regard. For me, it is within the context of *lived* history and sociality that I prefer to philosophically engage race and racism. Race functions as a "ready-to-hand" phenomenon which is performed in complex ways. I think that this became clear to me when I was a graduate student at Yale University. While at the University of Pittsburgh, I worked with philosopher Wilfrid Sellars and thought that after graduating I would work on something within the area of epistemology. I was specifically interested in sense data theory and problems regarding how we theorize and discuss the dispositional and occurrent properties of sensible objects. However, while at Yale, I took a course on hermeneutics with Georgia Warnke. The course really made me think about the dynamics of history and interpretation. In fact, I became interested in questions raised by Thomas S. Kuhn and Mary B. Hesse regarding scientific paradigms and questions of communities of intelligibility. I became fascinated with the issue of how epistemic subjects are impacted by context and history, and how knowledge claims are indexed to time and place. With the influence of Spady on my expanding knowledge of the history of Black philosophers, and the meaning of Black philosophy, it was a small step toward theorizing a philosophical anthropology of the subject as *homo historicus*. So, I became suspicious of philosophers who implied that their philosophical practices were disembodied or unencumbered by social context, the force history, and the mediating power of discourse. This is why, for me, African-American philosophy is fundamentally shaped by questions of resistance, agency, oppression, trauma, and identity specifically within the context of America's racist past and present. More broadly, when it comes to race, lived history plays such an important role for me, especially as Blackness and whiteness (as "racial" categories) are *not* objective, biological facts, but sites of lived meaning, social and historical constitutionality.

Davidson: You take on some of the complexity of the "lived experience" of Blackness by engaging with gender difference. How and why do you see specifying the valence of Blackness as masculine or feminine as important to one of your most famous books like *Black Bodies, White Gazes*? How do you see the "terrain of Blackness" as a lived site of meaning today? Do you see "Blackness" as we understand it in the United States changing, and how we in Black Studies might meet this challenge?

Yancy: I like how you've contextualized my work. I have been accused of speaking mainly on behalf of Black men. Then again, when I engage theory, I do it from the perspective of my own embodied subjectivity as a Black male, but I remain cognizant of the reality that I may, through that focus, place under erasure the embodied reality of Black women or women of color. *Black Bodies, White Gazes* (the 2008 edition) is a prescient text. I say this because of the horrific ways in which Black bodies, inordinately more Black male bodies, have been unarmed and gunned down by white state authority or its proxies since the publication of the first edition. In the wake of so many horrific deaths, the expanded and updated version of *Black Bodies, White Gazes* (2017) frames in powerful ways the tragic killing of Trayvon Martin, Eric Garner, Tamir Rice, Sandra Bland, Renisha McBride, and others. It is a text that theorizes, at the level of embodiment, how Black bodies are distorted under the white gaze, which is a deeply insidious practice. However, I do so in ways that don't conflate Black women's experiences of that gaze with Black men's experiences of that gaze. After all, Black women, within the context of white racist discursive constructions, have been and are defined as "whores," "welfare queens," "nymphomaniacs" "desiring to be raped," "mammy" figures, "matriarchs," "sapphires," and as having bodies that are sites of reproductive pathology. This is not a discourse that applies to women qua women. Rather, the white racist discourse speaks to the problematic ways in which Black women experience racist state violence, white perceptual gazes, as *Black women*, not as *Black* women or as Black *woman*.

On this score, Black women are not free from racist subjugation and experiences of tragic death through white state violence. Moreover, it does not follow that Black women are the "collateral damage" that results when the target of white state violence is really intended for the Black male body. To assume such a position would characterize Black women's experiences of anti-Black denigration and gratuitous violence as incidental, which would be fundamentally false, misleading, and an added level of violence. And while I think that *Black Bodies, White Gazes* (2017) helps to make sense of the tragic situations of Sandra Bland, Renisha McBride, and the profiling of Dr. Ersula Ore, a Black professor at Arizona State University, who was eventually thrown to the ground for "Jaywalking," I do admit that I am obligated to engage in a more detailed examination of Black women's experiences, not simply in terms of the white gaze, but also under patriarchy. This was brought home to me recently. I had just finished giving a talk on how it is that whites fear Black male bodies and how that fear is predicated upon a history of white myth-making. A young Black woman raised her hand and asked me to share my thoughts on Black women's fear of Black men. My sense is that she was also referencing her own lived experience vis-à-vis Black men. I was hesitant to respond as I didn't want to give fodder for nurturing white racist appetites, especially those whites who could use this issue as a way of justifying their own irrational fears. The easy way out would have been to say that some Black women are also operating with white racist assumptions about Black men. After all, I think that this is true. I think that this is also true of Black men. We are not immune to internalizing the same racist myths about Black men that whites perpetuate. I recall that I responded by saying that the question that she posed was a vital one that needs to be taken up by Black women and Black men in greater detail. Truth be told, I missed a significant opportunity. In fact, I may have inadvertently placed under erasure the *personal* dimensions of her critical question. Her point was a powerful one; it was one that implicated *me*. We can't collapse *all* Black women's experiences with Black men into whites' distorted projections upon Black men. In my book *African-American Philosophers, 17 Conversations*, I interview, among sixteen other Black philosophers, Adrian Piper. She critically discusses how Black women are perceived in academia as prostitutes. Let's be candid. Black men have not escaped this way of fantasizing about Black women and women of color. White men don't have a monopoly on ways to dehumanize Black women. I think that this is what this young Black woman was after. She wanted me to speak to levels of violence experienced by Black women who live with Black men who control their lives and how they move through space, who commit heinous acts of sexual abuse, domestic violence, and sexual objectification. She brought this point home to me. By the way, this isn't to say that Black men or men of color or Black boys or boys of color have not been abused, especially sexually abused, by Black women, women of color, and white women. Those cases, that history, *cannot* be erased. But with respect to Black women, they don't constitute a *systemic* force that violates Black male physical and psychic integrity. And even if there is an argument to be made about the ways in which Black men fall short of being recognized through the logics of patriarchy, where that concept is one exclusive to white men, it is senseless to conflate the ways in which Black men undergo forms of oppression with the ways in which Black women do. Black women are treated in ways that I have referred to as the third of the second sex.

So, I think that it is of utmost importance to keep track of the differential valence of Blackness as masculine as opposed to feminine. Black men and men of color are also to blame for doing violence to Black women and women of color. To what extent do we see Black women and women of color, both within the United States and transnationally, as "incompetent," "inferior," and as not belonging within academic spaces where engaging theory is believed to be a "masculine" game? To what extent have we embodied forms of toxic masculinity where we define women of color as "hoes," "bitches," "tricks," and "exotic"? To what extent do we fantasize about confining Black women and women more generally to the space of the bedroom, perhaps bound by chains and ropes, and enacting what we, through patriarchal constructions, imagine they want sexually? With that in mind, what is the relationship between the three women (Amanda Berry, Gina DeJesus, and Michelle Knight) who were eventually found in Cleveland, Ohio, after being held captive and sexually abused by Ariel Castro for so many years, and rapper Lil Wayne, though he did later apologize, who performed on Future's "Karate Chop (remix),"[4] who rapped about how he would "beat that pussy up like Emmett Till"? These are not simply anomalies. My point here is that there are common lethal manifestations of masculinity across race and class that speak to a larger and systemic form of a pornographic imaginary that does violence to women. As a Black male who is implicated within an androcentric culture, I think that there is more to be done, and I wonder to what extent I have dropped the proverbial ball. Then again, I think that it is important that Black women and Black men don't become entangled in a destructive phallic tug of war where we both become seduced by toxic forms of domineering logics.

I have another way of addressing your question about the "terrain of Blackness" in terms of the changing landscape of Blackness. In *Black Bodies, White Gazes*, as you know, I point to the Middle Passage as the crucible in terms of which Black identity is marked. It functions as that space of death, docility, amalgamation, and resistance that is important to understanding Black people in North America. So, it becomes a central existential and ontological motif through which I theorize what it means to be Black. Yet, it is important to note that those bodies were scattered and not confined to North America. So, I think that it is important to theorize the ways in which that oceanic experience shaped other Black bodies that were dispersed throughout the world. As such, then, and I must admit that I'm improving my scholarship within this area, one must examine the different genealogies and phenomenological configurations that speak not only to those bodies that were not enslaved in North America, though came through the Middle Passage, but also speak to those Black bodies that did not arrive at their "destinies" through the transatlantic slave trade at all. This raises important questions regarding the *lived* meaning of "Blackness" and how Blackness is differentially defined diachronically and in terms of points of geographical origin. Furthermore, this raises questions about how Blackness is permeable and protean. This also raises the issue of the meaning of 1619 and how Black identity and Black subjectivity can be erroneously tied to that moment in time, which then raises the issue of how a specific Black historical narrative can function monolithically and thus exclude those Black bodies that don't conceptualize 1619 in the same way or even at all.

Yet, from my perspective, the "terrain of Blackness" remains configured or portrayed as a site of social pathology through the white gaze. Think here of Amadou Diallo, an immigrant from Guinea, who, in 1999, was killed by an "elite" team of white police officers. They fired a total of forty-one shots. Diallo was hit by nineteen bullets. Or, think about Haitian immigrant Abner Louima who, while handcuffed at the police station, was sodomized with a stick by a white police officer. Both Black bodies were deemed *problem* bodies; one brutally killed and the other viciously dehumanized. Both were deemed in need of white disciplining. While it is important to recognize the differences in points of geographical origin, and how the meaning of Blackness is inflected by those points of origin, at the end of the day, those two bodies suffered a fate whose narrative is all too familiar to Black bodies regardless of place of origin. So, yes, given the influx of different African diasporic Black identities to North America, I think that the meaning of Blackness, out of necessity, is changing and must change. This is important because it calls for a multiplicity of origins and formations, even though the epistemology of whiteness re-inscribes a racial Manichean divide with whites on the "good" side, and those differences among Blacks relegated to ontological sameness. This epistemology of whiteness, by the way, reinforces a Black/white binary. I have been critiqued for reinforcing this binary in my work by not focusing on white racism vis-à-vis other people of color. Yet, it is whiteness that sustains this binary through its transcendental status in relationship to Blacks in the United States *and* other people of color. In fact, I argue that whiteness is structurally binary; it *needs* the "other." In terms of Black Studies, however, the protean character of Blackness demands that we be attentive to the shifting ways in which the meaning of Blackness is narrated, the pluralization of historico-social ontologies, the diversity of geographically Black "racialized" body semantics, and that we grapple with epistemologies that are diverse and specific to localized places of origin throughout the African Diaspora. I think that Michelle M. Wright's text *Physics of Blackness: Beyond the Middle Passage Epistemology* (2015) importantly speaks to questions regarding the shifting meaning and reality of Blackness.

Davidson: You are known for work on understanding the material and ideal valences of Blackness in the United States, but, as you also note, you have helped to spearhead philosophies of whiteness. Your book *Look, a White!* is a core text in the field. How do you understand the benefits and dangers of this field? What do you think are some of the largest misconceptions about it?

Yancy: Let's take the dangers first. One concern is that white scholars who pursue the issue of whiteness through the disciplinary lens of critical whiteness studies may do so for careerist purposes. While I understand the link between pedagogy and the larger institutional, *materialist* economic implications of what it is that we do as academics, I fear that white scholars might engage this work opportunistically. I say this because I get the sense that some white graduate students see the impact of whiteness studies in academia and jump on board as a way of increasing their expertise, their marketability. I fear that the critical edge intended by the field might be compromised because of this. Linked to this is that the field can also become overly intellectualized, treated as a process of mastering a set of concepts as one might master concepts in calculus. The field, however, demands something more. It seems to me that whites who do critical whiteness studies (in philosophy, history, feminist studies, cultural studies) really have to remain engaged in serious processes of *self-interrogation*; they must explore the ways in which their own academic expertise is performed disjointed from the additional work that needs to be done on their own white selves at the level of working through aspects of a contradictory life. Put explicitly, these white scholars engage the discourse of critical whiteness studies, but continue to treat faculty of color as less than human, as ersatz, and, as not belonging within academic white spaces. Another danger is that white scholars and the field itself may re-inscribe whiteness as the center of discourse and concern, where this becomes another site of white narcissism, white monopoly, white conceit, white interest, and white power and control. In this way, the field would become a site for white self-pleasuring.

After all, the motivational features of the field don't grow from the head of Zeus. It is a field that is historically grounded in critical discourses developed by Black scholars and Black people, and people of color, who have had to deal with the experiences of white terror, white brutality, and white arrogance on a daily basis. So, navel-gazing is not a process at the heart of engaging whiteness, but, rather, liberation from white supremacy and white habituated modes of being. Thus, it is politically a centrifugal process. It is not an intellectualist project, but a project of overthrow, of undermining the ways in which whiteness continues to exist as the normative center. Whiteness studies is not a site for making a fetish of discourse and conceptual analysis regarding whiteness, but one of engaging radical ways of undoing whiteness, of being-in-the-world in the mode of constantly, ontologically resisting whiteness. So, white scholars must realize that the field itself calls for *loss*. A radical conceptualization of the field is *not* designed to make white people feel good about the fact that they are the "enlightened" ones. This is too easy; and whiteness is far too messy and dense. The radical way in which I conceptualize the field would entail whites to become what I have come to call being *un-sutured* from the ties that bind them to structures of power, to undergo experiences of *crisis* and productive disorientation, where the normative structure of whiteness fails as a place of shelter. What are whites really prepared to lose? That is a powerful and frightening question for white people. White scholars can become seduced into thinking that they are doing really important work *for* Black people, thus installing white paternalism. They can become seduced into thinking that they are "radical" when in fact that radicalness doesn't reach beyond the confines of their classrooms. And then there is the issue of having a space (or being given a space) to teach critical whiteness studies while as a white scholar one benefits from the material support of that predominantly white institution. This is also a question that Black scholars and scholars of color need to raise. I don't have a quick and easy answer, but I do want the point to trouble how we construe our "radicalness," how we bask in it.

While there is often a sense of critical discourse alliance with people of color, there is no alliance to undo whiteness as a site of institutional, material power, there is no alliance where white bodies actually dwell together on an equal basis with bodies of color. My point here is that white academic institutions can *accommodate* these critical discourses and thereby render them weak. Then again, the academy can also accommodate the discourses coming out of Africana critical theory, queer theory, and feminist theory. I am worried about the tactics involved in the institutional capacity to accommodate "radical" discourses/voices. If the discourses don't force the system to expurgate them or if the discourses don't radically undo the system, to what extent have the discourses become digestible and tame? Is it fair to say that the discourses don't override the interests of white people? Then again, this reminds me of Derrick Bell's concept of "interest convergence," where white people are willing to support issues of racial justice only on the condition that there is something in that support from which they can benefit, where their interests are not compromised. This compromise preserves the hegemonic framework of whiteness. This angle of interpretation, it seems to me, lends credence to an Afro-Pessimist perspective, an approach which I see as a form of racial realism in the spirit of Derrick Bell. This is why I have come to take more seriously the idea of theorizing Black agency in terms of Marronage as opposed to the total dismantlement of the structure of white supremacy. On this model, we resist white supremacy during the day, we use the necessary energy to make it through that day, and then we return to spaces where we find comfort being in our skin, where we experience love and affirmation. I think that a major misconception, though, is the construction of the field as a site for inducing white guilt. While guilt may result, this is not and should not be the aim of the field; that being said, guilt can be deployed productively; it needn't result in an emotional dead-end. Moreover, critical whiteness studies is not a field designed to galvanize hatred *for white men*, or white people, more generally, a view that I think is implied by some who have objected to the existence of the field and have come to conceptualize it as a relatively new "academic fad." This is silly and indicative of a defensive posture. Black people *had* to study whiteness in order for us to survive whether in private or public spaces. It has never been merely an academic pursuit. One benefit of the field is to get whites to see the importance of how whiteness prevents them from becoming more deeply concerned about what it means to be human outside a philosophical anthropology that stipulates whiteness as normative. Returning to that sense of losing one's orientation, the field attempts to get whites to mark their whiteness, to render it peculiar, to make it an *object* of critical study, and to demonstrate to white folk that there is something there *to be seen as a problem* that they have been inculcated to think does not exist at all. White people have inherited forms of discourse that enable them to remain in denial about the problems of whiteness. Also, white people deploy deep psychological and emotional tactics for avoiding the need to look, to examine their whiteness. To those whites who are serious about issues of social justice, of undoing whiteness, of critiquing insidious levels of white opacity, it seems to me that the field is capable of providing a critical lens through which whites become cognizant of the ways in which their *lived* whiteness negatively implicates bodies of color. In short, they come to realize that they are not mere atomic, neoliberal, autonomous subjects, but deeply implicated in white racist structures and white meta-narratives that form a social integument in terms of which they are linked, in oppressive ways, to people of color. This, it seems to me, has the benefit of nurturing forms of epistemological and ethical humility, ways of being that bring white people closer to seeing or to recognizing their social locations vis-à-vis people of color. It is within the process of seeing that connection or that shared integument, that, for me, ought to haunt white people, ought to throw white people into a state of crisis. It is fear of this crisis, however, that can cause potentially dangerous blowback. I think that we need a form of *Bildung* or *Paideia* that actually cultivates vulnerability in white people, a space where they are wounded, undergo moments of trauma and narrative disorganization—that is, processes capable of troubling whiteness, of destabilizing *their embodied whiteness.*

This is not about having them undergo some form of white masochism. Rather, it is about growth, about being reborn, which is always a painful process. Yet, it is also about realizing that this rebirth is always a penultimate process. If one thinks about the Christological meaning of the term kenosis, it means that moment where Jesus empties himself of his divinity, becoming, paradoxically, fully human. Well, white people need to undergo forms of emptying, of getting rid of internalized forms of whiteness. Yet, this emptying is a process; one does not become empty of insidious forms of whiteness in one fell swoop. Kenosis vis-à-vis whiteness is a process. And to the extent that whiteness has become idolized as a god, as a site of exclusive "virtue," "purity," "light," "divinity," then the term kenosis is even more suggestive. In this case, white kenosis is a process of spewing out the ways in which one has subtly internalized the "sacredness" or "specialness" of being white. And to those whites who are doing this, I would like to see your wounds. Doubt, within this context, is justified. Unlike in the case of doubting Thomas or the Apostle Thomas, the history of whiteness cannot be trusted. So, show me evidence of the un-suturing, let me see and touch the opened wounds.

Davidson: In the conclusion to *Look, a White!*, you distinguish yourself from those theorists who assert that the "white anti-racist" is an oxymoron. You raise a crucial nuance where you argue that being a white anti-racist and yet being racist is not mutually exclusive. How can we change academic epistemologies for the better, that is, exactly as you suggest, academic disciplines based on mythological notions of "whiteness" as neutral, invisible? Should they be forced to name themselves? If it were up to you, where would you want to see changes first and foremost—and why? Put another way, for those white readers inspired by your call to join the fight against entrenched racism, where would you encourage them to focus?

Yancy: The idea of the anti-racist racist is a way of theorizing the complexity of what is involved in "undoing" whiteness. This is what I meant previously about the rebirthing process being one that is penultimate. The white anti-racist is not a noun, but more like a verb, which means that the anti-racist is always in process, always making a decision, choosing her life, as best she can, through an anti-racist lens. Yet, I theorize this existential freedom within the context of heteronomous and structural forces. It is at this point that many whites with whom I've shared my work begin to retreat and want to hold on to the idea that they are neoliberal selves who are not bound by contextual, historical, or psychic forces, who are not racists.

Invisibility is one important metaphor for thinking about whiteness, but there are others that complement this one, which augment the ways in which we think about whiteness. In *Black Bodies, White Gazes*, I introduced the powerful metaphor of "ambush," which involves a process where whites are attacked by deep layers of their own racism of which they are unaware. In that book, though, I had not theorized the basis for this ambush. I carry this analysis further in my authored book, *Look, a White!* Through many of the assumptions in Judith Butler's book *Giving an Account of Oneself*, I deployed the concept of psychic opacity, which claims that white people have undergone processes of cultural "hailing" that have resulted in levels of white racism that are opaque, a position that calls into question the assumption that consciousness is a totally transparent process that makes available the inner contents of one's white racism. Introspection is not sufficient to ascertain the limits of one's embodied racism. By the time whites begin to explore their own racism, I argue, they have already been given over—through and through—to white racism. On this score, whites are strangers to themselves vis-à-vis the sheer complexity and depth of the opacity of their own racism, which does not, by the way, let them off the proverbial hook. While I will not pursue this issue here, in *Look, a White!* I argue that Black people and people of color can function as "gift-givers" because they are gifted at seeing whiteness given their racialized epistemic locations. This is what W. E. B. Du Bois eludes to as a form of clairvoyance. Through the insights of Black people and people of color, whites can be encouraged to develop a white form of double consciousness in terms of which they begin to see, with greater clarity, how racism operates. I think that both metaphors, "ambush" and "opacity," help toward critically exposing the complexities of lived whiteness and adding to a critical vocabulary that can be used to unpack whiteness. Yet, both metaphors are hard to swallow for white folk as they indicate the reality of dispossession. All of us are dispossessed in some way. For example, we can't control for the inevitability of death; it has already claimed us from the womb. For whites, however, their lives have also been claimed by racist norms, practices, desires, bodily dispositions, historical meta-narratives, explicit and implicit racial fantasies, racial frames of reference, and so on. So, being an anti-racist racist does not guarantee either a decisive or an immediate victory. I even gesture toward there being no exit at all, which does not occlude resistance. Anti-racist racists would need, given the messiness of white racism, to begin giving accounts of themselves, critiquing themselves, and continuing to reimagine themselves. I think that this critical effort would help to militate against hegemonic academic epistemologies that privilege white ways of knowing and being-in-the-world, white ways of doing theory, of defining the aims of philosophy, of defining what is and is not important philosophically, historically, and culturally. This isn't easy. Within this context, I want whites, especially those white academic liberals who deem themselves free of any racist dispositions, to begin to mark their identities as racist, to mark their spaces of knowledge production as saturated with white normative assumptions. Given that whites are always already embedded within white racist institutions and effective history, and given that they are also constituted as relational selves that have undergone anterior white racist self-formation, where white opacity results, I think that whites need to approach themselves with epistemic humility, to be prepared to face the reality that they *don't know* the depths of their racism. Tarrying with non-white voices, then, becomes so important within this context. This does not mean that Black people, for example, ought to be at the epistemic beck and call of white people. My sense is that whites have failed to take seriously the ways in which they continue to be racist, in and outside of the academy. Part of the problem is that they don't "know" people of color. They refuse to tarry with us, to dwell near us. They assume that they know us, but they don't. They only know what they imagined us to be, which is predicated upon a false construction of how they imagine themselves to be. So, I want whites to tarry with those critical voices of color that challenge the foundation of their white modes of being-in-the-world. In this way, whites are able to begin the process of seeing themselves differently and thereby seeing us differently. The process is dynamically relational.

The "browning" of America does not guarantee the overcoming of whiteness or white supremacy. And for all of those who claim this to be true, Trump should be sufficient evidence to the contrary. Whiteness knows how to survive—*and it will by all and any means necessary.* If, as suggested previously, Derrick Bell is correct, then whites will only reinforce their sense of supremacy and hunker down to protect what they see as their "manifest destiny."[5] This unabashed reinforcement of a white America is what Trump has galvanized and in terms of which so many white Republicans have remained silent. The browning of America might increase, but its political power might prove nugatory. After all, whites in South Africa continue to have disproportionately more power, though it is a "post-Apartheid" South Africa. When it comes to the browning of America, whites, on my view, will simply redraw lines of ideological alliance, but do so in such a way that the core of their white interests prevail. So, again, we need a form of *Bildung* where whites can cultivate vulnerability, exposure, and risk, and rethink and undo various white racialized forms of self-protection and affectivity. We need a form of *Bildung* that will cultivate a culture of loss among whites while installing new forms of white relationality that are non-agonistic vis-à-vis people of color. As said earlier, this form of *Bildung* would create a space where whites can be wounded and undergo crisis. Given that they have lived with a multitude of lies about their "natural supremacy" and "entitlement" for such a long time, they will also need, as my colleague Kathy Glass says, to grieve: to grieve the loss of an imperial self, and to grieve in the form of *gravitas/heaviness*, which, on the flip side, may lead to a form of ethical responsibility or maturity, requiring constant ontological renewal. You should know that I am not optimistic here. Whiteness can absorb attempts to overthrow its hegemonic power. I have no reason to think that the majority of whites will relinquish their power through an unconditional ethical act or through an unconditional act of goodwill.

My point here is that, contrary to my impression that I was the only Black philosopher, African-American philosophy or philosophy in Black has a rich tradition whose conceptual parameters, historical trajectories, discursive possibilities, intuitions, meta-philosophical concerns, community composition, and canonical construction and reconstruction are in process. And how we address these various sites will not be through a priori rules, but through an active and generative self-corrective exegesis and by sustaining a strong space for socially shared and overlapping philosophical practices and orientations that are never hermetically sealed or *transcendentally* delimited. This is partly what makes African-American philosophy so vibrant to me. There is so much exciting philosophical, meta-philosophical, historical, and archival work to be done. And it is important that as a critical mass of professional philosophers, we never forget the deep political struggles and sacrifices to which we owe our existence. There are so many who created the necessary foundational shifts, disruptions, and fissures in both the larger racist institutional practices within the academy and within departments of philosophy which were (and still are) governed by the conceptual logics of whiteness. I have never taught in a philosophy department where I am one of even two Black philosophers. Hence, even though I now have deep connections with African-American philosophy and African-American philosophers, there is still often that feeling of being "the only Black philosopher."

In retrospect, my desire and eagerness to engage in primary and archival research on African-American philosophers Thomas N. Baker, Sr., Gilbert Haven Jones, and Joyce Mitchell Cook was a way of addressing that feeling of being the "only Black philosopher." With respect to these pioneer U.S. Black professional philosophers, my aim was to uncover something about the lives and philosophical reflections of those whose philosophical voices had not been theorized at all in any appreciably extensive way. So, that was my aim. My other aim was to help carve out a collective space, to cultivate textual sites, where African-American philosophical voices critically engaged questions regarding race, whiteness, autobiography, gender, meta-philosophy, and Black philosophy. This is what also motivated *African-American Philosophers, 17 Conversations*, and a number of other edited books, including *Cornel West: A Critical Reader* (2001); *What White Looks Like: African-American Philosophers on the Whiteness Question* (2004); *White on White/Black on Black* (2005); *Philosophy in Multiple Voices* (2007); and *Reframing the Practice of Philosophy: Bodies of Color, Bodies of Knowledge* (2012), and special journal issues focused on Black philosophy and specifically Black women philosophers in *The Black Scholar* and *Hypatia: A Journal of Feminist Philosophy*, respectively. With respect to Black women in philosophy, I continue to be challenged by Desirée H. Melton's question, "In the quest to become audacious enough to think themselves agents of history, gaining self-confidence, and self-consciousness to be universal, are white women philosophers and nonwhite male philosophers stepping on the backs of nonwhite women?"[1] I have also been committed to engage Black philosophical voices through the incredibly important venue of *The New York Times* philosophy column, "The Stone."

"Doing philosophy in Black" is not a chromosomal project. Rather it points, for me, rather directly or indirectly, to the lived experiences of Black people, a people who are not philosophically monolithic. Yet, I do work with the assumption that we are talking about Black philosophers of African descent. The pioneer Black philosophers within this section are exclusive to the United States. Yet, doing philosophy in Black is another way of marking Africana philosophy which, of course, is broader than the U.S. context. I am especially delighted to include chapters within this section on African-American philosophy and African-American philosophers. There is something honorable about refusing to allow their names to fall into oblivion. There is also the historical and epistemic responsibility that we have as philosophers of African descent to augment the existence of our philosophical traditions. Within the context of forms of white academic and curricular hegemony, it is our duty to continue to create counter-discursive moves, counter-canonization interventions, counter-curricular formulations, and counter-monochromatic (white) occupied spaces. This is our duty to Black philosophers to come. Of course, doing philosophy in Black is not *necessarily* predicated on countering the logics of whiteness. Given our collective diasporic history vis-à-vis white colonialism, fictions of universal white reason, and being on the underside of modernity, whiteness is a problem and must be contested. Moreover, historically, we were forced to theorize who and what we are against the backdrop of whiteness. That relationship with whiteness, though, is a historically contingent relationship. My point here is that "doing philosophy in Black" can begin from a departure that is non-referentially white.

Within this section, each of the Black pioneers in philosophy was situated within the belly of the white beast—Baker, in fact, being enslaved. So, engaging their situated existence within the context of U.S. racism was inevitable. I further emphasize the particularity of this U.S. racist context in terms of what I'm calling "the weight of the present." Hence, by ending this section with the insightful and parrhesiastic voice of Anita Allen and my own voice, my objective is to communicate as clearly as possible to readers just how far we still must venture and how difficult the journey will be. This, however, does not leave us in a state of Black pessimism. Our collective Black philosophical efforts and the fruits that they will bear have not been foreclosed by a preestablished historical trajectory. History is open. We have much to do. My hope is that this section contributes to the ever-growing panoply of doing philosophy in Black.

Chapter 14

African-American Philosophy: Through the Lens of Socio-Existential Struggle

THE INTERPRETIVE MATRIX OF STRUGGLE

I make no claims to provide *the* last word on the subject of African-American philosophy—as if there is such a thing. My approach to African-American philosophy, and the assumptions that inform that approach, as with every hermeneutic framework, both disclose and yet conceal. One always begins an inquiry *in medias res*. There is no hermeneutic perspective from nowhere. Every perspective (etymologically, "to look") is a partial, *unfinished* look, a beckoning for one to look again. By foregrounding the social and historical *struggle* of Black people,[1] African-American philosophy reconfigures certain perennial meta-philosophical assumptions about the nature of philosophy and the philosopher as conceived within the context of mainstream Western philosophy. Theorizing African-American philosophy within the social matrix of anti-Black racism situates philosophical reflective thought within the concrete muck and mire of *raced* embodied existence, thus deconstructing the myth of philosophy and the philosopher as Olympian, god-like. Within the context of discussing the preponderance of African-American philosophers who deal with issues in the area of value theory, political and social philosophy, Robert Birt argues that "the leisure and liberty to dwell on metaphysical concerns with Olympian composure . . . isn't so easy for an outcast and denigrated people."[2] Bodies that suffer, bodies in pain, unarmed shot and killed bodies, lynched bodies, and mutilated bodies constitute the existentially *lived* reality of Black people in North America. I argue that it is within the context of such pervasive suffering that African-American philosophy articulates its normative concerns. In stream with Cornel West, any really serious philosophy that grapples with life must make sense of what he calls the "guttural cry."[3] For my purposes, African-American philosophy is a critical process of rendering that cry, that scream, and that struggle hearable, visible, and intelligible. It is an approach that unconceals the stench of existential pain and suffering. Charles Mills is also cognizant of the "rage . . . of those invisible native sons and daughters who, since nobody knows their name, have to be the men who *cry* 'I am!' and women who demand 'And ain't I a woman?' "[4] Within this context, Mills explicitly emphasizes the importance of this rage in terms of its meaning for persons of African descent who have been deemed sub-persons/*Üntermenschen*. In line with Mills, I theorize the meaning of African-American philosophy within the context of Black "sub-personhood." After all, Black people have had to engage in socio-existential struggle to redefine themselves against long-standing historical racist acts of dehumanization. They have had to create counter-narratives—philosophical, aesthetic, discursive, performative—that sustain them within the belly of the beast of white racism.

My discussion of African-American philosophy is defined in relationship to its explicitly non-Cartesian or anti-Cartesian assumptions. This is not a novel approach, but it transcends the familial "Oedipal conflict" subtext that is often associated with so many thinkers who are eager to unseat the patriarch of modern philosophy. To think of the history of Western philosophy as constituting a family with cross generational (monochromatic) ties, it is important to note that Black people were not deemed part of that family; they were always already outsiders, deemed permanently unfit to participate in the normative (white) philosophical community.[5] A non-Cartesian approach to African-American philosophy is conceptually fruitful given the oppression of persons of African descent during European modernity. Black people and other people of color, within this context, are those who occupy the *underside* of modernity; they constitute the primitive "Other" of modernity's self-understanding, which is predicated upon a binary structure, one that already had profound implications regarding the capture and enslavement of Africans as "fit" for slavery earlier than 1492. Indeed, the Portuguese were already invested in the denigrating practices of rendering Black bodies "things" to be sold. "By 1449," according to Molefi Kete Asante, "there were an estimated 900 Africans living in Portugal alone."[6] And capturing what speaks to a problematic and hegemonic philosophical anthropology within the context of modernity, Nelson Maldonado-Torres writes, "1492 is . . . the year in which the conquest itself and colonization of the Americas began and the moment to which one can trace the emergence of a firm imperial Europe conceiving itself as the center of the whole world and as the telos of civilization."[7] Of course, by 1619, which some see as the first time enslaved Africans (twenty in this case) were brought to the British colony of Jamestown, Virginia, Descartes was in his stove-heated room rethinking the foundations of the sciences and engaging questions of indubitability after he had three powerful dreams.

So, in 1619, Descartes sleeps and twenty Africans are wide awake at the beginning of white terror and Black death within North America.

There are various Cartesian epistemological assumptions and moves that are crucial to modernity. Hence, the Cartesian predicament becomes, as Mills demonstrates, "a kind of pivotal scene for a whole way of doing philosophy and one that involves a whole program of assumptions about the world and (taken-for-granted) normative claims about what is philosophically important."[8] Given the materially and ideologically reinforced "sub-personhood" status of Black people in America, African-American philosophy is referentially *this*-worldly; it is a site of conceptualizing the world that looks suspiciously upon and rejects the *a-historical* nature of the epistemic subject. African-American philosophy's point of critical embarkation is not preoccupied with "the danger of degeneration into solipsism, the idea of being enclosed in our own possibly unreliable perceptions, the question of whether we can be certain other minds exist, the scenario of brains in a vat, and so forth."[9] To get a sense of the non-Cartesian, *this*-worldly constitution of African-American philosophy, consider a few philosophical assumptions held by René Descartes.

In his *Meditations on First Philosophy*, Descartes assumes the posture of a skeptic. After describing what he depicts metaphorically as having fallen into a whirlpool, a vortex that has tossed him around and thrown him off of his epistemological footing, he reaches his Archimedean point, the indubitable insight that " 'I am, I exist' is necessarily true every time I utter it or conceive it in my mind."[10] Knowing incontrovertibly *that* he exists, Descartes will shut his eyes, stop up his ears, and withdraw all of his senses in order to uncover the nature of the self. As he says, "I will attempt to render myself gradually better known and more familiar to myself."[11] This approach has embedded within it the assumption that the self can be "better known" through withdrawing from (or radically doubting) the social world, thus challenging the notion that the self is fundamentally socially transversal, constituted historically, and thereby inextricably linked to the reality of the social world, its dynamism, its symbolic constitutive processes, its force of interpellation, and its power to dispossess.

The Cartesian approach also presumes that the predicament of the Cartesian self is a universal (de-contextualized) predicament,[12] one unaffected by the exigencies and contingencies of concrete history. In short, Cartesian epistemic subjects (denuded, as it were, of historical and corporeal *particularity*) are substitutable or fungible pure and simple, and faced with the same epistemic global problems. This substitutability or fungibility assumption places under erasure important markers of African-American philosophy, how African-American philosophy, with its questions, problems, dilemmas, and intuitions, evolves out of a context where *raced* embodied subjects undergo shared existential catastrophes and struggles within the context of anti-Black racism. This does not mean that African-American philosophy does not share philosophical concerns with other philosophical traditions and paradigms. However, to understand African-American philosophy one must reject the substitutability or fungibility assumption in favor of a perspective that focuses on and highlights the relationship between social ontology and particular aspects of Black *Erlebnis*, that is, the range of ways in which Black people make meaning within the context of various historical occurrences and experiences where, in this case, anti-Black racism is salient. In this way, African-American philosophy, with its specific philosophical concerns and articulations, does not aspire to forms of abstract universalism that obfuscate modes of particularity. Moreover, African-American philosophy does not presume to speak for *all* epistemic subjects *simpliciter*. Its point of philosophical embarkation does not rest upon the assumption of a fixed set of abstract and universal problems or solutions. Leonard Harris eludes to this view where he argues that "as a genre, it [African-American philosophy] is dominated by issues of practicality and struggle, which means that it is not committed to a metaphysics in the sense of having a singular proposition out of which all other propositions arise."[13] And describing his important first anthology, published in 1983, a text which was/is historically pivotal in terms of gathering together important Black philosophical themes and figures, Harris writes, *"Philosophy Born of Struggle* is predicated on the assumption that a good deal of philosophy from the African-American heritage is a function of the history of the struggle to overcome adversity and to create."[14] It is important to note that the very publication of Harris' text grew out of struggle. Within a context where "important" philosophical texts were/are shaped by white consumption and white norms of canon formation, Harris notes, "There wasn't anybody who was willing to publish it. Not a single publisher in philosophy."[15] Even Howard University Press, the press of an important Historically Black Colleges and Universities (HBCU), would not publish Harris' text because of its narrowly defined "Negro genre."[16]

While the complexity of African-American philosophy should not be reduced to struggle, its historical genesis as a professional field of inquiry, its salient themes, and its forms of praxes, presuppose a world of white supremacy, a world that is fundamentally anti-Black. Unlike Descartes, Black self-understanding grows out of a social matrix of pain and suffering, a site where the Black body is a site of marked inferiority, difference, and deviance. To withdraw from the senses in the style of Descartes, which is a form of negating embodiment as a necessary condition for self-understanding, is to presume an abstract subject from nowhere. As such, this move actually renders the self incapable of knowing itself, as self-understanding is always already from an embodied *here*, a place of lived embodied knowledge, a *here* that presupposes a specific *community* of intelligibility, shared history, and a shared linguistic community. Hence, to understand Black *lived* experience, and to understand African-American philosophy, it is important to begin with embodiment, history, and *lived* social context, a context within which Black people were/are reduced to an epidermal logic that signifies pure external-ity, thus denying any subjective interiority to the Black body. The Black self, then, is not enclosed within a solipsistic bubble free of interpellation and oppression. The Black self has struggled to understand and define itself within a context where whiteness functions as the racial transcendental norm, where white embodied others' ego-genesis is parasitic upon the ontological distortion and nullification of Black bodies. Hence, whiteness as synonymous with humanity is purchased not only through opposition, but *negation*. The Black body is raced and so rendered non-normative [read: not white]. On this score, whiteness is deemed normative and un-raced. As James Cone notes, "Whites can move beyond particular human beings to the universal human being because they have not experienced the reality of *color*."[17]

To understand Black-being-in-the-world, and the historical context of African-American philosophy, the self–Other dialectic is crucial. Not only is it a fundamental assumption of African-American philosophy, but the self–Other dialectic captures the concrete reality of racism. While racism is not a necessary feature of the self–Other dialectic, the former presupposes the latter. Hence,

1. the self is dynamically plastic;
2. the self does not exist anterior to the existence of Others, or, the self is not pre-given or the result of autogenesis; and
3. the self is always already ensconced within a larger historical context of prejudices and value-laden assumptions that mediate and shape self-understanding and the understanding of the world and Others.

In their effort to delineate various generative themes that give rise to the views of Black philosophers within their text, *I Am Because We Are: Readings in Black Philosophy*, Fred Lee Hord and Jonathan Scott Lee emphasize the self–Other dialectic as one important theme. They argue that "constitutive of the black philosophical tradition . . . is the idea that identity of the indi-vidual is never separable from the sociocultural environment. Identity is not some Cartesian abstraction grounded in a solipsistic self-consciousness."[18] The *sum* (I am) of the self is not self-constituted; rather, "I am" presupposes "they are."[19] The Cartesian self, in its isolated self-certainty has no need for the category of sociality. African-American philosophy, however, does not begin with an ego-logically fixed and estranged self; for "the experi-ence of the self with other selves is the meaning of 'sociality.' "[20] And while the we-relationship that constitutes any particular self might be taken-for-granted, the reality of the we-relationship is decisive and its constitutive dynamism precedes the performative "I am." As Maurice Natanson notes, "We are before I am."[21]

Read through the lens of racism, the point here is that African-American philosophy presupposes a social ontology where the self, in this case the Black self, is positioned by anti-Black racist forces in terms of which the Black self must contend. In its racially configured form, the self–Other dialectic is captured implicitly by Cornel West where he asks, "What does it mean to be a philosopher of African descent in the American empire?"[22] West's question raises the issue of philosophical identity beyond the sphere of pure contemplation and *thinking substances*. His question also presupposes an identity in context, a situated self, one that is anti-essentialist in its constitution. Indeed, when I think about West's question within the context of my own philosophical writings, the American empire appears in the guise of white terror, a site of hegemony that not only questions my identity as a philosopher, but where many white people are prepared to threaten my very life for speaking truth about a systemically racist country like the United States. Hence, within the context of racist hegemony, the centrality of the American empire becomes a crucial and toxic axis around which African-American philosophical identity is defined. Lucius Outlaw even sees the very attempt by Black people to address important meta-philosophical concerns around the issue of whether or not there can be a Black philosophy as an outgrowth of struggle. He notes that confronting "this issue of 'Black philosophy' is the expansion of the continuing history-making struggles of African and African-descended peoples in this country (and elsewhere) to achieve progressively liberated existence as conceived in various ways."[23] Indeed, while African-Americans received PhDs in the field of philosophy prior to the activism and liberating struggles to establish Black Studies Programs in the 1960s and 1970s, it is important to note that the overall raising of consciousness during this period functioned as a catalyst for African-Americans who entered advanced degree programs in the area of philosophy. It is also important to note, however, that African-American philosophy and African-American philosophers have not only been neglected in mainstream philosophy, but also in the area of Black Studies. After examining two early pivotal Black Studies reference books published in the early 1970s, John McClendon found both to be wanting. In *Black American Writers, 1773–1949*, he found that the section on philosophy only included theologians and psychologists. And, in *A Bibliography of Doctoral Research on the Negro, 1933–1966*, there was a subsection on the humanities, but not any reference to philosophy.[24]

The question regarding philosophers of African descent within the context of the American empire bespeaks the role of power and oppression as important foci of African-American philosophical engagement. The philosophical embodied selves that are implicated in West's question are embodied selves that take seriously "the worldliness of one's philosophical project."[25] West also rejects the Cartesian presumption regarding "the absolute autonomy of philosophy."[26] For West, Cartesians assume that "philosophy stands outside the various conventions on which people base their social practices and transcends the cultural heritages and political struggles of people."[27] He concludes, "If the Cartesian viewpoint is the only valid philosophical stance, then the idea of an Afro-American philosophy would be ludicrous."[28] Indeed, any philosophy that takes seriously the importance of struggle against oppression through the exercise of human agency rejects philosophy as a practice that transcends the horror, messiness, and joy of human existence.[29] Within the context of this chapter, existential struggle not only denotes the historical matrix out of which African-American philosophy evolved/evolves, but the motif of struggle also functions as a source for meta-philosophical insight. Hence, struggle, as used here, is not only descriptive,[30] but heuristic.

Out of his successful effort to teach an introductory course in African-American philosophy for the first time, Mills shares that he effectively deployed the unifying theme of "the struggles of people of African descent in the Americas against the different manifestations of white racism"[31] as an important point of critical and insightful inquiry. Mills especially emphasized how Black people were/are defined as sub-persons and how this sub-personhood is an example of what he terms *non*-Cartesian *sums*. Mills' approach helps to flesh out in insightful ways West's point regarding the non-Cartesian sensibilities of African-American philosophy. Mills argues that if we take seriously the conception of sub-personhood, and how such a status presupposes a certain social ontology, then the morphology of philosophical questions that are posed and which philosophical issues and themes are deemed serious and relevant will be different. He contrasts a Cartesian *sum* with a non-Cartesian *sum* or the kind of *sum* that is portrayed in Ralph Ellison's text *Invisible Man*. Descartes was pained with questions about solipsism, whether or not he could know with certainty that the external world exists, and whether or not he could distinguish between when he was dreaming as opposed to being awake. These sorts of questions presuppose a range of implicit assumptions about the self, the world, and one's *lived* experiences. Ellison's invisible man does not doubt his existence in the privacy of a stove-heated room; rather, he is made to feel invisible, he is made to feel insignificant, within an anti-Black public transactional space where whites refuse to see him, refuse to respect him, refuse to value his life. The drama of his invisibility takes place *between* selves and within a larger racial Manichean divide. Of course, the Black self is not deemed a "Thou," but an ontologically truncated "It." As Descartes *doubts* his own existence, Ellison's invisible man is constantly *reminded* of the denial and diminishment of his self/existence. Within the context of a white hegemonic world, there are white narratives, myths, symbols, body comportments, and gazes that "validate" the view that the Black body is a "problem body." According to Ellison's invisible man, "I am invisible, understand, simply because people [in this case white people] refuse to see me."[32] Lynch mobs make a mockery of Cartesian hyperbolic doubt. The vitriol of white racism forces one to be ever cognizant of the existence of other minds, not in vats, but as embodied and raced. Solipsism has no place in a world where Black bodies are mutilated and burned for the pleasure of others.[33] Indeed, that brutal reality mocked the very presumption of a "Black solipsism." Hence, for Black people, the philosophical problem is not whether one exists or not, but how to *collectively* resist a white supremacist world of absurdity where one is degraded, marginalized, humiliated, oppressed, and brutalized. On this score, taking flight into the sphere of a private subjectivity is overwhelmed and derided by the sheer weight of racial violence. Within the context of colonization, Frantz Fanon suggests that this hermetic turn inward is an idol that the colonized will abolish. He writes, "The colonialist bourgeoisie had hammered into the native's mind the idea of a society of individuals where each person shuts himself up in his own subjectivity, and whose only wealth is individual thought."[34] For Fanon, the very concept of friend within the colonial context belies subjective withdrawal. Friendship presupposes an always already preexisting social matrix and signifies a centrifugal process of mutual recognition. Fanon notes, "Brother, sister, friend— these are words outlawed by the colonialist bourgeoisie, because for them my brother is my purse, my friend is part of my scheme for getting on."[35] In stream with Fanon, in our contemporary moment, neoliberalism can function as a cover to undo forms of Black solidarity and collectivity—privileging the performance of an abstract individualism that is always already belied by the logics of white hegemony.

Sociality is the matrix within which racist action takes place. It is within the mundane everyday world that Black people struggle *to be and attempt to make sense of their existence*. Existence in Black, then, which is a fluid site of identity formation and the articulation and re-articulation of meaning within the matrix of sociality, presupposes a set of social ills that are conspicuously absent vis-à-vis an ego that takes itself to exist as an island unto itself. As socially embedded and embodied, existence in Black speaks critically to the narrowness of the field of philosophy. To do philosophy in Black within a social context of white racism, where one's very existence is at stake, where one is reduced to a "sub-person," even by those white philosophers who have been canonized within the Western philosophical tradition (Hume, Kant, and Hegel, to name a few), one must critically engage and overthrow Western philosophy's misanthropy. Even Friedrich Nietzsche, though critical of philosophers who "pose as if they had discovered and reached their real opinions through the self-development of a cold, pure, divinely unconcerned dialectic,"[36] and whose work is held to have critical affinities with African-American thought,[37] argued that Negroes are representative of pre-history and that they are able to endure pain or "severe internal inflammations that would drive even the best constituted European to distraction."[38] Moreover, to do philosophy in Black, one must critique Western philosophy's thanatotic normative assumptions. Indeed, one must be suspicious and critical of *dead* philosophical idols and metaphors, fossilized and existentially inconsequential, that fail to speak to the lives of Black people. Within this context, West emphasizes the importance of de-disciplinizing modes of knowledge. Offering a pragmatic approach, he writes, "To dedisciplinize means that you go to wherever you find sources that can help you in constituting your intellectual weaponry."[39] Disrupting the disciplinary "purity" and marshaling discursive material that speaks to the lives of Black people is what Angela Davis did as early as 1969. When she began to teach philosophy at UCLA, she discovered that "there was not a single course that had anything to do with African-American ideas."[40] She decided to design a course where she got students to compare Frederick Douglass' understanding of the slave–master relationship with particular passages in Hegel's *Phenomenology of Spirit*. She notes, "I found that it was extremely important to legitimate the production of philosophical knowledge in sites that are not normally considered *the* philosophical sites."[41]

Drawing from the work of William Barrett, Outlaw argues that professional philosophy is a site of deformation. This deformation is "evidenced by the degree to which the 'problems' of philosophy continue to be, even in these very problematic times, discipline immanent, thus without foundation beyond the boundaries of the discipline itself. *They have not emerged from the practices of life*."[42] The fact that some philosophers of African descent leave "philosophy" or are unwanted in various philosophy departments is linked to the disciplinary hegemony, philosophical narrowness, and racist practices of so many Anglo-American departments of philosophy. Not only does Lewis Gordon point out that he was denied a position in a philosophy department because it was said that he might attract "too many Black people,"[43] but he argues that even those Black philosophers who primarily do logic and epistemology are at risk of not being hired by particular philosophy departments if they also raise serious questions about what it means to live in a racist culture as Black people, that is, questions that counter the legitimating practices of mainstream philosophy. And while in 2019, just over twenty years after I initially interviewed him, things may have slightly shifted, at that time Gordon argued that if the universities found this out "then that person is automatically not going to be considered at that institution in the department of philosophy."[44] Commenting on the need to have African-American philosophers well placed in departments of philosophy, Laurence Thomas notes, "I believe that no philosophy department in America would hire a Black who would trouble the waters."[45] What becomes obvious is that philosophy's disciplinary myopia and its prevalent monochromatic membership have militated against the presence of Black people. Harris describes the case of Broadus N. Butler, who received his PhD in philosophy as early as 1952 from the University of Michigan, to illustrate an important point about racism and the profession. After he received his doctorate, Butler applied to teach in a mostly white university. According to Harris, Butler found out that his letter of reference stated, "'a good philosopher, but of course, a Negro,' and the one-line response, 'Why don't you go where you will be among your own kind?'"[46]

Gordon insists upon "raising the question of whether philosophy has been responsible to itself in terms of what it is."[47] Anita Allen asks, "With all due respect, what does philosophy have to offer to Black women? It's not obvious to me that philosophy has anything special to offer Black women today."[48] While it is true that Allen became the first Black woman to be president of the American Philosophical Association (APA) in 2018, this does not render her observation moot. The question can and must still be posed. Does philosophy have anything special to offer Black women—epistemologically, ontologically, aesthetically, normatively, sociopolitically? Given the weight of this question's continued significance, what becomes especially relevant is West's observation that "a relativizing of the discipline's traditional hierarchies of importance and centrality thus becomes necessary."[49] The logic and significance of West's observation is captured in an example provided by Allen where she talks about studying analytic metaphysics at the University of Michigan. She notes:

Yet as a Black person it felt odd to sit around asking such questions as "How do you know when two nonexistent objects are the same?" There you are in the middle of the era of affirmative action, civil rights, women's movements, etc., and you're sitting around thinking about nonexistent objects and how to tell when they are the same.[50]

Albert Mosley also experienced this tension after he was invited by prominent philosopher of science Rom Harre to study with him at Oxford. Mosley was passionate about conceptual problems in the philosophy of science. Important among these were incommensurability, scientific realism, and the differential accounts of science given by Thomas S. Kuhn and Karl Popper. Mosley applied for a Fulbright and received it. "But," as he says, "1966–1967 found me torn again between scholarship and activism. I almost refused the Fulbright scholarship because I felt guilty that I was not actively involved in the civil rights struggle."[51] And while Bernard Boxill was steeped in Bertrand

Russell and Alfred North Whitehead's *Principia Mathematica*, and works by Alonzo Church and W. V. O. Quine, he was passionately attracted to all of the discussions and political upheavals around 1965. Boxill eventually wrote his dissertation on the Black Power debate through the lens of Frantz Fanon's work. It is important to note, though, that Boxill did not abandon the tools of analytic philosophy; rather, conceptual analysis was used to grapple with complex and significant issues such as social justice and affirmation action vis-à-vis the lives of Black people.[52]

The insights of Mills, West, Outlaw, Davis, Gordon, Allen, Mosley, and Boxill raise the issue of critically rethinking and contravening the narrowness of philosophy's self-image. Concerning the paucity of Blacks in the field of philosophy, West maintains that philosophy has not been made attractive enough. The image of the philosopher that we have is "the analytic philosopher who is clever, who is sharp, who is good at drawing distinctions, but who doesn't really relate it to history, struggle, engagement with suffering, how we cope with suffering, how we overcome social misery, etc."[53] Linda Selzer is correct where she observes, "Not surprisingly, many Blacks in philosophy found themselves drawn to Marxism, existentialism, phenomenology, and pragmatism, philosophies whose insights seemed directly applicable to the economic, historical, and psychological status of marginalized groups."[54] And even as these philosophical paradigms are still dominated by white philosophers, they raise important questions—intersubjectivity, freedom, dread, power, responsibility, history, embodiment, agency, habit formation, anti-foundationalism, oppression, *lived* meaning, the life-world—that are germane to Black people and their historically situated and symbolically mediated experiences of being defined and treated as sub-persons. "The *sum* here, then—the *sum* of those seen as subpersons—will be quite different."[55]

African-American philosophy's point of embarkation, then, will begin with a different set of existential problematics. W. E. B. DuBois points out that, for whites, Black people don't simply have problems; rather, they are a problem people, ontologically so. The very wish "to make it possible for a man to be both a Negro and an American, without being cursed and spit upon by his fellows, without having the doors of Opportunity closed roughly in his face"[56] already raises significant issues around the struggle for self-definition, political power, and survival. The existential weight of this struggle, which, again, speaks to the reality and importance of sociality, presupposes the capacity of whites who have the relational political and material power to make non-whites suffer. When one shouts a greeting to the world and the white world slashes away that joy, and one is told "to stay within bounds, to go back where [you] belong,"[57] one must begin with opposition; one must take a stand, one must rethink and critically evaluate one's status within the polity, one must engage in forms of critical thought that enable one best to navigate the terrain of anti-Black racism. Indeed, one must take to task the hidden philosophical anthropological assumptions upon which the polity was/is founded. One must raise the question of philosophy's duty to *this* world, the world of the "cave," where white ghostly appearances have killed and brutalized Black bodies in the night. On this score, situated Black bodies within the context of white gazes generate questions regarding the *here* of *embodied subjective* integrity in ways that are more urgent and immediate than traditional philosophical discussions regarding the mind–body distinction. Allen notes, "Two very prominent [white] philosophers offered to look at my resume (I was flattered) and then asked to sleep with me (I was disturbed)."[58]

The objective was to reduce Allen to her Black body; for the two of them, she was the quintessential object of their white sexual fantasies. Here is a context where armchair discussions regarding the conundrums of the mind-body distinction are transformed into serious matters of ethical and political urgency because of the reality of lived *embodied* trauma. The white male gaze, in this case, attempts to reduce her to a form of hypersexual embodiment that they know for *certain*. To those prominent white philosophers, Allen was perceived as a "Jezebel," the so-called Black slut whose interiority is nullified through the racist mythology that Black women are, as it were, solely constituted as lustful and lascivious. Within the context of white racist myth-making regarding Black women, T. Denean Sharpley-Whiting notes, "Epitomizing hypersexuality, driven by some racially coded instinct, the Black female renders herself available, even assailable, yet simultaneously unassailable, sexually invulnerable, in effect, unrapeable, because of her 'licentiousness.' "[59] Dorothy Roberts argues that in 1736, the South Carolina *Gazette* depicted "African Ladies" primarily as women who had a "strong robust constitution," capable of long sexual endurance, and "able to serve their lovers 'by Night as well as Day.' "[60] Then again, perhaps those two white philosophers knew exactly the complexity of Allen's philosophical brilliance. Threatened by a Black woman's philosophical perspicacity, they sexualized the situation in order to flee their own experienced philosophical impotence.

Adrian Piper, the first African-American female philosopher to receive tenure, notes: "I think the primary problem [facing Black women entering the profession of philosophy] is that everybody assumes that Black women are basically maids or prostitutes and so you have a lot to get over when you go into a [philosophy] department."[61] To be hailed as a prostitute, to be defined as sexually insatiable, to be reduced to one's genitalia, and deemed a prisoner of a presumed "racial essence," points to the lived experience of radically non-Cartesian *sums*. Such experiences are not forms of de-contextualized universality, where epistemic subjects are substitutable. In fact, such a false universality does an injustice to the intersectional, heterogeneous, *lived* reality of Black women and women of color. Out of the complexity of such experiences grow philosophically descriptive and explanatory categories and problems that render philosophical homogeneity deeply suspect. Within this context, for example, issues regarding self-interrogation and the "nature" of the self are not derived from a *universal* conundrum having to do with abstract skepticism. Rather, "systematic negation of the other person and a furious determination to deny the other person all attributes of human-ity" forces Black people to pose constantly: "In reality, who am I?"[62] The exclamation, "Look, a Negro!" has the power to objectify and ontologically truncate. The posed question does not grow out of some form of abstract skepticism, but results from toxic forms of racist interpellation. The hail-ing has the power, as Fanon says, to cause "a hemorrhage that spattered my whole body with black blood."[63] "A Black man did it!" has ignited forms of racist fanaticism that have resulted in unspeakable forms of bloodlust. Given the existential stakes, African-American philosophy is a form of critical thought-*cum*-action. In other words, given the fact of pervasive and systemic anti-Black racism, one way of thinking about African-American philosophy is in terms of a discursive and praxis oriented activity in which philosophers engage in second-order critical reflection on the lived experiences of Black people as they struggle against racist epistemic and normative orders that degrade, dehumanize, and militate against Black self-flourishing. In stream with Herbert Marcuse and Outlaw in terms of their characterization of criti-cal thought, I would argue that African-American philosophy is a species of *dialectical thought*, a mode of critical engagement that refuses to leave the world unchanged and static in its hubristic and procrustean ways.[64] In this regard, African-American philosophy is *negative*. African-American philoso-phy strives to destabilize the rigid conceptual terrain and normative landscape of Western philosophy's self-constituting and self-perpetuating narrative that presupposes whiteness as normative. Yet, understanding Black existence as a site of historically superimposed unfreedom, African-American philosophy deploys its hermeneutic energies toward the *positive* aim of liberation strug-gle, of securing and asserting *lived* freedom, and telescoping the various ways in which Black people create frameworks of meaning that promote and sus-tain that freedom. On this score, African-American philosophy inspires hope and engages in self-validating practices and thereby affirms one's agency and the restructuring of social structures of power in the quest for equality and the positive advancement of social transformation.[65]

Given the historical facticity out of which African-American philosophy grew/grows, questions of identity, community, resistance, and survival become philosophically indispensable, themes that get configured and recon-figured within the context of a collective journey through the crucible of North American racism. Mills notes, "African-American philosophy is thus inherently, definitionally *oppositional*, the philosophy produced by property that does not remain silent but insists on speaking and contesting its status."[66] In this way, African-American philosophy asserts a philosophical anthropology that opposes misanthropy and calls into question many of the normative (white) assumptions of modernity—the nature of rationality and who qualifies as human. Against the racist procrustean tendencies of modernity, Blacks have had to engage in "heroic efforts to preserve human dignity on the night side of modernity and the underside of modernity."[67] Such efforts are not carried out by monadic subjects, but within the context of a shared community, a shared sense of we-experiences that ground the sense of community, but should not stifle its augmentation and complexity. Harris is critical of thinking about African-American philosophers as constituting a community through a specifically shared *philosophical* vocabulary. After all, there are philosophers of African descent who are Marxists, existentialists, phenomenologists, and pragmatists who conceptually dwell within different and conflicting discourse communities. Yet, Harris argues that there is an overriding aim which African-American philosophers share that constitutes them as a community. It is the engagement "in the common project to defeat the heinous consequences of racism. That's the kind of community that it is . . . that binds them together regardless of their philosophy."[68]

There are some African-American philosophers who do not see their philosophical reflections as primarily informed by the fact that they are African-American philosophers or that their philosophizing is primarily informed by the concrete *lived* struggle of being Black in America. For example, when asked this question, Thomas was explicit: "My answer to that question is, I would say, no."[69] He does admit, however, that there are certain sensibilities that can give rise to various complex insights that are tied to being Black. He notes, "W. E. B. DuBois talked about double consciousness and Ralph Ellison talked about invisibility, etc. I think that those are insights that come with the Black experience."[70] Michele M. Moody-Adams has written about moral psychology and moral responsibility without mentioning race. She does not see herself as starting with a set of fixed questions/problems that have been defined by Alain Locke or DuBois, for example. Yet she admits, "I may never mention race but I know that deep down that what is egging me on intellectually is a set of problems that come out of my experience."[71] Birt argues that even African-American philosophers who are clearly interested in ontological and metaphysical questions "think and rethink such questions . . . in social terms."[72] And even African-American philosophy done through an analytical philosophical lens, what Paget Henry calls "political logicism,"[73] constitutes a critical space that involves "the application of Anglo-analytical philosophy to the study of black problems, most significantly those that are a function of the impact of race and racism on the lives of black people."[74] African-American philosophy, unlike Cartesian *sums*, takes seriously sociality.

As a project that takes seriously human embodiment-*cum*-others,[75] and that thereby emphasizes the importance of social constitutionality with respect to the self, African-American philosophy avoids abstract pretentiousness, decontextual assumptions regarding what constitutes a philosophical problem, what constitutes the self, and the bad faith of exclusive transcendence. Thus, the question of African-American philosophy ought to be raised within a social and historical context of emergence. Not only at the heart of its discursive concerns is African-American philosophy dialectically linked to struggle, but African-American philosophers have also struggled against various efforts by communities of white philosophers who have refused to take Black people seriously as philosophers, and who have characterized philosophical problems that evolve out of the Black experience as ersatz and sociological in nature. Hence, it is important to give attention to early African-American philosophers, which gives concrete historical testament to the preoccupations and strivings of "African-American philosophy against all odds."[76] As I will show shortly, from a contemporary perspective, the existential motif of struggling against all odds speaks to the importance of building intellectual community. Such community efforts are not simply done to overcome alienation within the field, but such efforts also function as a remedy to the kinds of philosophy undertaken by Descartes. Community building underscores the point that African-American philosophers engage in endeavors that are inextricably linked to the social world through the *mediation of the body* which, as I have argued, is precisely the site of white anti-Black hatred and vilification.

PIONEER AFRICAN-AMERICAN PHILOSOPHERS

Philosophers and historians have not given due attention to African-American philosophers who received PhDs in philosophy prior to the 1950s. In fact, in Bruce Kuklick's *A History of Philosophy in America: 1720–2000*, with the exception of DuBois (who received his BA in philosophy from Harvard in 1890), there is no mention of a single credentialed African-American philosopher.[77] One is left to believe that Black people did not receive advanced degrees in philosophy and did not produce any philosophy in North America. One would think that Kuklick would have provided some space for Cornel West, especially given West's prominence and visibility as an American philosopher of African descent.

While there are very important and indispensable contemporary philosophical texts that focus upon philosophical figures of African descent, there is still the need to do the important *archival* work necessary to ascertain the history and conceptual morphology of African-American philosophy. "It is from here," according to McClendon, "that we can move to definition and interpretation, knowing full well that the limits of our inquiry into the history of African-American philosophy is empirical research."[78]

Some important early figures include Richard T. Greener who became a professor of mental and moral philosophy at the University of South Carolina as early as 1873.[79] He not only taught philosophy, but taught in the Departments of Mathematics, Greek, and Latin. Greener was also the first African-American to graduate from Harvard with an AB degree. Albert Millard Dunham, Jr. received his PhD in philosophy from the University of Chicago in 1933, William W. Fontaine from the University of Pennsylvania in 1936, Charles Leander Hill from Ohio State University in 1938, Forrest Oran Wiggins from the University of Wisconsin also in 1938, Cornelius Golightly from the University of Michigan in 1941, Eugene C. Holmes from Columbia University in 1942, and Francis Monroe Hammond from the Université Laval in 1944.[80]

Within the context of delineating the historical origins of African-American philosophy, many scholars and philosophers begin with Alain Locke who received his PhD in philosophy from Harvard University in 1918. However, at least three African-Americans received PhDs in philosophy prior to Alain Locke. Remarkably, the first two African-Americans to receive PhDs in philosophy were born under the legalized system of institutional slavery. Marked as inferior, deemed chattel from birth, they struggled against racist mythopoetic constructions of the Black body and fashioned themselves as lovers of wisdom. Patrick Francis Healy (1830–1910) was the first African-American to receive the PhD in philosophy. He received the PhD in 1865 from the University of Louvaine in Belgium, which was prior to the first PhD granted in philosophy by an American University.[81] He also received an undergraduate degree from Holy Cross in 1850. Healy's Irish father, Michael Morris Healy, was his slave owner. His father took Mary Eliza, an enslaved woman of light complexion, as his mistress. Healy taught philosophy at St. Joseph's college and Georgetown. He eventually became President of Georgetown in 1874, the first African-American philosopher to teach at a predominantly white institution of higher learning. While Healy was the first African-American to receive the PhD in philosophy, Thomas N. Baker (1860–1940) was the first African-American to receive the PhD in philosophy from an American university.[82] He completed the degree in 1903 from Yale University. Just six years after Baker, Gilbert Haven Jones (1883–1966) received his PhD in philosophy from the University of Jena in Germany in 1909.[83] Sixty years after Baker was the first African-American male to receive the PhD in philosophy from an American University, Joyce Mitchell Cook (1933–2014) was the first African-American woman to receive the PhD in philosophy, also from Yale University.[84] In the next three chapters, I will explore the life and work of Baker, Jones, and Cook, three important pioneers of African-American philosophy.

COMMUNITY BUILDING: AFRICANA
PHILOSOPHICAL SPACES

Within an institutional context where white bodies numerically dominate the profession of philosophy, and where the image of the philosopher unconsciously signifies whiteness, African-American philosophers have endured oppressive feelings of alienation, of drowning in a sea of whiteness. The alienation is not simply felt at the level of numerical underrepresentation, but at the level of *normative* (white) philosophical hegemony, at the level of concepts, interests, and ways of looking at the world that do not speak to the Black experience. It might be argued that for many Black philosophers a feeling of philosophical homelessness, a form of alienation and disorientation, is experienced within classrooms, at conferences, on committees, editorial boards, faculty meetings, and so on. Through collective praxes, philosophers of African descent have fought against marginalization and alienation within the profession. Indeed, despite the fact that Blacks constitute a little over 1 percent of the profession, they have forthrightly engaged in efforts to build community and institutional support for their philosophical efforts.

The Committee on Blacks in Philosophy was founded in the early 1970s by William R. Jones (the first chair) and others. Jones was aware of the *crisis* regarding the lack of Black philosophers in the profession of philosophy and fought to get the APA to finds ways of remedying this. Jones pointed to the "ominous gravity" of the situation. "Although blacks constitute more than 10% of the general population, they comprise less than 1/100 of the personnel in philosophy. Accordingly, to approximate their proportion in the general population black representation in philosophy must increase ten-fold."[85] The response from the APA in reference to the problematic paucity of Black people in the field of philosophy, according to Jones, indicated that they did not see the reality of oppression that exists within their structures or within the context of their policies. This failure, according to Jones, was because the APA was not looking at itself from the angle of analysis that would in fact reveal such things as racist oppression. During an early interview with Howard McGary, he attests to the APA's lack of will to create infrastructural support for the advancement of Blacks in philosophy. He says, "I think that the APA has done very little as an organization. Very little."[86] The Committee on Blacks in Philosophy was the fruit of a collective effort on the part of Black philosophers to achieve self-determination within the context of a white association that was founded in 1900. Tommy Lott, who served as chairperson of the Committee from 1993 to 1996, observed that the Committee was "necessary to promote the interests of African-American philosophers by ensuring that they're included in the program and that the concerns of the African-American community, . . . students in departments, professors going through tenure, get represented in the organization."[87] The Newsletter on Philosophy and the Black Experience (NPBE) was later sponsored by the Committee. The NPBE began in 1991 and was pivotal in terms of informing readers of the Committee's efforts, encouraging the examination of issues that grew out of the Black world, encouraging the end of racial discrimination, highlighting the various complex traditions and legacies within the context of the Black world, and providing critical reflection on current philosophical works that explored the subject of African-American philosophy and philosophy of the Black experience.

Within a context where philosophical and (white) monochromatic inertia militate against the creative efforts of African-American philosophers to engage issues that are pertinent to their *lived* experiences, issues that challenge the Western philosophical canon and its normative assumptions, *Kujichagulia* (or self-determination) functions as an indispensable axiological principle deployed against continued marginalization. J. Everet Green experienced firsthand this sense of marginalization at APA conferences. Green knew that persons of African descent needed their own forum. As a result, Philosophy Born of Struggle, an annual conference named after Harris' important text, was conceived by Green and founded in 1993. According to Green,[88] he wanted a space where people of African descent could come together and where students could find a voice and mentoring could take place. The choice of name for the forum was apropos given the struggle of persons of African descent within the normative (white hegemonic) context of European philosophy. Green argued that it was believed that Black people did not have the intellectual capacity or tenacity that philosophy required. The presumption is that "real" philosophy grew out of Europe, but originated within Greek culture, which is believed to be the cradle of civilization and the origin of reason. Philosophy Born of Struggle is itself a site of struggle; it is a site of resistance to the long-standing and current assumption that to be a *Black* philosopher is an oxymoron, a bizarre creation like Frankenstein's monster—a site of teratology.

For the last forty years, the Society for the Study of Africana Philosophy (SSAP), previously known as the New York Society for the Study of Black Philosophy, has sustained a critical space for challenging the presumption that the activity of philosophizing is exclusively a Eurocentric phenomenon. The group has a long history of encouraging a diversity of Africana philosophical voices to engage ideas pertinent to the Black experience. Such a forum has been absolutely crucial not only in terms of nurturing philosophical ideas, but for creating a space for Black philosophical identity formation and for creating a space for white philosophers who are deeply interested in the philosophical problematics that grow out of the Black experience. Seminal to its creation was Alfred E. Prettyman, who both founded SSAP and who continues to host the meetings out of his apartment. Prettyman's demonstration of creating and sustaining a critical and fecund space for the importance of Africana thought is legendary. Asked about the importance of SSAP, West says, "Well, for me, it was crucial. It was monumental in terms of facilitating a context in which persons concerned with philosophical reflections of the Black experience could meet regularly at Al Prettyman's place there in New York."[89] During the meetings, papers were given and critically discussed. Also, encouragement was nurtured. There was a real sense of community building. For West, they "constituted an intellectual neighborhood, a real *community of inquirers* wrestling with the construct of race to philosophical traditions."[90] Howard McGary also remembers SSAP as a place "where people could come and give papers and many books and chapters of books were tried out in that forum."[91]

More recent critical spaces created for the purpose of examining the critical reflections of philosophers of African descent include the Caribbean Philosophical Association (CPA) and the Collegium of Black Women Philosophers (CBWP). CPA was founded in 2002 by a collective, which included George Belle, B. Anthony Bogues, Patrick Goodin, Lewis Gordon, Clevis Headley, Paget Henry, Nelson Maldonado-Torres, Charles Mills, and Supriya Nair. A central theme of the organization is to engage in shifting the geography of reason. This is an important move as it deconstructs the presumption that reason is the property of one group and one place. Indeed, it counters the epistemic and axiological hegemonic orders that privilege whites as the sole inheritors of reason. As a result, the organization debunks the myths supporting the racist philosophical anthropology that sees whites as those who stand at the apex of human history. The group is not limited to those with degrees in philosophy and encourages South–South critical dialogue. As such, CPA emphasizes a genuine interdisciplinary critical conversation, thus avoiding various forms of interdisciplinary hegemony. Philosophical reflection is understood as one site of a more complex space of critical theoretical engagement with issues that we as human beings face. In this way, philosophy is unmoored from its disciplinary confines and "special" access to the truth as such. The Diaspora is treated as a rich confluence of ideas and epistemic practices that grow out of and speak to issues of colonialism, sexism, racism, global suffering, and questions of freedom and creative expression. Indeed, in this way, CPA gives attention to multiple forms of knowledge production vis-à-vis plural *undersides* of modernity.

CBWP was founded by Kathryn Sophia Belle (formerly known as Kathryn T. Gines) in 2007, while at Vanderbilt University. This annual conference/organization is particularly important to community building among Black women in the field of philosophy, especially given that there are currently so few Black women in the profession. As a critical community, CBWP has a number of objectives that are designed to nurture Black women at various stages in their development as philosophers. The organization provides an important space within which Black women are able to militate against the sense of dissonance felt within predominantly white and male philosophical spaces. In the spirit of Black women who have struggled mightily for their own voices, CBWP is designed to help burgeoning Black women philosophers find and cultivate their philosophical voices, to help with the often intimidating process of finding a teaching position, of moving up within academia, of completing the PhD, and of creating a critical space to share ideas that can lead to publication of articles and books. The organization also engages in proactive efforts to locate and nurture Black women at the undergraduate stage who might be interested in pursuing philosophy as a career.

CBWP is grounded in the bold spirit of the efforts of early African-American women who received PhDs in philosophy. As noted earlier, Joyce Mitchell Cook was the first Black woman to receive a PhD in philosophy. She was also the first Black woman to teach philosophy at Howard University (from September 1970 to June 1976). In the 1970s, within the context of various conferences and panel discussions, Cook was actively involved and instrumental in articulating the conceptual parameters of what constitutes the nature of Black philosophy. For example, in 1974, Cook presented "Prolegomena to a Black Philosophy," which was an address presented at Springhill College in Mobile, Alabama. She presented a paper entitled "The Concept of Black Experience" to the APA (Western division meeting in Chicago, Illinois) in 1975. Additionally, in 1976, Cook, along with William R. Jones and Robert C. Williams, participated in a radio broadcast conversation regarding the meaning of Black philosophy.[92] Angela Davis (1944–) received an honorary doctorate in 1972 in philosophy from Lenin University. As mentioned earlier, she taught a philosophy course as early as 1969 at UCLA. It was entitled "Recurring Philosophical Themes in Black Literature." At the time, this was unprecedented at UCLA. Blanche Radford Curry (1949–) received her PhD in philosophy from Brown University in 1978. She was among a group of early Black philosophers[93] who worked together "to define a place for [themselves] within the philosophy profession, socially and intellectually, on terms that took into account and expressed [their] consciousness of being *black*."[94] Curry continues to address philosophical issues that are relevant to the lives of Black people. Adrian M. S. Piper (1948–) received her PhD in philosophy from Harvard University in 1981 and, as noted earlier, has the distinction of being the first tenured Black woman philosopher.[95] She is a Kantian scholar and a leading contemporary artist. Her philosophical and artistic work explores issues of racism and sexism. Her work on Kant and xenophobia relates to the concrete problems of Black people. For example, while arguing that Kant's "conception of the self affords potent resources for understanding xenophobia as a special case of a more general cognitive phenomenon"[96] that has to do with resisting anomalous data to preserve a unified sense of self, Piper is aware that xenophobia "is of particular concern for African-Americans. As unwelcome intruders in white America we are objects of xenophobia on a daily basis."[97] There is much work to be done detailing the lives, struggles, aspirations, conceptual trajectories, theory building practices, and career journeys of Black women in the field of philosophy.

Chapter 15

Thomas Nelson Baker, Sr.: On the Power of Black Aesthetic Ideals

When it comes to our knowledge of African-American philosophers, there is often a stark paucity of information. This chapter, based upon primary research, provides a profile of the life and thought of Thomas Nelson Baker, Sr., the first African-American to receive the PhD in philosophy from an American university. This chapter demonstrates Baker's early radical insights concerning the connection between Black aesthetics, ethics, political praxis, and the radicalization of Black consciousness. It is shown that Baker's aesthetical insights precede both the New Negro ideology of the Harlem Renaissance and aspects of the revolutionary Black aesthetic semiotics of the Black Arts Movement. The reader gets a clear sense of Baker's early Black cultural "nationalist" sensibilities. Indeed, Baker's insights engage an early alternative to the problematic manifestations of what W. E. B. DuBois called "double-consciousness." Baker argues for the psychological importance and primacy of Black aesthetic ideals. Moreover, Baker's life and thought demonstrate an early appreciation for the unity of reflective thought (theory) and emancipatory action (praxis).

Once we de-mask the ahistorical pretentiousness of Western philosophy, what topics and which philosophical figures get valorized reveal a powerful ideology predicated upon a deeply entrenched racial axiological structure that impacts how processes of meta-philosophy and canonization are conceptualized. For example, when the British philosopher Bertrand Russell wrote *A History of Western Philosophy*, his very act of writing this text was both mediated by and helped to construct and sustain the hegemony of the Euro-American philosophical canon. And the principal white philosopher-actors (e.g., Plato, Aristotle, Francis Bacon, Voltaire, Immanuel Kant, Arthur Schopenhauer, George Santayana, and William James) within the historical narrativity of Will Durant's *The Story of Philosophy: The Lives and Opinions of the Greater Philosophers* are presented as the exclusive preeminent histori-cal agents of philosophical knowledge production. In other words, the two texts function as quintessential sites of racialized philosophical normativ-ity. Hence, the two philosophical texts are themselves literary, cultural, and philosophical sites of "Othering"; indeed, they function as configurations of white cultural hegemony, sustained and reinforced by white male institu-tional power and scholarship. Along a similar line of contention, perhaps the African-American philosopher Leonard Harris is right when he maintains, "The *Encyclopedia of Philosophy* should be renamed the *Encyclopedia of Eurocentric Nationalism.*"[1] In short, there is the recognition that presumed ahistorical, philosophical "verities" are actually grounded within a certain white nationalist discourse of value, culturally preserved, reproduced, and disseminated.

Western philosophy often functions misleadingly as a pristine, noble, and stable referent. Its apparent "stability," however, is maintained by cultural gatekeepers who are in positions of institutional power to reproduce, sustain, and disseminate a "master philosophical narrative," that is, a totalizing nar-rative that is fundamentally structured by tropes of whiteness. Within the context of their dramaturgical self-presentation, Anglo-American and Euro-pean philosophy are constituted in and through discourse governed by white historical, material, and institutional power. Western philosophy constitutes itself as a sovereign philosophical voice, a voice of "oracle" authority.[2] By implication, of course, all other philosophical voices are rendered marginal and pre-critical; further, Western philosophical knowledge is linked to sites of social and cultural relationships of racialized power that conceals itself as free of race. Recognizing this, the history of Western philosophy is no longer rendered an unproblematic exemplar of the human mind at its reflective best, ruminating in perfect freedom, and unencumbered by murky relationships of power, race, class, and gender. In short, Western philosophy is uncovered as a site that signifies white male hegemonic power; the power to marginal-ize, exclude, and silence; and the power to effectively render invisible other voices and philosophical traditions. The African-American philosopher Wil-liam R. Jones recognizes and challenges the significance and consequences of the power of the logics of white self-definition where he maintains:

What is at stake here is the power and authority to define. Is the white philoso-pher to be the sole definer of reality? Is his perspective alone to be afforded philosophical merit? With this understanding of what is at stake, it is unob-scured that blacks dehumanize themselves if they do not insist upon the right to make their history the point of departure for their philosophizing. Blacks forge their own chains if they fail to demand co-equal authority for their vision of reality. Blacks announce their own inferiority if they do not force the

established philosophies to revalidate themselves and reconstruct their normative apparatus in light of the black experience.[3]

This chapter on Thomas Nelson Baker, Sr. should be seen within the larger
context of creating a rupture of sorts within the philosophical canonical fabric
of texts like Russell's *A History of Western Philosophy* and Durant's *The
Story of Philosophy: The Lives and Opinions of the Greater Philosophers*.
By focusing on the life and thought of Baker, there is an emphasis placed on
the recognition that different sets of experiences involve crucial and important epistemological and ontological sources of meaning. More generally,
"the Black experience" is extricated from its subjugated status as a domain
devoid of philosophical content, *Geist*, and world historical significance. In
short, there is no room here for Hegelian dialectics regarding Black people,
especially where Black people are deemed "beneath" recognition.

As aforementioned, Thomas Nelson Baker, Sr. is the first African-American
male to receive the PhD in philosophy[4] from an American university.
Although Baker's writings have been considerably neglected, his philosophical views on issues of Black aesthetics, Black cultural identity, axiology,
ethics, metaphysics, and philosophy of religion—broadly undergirded by a
philosophy of Black self-definitional agency—constitute an early and significant philosophical precursor to the Harlem Renaissance (roughly, from 1917
to 1935). Indeed, Baker is a very early precursor (though unacknowledged)
to the Black Arts Movement with its stress upon a radical Black cultural
semiotic reordering of the Western cultural aesthetic. As early as 1906, before
the Black philosopher Alain Locke envisioned the end of the days of "Mam-
mies," "Aunties," "George," and other caricatured images, Baker had already
begun to lay the aesthetical, ethical, and psychological groundwork for the
possible conditions in terms of which the "New Negro" might emerge. Therefore, linked to a general cultural and historical growth of Black consciousness
and identity, Baker can be viewed as helping to foster a sense of thematic
continuity concerning issues involving the cultural and identificatory integrity of Black people.

Where Locke spoke of a "spirit of cultural nationalism, based on the pride
in the Negro's own traditions and folk arts,"[5] Baker forthrightly fought to
influence the dissociation of Black aesthetic sensibilities from the prevail-
ing and delimiting framework of forms of white cultural hegemonic power.
Hence, more specifically, Baker is a very important philosophical figure of
the twentieth-century Black intellectual vanguard who attempted to radically
change the discourse of race pride and identity.

Thomas Nelson Baker, Sr. was born enslaved on August 11, 1860, to
enslaved parents, Thomas Chadwick Baker—a Civil War veteran—and
Edith Nottingham-Baker, on Robert Nottingham's plantation in Northampton

County, Virginia. Edith was the daughter of Southey and Sarah Nottingham of Northampton County. Thomas was one of five children.[6]

How does an embodied Black consciousness—one especially caught within the matrix of that peculiar institution known as American slavery, which was designed for a "subhuman" race of people—come to understand itself in expressly philosophical terms? How does a Black person, living within the grips of a powerful white *Herrenvolk* ideology, choose him/herself as having the possibility of philosophical promise? How is it possible for an embodied Black self "to win itself," as it were, within such a white oppressive and malevolent context? Baker writes, "this making of itself in the sense of realizing its possibilities is the soul winning itself."[7] Indeed, it is here that one might explore how the social matrix of American slavery evokes the humanity of Black people which leads to a powerful sense of philosophical criticality and existential examination in the very souls of Black folk. Clearly, Baker is referencing a powerful sense of achieved possibility within the historical situated facticity of American slavery and oppression. The enslaved, despite the hegemonic order of things, engaged in various acts of ontological and historical self-interrogation: why am I this being, here and now, and not some other being, not here and not now? What kind of being am I such that I am supposedly "fit for slavery"? What makes my Blackness an "ontological deficit"? How do I escape the negative epidermal over-determination of what and who I am? What is it about the surface of my skin, under the institution of American slavery that renders my subjectivity and agency suspect? Why is it that my inner being is constantly reduced to my phenomenal appearance? Am I, therefore, any different from the inanimate, surface objects that I see phenomenally before me? How do I avoid internalizing the white gaze and the normative "aspirational ideals" of whiteness? How do I avoid seeing myself as denuded of an inside, a *thing* spread out and subjected to the projections of the white gaze? As Frederick Douglass asks, "Why am I a slave?" Raising profound issues of theodicy, Douglass writes:

> When I saw the slave-driver whip a slave woman, cut the blood out of her neck, and heard her piteous cries, I went away into the corner of the fence, wept and pondered over the mystery. I had, through some medium, I know not what, got some idea of God, the Creator of all mankind, the Black and the white, and that he had made the Blacks serve the whites as slaves. How he could do this and be good, I could not tell. I was not satisfied with this theory, which made God responsible for slavery, for it pained me greatly, and I have wept over it long and often.[8]

The field of philosophy is saturated with the "aspirational ideals" of whiteness. Philosophy, after all, was deemed a field of high intellectual endeavor (read: white), not the sort of activity that Black people were thought capable of engaging. The idea of a Black philosopher was seen as a "square-circle," a contradiction in terms, blatantly foolish. After all, to engage in philosophical reflection is to assume a critical perspective. Black people, however, were constructed as intrinsically devoid of subjectivity, interiority, and perspective. In short, so it was believed, there was *no here* from which Black people made sense of themselves and their world. Baker, however, indefatigably negotiated his way through the labyrinth of white racist oppression and ideology and managed to receive the PhD in philosophy from Yale University as early as 1903. Contrary to the African-American historian Kennell Jackson's claim that Carter G. Woodson "was the first Black of slave parentage to earn a doctorate in the United States,"[9] Baker earned his doctorate nine years before Woodson, who received his PhD in 1912 from Harvard University.

In an article, printed in around 1896, which covered Boston University's announcement that Baker was "the first colored man to be elected a commencement speaker from any department, and is worthy of the honor,"[10] Baker was pressed to give a synopsis of his life. He recalls:

> My mother taught me my letters, although I well remember when she learned them herself. My first reading lesson was the second chapter of Matthew, the Bible being the only book we had. I never read a bad book in my life which is one of the blessings I got by being poor. I began to attend the common schools at eight and learned to love books passionately. I used to read through my recesses. Evenings I read the Bible to my parents and grandparents, while they listened with weeping eyes, thankful that I had received the great blessing of being able to read.[11]

In 1872, at age twelve, Baker's father found it necessary to take him from school so that he might help to meet rent payments for the house, which the family occupied. So, for the ten years between 1872 and 1881, Baker worked as a farm hand, which, as he says, "broke all connections with books and schoolmates."[12] But Baker's quest for an education was not abated. He says, "But on becoming of age I was again seized with a burning desire to get an education."[13] In 1881, Baker entered Hampton Institute in Hampton, Virginia, where he studied for the next four years. During his first year of attendance, he worked during the day and attended the night school. The last three years, however, he attended the day school. Upon leaving, Baker taught for a year in a wild marshland region known as the Dismal Swamp.

In May of 1886, Baker entered Mount Hermon School in Massachusetts (also known as Rev. Dwight L. Moody's "Boys' School") where he received training for entrance to college. While at Mount Hermon, Baker was one of the only two Black students in attendance; moreover, during his first year there, he acted as drillmaster.[14] Also, while at Mount Hermon, to earn money to pay his college expenses, Baker would act as principal whenever the regular principal was on summer vacation. He graduated in June of 1889.

It was around 1890 that Baker entered the Liberal Arts School at Boston University and he graduated in the class of 1893 with a Bachelor's degree. It was from 1896 to 1900 that Baker studied philosophy and psychology at Yale Graduate School. Coupled with pastoral duties between 1896 and 1901 at the Dixwell Avenue Congregational Church in New Haven, Connecticut (where he was ordained in 1897), he completed his PhD in philosophy in 1903. Baker possibly wrote a great deal of his dissertation, "The Ethical Significance of the Connection Between Mind and Body," while living in Pittsfield, Massachusetts, where he became the minister of the Second Congregational Church (the second minister in the Church's history) in that city from 1901 to 1939. He was made minister emeritus from 1939 to 1940.

Baker was married to Elizabeth (Lizzie) Baytop (a Hampton Institute alumna), daughter of Harry and Millie Bright Baytop on September 18, 1901, in Capahosic, Virginia. In a personal letter, dated May 31, 1898, Baker writes about his future wife referencing that he has "met my 'Waterloo'" and shares that he is engaged to Miss Lizzie. He ends his letter by noting that he feels "like a new man."[15] The two of them eventually had four children: Edith, Harry, Ruth, and Thomas Baker, Jr. All four of their children excelled academically. Edith received her Bachelor of Arts degree from Oberlin in 1926, a BSM in 1928, and a Master of Arts degree from Columbia University in 1933. She went on to become head of the department of music in Winston-Salem, North Carolina. Harry received his Bachelor of Arts from Oberlin in 1929, and a degree in music from Syracuse University in 1935. He became an instructor of music and English at Winston-Salem Teachers' College in North Carolina. Ruth received her Bachelor of Arts from Oberlin in 1933 and a BSM in 1934. She became a public-school teacher in Harlem, New York. Thomas N. Baker, Jr. received his Bachelor of Arts from Oberlin in 1929 and his Master of Arts in 1930. In 1941, he received his PhD in chemistry from Ohio State University, becoming the first African-American to do so in chemistry from that university. He later taught as a professor of chemistry at State College in Petersburg, Virginia.[16] In a personal correspondence with Newman Taylor Baker, the paternal grandson of Baker, Sr., and prominent jazz drummer and musical washboard player, he clarified a potential confusion in name usage:

My grandfather chose to use "T. Nelson Baker" instead of Thomas N. Baker. In our research we found that he made the change during his junior year at Boston University. I learned of that choice very early in my childhood because there are three T. Nelson Bakers—[my grandfather], my father and my brother—and all achieved PhDs. Two were in Organic Chemistry (Ohio State University and

Cornell University). My father was the first U.S. African to receive the degree
in Chemistry at Ohio State University. It was important to all three to use T.
Nelson Baker.[17]

In 1926, Baker had the honor of being the only Black pastor to deliver an
address at the mound of the unknown dead in Pittsfield Cemetery on a Memorial Day.[18] He was also the dean of clergymen in Pittsfield, Massachusetts. On
February 22, 1941, Baker died due to accidental illuminating gas poisoning
and was buried at the Pittsfield Cemetery.[19]

From the aforementioned, Baker was no doubt exposed to a rich oral
tradition of African-American homiletics. Indeed, as the commencement
speaker at Boston University he was said to have "marked oratorical ability."[20] For Baker, the pulpit became the site of philosophical and theological engagement. But he also participated in the early production of a corpus
of texts written by race conscious African-Americans. In short, Baker
participated in both oral and written philosophical transmissive mediums
with ease.

Baker's "Not Pity but Respect" is clearly reminiscent of the Washingto-
nian–DuBoisian philosophical polemic involving issues of resistance and
self-respect. Undergirding Baker's essay, however, is a profound call for
the psychological destruction or decolonization of the Black self as defined
vis-à-vis the dominant white American culture. In other words, the self-
defeating ethics and deforming aesthetics of living Jim Crow must be
rejected. Baker states:

> All would destroy the "Jim Crow car." Some would do it by destroying the laws
> that made these cars; others would do it by destroying the causes that made the
> laws; some would destroy the "Jim Crow car" so that white and colored can
> travel together; others would destroy the "Jim Crow Negro," so that the so called
> "Jim Crow car" would be the best car in which to travel. This is the longest way
> round, but the surest way home.[21]

Baker believed that all self-respecting Black people were agreed that the
wrongs committed against them must be fought to a finish. Indeed, Baker
was cognizant that race oppression in North America was founded upon
and sustained by what he termed "drunken humanity" and "moral insanity."
Baker was quite aware of white colonial hegemony and its inhumane and
pathological manifestations. What is clear is that Baker understood whiteness
as operating according to an expansionist logic that claimed everything standing in its egomaniacal path. He writes:

> Everywhere the colored man sees built into the steamboats, trains, and waiting
> rooms the teachings of Nietzsche: "All that is best is for my folk and for myself.

If it is not given us, we take it. The best land, the purest sky, the best food, the most beautiful thoughts and the most beautiful women."[22]

However, Baker held that the issue of "who" and "what" we are constituted deep psychological and conceptual issues anterior to "where" we are. He argues, "not where we are, but what we are is the great and final question that should concern us."[23]

Baker is concerned with the symbolic re-orientation of Black consciousness. As early as 1906, his views concerning Black self-identity involved an advocacy for independence and autonomy at the level of self-conceptual reconstitution. His was a deeply ethical concern: are we to see ourselves from the perspective of white symbolic ordering or should we conceptualize ourselves from the departure of our own meaningful, symbolic, and positive Black self-constructive discourse?

In a highly suggestive passage, Baker writes:

The young Negro must be taught that his task in this nation is not to run away from himself and hide his face in the snow, but his task is to make the name Negro not a sign for "tender sympathy" and pity, but a sign that stands for manhood and womanhood that always and everywhere demands respect.[24]

Baker concludes that the watchword of Black people should be, "Not Pity but Respect."[25] In short, by stripping away the identity of "helplessness" and "lethargy" as imposed from the perspective of whiteness, eliciting nothing but white pity, Black people say to their oppressors in certain and unequivocal terms that the "Jim Crow Negro" personality is dead, that they as Black people will resist the toxicity of whiteness and create a space for their own self-worth and self-value. It is important that we appreciate this delineation of a counter-white semiotics advanced as early as 1906 by the first Black male to receive the PhD in philosophy. Within the context of early professional Black philosophers, Baker is uniquely engaged in a deep social ontological, cultural, and identificatory project that has important philosophical implications for Black identity today.

Baker's contention that one important task of Black people is not to run away from themselves and hide their faces in the "snow" (a trope for whiteness) is grounded in aesthetical terms in his essay entitled "Ideals" (Parts 1 and 2): "It is the perversion of the aesthetical sense of physical beauty that the American Negro has struck his lowest depths of racial degradation."[26] In the *Southern Workman*, suggestive of a critical pedagogy painfully aware of how whiteness functions in quotidian ways and how it shapes the self-perception of Black students, Baker states: "The pictures of the boys and girls in school are just what the Negro child needs to see. If there is to be any real race love, the Negro child must be taught to see beauty in the Negro type."[27] Baker is arguing for the importance of re-signifying the educational spaces inhabited by Black children with pictures of Black boys and Black girls for the purpose of instilling Black self-love within a white nation bent on crushing Black self-respect. More generally, Baker's emphasis on the significance of taking pride in one's own racial aesthetic ideal is clear where he writes: "The artists who have made the canvas glow with divine beauty as none others have, have been those who were most religiously devoted to their own racial and national types."[28] While Baker doesn't consider this here, it is important to note how being "religiously devoted to [one's] own racial and national types" is often undergirded by forms of racial, cultural, or national supremacy, forms of fanaticism that can easily lead to the denigration of others. Baker's primary point, though, is that aesthetic devotion to and love of Blackness is a counter-symbolic force, not a form of fanatic devotion whose aim is to render others aesthetically nugatory. Within North America at the time that Baker is writing, he understands how whiteness functions as the transcendental norm, how white breeds Black dysfunctionality. For Baker, right ideals are very important: "Wrong ideals are the worst of all wrongs, for they turn the efforts of the soul in the wrong direction. The ideal is the lamp of the soul; but if the ideal be evil the whole soul will be full of darkness."[29] The process of Blacks internalizing wrong ideals (read: white ideals) involves a systematic process of maintaining and policing the myth of whiteness as supreme. Baker realizes that issues of self-respect and living one's Black body healthily are inextricably linked to the process of contesting wrong ideals or white ideals. Toni Morrison's fictional character Pecola Breedlove and Wallace Thurman's fictional character Emma Lou Morgan both know what it means for the soul to be, as Baker says, "full of darkness." Pecola, as portrayed in *The Bluest Eye*, eventually goes insane for want of blue eyes. Emma Lou Morgan, as described in *The Blacker the Berry*, although in the end she begins to rebel against whiteness, is deeply troubled by the fact that she is *too* Black. The epidermal Black flesh has taken on a metaphysical status of ugliness and deformation. Both Pecola and Emma come to experience their racially somatic constitutions through the white gaze. Epistemologically, through knowledge/power regime of whiteness, they have been made to perceive themselves as somatically wretched and aesthetically inferior. As Charles Mills explains:

> Because of the deviant standing of the flesh of the non-white body, the body is experienced as a burden, as the lived weight of subordination. So one gets what could be called a "somatic alienation," more central to one's being than any Marxist notion, since what is involved is not the estrangement of the worker from his product but the estrangement of the person from his physical self.[30]

Apart from Baker's discourse which suggests racial typological assumptions, his argument that Black people rid themselves of a white perverted

aesthetic has broader implications concerning issues of ethics, Black symbolic self-construction, the plasticity of the Black self as constituted through
productive and generative social meanings, and the phenomenology of
double-consciousness.

For Baker, the aesthetical ideal and the ethical ideal are inextricably linked.
That Black people ought to internalize their own conception of beauty is
really a call of duty which is grounded, as Baker says, in the uniting of both
the will and the category of feeling. Baker says, "It is when duty comes in the
person dressed in the beauty of holiness that the person can be depended upon
to lay down his life for duty's sake."[31] Baker clearly understood the serious-
ness of the issue of Black aesthetic symbolization; it was an issue of our very
survival within a racist cultural and institutional symbolic space designed to
create Black self-alienation/somatic self-destruction. Although there is much
about Baker's views on Black women that is historically and conceptually
problematic,[32] in his essay, "The Negro Woman," he insightfully illustrates
the insane race-prejudice imposed by whiteness on the symbolic construction
of the Black woman. He says, "As a 'black mamma' the Negro woman is
all right, but as a 'Black Madonna' she is all wrong."[33] In short, for Baker,
the concept of a Black Madonna explodes the Western (racist) religious,
aesthetic, and canonical construal of what constitutes the "proper" image of
a Black woman or the Madonna. Within a racist value framework, however,
it is better that Black women are conceived in terms suggestive of abject
submissiveness and self-hatred. It is better that she remains a prisoner of
whiteness.

This theme of Black self-hatred is brought to bear on Baker's apologia for
a species of racial separatism. He demonstrates keen psychological analysis
of the internalization of Black self-hatred where he argues:

> This constant protest against everything like race separation has a deeper mean-
> ing than at first sight appears. There is a class of Negro leaders who in their
> blindness object to everything Negro. They object to Negro churches and call
> them a great wrong against the Negro; they object to Negro schools and feel
> that a great wrong has been done the Negro child who has not been allowed to
> attend school with white children, and in their heart of hearts they object to the
> Negro child.[34]

Broadly construed, Baker's argument is that Black people ought to create a cultural symbolic space which reinforces their own positive aesthetic,
social, and cultural ontology.[35] Over five decades later, the poet, dramatist,
and Black literary figure Larry Neal wrote:

> The Black Arts Movement . . . envisions an art that speaks directly to the needs
> and aspirations of Black America. In order to perform this task, the Black Arts

Movement proposes a radical reordering of the western cultural aesthetic. It proposes a separate symbolism, mythology, critique, and iconology.[36]

In a powerful sermon dealing with the prophet Moses, Baker raises such fundamentally linked issues as the maintenance of identity, the role of education, and the significance of community:

> Heir to the throne, he is so instructed in all the wisdom of the Egyptians that he grows to manhood mighty in words and deeds; one of the best educated men of the empire and the very best educated man of his own people. This brings us to that part of the picture which shows us how great, how truly great a man, Moses was. He does not forget his own people. His education has not made him a fool; has not made him feel that everything Hebrew is inferior and everything Egyptian is superior. He was not Egyptianized.[37]

Reading his sermon in terms of analogous significance for Black people in the United States, Baker, as early as 1919, had already begun to deconstruct the miseducation of the Negro and to lay bare the self-contemptuousness residing in the souls of Black folk. For Baker, education appears inextricably linked to a profound sense of community service. One might even reasonably infer that Baker saw the activity of philosophizing and theorizing as fundamentally linked to Black praxis. And what is also clear from the previous quote is Baker's staunch position against the aesthetic Europeanization of Black people.

However, Baker's cultural hermeneutic not only serves the purpose of creating the groundwork for the expression of greater depths of Black self-emancipation, but it also provides for the possibility of the "singularization," so to speak, of DuBoisian double-consciousness. Baker really provides an early plausible alternative to challenging the negative phenomenon of internalized double-consciousness. The idea is to contest and remove the internalized white voice. It is to disrupt the entire white panoply of white racist machinations that attempt to structure and control Black identity and Black existence. For it is precisely through the construction of our own positive Black aesthetic, and, thereby, the fissuring of the normative operations of the white gaze and the superimposed negative "pigmentization" of the Black body, that the imposed racist veil might be lifted and Black people begin to have a healthy sense of self-consciousness and positive self-regard. For Baker, to be at home in one's Black body is to have nurtured right ideals, ideals that celebrate the Black epidermis. Again, as Mills argues, "Resistance to subpersonhood thus requires an exorcism of this ghost [the ghost of whiteness] and a corresponding acceptance and celebration of one's own material being."[38]

Coupled with his views on Black resistance through the internalization of right aesthetical ideals, Baker tenders an early liberationist theological position that places the conception of a just God at the center stage of the drama of North American racism. It is the ideal of justice for which Black people long. But "slavery, oppression and race-prejudice," as Baker says, "cannot live in peace with such an ideal."[39] Indeed, the history of Black people in North America mocks such an ideal. This is why Baker calls for religious practices that are ethically robust. Baker understands religion as predicated upon a hermeneutic that places God at the center of social justice issues. Indeed, Baker places important value on a form of religious praxis which concerns itself not just with empty ritualistic incantations but with concrete, nonideal sociopolitical issues involving systemic injustice, racism, and the inequitable distribution of power. Baker writes: "If I were a southern white man I should be afraid—not of the colored man—but of the Almighty. If God does not damn such systematized and legalized injustice, then no one, it seems to me, needs to fear damnation."[40]

Hence, Baker is not simply concerned with an otherworldly abstract metaphysics. Indeed, it is his concern with socially pregnant, real life issues, and his understanding of moral agency qua bodily-being-in-the-world that informs the thesis of his Yale dissertation. Although it is not possible within the scope of this essay to consider the full philosophical ramifications of Baker's consideration of the mind–body problem, the reader will note that Baker was an interactionist; he held that the mind and body, though distinct in their origin and ontological nature, assume a casual influence upon one another. He writes, "We cannot remind ourselves too often that the mind and the brain are not identical, but that defective brain organization means, in one form or another, defective manifestation of mind."[41] Baker elaborates as follows:

> The body does not produce the mind, nor does the mind produce the body, and in a sense they are independent of each other. They are independent as to their origin, but interdependent as to their development. The mental states affect greatly the bodily states and vice versa. The wellbeing of the body is the condition for the wellbeing of the mind. Degradation of the body is always accompanied by the degradation of the mind.[42]

The last two sentences are very insightful, especially as Baker was born enslaved. Given the white peculiar institution of North American slavery, the Black body was degraded, viciously scarred, brutalized, and dehumanized. This clearly involved destructive corporeal conditions for the deformation of a healthy mental life. And given a white racist ideology that was designed and reinforced to instill feelings of baseness, ignobility, and inferiority in Black people, one can understand the impact on Black embodiment, how Black people are left facing difficulties vis-à-vis the development of their bodily schema. It is the interactionist thesis that is insightful here. For Baker, the body is an integral part of the facticity of our concrete here and now; it is the mind-body connection that constitutes the crucible of our actual moral and ethical victories and defeats. Baker does not postulate the existence of a nou-menal moral subject which ethically legislates outside the (social and physi-cal) ontology of the concrete everyday world. Indeed, for Baker, if the moral and ethical life is to be anything other than a mere empty possibility, moral and ethical agency must be executed within a real (bodily) volitional person, a person socially situated, limited, and constituted by heredity, circumstance, bodily health, and habit. Insightfully, Baker writes:

> Habit is often spoken of despairingly . . . and yet habit is indispensable for the existence of all intellectual life in the individual, enabling the subject to be a concrete immediacy . . . enabling the matter of consciousness, religious and moral, etc., to be his as the self, this soul and no other.[43]

Another central strain within Baker's life and philosophical project is his concern regarding service to others. Baker insightfully observed:

> Some boys and girls in colleges are ashamed to invite their parents to come and see them graduate. They have missed the best part of their education. They have gone through school, but school has not gone through them. The truly educated man or woman wants to be, not where they can get the most consideration and the most service, but where they can give the most of both.[44]

The theme of caring for others runs throughout Baker's life and work both in his teaching and his ministry. Moreover, Baker did not fetishize his Ivy League education, but demonstrated humility. In an important interview with Willie Singleton,[45] an eighty-four-year-old Black man who knew Baker, the view that Baker embodied a profound sense of unpretentiousness and human-ity is made evident. Part of the conversation is worth quoting in full:

> I first met Rev. Baker when I was 19. Baker was actually close to retirement when I first met him. I first came to Pittsfield, MA to work for General Electric. There were all white men working as engineers for GE. The engineers were from the South and they wanted someone who could cook southern biscuits for them. I could cook some real good southern biscuits. So, I got the job. It was at this time that I met my future wife, Magnolia, who was already attending the Second Congregationalist Church where Baker was pastor. Magnolia was on the choir. She could sing, but I couldn't. I was in love with her and the rest was history. I heard that Baker was a Yale man, but I did not know exactly what this meant, though I knew that a Yale man was special. Baker's son, Harry, was the piano player for the church. The church was very conservative. Baker didn't shout. Baker had a middle type voice. There were only Blacks in the congrega-tion at the time [1935]. The church was so conservative that if someone hollered

out "Amen," people looked around to see if something had gone wrong. Baker was a tall man with a long beard. I never saw Baker without it. Also, Baker did not change his speaking voice to fit his audience. Baker spoke the same in the company of other fellow Yale men and in the company of so-called "uneducated" people. He would visit people in the parish all the time. He was a very distinguished man and well respected. Baker was easy to talk to and he was never spoken of negatively. Baker was an outstanding Christian Gentleman. There was a pastor who followed Baker, who was also Black and a Yale man. But he was one who never wanted anyone to forget that he was a Yale man. So, he would only shake the hands of other Yale men.

There is still a great deal that remains unexplored that is of importance in the life and philosophical worldview of Thomas Nelson Baker, Sr. For example, as a child, for Baker, what was it like growing up in Northampton County, Virginia? How did his parents help him to deal with racism? Having been born enslaved and having inherited the culture of racist ideology, what impact did this have on Baker's self-esteem? Did he discuss his parents and how they experienced the sting of slavery firsthand? How did his parents help to counter the power of whiteness on his self-understanding? What did they say? What was it in the nature of Baker's character that provided him with such an inexhaustible desire to learn? As an African-American philosopher actually born enslaved, how did this reality mediate his own conception of the nature of philosophical reflection and analysis?

What impact should the life and philosophical thought of Baker have on contemporary African-American philosophers? Is there, at least implicitly, within the framework of Baker's thought, a burgeoning conception of what constitutes African-American philosophy and the role of the African-American philosopher? At what point did Baker begin to see himself as a philosopher? Did he believe that philosophers had a special duty to uplift the race? What was it like being the only Black person studying philosophy at Yale? And while at Yale, was Baker the object of ridicule and the white gaze? If so, how did this impact his identity and what was his response? Did Baker apply to teach philosophy at any other white institutions? Did Baker apply to teach philosophy at any Black institutions? If so, what was the outcome of each? Which philosophers at Yale impacted his philosophical reflections most? Which courses did he take? Are there any sermons yet to be uncovered? Are there any, as of yet, undiscovered letters of correspondence indicating the extent of Baker's contact with some of his Black philosophical contemporaries, for example, Rufus L. M. Perry, Jerome R. Riley, Alain Locke, and Gilbert Haven Jones? To what extent did the Harlem Renaissance movement influence Baker? And what was Baker's impact, if any, on this incredible cultural movement? More specifically, to what extent did he influence any of its key Black intellectual contributors? After all, on April 14, 1906, it was W. E. B. DuBois who wrote to Baker:

> Hitherto as your writings have from time to time come to my notice, I have read them with interest and considerable sympathy. I have not agreed with you always but thought I recognized a fellow soul striving for the light and have hoped that sometime we might see alike and work together.[46]

As of this writing, there are no letters found that reveal a response letter from Baker.[47] It is hoped that this chapter provides insight into some aspects of Baker's life and philosophical concerns, that it will push us closer to a recognition of Baker as an important African-American philosopher in the continuum of the cultural and historical growth of Black philosophical consciousness and identity.

Chapter 16

Gilbert Haven Jones: Early Black Philosopher and Educator

The exactions of a heartless world and the drive of a relentless nature will compel you to go on until the end.

—Gilbert Haven Jones

This epigraph speaks to the indomitable spirit of Black people of African descent throughout the world. Gilbert Haven Jones was fully cognizant of the dynamic spirit that moved in the souls of Black folk. Living within a social polity where white supremacy ruled and continues to rule, Black people were forced to make a way out of no way, overcome, and rise up (*aufhebung*) against and over circumstances historically and socially imposed upon them. The process of overcoming is a central existential motif in the African-American experience. Thematic cognates of overcoming—transcending, enduring, and struggling against—defined part of the crucible out of which Black people in the United States forged a sense of identity and dignity. Defined ontologically as a problem, Black people struggled against this white construction, envisioning their lives in ways that constituted a counter-white episteme, a mode of knowing and being that was deconstructive, reconstructive, and transformative of what it meant to be Black. Black lives in America have been shaped through the media of the chain, whip, and the cross. Enslaved, tethered like beasts of the field, beaten and battered, and with blood stained bodies that bore witness to white inhumanity, so many Black people maintained and nurtured a powerful sense of freedom, salvation, and victory. Through all of the existential turmoil, the cross spoke to Black people of what existed on the other side of white hatred, broken backs, self-deprecation, low moments of profound dread, broken families, violated bodies, and violated rights. The cross signifies (and signified) the burden of remaining moral in the face of immorality and the certainty that the future holds (and held) many positive possibilities yet unseen. My point here is not to endorse the position that to suffer "proves" one's "righteousness" or that all Black people conceptualized the symbolism of the cross to mean the same thing. By "cross," within this context, I'm pointing to a specific cruciform structure, where the cross signifies *horizontal* historical suffering and where it also signifies a *vertical* form of transcendence. It is blues-like in structure. We touch the pain, but never become prisoners of that pain.

Jones' epigraph, as he is writing within the context of the United States, speaks to Black *lived* experience as a process of being between facticity and possibility. It is "the exactions of a heartless world" that constitute our facticity. It is "the drive of a relentless nature" that speaks to who we are as a possibility. In "A Message to the Class of '39"—from which the previous epigraph is taken—Jones, who was then Dean of the College of Education and Industrial Arts at Wilberforce University, is very much aware that the graduating class of 1939 would face moments of "disillusionment, disappointment, remorse, and the possible breaking of your own spirit."[1] However, he goes on to say, "But, albeit, you will not be able to turn back. This will be impossible."[2] What is clear is that Jones is aware of the indefatigable spirit of Black people, a relentless courage that refuses to submit. Nevertheless, he is also emphasizing the significance of a Wilberforce University education, that is, the solid training and acculturation that should enable Black students to endure the storms of white America and the challenges of life, more generally. He writes:

> What the world holds for you, good or evil, no one can tell now, but if you have caught the spirit of Wilberforce and absorbed its philosophy of life, in success and failure, in happiness and in remorse, your spirit will cling to, and your soul light up with the eternal traditions of the great souls of Wilberforce who lived and labored ahead of you that these blessings might be yours.[3]

Jones, of course, also benefited from a Wilberforce University education and embodied the spirit of the African Methodist Episcopal (AME) Church. In short, he was a product of those Black folk who endured in the face of white racism and were determined to make a way out of no way. It is here that Richard Allen (1760–1831), who was formally enslaved, functions as both sign and symbol. Indeed, whites—at St. George's Methodist Episcopal Church in Philadelphia, Pennsylvania, where Allen had already established himself as a significant preacher and had quite a following—did not have the last word in terms of defining Allen and other Black Methodists as a "problem" or "plague." Literally pulled from their feet in the very process of supplication, white ushers reminded Allen and the other Black Methodists (including Absalom Jones and William White) that no act is too holy when it comes to the power of Jim Crow. They were removed from the white section, a site of the quintessentially "sacred," and told they had to sit in their "natural" place of worship. In a spirit of independence, a keen sense of justice and righteous indignation, Allen was fueled with the fortitude and vision to see possibility over facticity, hope over despair, and self-respect over humiliation. It was precisely this sense of constructive and generative counter-hegemonic self-narration and anti-white hegemonic praxis that led to the founding of the AME Church in 1816. It is this same fortitude and vision that is emblematic of the life and philosophy of Jones.

Gilbert Haven Jones was born on August 23, 1883, in Fort Mott, South Carolina. His father, Bishop Joshua H. Jones (born in Pine Plains, Lexington Co., SC, June 15, 1856) was a former president of Wilberforce University (1900–1908) and an AME Church Bishop from 1912. Joshua H. Jones was an AME preacher as early as age eighteen. He served as pastor to congregations in South Carolina; Wheeling, West Virginia; Wilberforce, Ohio; Lynn, Massachusetts; Providence, Rhode Island; and Columbus, Ohio. He was also presiding elder of Ohio's Columbus District from 1894 to 1899 and a pastor in Zanesville, Ohio. Joshua Jones was well educated, having received a Bachelor of Arts degree from Claflin University, South Carolina, in 1887. He was also a student at Howard University, Washington, DC. He received both his Bachelor of Divinity (1887) and his Doctorate of Divinity degrees (1893) from Wilberforce University. He was married to Elizabeth (Martin) Jones in 1875. Elizabeth or "Lizzie" was Gilbert Haven Jones' biological mother. It is not clear why Bishop Jones married a second time, but in 1888, he married Augusta E. Clark.[4]

Gilbert Haven Jones was still a young boy when his parents decided to move from South Carolina to Providence, Rhode Island. While living in Providence, Jones was educated in public schools. The family then moved to Columbus, Ohio, where he graduated from Central High School at the age of fifteen. He then attended the College of Arts and Sciences at Ohio State University for three years. Subsequently, he transferred to Wilberforce University, where he received his Associate of Business degree in 1902. Just a year later in 1903, he received his Bachelor of Science degree from Wilberforce, where his father was president at this time. After his graduation, Jones was principal of Lincoln High School in Carlisle, Pennsylvania. He was also studying for a Bachelor of Philosophy degree at Dickinson College in Carlisle. It is unclear whether he received the degree in 1905 or 1906. In 1907, however, he received the Master of Arts degree. After accepting a new position chairing classic languages at Langston University in Langston, Oklahoma, and working there for one year, Jones decided to complete his studies abroad.[5] He studied at the University of Gottingen, in Berlin, University of Leipzig, University of Halle, University of Toulouse, and at the Sorbonne in Paris. In 1909, he received his PhD in philosophy from the University of Jena, Germany. Jones' (inaugural) dissertation, to which I will return, was entitled "*Lotze und Bowne: Eine Vergleichung ihrer philosophischen Arbeit*" or "Lotze and Bowne: A Comparison of their Philosophical Work." This also qualifies Jones as the first African-American to complete his PhD from a German University.

Jones received honorary degrees from Dickinson College (LLD), Wilberforce University (LLD and LHD), and Howard University (LLD). Clearly, Gilbert Haven Jones was under the influence of both his father's educational values and the AME Church's emphasis on educational excellence. Historically, the AME Church is known for its forward-looking vision and activist social gospel. Not only were AME pastors involved in bringing pressure upon segregation in American public schools during the 1950s, but the AME Church was also involved in the assurance that Black people obtain a quality education. After all, as early as 1863, Bishop Daniel A. Payne was engaged in founding Wilberforce University, one of many colleges founded by the AME Church. Both father and son were exposed to a rich classical education. Black schools such as Clark Atlanta, Fisk, Wilberforce, and Howard Universities operated on the model of European universities (Germany, in particular). Each school emphasized Latin and Greek. As William M. Banks notes:

> W. E. B. DuBois, after returning from graduate work at the prestigious University of Berlin, took a position teaching Latin at Wilberforce University, a small black normal school in Ohio, not because he had aspired to such work but because at that time it was the best job available to a black with a PhD from Harvard.[6]

This classical orientation, however, did not last given the labor demands of burgeoning corporations. American colleges began to develop programs of study "that prepared students for the emerging industrial order."[7]

Jones married Rachel Gladys Coverdale on June 10, 1910. She was born in Germantown, Pennsylvania. They had four children: Gladys Havena, Gilbert Haven, Jr., Ruth Inez, and Donald Coverdale. Jones was not only a member of the AME Church, he was also the "Ohio state superintendent of the Allen Endeavor Society of that church."[8] Like his father, Jones served as the fourth president of Wilberforce University from 1924 to 1932. He also served as the University's vice-president. While president, Jones was described as "proud, brilliant, versatile, and of good appearance."[9] During Jones' first four years as president, his father was president of the board of trustees and shared many of the challenges his son faced with the school's administration. During the last four years, Jones' father was both a vice-president of the board and very active member of the executive committee. F. A. McGinnis concludes,

"Therefore, it is safe to say that the influence of the elder Jones was much in evidence in the policies of his son, although perhaps not to the disadvantage of the latter."[10] Gilbert Haven Jones accepted the presidential position after having a great deal of work experience in a university atmosphere. He was Dean of the College of Liberal Arts at Wilberforce University, from 1914 to 1924, yielding him with ten years of experience. It was noted, after assuming the role of Dean of the College of Liberal Arts that Jones "modernized the procedure in that department, has expanded the work to include general biological research, securing for that department an admirably equipped laboratory, and has directed special summer-school work there."[11]

As president, Jones expended a great deal of energy, bringing to fruition the standardization of the university. The Great Depression, as we know, hit Black people especially hard. It also negatively impacted Jones' efforts for standardization. At Wilberforce University, the Depression caused the reduction in teachers' salaries and a reduction of about 14 percent of the faculty personnel. In his quadrennial report to the 1932 General Conference, Jones notes, "This retrenchment program has kept us from furthering our program of entering the North Central Association of Colleges and Secondary Schools, the standardizing body for this area, but is not precluded the same next year."[12] In the midst of this retrenchment, however, Jones added:

> The buildings and grounds have been kept in much better condition. There are more books in the library and an assistant librarian has been employed. The laboratory equipment has been improved and increased and the health of the students has been improved. The adding of a Health and Physical Education Department has done much to contribute to this. The health program for the students is under the direction of a faculty committee and this program has done much to improve the general conditions.[13]

The student body at Wilberforce University, no doubt due to the missionary efforts of the AME Church, consisted of a diversity of Black students, coming to Wilberforce University from various places within the United States as well as South America, Canada, England, France, Panama, Bermuda, Honolulu, West Indies, South and North Africa, and the interior of Africa. Despite the broad geographical distribution of the student body, Jones was aware of the troubles Wilberforce University faced. He observed that "Wilberforce University, like all church schools, has been subjected to a falling off income, has in many instances, reached the point of danger and even destruction. Wilberforce suffers from a heavy debt which was inherited from other administrations."[14]

While president, however, Jones appears to have made progress in terms of lessening the University's indebtedness and creating a greater operating surplus.[15] Jones, while showing a great deal of doubt about the financial strength of the church to maintain its schools, seems never to have abandoned the centrality of the church's role at Wilberforce University. Within the context of the question of church support of specific kinds of training, Jones' pessimism is clear. He wrote:

> From the results it seems that the church cannot support the number of schools that it now has on the basis of the newly made financial demands upon it in this new program of standardization. Without standardization, no worthwhile schools; without worthwhile schools, no educational program; without an educational program, no promise for the future church through the education of its young, its own or Christian influence. The question of financing modern education is the big problem confronting us today [sic]. With that program solved the whole program will take care of itself.[16]

On the other hand, Jones spoke positively about the actual progress of the church-supported dimensions of the school and expressed a more general sense of optimism. For example, he noted:

> The educational program and training of the faculty have been improved so that our teachers on the pay roll have been getting their master's degrees from one or two a year to six and eight a year. At the close of this school year, according to promise and prospect, there will not be a teacher employed by us here in the Church supported Branch, without his master's degree, while several will be near their doctorate.[17]

Jones added:

> The support and cooperation between the church and the State is better and the rating of Wilberforce is better. The recognition of the president as an official radiates, ramifies and affects the school life as perhaps never before. The relationship of the church to the general educational program of the institution is as never before. The present standing of Wilberforce should bring pride to all Negroes and all churchmen should resolve to make it a university second to none.[18]

As an administrator of Black educational institutions, Jones moved with great passion, vision, and fortitude. African-American philosopher Charles L. Hill also served as president of Wilberforce University (1947–1956). Hill received his PhD in philosophy in 1938 from Ohio State University. I am told that Hill not only functioned at the administrative level, but could be seen painting buildings, teaching courses, raising money, and so on.[19] While Hill was president, Jones provided support to him in terms of recruiting new students. Jones also became head of the philosophy department. It is not known which philosophy courses Jones taught. I wonder, though, about the philosophical exchanges between Jones and Hill. Did either of them know Thomas Nelson Baker? Did they know of the existence of Patrick Francis Healy? Perhaps there are letters yet to be found that shed light on these and other questions.

Jones invested greatly in Wilberforce University. His father, Joshua, as was noted, also invested time and energy in the university. They were two AME Church warriors fighting for the education of Black people. In fact, Jones' father was instrumental in erecting the Shorter Hall building, containing one of the best auditoriums in the state. It was known as the "Jones Auditorium," named after Joshua.[20] Gilbert Haven Jones was well known as a great administrator, enthusiast for the maintenance of Black institutional power, and brilliant scholar. He appeared in "American Who's Who in Colored America," "International Who's Who," the "British Lauded Gentry," and "Leaders in Education." He was also a member of the American Academy of Political and Social Science and Advisory Board member for Northeastern Life Insurance Company in New York City. Lastly, he was the former Treasurer and member of Kappa Alpha Psi. Besides his (inaugural) dissertation, Jones authored a number of magazine articles and other publications.[21] He authored *Education in Theory and Practice*, published in 1919, the year known as the Red Summer. It was indeed a year of Black unrest. There were at least twenty-five race "riots" involving the death and injury of both Blacks and whites. Ironically, it was an early Black philosopher—trained at some of the best universities around the world—whose treatise on education was published in the very midst of Black protest, white mythmaking, white anti-Black racism, discrimination, segregation, and white madness. The point is that Jones, an early Black philosopher, engaged in the conceptualization of the very foundations of education as early as 1919, while the "intellectual inferiority" of Black people was taken to be true a priori by white people. This is clearly a manifestation of Jones' scope of social consciousness, depth of knowledge, and critical mind. Indeed, his race and class-consciousness permeated his treatise on education. Central to the text is the motif of Black Power. Gilbert Haven Jones died in 1966, the same year that Blacks shouted "Black Power!" "Black Power!" Jones is part of a long and arduous continuum of Black struggle, a struggle to gain dignity, respect, and power for Black people.

"Lotze and Bowne: A Comparison of their Philosophical Work" was written in German and, with great delight, has been translated into English by African-American scholar Robert Munro.[22] Apparently, Jones requested copies of his dissertation so it might be translated by the graduate school of Boston University's philosophy department, with the intent of using it in certain philosophy courses. Permission was given and a graduate student began the task of translating it under the tutelage of philosopher Edgar S. Brightman.[23]

Brightman—with whom Dr. Martin Luther King, Jr. studied while attending Boston University—was a personalist. Prominent American philosopher Borden Parker Bowne (1847–1910), who Jones considers in his dissertation, can also be described as a personalist. His major philosophical work is entitled *Personalism*. As one might expect, he was a critic of both naturalism and positivism. He postulated the existence of an "infinite self" in terms of which we, as individual thinking selves, are manifestations. The thinking self (and all other thinking individual selves), in other words, is part of the ontological structure of reality. Notably, Bowne taught philosophy at Boston University for many years. This created another link to Brightman.

Rudolf Hermann Lotze (1817–1881), the other philosopher considered in Jones' dissertation, was a German philosopher and physician. Lotze's work impacted the development of experimental psychology. Given the idealist sentiments of Bowne's philosophy, it seems natural that Jones might compare his views with those of Lotze. After all, Lotze was interested in the reconciliation of idealism with a mechanistic form of scientism. Starting from a nonpersonalist metaphysical framework, Lotze began with the thesis that all empirical phenomena consist of atoms. However, Lotze seems to have had an idealist strain in his thought as well.[24] Perhaps this is why Bowne, although greatly influenced by George Berkeley (given Berkeley's idealism and the importance for God in his system) and Immanuel Kant (given Kant's Copernican revolution with its stress upon the constitutive aspects of the mind), embraced aspects of Lotzean philosophy. Lotze wrote such works as *Allgemeine Physiologie des Korperlichen Lebens* (or *General Physiology of the Physical Way of Life*) and *Medizinische Psychologie oder Physiologie der Seele* (or *Medical Psychology or Physiology of the Soul*). The texts were published in 1851 and 1852, respectively. Interestingly, as already noted in chapter 15, Baker's dissertation, "The Ethical Significance of the Connection between Mind and Body," also explored the relationship between mind and body. Like his forerunner Lotze, George T. Ladd—who taught at Yale while Baker was there and was on Baker's dissertation committee—was interested in the biological substratum of mental reality. Both Jones and Baker explored deep philosophical and psychological issues in their dissertations. Jones also drew heavily upon psychology in his treatise on education.

Given the relatively undefined field of psychology in the United States around the time that Jones received his dissertation, until the work of Wilhelm Wundt, it is fair to say that Jones was probably the first Black to teach psychology as a species of philosophy on a university level. Indeed, Robert V. Guthrie is more emphatic. He writes, "Jones was the first black person with an earned doctorate to teach psychology in the United States."[25]

Wundt undercut the link between psychology and physiology. He envisioned an experimental psychology that was independent of physiology. Wundt is credited with having launched psychology as an independent science. The founding of his laboratory (in Leipzig) in 1879 also contributed to the autonomy of psychology.[26] As I have not yet read Munro's translation of Jones' dissertation, I continue to wonder: what did Jones have to say about the mind? Was he an idealist or personalist in the tradition of Bowne? Did he emphasize more of the physiological basis of mind, resulting in some kind of epiphenomenalism? Now that the dissertation has been translated, I am sure that Munro's work has provided an important framework for addressing these questions. Given the philosophical aspects and scope of Jones' book, *Education in Theory and Practice*—dedicated to his father for having led him to the love of study—it is possible to discern philosophical claims that appear to point to his earlier thoughts about the mind–body relation, perhaps a philosophical position wedged safely between the Scylla of idealism and the Charybdis of materialism.

Jones, from what I can tell, is the first Black scholar, and certainly the first Black professional philosopher, to publish a treatise on the nature of education. His 396-page dissertation dealt with a broad range of both practical and theoretical issues in education. Likewise, Jones' *Education in Theory and Practice* is a variegated pedagogical text. He explores issues in the area of discipline in the school, importance of the field of psychology to education, use of playgrounds, issues of hygiene, body comportment, manners, dress, social development, heredity, mnemonics, means of teaching patriotism, religion, habit, interest and attention, teachers and the community, length of school hours, rewards used in school, dynamics of the physical and social environmental aspects of the school and classroom, lighting, equipment, heating, intellectual, cultural, and practical education, and arts and sciences. Most importantly, however, the text is undergirded by a dynamic conception of what education presupposes. Jones' framework for understanding the dynamics of education includes a theory of the self as dynamic and capable of growth, movement, progress, and change. It is the nurturing element inherent in the process of a good education that Jones finds significant. He writes:

> From the author's viewpoint, Education is a process through which individuals *go*, or are taken (more often the latter) which is intended to fit them for social efficiency, i.e. for an *active aggressive life of service among their fellows*. It aims to remove from the individual defects with which they are born or through any cause have acquired, and supplant them with the capacity to live harmoniously with their fellows and to share equitably with them the duties and responsibilities as well as the material goods of this life. Its purpose or end is to create for mankind social advantages and *opportunities in life by nurture* which they could never hope to attain by nature.[27]

Given the aforementioned, Bowne's idealism is far too abstract for Jones. The self as grounded within and fundamentally linked to circumstances seems far too this-worldly for Bowne. The theory that only thinking persons are real undermines the very concrete reality that involves the social and cultural material conditions that make who we are as thinking embodied persons even possible. On Bowne's view, our relation to the material world and to other embodied persons in social and material relations, takes a metaphysical backseat to our dependent relationship on the "supreme person." However, a thoroughgoing materialism can also undercut the open dynamism operative in Jones' conception of education and who and what we are. If we were reducible to our material circumstances, then education would do very little in terms of stimulating growth from within, from an interiority that seems, for Jones, to be mentally purposive given our identities as free persons. The very process of nurturing suggests an ability to be more than we are vis-à-vis our material circumstances. For Jones, the concept of nurturing suggests that we are persons irreducible to a materialist causal nexus. What is also interesting about Jones' theory of education is that he recognizes education as a living process, one taking place during the entire narrative journey of a person's psychological and social life. Education is not limited to a physical building. For example, he writes:

Looked at from this view point [that is, from a broad perspective] the educational process begins with the earliest prenatal evidences of life and continues till the last signs of conscious life disappears in death. It is a process co-extensive with life itself, and, in the process, the regular routine of school plays as small a part as is the actual fractional portion of life that is spent in the schoolroom. In the broad sense of education the world is the school, mankind the teacher, and life itself the school period.[28]

Concerning the issue of mind, Jones allows that the mind is—in certain limited respects—independent of the body. Nevertheless, this does not seem to be an ontologically robust idealist position. In the matter of education, however, Jones argues the "mind is apparently almost completely dependent upon the body and its relation to other bodies."[29] This is not, however, a crude reductionism of the mind to the body. After all, knowledge itself is not spatial. According to Jones, education "is not restricted within spatial limits."[30] He writes:

Though the brain and body which contain the mind and furnish it with media for gaining knowledge are spatial as well as temporal the mind itself is not by all so regarded, and hence cannot necessarily be said to be limited in this way.[31]

Jones assumes we do indeed have a mental life, but it is situated; hence, he suggests a dynamic relationship between mental life and our material situatedness. This is the context of the *lived* body. Jones is interested in the intimate reciprocity of our mind-body unity for the purpose of offering a radical educational theory that will provide maximal growth and achievement within the lives of all people. For him,

> The study of education proper will involve, therefore, a two-fold aspect, one, the psychological which considers the general mental nature and temperament of the individual, the other the physiological which considers the physical organism, its nature and its general adaptitude to its environment during the period of the educative process.[32]

There seems to be more at stake here than an abstract discussion of metaphysics. Jones is doing metaphysics and philosophical psychology in the service of Black political freedom. To argue that the mind is completely separate from the body and material circumstances, it would be easy—no matter how fallacious—for one to argue that certain minds are ontologically inferior to other minds. Certain minds are inferior to other minds because, as the white racist paradigm would argue, it is true a priori that Black people are "inferior." According to this racist logic, Black people would be considered inferior through a "low-grade" form of "spiritual substance" out of which their minds are composed. With no significant connection to material conditions, one could not argue that depleted, inferior, and poor material conditions make for inferior minds. By implication, of course, other minds, which are superior a priori (that is, "white minds"), are superior due to a "high-grade," superior "spiritual substance." The conclusion would be that white minds are not "superior" because they have been generally exposed to the most beneficial material conditions, but that they are ontologically superior due to the superior "spiritual substance" which constitutes their very being. Jones nicely anticipates the weakness of such a move where he writes:

> But is there "a divinity in some of us that makes us great whether we will it or not" which the others of us do not possess? If there is such a divinity there it certainly does not do much for us apart from opportunity and circumstance.[33]

Interestingly, throughout *Education in Theory and Practice*, Jones uses the word "Negro" only a few times. In a text of this size, authored by a Black philosopher and published in 1919, one would expect references to the Negro to appear on every other page. However, this is not the case. Why? After all, Jones is acutely aware of the political weakness, existential, and socioeconomic plight of Black people during the early 1900s. It was by no means easy, though, for Black scholars to find (white) publishers to consider their work for publication. It is not difficult to recognize just how caustic Jones' written words could have been against white racism. However, my sense is that he conceals his critique of white hegemony while still critiquing aspects of whiteness, but one has to look closely. This was not the adopted strategy of a coward or accommodationist, but the enactment of a skilled thinker and writer. This strategy of critiquing those in power—to their face—without them being the wiser is an old technique used by Black people under conditions of white dominance. Overall, Jones argued for a perspective on education that "looks to the uplift of humanity,"[34] which challenges the very normative structure of humanity as only white.

The deeper implications of Jones' progressive conception of education include the idea that education is by no means only for a few. How could Jones, who was imbued with the spirit of the AME Church, argue otherwise? The aim of education, for Jones, is "to equalize the opportunity of all in their access to the accumulated knowledge of the [human] race and give to one and all an equal opportunity to acquire skills in the use of its material achievement."[35] In more race-sensitive language, if one allows Black people to gain an equal quality education then one also opens up possibilities for them to gain greater control over their circumstances. Jones is certainly aware of how higher education is in the hands of the privileged, those who had special political opportunities "and maintained themselves in it by rigid caste rulings and regulations and a strong spirit of clannishness."[36] How could his educational text not have directed a critique of the political privileges, educational hording, and clannishness of white people in 1919 and earlier? Again, using race-sensitive language, Jones—although aware that different people have different intellectual proclivities—is aware that whites must maintain the illusion of their "superiority." He writes:

> The principal reason for the argument of the difference in the capacity of individuals is that there is present in such minds a tacit knowledge that the equal opportunity which education gives will rob them of their advantage and prevent the further exploitation of the ignorant by the intelligent, of the socially low by the socially high.[37]

Embedded within Jones' theory of education is a fundamental critique of power. He is fully aware of the fact that many of those who have economic power have acquired this power through "extortion, robbery and 'graft,' and unscrupulous and unprincipled plunder of the public goods and utilities."[38] It can be argued that Jones is not only putting forth a critique of white power as specifically manifested within a capitalist, socioeconomic context. Hence, his theory of education is structured by a critical analysis of both race and class. Concerning the latter in reference to aesthetic education, he argues it "has been and still is confined chiefly to the leisure class."[39] Jones delineates a radically democratic conception of education, a theory of education that challenges vast economic disparities, socially imposed, and racist epistemologically engineered, conceptions of who is inferior vis-à-vis who is superior, and the biological determinist view that we are who we are by *nature*. According to Jones, "Great minds, 'men of genius,' are not so much born so (by nature) as they are made so (by nurture)."[40] Politically, Jones is representative of an early Black thinker who saw through the socially constructed and interest-laden status of whiteness, refusing to yield to the ideology and mythology of "white superiority."

Central to Jones' conception of knowledge and education is that both should be used to make a difference in the lives of ordinary people. There is an important pragmatist dimension to Jones' educational theory. Intellectual activity (and knowledge production), according to Jones, ought to make a difference in how we live. In this sense, knowledge should never be completely removed from the relationships and activities that obtain within the sphere of our quotidian social life. He argues:

> Nothing has any value for its own unrelated sake, not even knowledge. In other words take away knowledge from its relation to human activities, its effectiveness and power in human affairs and make it of no use or value except for knowledge and it can be of no use or value to man.[41]

Jones is committed to the thesis that knowledge should make a material, social, and interpersonal difference in the lives of ordinary folk. He understands that there should be a relationship between the equitable distribution of education qua knowledge and the equitable distribution of material goods, aesthetic goods, goods for the body, and the maximization of a happy and productive life (through good health, nutrition, and decent living conditions). Of course, the moral element is also central to Jones' conception of knowledge production and acquisition. In "A Message to the Class of '47," Jones observes:

> The whole concentration in the past has been on knowledge-getting without regard to who did what, and how. The new concentration is going to be on knowledge-doing. By that I mean knowing the right and doing the right. Only by facing these values can we realize our hopes for the future.[42]

My work within the context of doing philosophy and doing public intellectual work is significantly about knowledge-*doing*. Much of philosophy has lost its sense of responsibility for those outside of the pristine walls of academia or armchair reflection. Philosophers must commit beyond the narrow confines of knowledge-*getting*. Knowledge-doing is essential to philosophy as a process of critical, meta-reflection on what philosophy means vis-à-vis radical forms of *doing* collective justice work—the work of love. It is within the space of deeds, and not simply within the space of philosophical abstractions, where we must strive for excellence. Jones is aware, though, of how we have learned to look in the wrong direction. He posits, "Man has been a wonderful being and achieved wonders. Most of it has been outside of himself and often on forms and elements other than himself."[43] What is this but the Socratic injunction to live the examined life? Hence, Jones' philosophy of education (*educare* or "to lead out") places a deep social and personal demand upon how we ought to live and calls for a radical understanding of democracy, a radical exploration of new forms of praxis, and a radical cultivation of new educational values, all for the sake of a better world. According to Jones, "Men [and women] afraid of opposition and criticism never turn the world upside down by their 'doughty deeds.'"[44] Like Frantz Fanon, James Meredith, Kwame Ture (formerly known as Stokely Carmichael), Martin Luther King, Jr., Malcolm X, Audre Lorde, bell hooks, Ida B. Wells-Barnett, and millions of other Black people, Jones knew what it meant to march against fear; moreover, he knew the challenges involved in attempting to turn the world upside down.

Chapter 17

Joyce Mitchell Cook: Autobiographical and Philosophical Fragments

I

In 2007, the Collegium of Black Women Philosophers, founded by Kathryn Sophia Belle, held its first conference, which took place at Vanderbilt University. The room was filled with professional Black women philosophers and Black women whose work intersected with Black feminist theory, critical race theory, critical philosophy of race, and other philosophical traditions (e.g., variations of both analytic and continental). It was an unprecedented historical gathering, a philosophically fecund space, one filled with tremendous energy, pride, mutual validation, respect, and creative and critical philosophical dialogue. It was within this same space that Joyce Mitchell Cook, the pioneer Black woman who was the first to receive the PhD in philosophy, received a beautiful public recognition from a critical mass of other Black women philosophers. I was elated to be there on such a momentous occasion. As I recall, there were only two other male philosophers of color in attendance: Lucius T. Outlaw and Ronald Sundstrom.

It was during her speech that Cook said publicly: "If it wasn't for George Yancy, I would not have been known." I was deeply moved by her public recognition, especially as I had no idea that she had conceived of my role in her life in this specific way. More importantly, however, her words spoke to me of her sense of humility and thankfulness. They spoke to me of our friendship and mutual trust. She was, after all, already known as the first Black woman to receive the PhD in philosophy. She had already paved the way, made her historic mark. Yet, I understood what she meant. She was referring to the precious time that I had spent with her, engaging her life and philosophical worldview, and making sure that her voice and achievements, and the details of her life, were made public and available to the broader philosophical community and to the world.

Back in 1997, I met Cook for the first time. It wasn't face-to-face, but over the phone. I was the one who was unknown at the time. So, I was the real stranger who Cook allowed into her private life. It has been my sense that Cook has, for the most part, lived a very private life, one filled with just a few valued friends/insiders. This would later be confirmed as we became friends. Cook was very selective in terms of whom she befriended. In fact, in 1997, it was Adrian Piper, the first tenured Black woman philosopher in the United States, who introduced me to Cook, which was done over the phone, by conference call. I will be forever thankful to Adrian for arranging my conversation with Cook. Adrian was an incredible ally. She actually mediated our conversation, assuring Cook that I was a burgeoning philosopher on the philosophical scene and that the idea that I had for interviewing African-American philosophers for a volume under contract with Routledge was groundbreaking. I had already completed my interview with Adrian; it was brilliant and philosophically engaging.[1]

So, I made my case to Cook. I could hear her reluctance through her moments of silence. I also got an early sense of her humility. Indeed, it was at that moment that I came to realize that Cook, while the first Black woman to receive the PhD in philosophy, was very unassuming about that distinction. Having broken that barrier was not uppermost on her mind during our conversation. Her real worry had to do with whether or not she had much to say and if what she had to say had any philosophical value were she to do the interview. It is important to note that Cook had been out of the professional field of philosophy for many years—in terms of attending conferences, delivering papers, and so on. I understood her concerns. Again, though, it was her humility and honesty that moved me. What became clear to me over the years is that Cook, while not participating in the sphere of professional philosophy, had never abandoned philosophy. Philosophy was her vocation, her calling. She was brilliant, a prolific reader and possessed a remarkable memory for details. Her knowledge of the history of Western philosophy was impressive in its breadth and depth.

With Adrian's steadfast encouragement, along with my communicated conviction that my book would not be complete without her voice, Cook agreed to do the interview. I was thrilled. In fact, her agreement to participate in the project helped to undergird my confidence in the project as a whole. I knew that her voice *had* to be in the book, especially as no one had interviewed her in terms of the extensiveness with which I had planned. The volume was entitled *African-American Philosophers, 17 Conversations* and was published by Routledge in 1998 and has since become an indispensable and celebrated philosophical text. More than a philosophical goldmine, the text also functioned as a form of historical service. I have had younger philosophers say to me that it was that book which encouraged them to become philosophers, especially as it provided the first detailed interviews of a critical cadre of African-American philosophers, tracing significant moments in their lives, detailing intellectual and academic influences that encouraged them to study philosophy, discussing books that they read, and revisiting personal and meta-philosophical challenges that they faced as Black men and women in a predominantly white and male field. I once had a Black graduate student say to me, "This book saved my life!"

My conversation with Cook was momentous. During our interview, and over the course of fifteen years, Cook shared significant details of her life with me, some of which she did not want to be made public. She made it clear that I understood that. I promised her that I would honor her wishes. I not only engaged Cook concerning her philosophical ideas, and spent many hours and days talking about her life, but we became close and wonderful friends. I became one of the few insiders; there was a shared sense of mutual care and profound trust. When visiting Cook for dinner, she was the perfect host; there was that unconditional sense of hospitality. And I loved her pecan pies, something for which she was well known. When Cook became ill, I was there for her as best I could. At one point, I helped her sip from a straw as she was very weak. I knew that her weakness wasn't a good sign. What struck me most about Cook during the time of her illness was her sense of extraordinary fortitude and optimistic attitude that she would not be beaten by anything. Even as she was too weak to move about, she would often talk to me about all of the things that she had to do around the house. And even as she greatly appreciated the assistance of an aid who had come over to help, I knew that she wanted her autonomy and privacy.

It was that sense of purpose and drive that moved me. On one visit, one of my sons and I sat with her, close to her bed. She was witty and confident, telling me that people believed that she wasn't going to get out of the bed. As I was afraid that I would not see her again, I instructed my son to take notes of what she said, of the little that we discussed. After we left, I felt that this would be the last time that I would see her alive. A few days later, I called Cook and to my surprise she answered the phone, her voice stronger; she sounded like her normal jovial self. Hers was the kind of voice that you looked forward to hearing. Even though this moment of "recovery" was short-lived, I was again moved by her tenacity. As I had done so many times before, I told Cook that we must begin working on her long-awaited book on the Black experience. A few weeks after that phone conversation, Cook's health began to worsen. There were times when she could barely hold the phone to her ear, though I knew that she wanted to talk with me. Once, after the aid had taken the phone to her, Cook said hello to me and I to her.

However, she would not say much more. I simply waited on the phone, sitting silently, listening to the latest news on her TV in the background, and not saying a word. My sense is that she may have forgotten that I was on the phone. It didn't matter to me. It was enough to know that she and I had that connection, even if only in silence.

After Cook passed away on June 6, 2014, I, along with my family, was invited to the funeral. It was beautiful and consisted mainly of her extended family members. When we arrived, I was asked to say a few words about Cook during the service. While very honored, I felt unprepared to be the first nonfamily member to speak. I spoke highly of Cook, saying what I thought needed to be said, especially to her many younger relatives who would not have been aware of the exact nature of her historical importance to the field of philosophy.

A little over a year later, I was invited by Yale University's philosophy department to provide the keynote address for "The Joyce Mitchell Cook Conference." It was philosopher Jorge L. A. Garcia, I believe, who conceived of the idea to have the conference in honor of Cook. She would have been profoundly honored to have received such recognition, especially from her Alma Mater. And, yet, knowing Cook as I do, she would have also been hesitant to receive such recognition. I say this because Cook was less concerned about honors bestowed upon her and far more concerned with whether or not she was living up to what it means to be the best human being that she could be. She stressed the importance of the ethical life and she was very keen to make sure that any claims that she put forward were consistent and valid. I recall that she would often immediately question the strength of what she had just argued. I admired her epistemic integrity.

Her epistemic integrity was also brought to bear upon what I would ask her or a certain line of reasoning that I would take up. She would not accept any idea that I had not thought through, forcing me to clarify the point. Yet, as I would ask Cook one question after the next, late into the evening, she was apologetic for not responding as she may have thought that I wanted her to. The truth of the matter is that her responses to my questions were always rigorous. I knew that she was working on her book on the Black experience and that her ideas were still in process, especially regarding questions about race. So, I communicated this understanding to her. Despite this, she said, "I can't imagine that the answers [that I'm giving] are sufficient. I'm not passing myself off as a philosopher, you know."[2] In fact, when asked if she defined herself as an African-American philosopher, she said: "I never referred to myself as a philosopher. I used to say that I was a student of philosophy."[3] Further clarifying her identity, she said, "No. I would not say that I'm an African-American philosopher. First of all I don't even use that language—African-American. I use the term Black. I'm trying to be neutral as I question the African connection. But I have no problem using the word Black."[4]

From politics to personal friendships, Cook emphasized the significance of deep mutual respect and integrity. I have met very few highly principled human beings in my life and she is right up there at the top.

As I gave my keynote address, I made it clear that this was not simply about honoring the first Black woman to receive the PhD in philosophy, but it was about honoring my friend and colleague, and keeping her memory alive. After her death, I was called by Cook's favorite niece[5] who told me that it was Cook's will that I become executor over her books (700+), and all of her published and unpublished papers, literally thousands of index cards of notes, and various correspondences. Cook kept everything that she deemed valuable. And we ought to thank her posthumously for doing so. She even kept the graded papers that she wrote as a graduate student for philosophers like P. F. Strawson. Cook kept notes and papers in meticulous order. Looking through the 700+ books is like reading a hyper-text as she made extensive notes in most of them. There are lines and lines of notes. This speaks to Cook's reading habits. She engaged books in critical conversation. There are some books where she created a separate index, organizing concepts and providing page citations, which is a practice that I have now begun to use. Her personal copy of *African-American Philosophers, 17 Conversations* is filled with marginal notes, Post-it notes, and many notes in red and black ink on the inside cover of the last page. She left our interview unmarked. I recall that she had told me that once the interview was complete, she had no plans of reading it again. She also said this of her other writings. Her objective was to go on to the next project. My sense is that she would have been far too critical of what she said, which is something of the perfectionist in Cook. I believe that this is one reason why Cook's authored book on the Black experience was delayed. Her objective was synoptic and rigorous, consuming everything that was relevant to the subject, which is evidenced by the sheer number of books that she had read that dealt in some way with the Black experience.

Given Cook's privacy regarding her unpublished writings, it is clear that she and I had developed a profound trust, friendship, and collegiality. Otherwise, I would not have been entrusted with her work, papers and notes that were of deep significance to her. For those who know Cook, she had been working on a book on the Black experience for many years. My aim is to see to it that some version of that book is published. I only wish that she had completed it. Unfortunately, she didn't leave a completed manuscript or even a half completed one, but there are published and unpublished papers that will serve to function as book chapters.

In the second part of this chapter, which includes some material used in my keynote address, I provide some fragments of Cook's life and philosophical intuitions. Why fragments? I am by no means an expert on Cook's philosophical work. In fact, no one is. There is too much that I have not yet read of hers. I have only looked at about one-third of the materials in the many boxes that I received. So, my aim is to provide fragments that at least help to scaffold a greater appreciation for the life and thought of Cook. The chapter also provides insights that she shared, but that were not published from our interview back in 1997. Furthermore, I have incorporated material from some of her published and some of her unpublished material. While overdue given her historical significance, the chapter is the first full-length piece written on Cook and her work.

If I had to use four words to describe Joyce Mitchell Cook, they would be: humble, rigorous, principled, and deeply ethical. Without pressuring her, I used as many opportunities as possible to remind Cook of the urgency and importance of writing her book. As she became ill, I began to lose hope that she would complete the book. As sensitively as I could, I would speak to her of her finitude/our finitude. The book, unfortunately, was not completed and, as indicated, there are only published and unpublished articles. What gave me hope, however, is that Cook would tell me that she was still in the process of taking notes regarding the Black experience. I had every reason to believe her; moreover, her many notes confirmed this. Having received Cook's extraordinary book collection, and her published and unpublished writings, it is with great honor that I thank her for trusting me, for sharing with me what I know she valued highly. You really had to know Cook's need for privacy, and the value that she placed on her work, especially in terms of how much she wished to perfect it philosophically before sharing it, to realize how monumental such a gift is to me, to us.

II

In this section, I provide significant fragments of Cook's life and philosophical views and intuitions. While I wish that I could provide a more detailed and synoptic engagement with her philosophical corpus, so much of her unpublished work still needs to be read and critically engaged. So, my aim in this chapter is to provide an overview that helps to scaffold a greater appreciation for the life and thought of Cook. This chapter greatly and indispensably benefits from insights not previously published from my interview with Cook conducted back in 1997. That interview, to my knowledge, was the first historically extensive interview that Cook allowed. Moreover, I incorporate material from some of her published and some of her unpublished material. One objective of this chapter is to provide for readers, for the first time, important aspects of Cook's life and thought. My hope is that the chapter will generate an awareness of Cook's work and to encourage others to engage it critically and more thoroughly than done here. So, I will *not* engage Cook's work across extant philosophical literature in normative theory or ethics or critical philosophy of race or Black feminist theory. This approach is *not* an oversight. It is to create a space for Cook's voice and thought. So, my objective is primarily descriptive. At the moment of this writing, to my knowledge, there is no article on Cook's work that engages it with as much detail as this one. It is with honor that I am able to do so. This would not be the case without Cook's invaluable assistance in the form of extended conversations and access to her unpublished material.

Historically, Yale University holds the distinction of not only being the university to grant the first PhD in philosophy to a Black man, Thomas Nelson Baker[6] (1903), but it also holds the distinction of being the first university to grant a PhD in philosophy to a Black woman, Joyce Mitchell Cook (1965). Significantly, Yale also was the first American university to grant a PhD to a Black person, Edward Alexander Bouchet (1852–1918), who received his doctorate in physics in 1876.

Not only does Cook hold the distinction of being the first African-American woman to receive a PhD in philosophy in the United States, she was also the first woman appointee to teach in the department of philosophy at Yale College (from September 1959 to June 1961). She was also the first African-American woman to teach philosophy at Howard University (from September 1966 to June 1968 and from September 1970 to June 1976). Historically, it is important to note that Howard University played an important role in hiring Black philosophers. Alain L. Locke, as chair of the department, played an early role in that regard. While Cook was there, her colleagues included Eugene C. Holmes, who was a Marxist and wrote on philosophical issues regarding space and time; Winston K. McAllister, whose areas were ethics and logic;[7] and William A. Banner, whose work included ethics, conceptions of the moral life, and work on St Augustine. According to Leonard Harris, it was Banner "who ends the era of philosophy at Howard in terms of being a source for Black intellectual activity."[8]

Joyce Mitchell Cook (from October 28, 1933, to June 6, 2014) was born in Sharon, Pennsylvania. She was the ninth of twelve children of the late Reverend Isaac William Mitchell, Sr., who was minister of the Church of God (headquartered in Anderson, Indiana and described by Cook as nondenominational), and Mary Belle Christman. Cook was educated through the Sharon public school system from elementary through high school. After coming across a life story of Madame Curie, Cook planned to major in chemistry and studied chemistry until her junior year in college. She traces an early penchant for philosophy, however, in what she describes as "an ear for consistency, one of the cardinal philosophical virtues."[9] Cook describes that in the ninth grade, one of her teachers, Mary McDowell, asked her to do an algebraic problem on the board. Out of all of the students, Cook was the only student who completed it. McDowell said to Cook: "I knew you could do it."[10] It was this vote of confidence that Cook describes as one important impact that a teacher had on her during her early educational experience.

As an undergraduate, Cook took her first philosophy course at Bryn Mawr College, and after switching majors, graduated with her AB in philosophy with honors in 1955. Her very first philosophy class was taught by Isabelle Stearns, who was the only woman philosopher at Bryn Mawr College at the time. Stearns became the director of Cook's honors thesis on Spinoza, which dealt with his ethics. It was entitled "The Individual in Spinoza's Ethics." Cook said that she studied Spinoza because of her interest in his geometrical method. At Bryn Mawr, she also studied under Dr. Geddes MacGregor, a Scotsman, who taught her medieval philosophy. When she entered Bryn Mawr College, Cook was one of only two Black undergraduates on campus.

After writing to Harvard University, indicating her interest in pursuing graduate studies, Cook was advised by Harvard to apply to Radcliffe College. Instead of applying to Radcliffe, Cook applied to Yale University and was accepted the same year that she graduated from Bryn Mawr. However, Cook wrote a letter to Yale requesting that they hold her dossier until she reapplied so that she could attend St Hilda's College, at Oxford University, in the United Kingdom (from 1955 to 1957). When she reapplied to Yale, she was accepted. Cook received her second BA with high honors in both philosophy and psychology in 1957 from Oxford University. While at Oxford, Cook studied with prominent philosopher Peter Strawson, one of the leading analytic philosophers at the time. She was also introduced to ethics from an analytical perspective while attending informal lectures given by John Austin, the prominent British linguistic philosopher. One of Cook's tutors at Oxford was Mary Warnock, who was a prominent philosopher who specialized in ethics, especially at the intersections of reproduction and ethics. She also wrote on Jean-Paul Sartre, existentialist ethics, and education. It was Warnock who referred Cook to Strawson. In the interview in 1997, Cook shared with me that being sent to Strawson was an indication of Warnock's confidence in her philosophical acumen. B. A. Farrell, who taught philosophy of mind, was also one of her tutors.

After graduating from Oxford with the BA, Cook entered Yale in 1957, where she was one of only a handful of female students (and the only Black female) in the graduate school studying philosophy. While a student at Yale, Cook also received an MA from Oxford University in 1961. Cook remained at Yale for four years. During the last two years (1959–1961), she was a teaching assistant in philosophy. This was the first time, according to Cook, that a woman was appointed to teach in Yale College in a field other than a foreign language. Also, during these two years, she worked as managing editor of the prestigious philosophy journal *The Review of Metaphysics*, which was established and edited by the American philosopher Paul Weiss. He showed a great deal of confidence in Cook's superb editorial abilities. She also worked at Yale University Press.

When her name was put forward to become managing editor of *The Review of Metaphysics*, Cook said that she asked herself two questions: "In deciding to take it or not to take it, I asked myself only whether I can do it and whether I want to do it. And the answer to both of those was yes."[11] Cook didn't hesitate to say that she thought that there was another person (whose name she did not provide) who she thought was also qualified for the position as managing editor. Significantly, Cook also commented that "you have to realize I'm not looking at this as I would after developing a racial consciousness."[12]

While at Yale, Cook studied with such well-known philosophers as Wilfrid Sellars, F. S. C. Northrop, Rulon Wells, John Smith, and Paul Weiss. In the unpublished portions of my 1997 interview with Cook, she shared that although she was not a convert of Weiss' brand of metaphysical speculation, partly due to the influence of Oxford University's view of philosophy, what she did learn firsthand from Weiss was his dedication to philosophy, his care for his children, and his extraordinary industry. Weiss also hired Cook during her first year at Yale to be a reader for his undergraduate philosophy of art class.

Cook describes herself as "always primarily interested in ethics," which she links with her religious background. She specialized in the area of value theory, which she says includes branches of logic "insofar as logic is interested in what constitutes a good argument."[13] Her dissertation was entitled "A Critical Examination of Stephen C. Pepper's Theory of Value." Pepper was a well-known American philosopher who wrote on ethics and aesthetics, among other philosophical topics. My aim in this chapter is not to engage Cook's 250-page dissertation. My point here is that while this chapter is historically the first chapter or article written on Cook's life and work, there are many others, more qualified than I am, in the area of ethics and even value theory, who will do the necessary work of addressing any conceptual lacunae that I have left unaddressed. Cook's work requires a long-term division of intellectual labor. So, I leave that to philosophers who are interested in exploring the complexities of Cook's dissertation as a way of understanding her value theory and conceivably for understanding the dissertation's importance to her work on race. Cook's interest in Pepper's work on ethics, though, is linked to her own Kantian deontological sensibilities. She was critical of Pepper's naturalist presuppositions, accusing Pepper of committing the naturalistic fallacy. In her dissertation, Cook notes that Pepper's theory is designed to provide light on the problem of how to make well-grounded decisions within the context of human affairs. Cook notes, "Seen in these terms, Pepper's theory fails to accomplish its purpose. It confuses (1) the problem of how to make well-grounded decisions with (2) the problem of how well-grounded decisions are made, and consequently falls into the naturalistic fallacy."[14]

It was Wilfrid Sellars who assisted Cook in formulating her dissertation prospectus before he left Yale to teach at the University of Pittsburgh, and then Paul Weiss stepped in as Cook's dissertation director. In the end, however, it was under the directorship of philosopher Rulon Wells that Cook wrote and completed her dissertation. Cook graduated from Yale with her PhD in 1965.

In addition to her teaching experiences noted previously, Cook also taught for one year at Wellesley College (1961–1962) and two years at Connecticut College (1968–1970). Part of Cook's experience at Connecticut College was inundated with toxic forms of race discrimination. She communicates this in a letter that she wrote to the editor of the college's school newspaper, *Satyagraha*. Cook's letter was in response to a letter written by then Black student, J. W. Walters. The letter, which has the caption, "Connecticut College—A Fraud," attempts to bring attention to the plight of Black instructors at Connecticut College. Walters indirectly mentions two Black instructors on campus, one being Cook, who he says have been targets of what he refers to as a "crime perpetrated by members of the philosophy department."[15] His charge of racism is clear. His objective was to rally students to support the few Black faculty on campus and to bring justice to bear on racist discrimination and the failure to treat Black faculty fairly at the college. Cook's response is a philosophical and political gem as she is clear not only about her intolerance of how she and others were treated, but she is emphatic about the degree to which she is willing to fight against racism, the larger issues at stake with respect to racist discrimination against Black academics, and the risk that she is prepared to take in being alone as someone who is willing to fight against racial injustice. Her response letter is worth quoting in full:

To the Editors:

I shall address myself to limited aspects of Mr. Walters' letter (this newspaper, March 10, 1970), reserving fuller comment for a later date and possibly another medium. At the time of this writing I have not had the opportunity to ask Mr. Walters what he has in mind insofar as he has called upon "all the students and interested faculty of Connecticut College" to help, apparently in regard to the matter of my not having been recommended by my department for a further appointment at this College. I was much pleased to learn that Mr. Walters had been concerned about my well-being sufficiently to write a letter to this newspaper. However, I found his general appeal to the College community as puzzling as it might have been embarrassing to others among us. I thought that in my discussion with him I had emphatically stated the opposite of what his appeal implies, to wit, that under no conceivable circumstances will I consider remaining at Connecticut College after the expiration of my present appointment in June 1970. To be sure, I believe that I have been trifled with by members of the administration of this College and unfairly treated by my department. However, my only public concern in the matter is to ensure as far as possible that there shall be no repetition of the same treatment for others who, broadly speaking, may be said, now or henceforth, to be similarly situated. I am interested, not in justice for myself, but in the truth which, touching as it does upon a number of major issues that are troubling colleges and universities throughout this country, I should hope will edify us all, however damaging it may prove to me personally. In this endeavor, there are those who are interested but who cannot help; and there are those who can help but who are uninterested. Thus it ever was and, I suspect, ever shall be. Happily, my silent meditation upon these matters for some months has prepared me, should I be required, to stand alone—a posture all too familiar to those who would dare to know the truth.

Yours sincerely,
Joyce Mitchell Cook[16]

In terms of other work experience, for about a year and a half, Cook worked for the State Department, where she worked as an analyst covering the affairs of various African countries. After leaving the State Department, she worked for the now-defunct Office of Economic Opportunity. Although she left governmental work in 1966, she returned to it when she worked for four years (1977–1981) at the White House under President Jimmy Carter.

Cook was the recipient of a 2004 Alain Locke Excellence Award in Africana Philosophy presented at Howard University. The award was given in part for Cook's early attempts to articulate, philosophically, the meaning of "Black philosophy." In the early 1970s, during the formative historical period when only a small number of Black philosophers were working on the conceptual parameters of what constitutes the field of Black philosophy, Cook was actively involved in a number of significant panels and conference discussions dedicated toward that end. In fact, in November of 1970, at a conference on philosophy and the Black experience at the University of Illinois at Chicago Circle, Cook delivered a paper entitled "A Critique of Black Experience." This conference was important as it brought together a critical cadre of Black philosophers. Later, in February of 1976, at the John A. Johnson Foundation in Madison Wisconsin, Cook, along with Black philosophers William R. Jones and Robert C. Williams, engaged in an extensive conversation about the nature of Black philosophy. During that period, Cook also served for two years on the Program Committee of the American Philosophical Association, Eastern Division, as well as on its Committee on Blacks in Philosophy.

Given the paucity of African-American women in the field of philosophy and the continued low percentage of African-Americans in the field of philosophy more generally (even as of 2020), Cook is a significant pioneer in the field of American philosophy, a figure whose very historical presence speaks to her incredible tenacity as a Black woman within a discipline that continues to be predominantly white and male.

This tenacity and sense of independence is linked to Cook's younger years. When talking about her experience during grade school (1–6), junior high (7–8), and high school (9–12), Cook communicated that "I was an independent personality type of person at a very early age."[17] She continued, "I loved school more than anything else."[18] In fact, Cook was not very happy when school let out for the summer. In addition, she says that from an early age she loved books, especially detective novels and the classic Nancy Drew Mystery Stories series, which were written for young girls. "I would just walk down the street reading and people would just honk their horns."[19] She remembers that remarkably she would always know when she came to the curb, though she didn't always look up. She discussed how her mother would give her lots of chores to do and how she would work to get them done well and quickly so that she could get back to her books. From these reflections it is obvious that Cook was a young bibliophile. However, she mentioned that it was not because her parents paid special attention to her that she was such a voracious reader. In other words, her parents didn't select her out in some special way such that this led to her love of books or learning. She says that she didn't need that, because her head was just always in books. My sense is that Cook was in love with learning as such and had an incredible sense of dedication toward learning at a young and formative age. Cook seemed to have always had an ethics of learning.

There is a race transcending cosmopolitan spirit in both the younger Cook and in the older Cook, though the older Cook is far more informed about race matters. In a short article published in 1973, Cook marks the importance of her raced and sexed identity and yet gestures toward an identity standpoint neutral to both philosophically. She writes:

> The sixties have raised the consciousness of us all. I cannot envisage future goals oblivious of the salient aspects of my being, i.e., black and female. Quite reluctantly I have acknowledged my responsibility to the social order in national conferences at which I read papers relating philosophy and the black experience. I say reluctantly because my own interests, philosophically speaking, indicate other topics. On the other hand, I cannot carry placards nor can I be a politician: reasoned discourse is my medium.[20]

By "placards," did Cook mean that she would not carry signs during the Civil Rights Movement or the Black Power Movement? Her desire not to be a "politician" perhaps speaks to her reticence to enter into a racialized *political* struggle. Or, perhaps she meant that politics is the space of sophistry given her emphasis upon *reasoned* discourse. In our current age of "post-truth" and "alternative facts," Cook's point is well taken. And then there is the reluctance, the hesitancy to embrace what she sees as her responsibility to engage the racial and racist social order critically by participating in various conferences dedicated to the Black experience.[21] More importantly, I think, is the impact that the 1960s had on her self-understanding regarding her identity as Black and female. Cook's observation here is consistent with many other Black philosophers who lived through the 1960s during the times that they were studying philosophy.[22] The white racist brutality on the proverbial streets in the United States belied forms of philosophical abstraction and ideal theory. In 2020, there continue to be meta-philosophical assumptions held by many professional philosophers that militate against the *philosophical* importance of historical, social, political, and existential issues that are of deep significance to Black philosophers and philosophers of color.

While it is true that Cook critically engaged the philosophical complexity of the meaning of the Black experience, she came to this critical approach later in life. In fact, she says, "I was always liberated whether you're talking [about] race or sex."[23] Yet, Cook seems to have realized how a certain level of ignorance functioned as a shield for her or perhaps even an affordance. She writes:

Lack of consciousness, or ignorance, if you will, meant indifference to obstacles both real and imagined. I should like to think that it also made possible the surmounting of genuine obstacles, economic as well as racial and sexist, with a modicum of grace.[24]

Recognizing the profound harm that results from the internalization of racist and sexist assumptions, specifically with regard to her pursuit of philosophy as a Black person and as a woman, she writes:

For my part, I am grateful that I enjoyed a protective shield long enough to work out my own defenses. Without such a shield the fulfillment of past goals— here I am thinking particularly of the long road to the PhD—would have been jeopardized. Kant and Hegel, not to mention Sartre, are difficult in their own right. Suppose my consciousness had been exposed to [William] Shockley's arguments on the one hand and male chauvinist propaganda on the other as I contemplated a career in philosophy. Very likely I should have regarded as my own obtuseness what I then quite correctly took to be the obtuseness of the writings themselves.[25]

And in a short article entitled "Who Harms My Soul," Cook observes:

I have argued for many years that the internalization of intimations—direct or indirect, real or imaginary—of racial inferiority is responsible for many, if not all, of the negative aspects that characterize the black experience in America. The greatest harm resulting from racial discrimination is measurable, not in terms of a lost economic opportunity (severe as such a loss is), but rather in terms of one's being made a lesser person than one otherwise would be.[26]

And in an unpublished paper entitled "Values: Black/White," Cook writes:

In my experience teaching black students I have observed that some are so brainwashed by the propaganda of racial inferiority they readily interpret any difficulty they may have in grasping certain ideas as proof of their intellectual inferiority. It seems to me that such students might well take to heart the statement Spinoza makes at the end of the *Ethics*, that "all things excellent are as difficult as they are rare." Even geniuses, white and black, we are told, work hard.[27]

What is clear from the aforementioned is that Cook understood all too well the dangers regarding the internalization of racist and sexist myths. Moreover, she highlights the myth of racial inferiority as an important aspect of how she theorized the Black experience vis-à-vis its historical context, though not reducing the Black experience to that aspect alone.

Cook's passion for philosophy would have functioned as an important rejoinder, as it were, to any racist and sexist assumptions about her philosophical abilities. For Cook, as noted previously, "reasoned discourse is my medium." She provides a personal confession that speaks to both her passion for philosophy and her recognition of what philosophy demands. She writes:

Soon I shall be forty. How rightly to divide time, when to say yes and when to say no to the thieves of time: these are the questions. The committee assignments, the demands of family and friends, present obligations as educator and administrator and piano lessons[28] all compete with a compelling interest in studying philosophy unencumbered. I no longer think it possible to combine my professional interest with marriage and family. Philosophy, it seems to me, is a jealous taskmaster. A special and rare person such as I have not encountered would be required to understand and accept its claims upon me.[29]

Cook also speaks about the price paid for pursuing philosophy. She says:

And the price is high, you see. I tell students the only reason to go on in philosophy is because your life is unthinkable without it, because you have to pursue questions that are traditionally regarded as philosophical questions. That's the only reason to go into it. And then, if you have that kind of interest, you don't care whether you will make a salary, find a job, or not, you see. Now, perhaps I'm too much influenced by my own background. At a time when I made the decision to go into philosophy, there were very few women in philosophy. I saw one woman philosopher; I had never read anything from women, you see. But, I had that kind of interest which I contritely characterized as an interest in, and it made me go on in philosophy. And I think that this is the kind of commitment that one has to make.[30]

Cook embodied a bold and defiant spirit. Yet, there is a nagging tension of awareness on her part of something that militated against her sense of spirited philosophical wonder and intellectual independence. She felt the weight of the history of racist and sexist hegemony. When asked about her identity as a *Black woman* and how she does philosophy, she quoted Boethius. Cook said:

Boethius said, "Had you remained silent, you would have passed as a philosopher." And I saw the bitter irony of applying that to me. It's a terrible thing to say about anybody. But what I'm saying is that I see a special irony in *my case, because whether I speak or whether I keep quiet I would not be taken for a philosopher.*[31]

Given Cook's awareness of the deep racist and sexist assumptions regarding Black women, her reconfiguration of Boethius' point is very insightful. On this score, for Cook, silence is no protection. One is still "trapped." When asked if there were specific obstacles that Black women must confront in professional philosophy, Adrian Piper said: "Oh definitely, yes. I think the primary problem is that everybody assumes that Black women are basically maids or prostitutes and so you have a lot to get over when you go into a philosophy department."[32] Or as Anita Allen shares, "Two very prominent [white] philosophers offered to look at my resume (I was flattered) and then asked to sleep with me (I was disturbed)."[33]

Highlighting her bold and defiant spirit, those who knew Cook report that it wasn't about the grades or the accolades that she received, but it was the learning itself that motivated her. Whenever I spoke with Cook about being the first African-American woman to receive the PhD in philosophy, she seemed nonchalant about it. The impression here was evident in her voice, in her responsive discourse.[34] Yet, there was something more complex going on in Cook's life. Was she nonchalant because of her humility or because she wasn't that concerned about being the first *Black woman* philosopher? My sense is that it may have been a combination of both. This doesn't mean that Cook didn't understand the importance of being the first Black woman to receive the PhD in philosophy, but my sense is that she wanted to be careful not to be seduced by racial forms of totalization that place under erasure the important ways in which she saw herself as someone engaged in the human project of attempting to understand what it means to be, to know, to seek meaning, to seek truth. The human quest, one that she would see as racially non-tribal, for truth and philosophical rigor motivated her. When asked about her worldview, Cook said:

> I would say that I have to create whatever value there is in my life. I reject a religious point of view. I think that I'm here to make sense of my life and to give meaning to it. Now, I have arrived at that point of view beyond any considerations about color. And I think that it is true of me, of a white person, of a red person. What else can I say that would be more significant than I did? You see, if race has nothing to do with my view of whether there is an afterlife or whatever; has nothing to do with those other questions for me, then these other things [race, blackness] are of lesser importance. I don't mean to repudiate a whole sociological theory.[35]

In fact, Cook says that it was African-American philosopher Eugene C. Holmes, and a few other philosophers, who first mentioned to her that she was the first Black woman to receive the PhD in philosophy when she was teaching at Howard University. She had not thought about it prior to this.

It is her humility with which I wish to linger. This is so incredibly instructive for us as scholars, in general, and philosophers, in particular. We can be so ego-driven; out to slaughter through philosophical argumentation our interlocutors. I've witnessed this. It can be disillusioning and discouraging. Philosophers can be cocksure; waiting eagerly to show us (and to show us up by) their so-called *sui generis* brilliance. As philosopher Adrian Piper states during a discussion of the dilemma of getting more Black women in the profession of philosophy:

> It's not only that you yourself have to be subject to these power plays, Machiavellian schemes of one-upmanship, back stabbing, . . . but it really destroys your ability to believe that the field is about what it says it's about.[36]

There is so much that Cook has to teach us as philosophers about humility, critical dialogue, and mentorship. I would certainly call her my mentor. This leads one to ask: who was there for Cook as a Black woman? Was she encouraged, beyond the efforts of Winston K. McAllister, to pursue issues in Black philosophy? Who was there to help her negotiate the space of a predominantly male philosophy department?[37] Who was there to support her publishing efforts or even help her to negotiate an effective path toward acquiring tenure? Who headed Cook's tenure committee? Were there insidious forms of unfair faculty/administrative use of power against Joyce? From my perspective, there is no reasonable explanation as to why Cook did not receive tenure at Howard.

It is so easy and misleading to peg philosophers into holes that we our-selves want them to fit. As I prepared for writing this chapter, and so decided to listen yet again to my interview with Cook, a richer account of her life and thinking emerged. At one point in our interview Cook says, "Where do I fit into all of this? I can't accept any view of the Black experience that does not somehow make me understand why my life is different."[38] Taken together with Cook's unpublished papers, what emerges is an understanding of her as a person who was shaped by a certain set of experiences that did not, from her perspective, qualify as *the* Black experience. For example, in an unpublished, undated, and untitled paper, Cook writes:

> The question that immediately suggested itself to me was "Whose experience is black experience?" I remember philosopher John Dewey's caution that it is always appropriate, when someone speaks of experience, to ask whose experi-ence one is talking about. The question was particularly urgent for me since I could not for the most part identify with the experience being described by writers on the black experience. When I encountered someone who, like Countee Cullen, asked "What is Africa to me?," I instead asked what has this so-called black American experience got to do with me? If I cannot make a connection, I thought, then I might be allowing myself to be defined out of the human race. My skin color is unmistakably black. "Black—so what?" was my visceral response, which a family member talked me out of saying in public for fear of retaliation in the . . . 1960s. Colloquialism aside, I genuinely was puzzled about claims about the black experience.[39]

During our interview, however, it was clear to me that Cook was passion-ate about engaging and formulating a critical understanding of "Black experi-ence." She noted:

> By the way, I'm still trying to understand that. And I, to that end, read as much as I can. I've read Black history, Black psychologists, anthropologists, geneti-cists. I've tried to read work on the arts. And, I've tried to read some philosophy. In that order. I discovered that philosophy has changed a lot in the 20 years that I've been out of it. It seems to me that fewer people seem to know what it is anymore.[40]

"Whose experience is black experience?" is Cook's way of critically engaging certain race essentialist assumptions. Wondering where she fits within the complex racial identificatory landscape is an important inquiry for Cook. As Black people, we continue to struggle with these issues, especially in the light of the dynamic influx of various racialized "Black" bodies that are deemed bereft of the "Black experience." Cook was attempting to make sense of her life through a set of racial categories that did not prima facie square with various aspects of her life experience. As I now think about

Cook working on the problem of the "Black experience," I realize that she was struggling at a deeply experiential level to make sense of her identity. She was raising important issues about the epistemic status of her lived experiences vis-à-vis the historical moment in which she found herself, and the historically produced categories within which she had to negotiate. She was raising significant issues regarding essentialism, the socially constructed nature of experiences, issues regarding history and geography, phenomenology, and hermeneutics. I now better appreciate what was at stake for Cook, both philosophically and personally regarding clarifying the meaning of the Black experience.

When I asked about one of the central concepts that she was exploring within the context of the Black experience, Cook stated that she was interested in what she called the "Black epiphany," which she defined as "a revelation that you are Black, with an awareness that this has racial consequences for the future."[41] She maintained that there are those who argue that the Black experience *is not* a comparative concept. She responded, "I argue vigorously against that."[42] So, here Cook is arguing that the Black experience presupposes a white racist anti-Black world, a world in which she is deemed a "problem" in virtue of being Black. She understood the contemporary ways in which Black people undergo anti-Black experiences, and she was very interested in looking at slave narratives as sites of testimony to racist barbarism. When I asked about her personal experiences of anti-Black racism, she said:

> Well. See, I was lagging when it came to that sort of thing. I think that the junior high school experience . . . [described later] would have qualified if I had drawn more of a conclusion from it than I did. That was something that was pointing up my difference through the eyes of my mother and what she told me. But I didn't draw from that that there was an entire sociological problem out here. *I didn't know that I was part of a problem, in DuBois' language.*[43]

Cook went on to say that she only had snatches of such experiences. She went on to argue that the "Black epiphany" has to "hurt you; it has to be something that you take away in a negative way."[44] Cook locates at least two such "snatches of experience" that made her aware of anti-Black racism. Keep in mind that Cook grew up in a predominantly white space in Sharon, Pennsylvania. Throughout her entire educational experience, she was surrounded by white people. And even as she did have such snatches of experience, she says:

> I put no value on it. I was always a logician. This is my perception of myself. I always evaluated what was said to me no matter who the source was. And I was a critic based on that. I learned at an early age not to take as gospel what anyone said. And I remember applying that to my parents and my grandparents.[45]

One of the experiences that Cook mentioned was that when she became editor of her high school newspaper, the title of the editor was changed from "Editor-in-Chief" to "Managing Editor." She said that the change occurred because of her having become editor, thus removing the more prestigious title. Another anti-Black experience that Cook identified was in junior high. She was supposed to be the *highest* honors student as a result of receiving all As. However, three other white students, who were her friends, were said to have all tied with her, though they had not received all As. Cook says:

> At that point, my mother told me that my oldest brother and second oldest had also won the highest honor, but that they wouldn't give it to them, because the honor carried with it a year's membership in the private Boys' Club (or Girls' Club). Since the Club didn't have any Black members, they just didn't acknowledge my brothers having achieved the highest honors.[46]

So, Cook didn't receive the highest honors award, though she was Valedictorian in high school. Yet, a year after graduating, Cook went back to the school and was told that even this honor was given to her only after a number of teachers threatened to resign if she had not received the status of Valedictorian. Regarding the situation of being denied the highest honors award, Cook recalled:

> And my mother told me this only because she said she hoped that when I went to high school it would not discourage me as it had my brothers. But I told my mother that I was not studying in order to get grades. That's what I said and that's want I meant. I would say that it did not damage me in any way. I remember thinking that I will sleep well that night, but the Principal will not because he had done the wrong thing as my mother had made me understand it. But I'm not sure I would have even known that. She never mentioned race much. And I can see why; her mother looked white. Her mother was not white, but she looked white. She could pass for white. And my mother was very fair, but you would not mistake my mother as white.[47]

Again, referring to having not been granted the highest honors, Cook was clear: "That did not start me on the road toward consciousness of race. I dismissed it. If you said something that didn't make sense to me, I tended to dismiss it."[48]

Cook made it clear that she came to the philosophical question of the Black experience as late as 1970 when she was thirty-seven years old and that Howard University functioned as an important catalyst. She says:

> At that point, being at Howard and there is a student revolution out there, [it] was the first time that I'm hearing about people like W. E. B. DuBois. I never heard of him. I never heard of Alain Locke. I never heard of any of these Black

people with the exception of George Washington Carver and Booker T. Washington. In Sharon, Pennsylvania, in the syllabus in the schools in those days I believe that I ran across those two names.[49]

What Cook knew or didn't know about Black people, about Black history, was not a failure on her part, but the failure of an educational system to recognize the contributions made to America and the world by Black people and people of color. Sharing an important catalyst regarding her exploration of the Black experience during her time at Howard, she says:

In 1970, I was asked to give a paper at the University of Illinois, Chicago Circle. My chair [who was Winston K. McAllister at the time] was pulling my arm and I said "I don't know anything about this." And he thought that I would do just fine. [The paper] was a "Critique of Black Experience"; very presumptuous, I now know. I got some positive feedback, especially from [Paul] Weiss. Some Black people in the audience came up and said that they wished that they had thought of these things. So, I consider that positive.[50]

Cook also points to Frantz Fanon as essential to her work on the Black experience, though she is careful not to reduce the Black experience *in toto* to a negative framing.

I went on to propose a characterization of the Black experience. It was based very closely on something that Frantz Fanon had said, but I had expanded on. And that was the Black experience is the internalization of intimations of racial inferiority. I still think that there is something in that in so far as it is a topic of concern to anyone. I don't think that it would be singled out for discussion anyway if there was not some problem that is connected with all of that. I had to ask myself, "Where do I fit in all of this, even though I know that my experience is atypical." Subsequently, I gave a paper at Springhill College, a Jesuit school in Mobile, Alabama. And the thrust of my remarks were different, but I did trot out this notion of the Black experience. The chair, after the meeting was over, asked me if I had the experience that I was talking about and I said no, although I had been close enough to it to perceive it. There was kind of a smirk on his face. But I can turn that around: My skin is Black, shades of Black, you know, and I have to make sense of all of my experiences with Black people.[51]

By 1972, in an unpublished article, Cook articulates the role of the philosopher vis-à-vis anti-Black racism:

If we suppose that a strict philosophical analysis is not possible, must the philosopher remain silent while the color line projects itself as the problem of the twenty-first century? I think not; if as philosophers we cannot solve the problem of the color line, we may perhaps form some service to those who can and will by "irrevocably" joining "critical intelligence as an instrument and racial responsibility as a principle."[52]

Furthermore, in 1974, as the W. E. B. DuBois Fellow in the Department of Philosophy, and as a Faculty Research Associate in the Division of Behavioral Science Research, at Tuskegee Institute, Cook gave an address entitled "The Search For Personal Identity" where she critiques Orlando Patterson's "The Moral Crisis of the Black American." Arguing against what appears to be victim blaming ideology, she writes that the systematically applied restrictions against Black people are "a factual matter beyond dispute."[53] She also writes, "Seek ye first the kingdom of moral responsibility and political equality will be added unto you appears to me at best naïve, at worse harmful to the cause of black liberation."[54]

Cook also critiqued the Black experience in terms of its "unqualified" link to Africa. She said: "I also question the African connection. I mean, why not go radical?"[55] And here she references Søren Kierkegaard. She says that Kierkegaard posed the following question: "If your eternal salvation depended on it, would you accept the word of someone else that you had been baptized as an infant?"[56] Cook continues:

> I look at the evidence. What is the African connection? Going radical is even questioning the African connection. There are some people who want to embrace African values, but I'm saying what is that connection based on. I'm questioning pre-history, and I'm urging that the pre-history of Black Americans is in America.[57]

Cook's critical engagement with the meaning of the Black experience was not limited to its configuration in the United States; she was interested in important issues of historical, cultural origins. When asked about the social construction of the concept of race, Cook said:

> The concept of race is not useful to scientists; neither is the concept of God. I don't see that getting rid of race in our language or our thinking is going to get rid of the problems that we think that we have at times.[58]

So, Cook is arguing that despite the social constructed nature of race, its non-referential status, the social reality of race can and does continue. Because race doesn't cut at the joints of reality, this does not ipso facto mean that we inhabit a "post-racial" world; the social ontology of race/racism can and does persist. It is clear that Cook brought philosophical rigor to her attempt to understand not only the concept of the Black experience, but also racism. Her proclivity toward rigor is linked to her early upbringing. Indeed, it was within a familial context of daily debate that Cook grew up and was nurtured. She stated: "If you say something and there is a hole [in it], [it was said that] a Mitchell is going to drive through it."[59]

My interview with Cook was broad and multifaceted. For example, after discussing the issue regarding the ontological status of race, I asked Cook if she thought that philosophy put us in touch with something metaphysically absolute. Cook said:

> Well, I think that we should be satisfied in our claims to knowledge, have our reference be language. But I do believe that there is something beyond us. I don't believe that reality is entirely mind-independent. I always thought that people misunderstood Kant, the critics, I mean. I always thought that he was not denying a reality independent of mind, but that he was denying that we could know anything about it.[60]

Asked about the possible existence of God, one that transcends our experiences, a kind of "noumenal God," Cook responded:

> I'm more comfortable saying that I'm an agnostic than saying that I'm an atheist. And, as I get older, after all, and I will be 63 soon, down the road I don't see anything changing my mind. I would be ashamed of myself if I had a Bergsonian death-bed conversion.[61]

She laughed as she repeated those lines—"I would be ashamed of myself." Yet, Cook was an avid reader of the Bible. She shared that she once won an important Bible prize: "It was a contest in the whole valley. There were all sorts of esoteric questions about the Bible. I knew the Bible so well. I used to memorize just about everything that I came in contact with."[62]

Toward the end of our interview, following up on the issue of philosophy's access to reality *simpliciter*, I asked Cook about Richard Rorty's understanding of philosophy. This seemed to be a logical next step. She said:

> I don't agree with Rorty. [He], by the way, was a colleague of mine at Wellesley. But I read him because I asked Paul Weiss, "whom should I read?" And he mentioned Rorty and [Alasdair] McIntyre. I read *Philosophy and the Mirror of Nature* when it came out. You know, Rorty attacks the privileged position, but I think that he is wrong. I have another model of philosophy in my mind. You see, there are a lot of difficulties with my own conception because daily I struggle with the fact that I have thousands of notecards here, and I'm trying to take into account so many points of view. But there is a fallacy that is involved that because it is difficult for me that it can't be done or it ought not to be done.[63]

Later in the interview, Cook shared:

> I think that I'm probably back at square one. I sometimes have this sense of wonder [like] when I was just a kid, you know? I still have that and it still

motivates me to want to find out, "Well what do they think about this or what do they think about that and how does it all fit together?" At one point I was studying cognitive dissonance. I don't like [to be in a state of] cognitive dissonance.[64]

This last statement by Cook is revealing. She grappled with the concept of the Black experience for many years. It wasn't just *philosophical* puzzles that Cook was trying to solve, but a cognitive dissonance that was due to the juxtaposition between her actual lived experience within predominantly white spaces and the historical frames of reference that came replete with so many racialized social and value-laden assumptions, expectations, scripts, and horizons.

The scholarship on Cook has only just begun. As the first full-length article to date, my hope is that this chapter will encourage philosophers to begin to ask critical questions regarding Cook's philosophical corpus and to further explore her life and philosophical intuitions. I don't end this chapter with a delineated set of propositions regarding what Cook thought about the "Black experience," but have engaged a number of ideas, implications. My objective was to bring together important and very suggestive ideas that Cook held regarding the "Black experience." Another aim was to pull from Cook's published and unpublished writings to create a far more complex and manifold view of what she had to say regarding a number of important philosophical concepts. Feeling a bit like Diogenes Laërtius, I desire that Cook's philosophical ideas are preserved and that she is given full recognition. This is both a labor of love and a gift to a dear friend.

Chapter 18

The Pain and Promise of Being Black Women in Philosophy with Anita L. Allen at "The Stone," *The New York Times*

George Yancy: When I interviewed you more than twenty years ago for my 1998 book, *African-American Philosophers, 17 Conversations*, I asked you how African-American women had fared in the field of philosophy. Your response was very clear: "Extraordinarily badly." Why did you hold that view then, and has it changed?

Anita L. Allen: Let me preface my answer by noting it was an honor to have been included in your landmark book of interviews with African-American philosophers. Because I went to Harvard Law School after getting my PhD in Philosophy from the University of Michigan, I am sometimes viewed more as a lawyer than a philosopher. An active, licensed member of the Pennsylvania Bar and a member of the New York Bar, my official primary academic appointment is in the law school at the University of Pennsylvania. But, I view myself as very much a part of the philosophical community. I was pleased that you see me that way too. That said, my interview with you got me into trouble! One person thought I stereotyped Black women as tragically torn between heart and head—wanting family and wanting successful careers in philosophy, but unable to have both. A couple of others thought I was flat out advising African-American women to reject philosophy.

Why, two decades ago, did I say that women have fared "extraordinarily badly" in philosophy? Behind the remark were the personal stories, as I knew them, of the first half dozen women who entered the field. The first group of Black women to get PhDs in philosophy attended top universities. Angela Davis studied at the Humboldt University of Berlin. Joyce Mitchell Cook attended Yale University. Adrian Piper and Michele Moody-Adams went to Harvard University. I went to University of Michigan; LaVerne Shelton went to University of Wisconsin. Georgette Sinkler was a product of Cornell

University. Brilliant and rigorously trained, African-American women often faced rejection. Angela Davis was unlawfully fired by the University of California, Los Angeles in 1970, for her radical politics; Joyce Mitchell Cook was denied tenure at Howard University, an HBCU. LaVerne Shelton, now an inspiring poet, was denied tenure at Rutgers University, and left academia in the 1996. Adrian Piper, who got her PhD the same year I got mine, was denied tenure at University of Michigan, and, after a series of other good jobs in philosophy, retired to a massively successful international career as an artist. Michele Moody-Adams, Georgette Sinkler, and I avoided the trauma of tenure denials. Yet, as survivors, even flourishers, we faced bias related to our race and gender.

My perspective on philosophy and Black women has changed because the discipline has changed. I would point to two striking signs of change. First, as of July 1 (2018), I will be the President of the Eastern Division of the American Philosophical Association, elected last summer. I am the first Black woman to have this role, but I am sure I will not be the last. Second, there is a lively Collegium of Black Women Philosophers, a group organized by Kathryn Sophia Belle (formerly Kathryn T. Gines) at Penn State. The Collegium celebrated its tenth anniversary last fall, with a keynote by Angela Davis, as a place where African-American women can come to present their ideas in their own, unguarded voices. A few dozen women—some students, most faculty, a couple of freelancers, show up every time. It's terrific.

Yancy: Congratulations on such a significant and well-deserved position. While I hear your optimism, I continue to hear from undergraduate Black female students and female students of color about how they are discouraged from majoring in philosophy because the field doesn't speak to their philosophical passions. For example, they want to read more about Black feminist philosophy and be able to see themselves mirrored in what is still a predominantly white and male profession. I empathize and yet I want them to pursue philosophy. What should we say to them to keep them from getting discouraged?

Allen: To your general question, people get discouraged when they fail repeatedly at efforts to achieve a goal. I would like to know if this is happening to women trying to get training and jobs in philosophy. If they are failing, why are they failing? I suspect women are not being discouraged by patterns of personal failure, as much as by a lack of apparent opportunity. People get discouraged from making certain efforts where opportunity is limited by forces of history, traditions, social roles, and stereotypes. If my daughter wanted to become a philosopher, she would need to hear words of encouragement similar to those she would need to hear if she wanted to become a plumber, heart surgeon, or politician: it is very hard for women, it's even harder for African-American women, but you are smart and strong enough to do it, and I am here to help you. In addition to words of encouragement, young women benefit from role models, mentors, and financial resources. You are right to emphasize barriers but encourage pursuit.

I would add a message about the exciting, broad array of professions and careers open to women, many of which would engage their talents and interests as well as or better than philosophy. And help them meet their needs. Let's recognize our value. Put the burden on philosophy to make the case for us, rather than always assuming it's our job to prove we are worthy of philosophy. I share the commitment of the APA to support Philosophy in an Inclusive Key Summer Institute (PIKSI), and other efforts to recruit philosophers of all backgrounds. The University of Michigan, Brown University, and the University of San Diego have summer programs. Rutgers University hosted the twentieth Annual Summer Institute for Diversity in Philosophy in 2018. The University of Pittsburgh hosts A Summer Program in Philosophy of Science for Underrepresented Groups. Princeton hosted Athena in Action 2018: A Networking and Mentoring Workshop for Graduate Student Women in Philosophy. I have signed on to be an Athena in Action faculty mentor this summer.

Yancy: You mentioned Adrian Piper. As you know, she was the first African-American tenured philosopher in the United States. I recall asking her about some of the obstacles that Black women face in philosophy and she was rightly critical of what she saw as a racist and sexist perception of Black women in philosophy as "maids or prostitutes."[1] What's your sense of this? Do Black women in philosophy continue to be stereotyped in such denigrating ways?

Allen: Adrian Piper and I were colleagues at Georgetown University in the late 1980s. We were close friends for about a decade. I shared with her my stories of denigration, which may have contributed to what she said to you. My dissertation chairman was Richard Brandt. Once, after I had earned the PhD and was meeting with him, he stood over me, lifted my chin toward him and remarked that I looked like a maid his family once employed. About the same time period, early in the Ronald Reagan administration, an effort was made to rid central DC of the sex trade and shops that flourished along the 14th Street corridor a few blocks from the White House. I worked in nearby McPherson Square at the National Endowment for the Humanities, and as a volunteer at the NAACP Legal Defense Fund. One day I was walking near my office with a white male friend, an Ivy League PhD philosopher. We were stopped by the police who assumed I was a hooker and he a john. I had to answer questions and show ID. You may ask, is the denigration of Black women philosophers a thing of the past? Are we beyond being asked to fetch coffee for department chairs and worse? Regrettably, no. In October 2017 a very senior Harvard-educated white male philosopher, whose wife is also a philosopher, wrote to me seeking feedback on an op-ed he hoped to submit to *The New York Times* or the *Washington Post*. He did not like my feedback. He ended an email lamenting his lack of success getting more than "duncical shit" as feedback on his work by letting me know that he had recently seen my face in the photographs he used in masturbation! Incredible, right? I wrote back to explain why I was offended and to sever ties. I have to assume that if such things happen to me, some very, very serious harassment and racism must be happening to young women in the field.

Yancy: All of those experiences are degrading, Anita. Concerning the third one, though, he could have kept that to himself. Why would he feel the need to tell you this? Was it about control and dehumanization? Was it about impunity on his part? I think that we also need to keep in mind that he is white and that he shared it. This does not escape the history of white men and the racist depiction of Black women as "Jezebels." Please speak to these issues.

Allen: This all happened right about the time Harvey Weinstein fell from grace. For years I put up with demeaning comments from this individual. I should have let my true feelings be known and kept a greater distance. The email was the last straw. Ironically, although he came to me out of the blue for help with his article, when I was an Assistant Professor he had discouraged me from philosophy doubting, to my face, that I had "enough candle power (i.e., intellect) for philosophy" but saying I had "too much juice (i.e., sensuality) for philosophy." Unable to achieve intellectual domination, he attempted sexual domination to preserve the upper hand. The lack of respect for me and my marriage was infuriating. The lack of respect for his own marriage disturbed me, too. Cunning and disloyal, he had copied his wife and another senior woman philosopher on the original email asking for my help, but did not copy them on the defeated email in which he referenced his masturbation practice. To your point about sexual harassment and race bias, the lascivious Jezebel stereotype remains relevant to understanding the treatment of Black women.

Yancy: Are there obstacles that Black women and women of color face within academia, more generally, that white women and Black men don't?

Allen: Are you trying to pick a fight? Just kidding. We know that there are pay equity and status gaps between women and men that favor men, and that white women are better represented and perhaps more easily accepted in philosophy than women of color. However, everyone faces obstacles along the way, and I do not know that being a Black woman is necessarily a greater obstacle to career success than being a white woman or a Black man. I have known a white woman philosopher who was blind, and another who used a wheelchair. I have known a Black male philosopher who had to hide his sexual orientation for many years. My obstacles were not, and cannot be reduced just to my race and dark color, they include that my parents started out as penniless teenagers, high school dropouts living in the Deep South, their first child born when they were only sixteen. Other obstacles along my road have included parenting challenges and cancer.

Yancy: Earlier you mentioned recruiting and retaining African-American women within philosophy. To do so, it seems to me, also requires a shift in philosophical themes that reflect many of the social and political realities of Black women. I think that this is what my African-American undergraduate female students are getting at regarding the desire for Black feminist thought appearing more on the philosophical syllabus, as it were.

Allen: Philosophy departments that aspire to be inclusive of Black women can succeed if they take the time to learn about emerging and emergent trends, advertise positions for philosophical fields people of color specialize in, and expand curricula to incorporate what Black philosophers do. This is already starting to happen. The syllabus of the discipline is expanding. As you know, because of the work you have done, during the past sixty years new fields of specialization have emerged, variously termed Philosophy of Race, African-American philosophy, Africana philosophy, critical philosophy of race, Black feminist/Womanist thought, and so on. These have appeared in tandem with an increase in the number of professionally trained philosophers of Black descent. Among the APA's estimated 10,000 PhD trained philosophers in the United States today, an estimated 125 are Black, and 38 are Black women.

Back when I was a graduate student teaching assistant, a Black student approached me and asked why I didn't teach Black philosophy. I gave the then standard answer that philosophy addresses universal themes applicable to everyone. But it has proven really hard for undergrads to see why Plato's allegory of the cave, or Leibniz's windowless monads, or even Rawls' theory of liberal justice matter enough to make philosophy their majors or life's work. Tokenism in moral and political philosophy has proven unworkable as a method of inclusion. Devoting a class or two to affirmative action, and others to criminal punishment is not the way to make African-Americans feel included. Women need more than a class on abortion to feel that philosophy is a relevant and important discipline.

Some contemporary African-American philosophers teach and write about topics that do not explicitly or directly relate to African or African-American history and culture, in the traditional fields of philosophy like metaphysics and epistemology. A greater number of African-American academically employed philosophers publish scholarly articles and books on topics directly related to race or other aspects of the African-American experience. Indeed, at some point in their careers, most African-American philosophers seem to have found themselves deeply engaged in "social analysis" that deals with what M. L. King, Jr., as he sat in jail in Birmingham, referred to as "the hard, brutal and unbelievable facts" of the case.[2] Work by Black philosophers has addressed what philosopher Angela Davis identified from her jail cell as the ignorance of those who purport fairly and objectively to judge and legislate concerning Blacks while having "absolutely no idea" about the depth of African-American deprivation and vulnerability.

As I discovered when I set out to put together a course for Penn, "African-American Philosophy Since 1960," African-American philosophers have been critiquing law and government; analyzing power, and institutions and practices of oppression, subordination, slavery, class, caste, colonialism, racism, sexism, and homophobia; articulating the basis of African-American identities and the grounds of responsibility, community, solidarity, and collective action; expressing African-American existential, spiritual, psychological, and moral joys and discontents; celebrating and interpreting African-American art and culture; and assessing the discipline, the canon and history of Western philosophies, by reference to gaps, logical, and moral inconsistencies, methodological limitations, epistemologies, and exclusions. As our numbers grow, we can expect to see more Black feminist philosophy. Trails are being blazed by senior Black feminist philosopher Joy James, on the faculty of Williams College, and by junior scholar Lindsey Stewart, at the University of Memphis, among others.

Yancy: As President of the Eastern Division of the APA, what is your vision in terms of tackling such issues as we've been discussing?

Allen: I am excited about working with the APA, currently as a member of the Board of Directors and later as a President (2018). I am impressed by the ways in which the philosophers involved in the APA are working together toward a more inclusive professoriate that recognizes the contributions of racial and ethnic minorities, LGBTQ+ community members, and of part-time and adjunct faculty. The APA and its three divisions, Eastern, Central, and Pacific, boast diverse leadership teams. A standing Committee on the Inclusiveness of the Profession addresses issues of diversity and inclusion in the organization and the profession. The organization continues to have active Committees at the national level, devoted to the flourishing of Black, Asian/Pacific, Hispanic/Latinx, and Native/Indigenous Groups. As for the core intellectual mission of the APA, the program committees work toward annual meetings that reflect the changing demographics of the profession, as well as new methods and the growth of new specialties and sub-fields. In short, my vision is for a more inclusive and self-aware profession; a senior leadership that is more consistently and intentionally engaged with the public and that serves as strong ambassadors for our vital share of the Humanities.

Yancy: But how might you (we) specifically impact a greater awareness of the forms of male violence either against well-established women in the field of philosophy or female graduate students?

Allen: You are not going to let me end our conversation on an artificially cheerful note. We must acknowledge that sexual harassment, stalking, and sexual assault by academics are a reality. Philosophers in the academy are no exception. To achieve greater awareness, academic leaders have to be willing to speak openly about our degrading experiences as well as our soaring successes. Mentoring junior faculty and students should include facts and "lessons learned" about unconscious bias and mistreatment. In our roles as department chairs, deans, vice provosts, provosts, and presidents, we have to work to push for norms and policies that make the academic realm safer. I am troubled that so many universities hold on to policies from decades past that permit faculty to date and have sex with students, even undergraduates. The APA has recently sought to make sexual harassment less likely at its annual meetings by, for example, prohibiting job interviews in convention hotel bedrooms. Those of us involved in the APA leadership and the leadership of other philosophy associations should continue to press for change.

Chapter 19

Hateful Speech: The Perils of Being a Black Philosopher with Brad Evans at "The Stone," *The New York Times*

Brad Evans: In response to a series of troubling verbal attacks you received following your "Dear White America" op-ed, which concluded the series on race in this column, the American Philosophical Association (APA) put out a strongly worded statement criticizing the bullying and harassment of academics in the public realm. While the APA statement has been important in terms of highlighting the perils you personally faced in the efforts to confront injustice, some debate has arisen in respect to some of the key terms deployed. Not least the complicated lines between free speech and bullying. Instead of dwelling upon these academic points of contention, however, which often separate verbal assault from physical abuse, might it not be more considered to address the all too human realities of such hateful speech? In particular by questioning how discursive violence impacts directly upon the body of the person attacked?

George Yancy: Your point about discursive violence is an important one. Immediately after the publication of "Dear White America," I began to receive vile and vitriolic comments sent to my university email address, and verbal messages sent to my answering machine. I even received letters sent through the postal service that were filled with hatred. Imagine the time put into actually sitting down and writing a letter filled with so much hate and then mailing it off, especially in our world of the Internet. The comments were not about pointing out fallacies in my position, but were designed to violate, to attempt to leave me psychologically broken, and physically distraught. Words do things, especially words like "nigger," or being called a subhuman animal. One white supremacist message sent to me ended with, "Be Prepared." The discourse was threateningly "apocalyptic" in tone. I have been called "nigger" hundreds of times since the publication of the article.

The impact of that term, especially when you're called it over and over again, has a way of inflicting injury.

Given the history of the term, one feels the brutal racist longevity and hate-filled context of violence out of which that term grew. This points to the nonspectacular expression of violence. The lynching of Black people was designed to be a spectacle, to draw white mobs. In this case, the Black body was publicly violated. It was a public and communal form of bloodlust. There are many other forms of violence that are far more subtle, nonspectacular, but yet painful and dehumanizing. So, when I was called a "nigger," I felt violated, injured; a part of me felt broken. One person left a message that began with "Dear Nigger Professor." Another person left a message saying, "Somebody needs to put a boot up your ass and knock your fucking head off your shoulders." Only now have I really begun to recognize how discourse designed to hurt can actually leave its mark. I recall after reading so many messages such as the ones noted here that I began to feel sick, literally. So, words can debilitate, violate, injure; they can hit with the force of a stick or a stone and leave marks on the body. In this case, I began to feel the posture of my body folding inward, as it were, under the attacks. Frantz Fanon talks about this as not being able to move lithely in the world.

Evans: What you describe evidently points to something far more pernicious than the routine attacks often leveled at public intellectuals and critical thinkers who have the courage to speak truth to power. How does this relate to the intellectual history of racial persecution, oppression, and subordination, especially the denial of the right of Black people, and specifically Black intellectuals, to speak with their own voice in a public setting?

Yancy: I shared some of the malicious discourse used against me with some very prominent white public intellectuals. There was a brief exchange. The exchange was helpful to me; it helped me to understand what is at stake when engaging in courageous speech. What was immediately clear, though, was the absence of specifically racist vitriol directed at these white public intellectuals, which in no way downplays their pain. Yet, we must bring attention to the difference, to the perils of being a *Black* intellectual. Not only was I being attacked for my courageous speech; I was being attacked as a *Black man*. Yet, I was also being attacked as a *Black* philosopher. There were some very nasty remarks that were designed to question my status as a philosopher because I'm Black. The implication of those messages was that to be Black *and* a philosopher was a contradiction, because "niggers" can't be philosophers. So, yes, the discourse was far more racially pernicious. But to understand this is to come to terms with the history of white violence in this country used to control and silence Black people. To conceptualize what I experienced as episodic and anomalous is to deny the logic of the long history of white racist violence. Recall that bell hooks, as a child, says she thought of whiteness as a site of terror. In a country in which white people would brutalize and kill a Black person on a whim, it is far from irrational to see whiteness as a site of terror.

While 9/11 was a tragic and horrible moment for the United States, it is not the case that this was the first terrorist attack on African-Americans. For centuries, Black people lived in fear of white terror. That fear partly captures the contradiction of being Black and an American. It is important that Black people name the reality of their experiences under white supremacy. The naming process helps to complicate how the American "we" is defined. Black people were not the American "we," but the terrorized other. The symbols of white sheets and cross burnings must be recalled. Think here of Black WWII veterans who returned home from the war and were severely beaten and lynched by whites, even as they wore their uniforms. They fought against Hitler only to return home, to the land of "democracy," to be attacked by what I would call white terrorists. Or think here of the slave trade, the institution of American slavery, Black codes, convict leasing, the lynching of Black men and women and the flaying of Black flesh, the castration of Black men, being burned alive. Violence, within these contexts, is a specific racialized form of inculcating Black people with fear, and controlling their social mobility. There is nothing episodic about it; this form of white violence is historically grounded, systemic, and systematic. Personally, I will never allow the United States to forget its history, and current manifestations, of white supremacy, white violence against Black people.

The coldhearted use of white violence was very effective. Not only was one actually beaten, but there was the fear of possibly being beaten. So, the Black imagination, though never defeated, was weakened. The lynching of a Black person wasn't just a form of theater (where the root meaning suggests a kind of "beholding"), but a way of communicating fear and terror through mass displays of violence. For someone white, the spectacle was a sport, a kind of national pastime activity, but for a Black person, one could always imagine that "one is next," and thereby stand in fear of what *could* happen at any moment.

Cornel West insightfully delineates what he calls the "death shudder." It is a deep existential moment of realization that one is finite, that death is inevitable. I think that as human beings, though many of us attempt to flee that existential fact, we are all open to experience that dreadful sense of our existence coming to an end. However, when Black life is forever in a "state of exception," it is an additional weight. Black people not only experience the death shudder, but a specific kind of shudder that involves an emotional intensity that speaks to the disposability of Black life, the valuing of Black life on the cheap in this country.

Evans: These connections between the continuum of racial violence and the terrors of the everyday are crucial to understanding the normalization of humiliation and the outright denial of the most basic qualities that make people feel part of a society and "human" as such. This demands a more serious intellectual engagement with the "marking out" of the Black body as something incapable of philosophical thought and deliberation. Not least, how do we conceptualize political rights, including the most important, the right to critique? Does this make a return to Frantz Fanon all the more relevant in the contemporary period?

Yancy: Yes. And racial violence takes many forms and raises larger issues. For example, of importance is Judith Butler's concern about questions of grievability. Racial violence is inextricably linked to forms of racial vulnerability, disposability, and our tendency as a nation to grieve the deaths of certain racialized persons and not others. The disproportionate number of poor Black people affected by Hurricane Katrina, or the sentencing disparities when it comes to locking up Black people for nonviolent offenses, or the shooting in the back of fifty-year-old Black male Walter Scott by white police officer Michael Slager are all examples of forms of racialized disposability. They speak to how Black humanity is deemed of little or no human value. These examples are manifestations of a racialized, selective misanthropy. This is why I have such a negative visceral reaction to Donald Trump's promises to build a wall along the Mexican border. That discourse is one of labeling certain bodies as "unwanted," "deviant," "sub-persons." And to say that Mexico is sending "rapists" to the United States is a form of deep insult, of marking certain bodies as violent and pathological. Trump is, sadly, able to play on the racist biases and fears in many people. It is a divisive tactic that exploits both latent and manifest bigoted assumptions in many white Americans. It is not by accident that David Duke, a former Grand Wizard of the KKK, supports him.

And the process of marking the Black body as incapable of philosophical thought is long-standing. It is one of those major myths that grew out of Europe, even as Europe championed "humanism." Negritude poet Aime Cesaire, through immanent critique, knew that European humanism was a farce. Of course, Jean-Paul Sartre knew this as well. And Fanon knew what it was like to embody reason and have it denied to him. In *Black Skin, White Masks*, he argued that when he was present, reason was not and when reason was present he was no longer. So, one might argue that reason and Black embodiment, from this perspective, are mutually exclusive. And yet, at the end of that text, Fanon says, "My final prayer: O my body, make me always a man who questions!"[1] Fanon seems to appeal to something that is beyond abstract political rights discourse. He appeals to his own body, something concrete and immediate. Fanon asks of his body not to allow him to be seduced by forms of being-in-the-world that normalize violence and dehumanization. Doubt can be linked to critique. In a society that hides beneath the seductions of normalization, critique is undesirable and deemed dangerous. Yet, in our contemporary moment, the fulfillment of Fanon's prayer is desperately needed.

Evans: As you point out, a conceptualization of political rights must also include the right for the marginalized to critique power. Does philosophical inquiry have to do with the ways we might reconceptualize the meaning of rights, especially considering that the denial of persons' humanity often occurs within normative legal frameworks?

Yancy: Absolutely. After all, slavery, which was a vicious, death-dealing, and violent institution, was legal. I think that rights-based discourse is necessary, but there is this sense in which rights can be given and, by implication, taken away. Within this context, I think that America needs a movement that transcends the Civil Rights Movement. Applicative justice might be necessary, but not sufficient. Imagine a scenario where justice is being applied across the board, and the rights of people are being upheld. In a country like ours, saturated by racism, that scenario might still involve Blacks being hated, seen as "inferior," as "sub-persons." In such a world, white people can continue to insulate themselves from the Black "others."

We are desperately in need of a movement that shakes us at the very core of how we think about ourselves as individuals, masters of our own destiny. While this isn't philosophically fashionable, I want to know what it means to love with courage. What would it mean to make love an integral feature of moral reasoning, the kind of love that risks profound ways of being mutually vulnerable, of placing no limits on who we call our neighbors? This means radically changing how we currently relate to one another. I recall when we killed Osama bin Laden in 2011 that there were Americans who were cheering. As unpatriotic as some will say I'm being, we must keep in mind that bin Laden was someone's son, father, and husband.

This speaks to the limits of our moral imagination as a nation. Can you imagine President Obama saying at a press conference that he is sorry that we killed bin Laden, that we loved him as a human being despite his violence? Can you imagine what would happen if Israelis and Palestinians were to cease their "peace" talks and radically deploy a discourse of love? Imagine the many whites who read "Dear White America" saying to me: "We return the love to you that you've shared with us!" I think that we are an impoverished nation when it comes to loving our "enemies." God bless America is an empty politicized gesture if we are not also saying God bless our "enemies."

Evans: There is an ethical aspect to "Dear White America"—particularly the honest reflections put forward regarding your own prejudices and fallibilities when it comes to relations of power. While a critique of violence demands attention to historical forces of domination and exploitation, it also asks how all of us shamefully compromise with power, often against our better judgments.

Yancy: Yes. This raises the issue of complicity. As I discussed in the essay, there are ways in which I have been shaped to believe that looking at women with a dominating gaze or desiring women only for sexual pleasure is "normal." Yet it is this process of "normalization" that produces a kind of "walking dead" mentality where many of my social practices (sexual desire being one, fixed gender role expectations being another) support the oppression of women. The process of normalization is often so effective that there isn't much resistance coming from one's "better judgment," especially as one's better judgment has already been defined by the terms of normalization.

In this case, one's "better judgment" has already been compromised, has already become an extension of the power of normalization. Your use of the term shameful is important. Shame implies a powerful sense of disgrace. It is not limited to the assignment of blame, which is more like guilt. Shame suggests the sense of disrupting one's ethical "certainty," or business as usual. After all, one can be guilty without ever feeling shame. So, violence, for me, has to be attended to at those levels where we are going about our business as if we are not doing violence to other individuals.

The fact that we don't hear cries of pain doesn't let us off the hook. Ethical discourse and practice must be imbued with an effort to remain honest, especially about one's own ethical shortcomings and the pain and suffering that we cause others.

A critique of violence must include an understanding that one doesn't escape the many ways in which one perpetuates violence—violence against those who we may never see face to face, violence against those who are closest to us, violence against the earth, and perhaps even violence against one's own sense of self-integrity.

Violence is all around us. Yet we prefer to remain asleep—the walking dead. For me, personally, the more I become aware of the magnitude of violence in our world, what many of us would rather deny or not see, the more I enter into that space of the "dark night of the soul," a place where dread and hopelessness reside. The objective, though, is to continue, to remain awake, to keep fighting for a better world even as one endures the dark night of the soul.

Part 4

MEANING-MAKING AND THE GENERATIVE SPACE OF BLACK PERFORMATIVE DISCOURSE

The chapters within this section, and their common assumption about communities and their dynamic discursive practices, point back to my conversation with Maria del Guadalupe Davidson in chapter 13. When I was a graduate student at Yale University, I was convinced that I would write my dissertation on some aspect of language. As stated earlier, philosopher Georgia Warnke's course on hermeneutics had such an important impact on my thinking at that time. In fact, I was interested in writing on religious speech acts, trying to figure out their meaning, how they were intended, the emotional content communicated through them, how they compared to poetic and scientific discourse, their epistemic status, and their truth-value. At that time, given my assumptions, I would have defended some form of fideism that supported the view that religious discourse was certainly *meaningful*, but embedded within its own community of intelligibility, where "scientific claims" were part of a different community of intelligibility. Hence, I emphasized the importance of religious life-worlds and how they were generative and spiritually edifying practices that were largely shaped by the logics, pragmatics, and norms embedded within those life-worlds. Of course, I was conceptually troubled by the incommensurability and forms of relativism that seem to result from the idea that there are autonomous forms of religious life that are predicated upon *their own* "truth-claims." This background information speaks to the ways in which I've come to think about the significance of Black cultural practices, broadly construed, as matrices of meaning-making, speech acts, stylizations, and embedded forms of cognition. At the time, I could not envision the overall impact, both explicit and implicit, that the course on hermeneutics would have on shaping the background assumptions that I brought to bear on Black culture.

Each chapter within this section engages cultural spaces of Black discursivity and the ways in which Black people have created modes of expression and cultural practices that point to their agency, meaning-making, and cultural world-making. What better section to end on—a space of Black cultural and Black identificatory fecundity. Within our current political climate, where unabashed white supremacy is on the rise and where the POTUS himself has a perverse desire for white authoritarian and neofascistic rule, the significance of Black generativity as *lived* within a space of their own, a space of discursive play and social ontological resistance, is especially vital. Yet, as was shown, particularly in chapter 1, Black fugitivity has always already haunted Black life. I have no illusions about the terror of whiteness, its insidious structure, its perceptual habits, its unconscious and opaque dimensions, the gaps within, and the resistances to, its problematic epistemic framing of social reality, its institutional systematicity, its expressive and contextual forms of privilege, and its anti-Blackness. And even as I understand how Black people, within the context of (and for) their embodied health, must put whiteness at a distance—or certainly certain expressions of whiteness— whiteness is too pervasive and perhaps even permanently fixed to completely leave behind. It is, after all, a global phenomenon. And if the global spread of right-wing white nationalism tells us anything it is that Black people (we) are not safe. But we have never been safe in the United States. So, this corrosion of democracy is not new to us. And, yet, we survive, we thrive, we create spaces of our own making.

So, in this section, I open with a conversation with Robert L. Williams as a way of bringing attention not only to African-American English or Ebonics, but as a way of demonstrating the interlocking ways in which language is not a culturally neutral site, but one that implicates racialized hegemony, questions regarding assessments of cognitive ability (or lack thereof), linguistic agency, self-determination, and educational success or failure. The interview with Williams is a powerful segue to my speculative ruminations on using African-American language or Ebonics within the context of traditional forms of Anglo-American and European philosophical expression. The work of Geneva Smitherman provided the generative linguistic framework for this next chapter. Part of the idea here was to mark my own lived experience as a site of a fluid and complex linguistic vector—the language of my nurture. The piece is discursively animated and playful as all spoken languages ought to be. I imagine that there are many Black philosophers who will say: "I've never spoken that way." Indeed, as Fanon might say, there are many Black folk who will not find themselves in what I've theorized. I'm fine with that, especially as my *lived* cultural world, my shared reality with so many Black folk, isn't diminished because of that fact. The important point is that there is much more work to be done by philosophers of language who find the complexity of Black vernacular, and its deep historical and cross-cultural forms of configuration, of *philosophical* interest.

The last chapter within this section continues within a cultural space of Black agency through deep performative practices—from discourse, spatial embodiment, to the rawness and beauty of living within Black urban spaces to Black imaginative creativity—that result from the genius and the acuity of rap and Hip Hop self-consciousness. Rap and Hip Hop are global phenomena, but they are fundamentally grounded within origination within a specifically diverse Black stylized space. Spady's work is incredibly sensitive to and profoundly cognizant of the cultural *specificity* and the cultural *global* dynamics—and their interplay—within the context of rap and Hip Hop. His work in the area of rap and Hip Hop is driven and informed by an epistemology of both spatially shared meaning and the dynamics of shared ontological space/place that constitute matrices that presuppose mutually shared intelligibility. In short, as a quintessential actor-participant, Spady has remained *grounded*, which means that he has remained true to Hip Hop beings who activate and are activated by their own legitimation practices. This section is about naming and claiming, being and becoming.

Chapter 20

The Scholar Who Coined the Term Ebonics: A Conversation with Robert L. Williams

On December 18, 1996, a controversial resolution was passed by the Board of Education of Oakland, California, that recognized the legitimacy and significance of Ebonics in the cultural lives and in the education of African-American children. The resolution, which was eventually amended, particularly regarding the implications that Ebonics was a "genetically based language," created a firestorm of national debate, a great deal of media attention, and much misunderstanding. The Ebonics debate was linked to questions about ascertaining and employing effective and actionable strategies for improving test scores and the educational experiences of African-American children. The Ebonics debate also raised profound issues concerning questions of linguistic hegemony, race, self-esteem in African-American children, questions of cultural linguistic autonomy and self-determination, and questions regarding intelligence testing and academic success/failure.

The argument articulated by the Board of Education was that Ebonics was a primary language used by African-American children that had deep cultural–historical roots in West and Niger–Congo African linguistic systems. Hence, not unlike other groups that benefit from a bilingual education (Asian American and Latin American groups, for example) whose primary languages are in fact *not* English, African-American children, under this assumption, would also benefit from a bilingual education. African-American children would be instructed in both their primary language (Ebonics) and English. The core of this debate was not only about how African-American children might be effectively educated given that their primary language was not English, but there was also the issue of their humanity, and treatment as equals guaranteed by the Fourteenth Amendment. In the end, the resolution and the unique vision of the Board of Education were nullified. In short, Oakland's African-American Educational Task Force was subjected to extraordinary political pressure, forcing them to hire a Public Relations firm to provide them with advice. The Task Force and School Board were making a case to use bilingual educational funds—a demand that logically followed from the assumption that African-American children speak a language other than English—for African-American students. "Bilingual educational advocates, primarily Latino and Asian groups, objected to calling Ebonics something other than English. The PR firm advised that it would be a mistake to continue to claim that Ebonics is not English. Their (Oakland's) Ebonics proclamation was revised, and they dropped the program because of unwelcome controversy. The superintendent resigned, and the incoming replacement wanted nothing whatsoever to do with Ebonics."[1]

Given that the national conversation regarding the resolution had become laden with a great deal of conflict and confusion, I thought that it was important to get a sense of the historical, social, and pedagogical context out of which the term Ebonics evolved. I knew that I would need to do primary research. Hence, it was out of the necessity for greater clarification that on February 1, 1997, less than two months after the historic resolution had been passed, that I conducted the following interview with Robert L. Williams (1930–) who actually coined the term Ebonics in 1973. The interview was to be published in the *Philadelphia Tribune*, the oldest and continuously published African-American newspaper in the United States, but did not come to fruition because of an editorial shift in focus.

At the time of the interview, Williams had appeared on Black Entertainment Television (BET) and the NBC News to discuss the controversial theme of Ebonics. Williams is currently Professor Emeritus of Psychology and African and African-American Studies at Washington University, St. Louis, Missouri. At that time, he had authored over sixty articles and two books, *Ebonics: The True Language of Black Folks* (1975) and *The Collective Black Mind: Toward An Afrocentric Theory of The Black Personality* (1981). He also authored *Racism Learned at an Early Age through Racial Scripting* (2007), a book that deals with how racism is perpetuated by parents, media, and schools, through a process called "racial scripting." As a critic of racial and cultural biases in the area of IQ testing, a theme that raises significant issues dealing with questions of cultural power, dominance, testing, and intelligence assessment, Williams is the developer of the Black Intelligence Test of Cultural Homogeneity. Indeed, early on, he has been a guest on several national television programs relating to IQ testing, including CBS' "IQ Myth" with Dan Rather, Prime Time Saturday Night, The Phil Donohue Show, and The Montel Williams Show. Williams is also a founding member of the Association of Black Psychologists. He has also served in the capacity as the association's second president.

After conducting the interview, it became clear to me that the controversy about Ebonics had profound implications for larger cultural questions. If indeed Ebonics was about the historical and cultural roots of African linguistic retentions and systems, and the constitution of a separate African-American language, then there were deeper questions to be asked about identity, cognition, colonialism, and reality construction. Concerning language, the Kenyan literary and social activist figure Ngũgĩ Wa Thiong'o argues that there are two important roles to consider. There is the role of language that functions in the capacity of "an agent that enables us to communicate with one another in our struggle to find the means of survival. The other is its role as a carrier of the history and the culture built into the process of that communication over time."[2] Frantz Fanon, the Black philosopher, political activist, decolonial psychoanalyst, and social theorist, also echoes the larger cultural dimensions of a language that transcend syntax and linguistic morphology. He reminds us that to speak means that we "assume a culture, [that we] support the weight of a civilization."[3] In short, then, the following interview with Williams raises significant issues pertaining to language and existential and cultural struggle and highlights questions regarding linguistic retention as a dynamic process of African cultural cohesion and integrity.

The specific themes that evolved out of the conversation are multiple and insightful, including the following:

- The significance of Ebonics vis-à-vis the presuppositions of the "Deficit Model School."
- The distinction between Ebonics, dialect, and "Black English."
- The importance of Ebonics as transcending a discussion of formal linguistics and how it is related to questions of cultural identity.
- The relationship between Ebonics and the perceived "lack" of language sophistication on the part of African-American children.
- The link between language, cultural capital, and self-determination.
- The connection between Ebonics and the Black underclass.
- The broader positive and negative outcomes of the Oakland School Board's Ebonics resolution.
- The issue of educational failures vis-à-vis African-American children.

George Yancy: What year did you actually coin the term Ebonics? Also provide a broader context for its emergence.

Robert L. Williams: I coined the term on January 26, 1973. If you look at the history of the literature on the language of Black Americans, most of it was done by white academicians such as William Stewart, William Labov, Joan and Stephen Baratz, Ralph Fasold, and others. Their writings had been rather pejorative in the description of Black language. In fact, many of them came out of what is called the Deficit Model School, meaning that our language was deficient. I had grown very tired of reading those writings and I felt that African-American scholars needed an opportunity to examine our own language and to do something about that. So, I called a conference on the cognitive and language development of the African-American child and I invited African-American scholars and Caucasian scholars and we all presented papers at this conference. It was at that conference that African-American scholars decided to become creative and define our language and develop a line of research for that particular language so that we could develop scholarship in that area. One evening the African-American scholars got together and it was at that meeting, without the Caucasian linguists, that we got together and decided to define our own reality. It was at that meeting that I put together the terms "ebony" and "phonics" to come up with Ebonics and the group essentially validated that term.

Yancy: Was the term well-received?

Williams: Yes, very enthusiastically received.

Yancy: So, the conference was a response to those who would have questioned the legitimacy of Black speech patterns.

Williams: Yes, it was. Basically, what we wanted to do was to take over that area and really nullify some of the research that had been done by the Euro-American scholars.

Yancy: Did your book *Ebonics: The True Language of Black Folks* grow out of that conference?

Williams: Yes, it did. It was two years later that I put together a number of the papers written by the African-American linguists to form the book. That was in 1975.

Yancy: Is there a distinction to be made between Ebonics and Black Language?

Williams: I think that Ebonics is a more positive description of our language. I think that Black English has a lot of negative or pejorative definitions and descriptions. I would say Ebonics aka Black English, but we've moved away from that because I'm not sure that there is anything that we can call "Black English." If you call it Black English, then you place limits on the roots of our language. You're saying that it's English rather than Ebonics which is an African based language that comes out of a family of African languages. I would say that Ebonics is the African-American's retention of African languages just as we have retained vestiges of African culture in our literature, food, music, etc.

Yancy: In the title of your book, *Ebonics*, how does the term "true" function?

Williams: Well, "true" means that there is an assertion that Ebonics is really the genuine language of African-Americans rather than the other descriptions such as deficient language, slovenly speech, Black vernacular, etc.

Yancy: Is Ebonics a dialect or does it constitute a language?

Williams: I think that dialect is subsumed under Ebonics as a language. Dialect is a regional expression whereas Ebonics can be traced back to Africa, and it's all over the Diaspora rather than just in a particular region. You see, the limitation here is that a dialect may exist in one area but in another area you may find a different dialect.

Yancy: What are some of the linguistic characteristics that make Ebonics a language?

Williams: First of all, I think there are grammatical and syntactical aspects of Ebonics, there are idioms, etc. Another aspect is that the purpose of language is to communicate and to solve problems and I think that Ebonics has those two dimensions. It is a way of communication and it is a way of solving problems and therefore it qualifies as a language.

Yancy: Is the issue as to whether Ebonics is a language really an issue concerning who has the power to define language?

Williams: Oh, certainly. I think that there is a very strong need here to decide who will define our language. African-Americans did not take that position for many years so that the white power structure simply eliminated or did not recognize the language of African-Americans. The white power structure referred to our language as slang or slovenly speech or ungrammatical speech rather than to look at the richness of the language. So, yes, those who are in power tend to define the language and decide what is correct or what is incorrect in that language.

Yancy: So, one might say that Ebonics is a challenge to the sociolinguistic hegemony of "Standard English."

Williams: I think that Ebonics is a threat to white supremacy in this society because it means that we have invoked the Second Principle of the *Nguzo Saba*, *Kujichagulia* or self-determination, in that we are creating and defining our own reality so that that becomes threatening to white America.

Yancy: In other words, there is a deeper cultural war that is at stake with regard to acknowledging Ebonics as a language.

Williams: Obviously, yes, because Ebonics is part of a culture. And though it's not the only part, it's one part. It's very similar to music or literature. No one would deny that we do have such things as African-American music, literature, church, etc., and that these things have certain very unique characteristics about them. The language, Ebonics, is a part of that totality of our culture. That's what culture really is. It is composed of a number of components which come together as a total culture of a people.

Yancy: Say more about the deeper issue of identity that is involved in this discussion about Ebonics.

Williams: At a micro-level my language is me. My language represents an extension of me, it represents how I come across and the kind of appearance I make to other people. It involves my self-esteem, how I see myself and how others see me because it is through my communication that I make contact with other people. So, at that particular level, language is very fundamental and it's very basic to an individual's identity. And one's identity is really linked to one's reference group or to one's ethnicity or to one's culture so that language encompasses, you see, my Black identity, it encompasses who I am. It is part and parcel of the totality of our culture. So, we communicate our culture through linguistic systems, and through Ebonics. Whether it's in music, in literature, in church or whatever, that is one characteristic of who we are.

Yancy: You spoke earlier about the issue of who has the power to define. Given the tight link between language and reality, it would seem that the issue of Ebonics is really an issue regarding how African-Americans choose to define their *own reality*.

Williams: Yes. Well, it's how we define our reality. And I think we have defined our reality in the terms of W. E. B. DuBois, that is, double-consciousness. We are aware that we are African-Americans and that we have Ebonics as a language, but we are also aware that in order to function in this broader society we have to master "Standard English" in order to be involved in that society. So, you have this double-consciousness. For example, I am an African-American who may speak Ebonics, but I'm also a person who needs to acquire certain tools in order to make it in the wider commerce.

Yancy: Consistent with the discourse of W. E. B. DuBois, one might say that African-Americans have a *linguistic* double-consciousness.

Williams: Yes. You know, I've got one mind for white folks to see and I've got another one that I know is me. "You don't know, you don't know my mind. When you see me laughin', I'm laughin' to keep from crying." That's a quote from Zora Neale Hurston's *Mules and Men*. What she was talking about there is the same kind of thing we're discussing here, our double-consciousness. We've always had this bilingual or this dual-consciousness as

African-Americans. And you might look at many African-Americans who go through this. With our homies, for example, we behave one way and in the broader society we may behave in another way. And we do this kind of code switching in language or we do this switching in identities because we play those roles, the role with our peers and then the role with the broader society.

Yancy: Why is the use of Ebonics so pervasive among the Black underclass?

Williams: Well, I think that it is pervasive for several reasons. The main one is that within the lower socioeconomic class, there is less education and there may be a lack of the acquisition of "Standard English" because of the fact that they're not in the middle class where middle-class people have acquired some of the characteristics of "Standard English." And I also think that there is an educational factor going on here rather than any kind of [natural] deficiency in the Black underclass. The acquisition of "Standard English" is associated with the level of education that one has. So, the lower socioeconomic class might not have acquired as much "Standard English" per capita as the middle class.

Yancy: But just because "lower-class" Black people have not acquired as much "Standard English" per capita as the Black middle class, this does not in any way have a negative impact on the cognitive functioning or intelligence of "lower-class" Blacks.

Williams: That's right. But you'll find that parents who have lower education will transmit more of the Ebonics to their children than parents who are in the middle class. The middle class will transmit less of that to their children because they have acquired more of the "Standard English." For example, I came out of a very low socioeconomic class and all through elementary and high school I spoke Ebonics. I never knew how to conjugate a verb because no one ever told me that verbs needed to be conjugated. I was in college before I really learned that there was something called "Standard English" that specified ways that I was supposed to talk. I took a French class in college and it was at that time that the instructor talked about conjugating a verb and I was shocked that verbs had to be conjugated. There was an English professor who also invited me into his advanced composition class and he helped me to work on my English. And the French teacher helped me through a method of contrast. Having now two languages I was able to understand and improve my acquisition of "Standard English."

Yancy: By acknowledging to young Black language users that Ebonics is a legitimate language, will this inhibit them in terms of giving them an excuse for not wanting to master "Standard English"?

Williams: I don't think so. I think that awareness helps people to understand the reality of what they're doing. If no one ever tells a person that there is, let's say, home-talk and school-talk, or street-talk and school-talk, or street-talk and talk of the broader commerce, then they don't have this contrast in mind and what they're doing is simply communicating the way that their peers are communicating or that their families are communicating. So, I think it brings about a certain recognition so that they can now identify language *A* versus language *B* and develop this code switching more aptly than before.

Yancy: What's your response to those who claim that Ebonics is "inferior" to "Standard English" acquisition?

Williams: Well, see, that's another thing. I don't really see Ebonics as being inferior. We could go from Ebonics to French or Ebonics to Swahili or whatever. We're not admitting to an inferiority. The inferiority issue comes in when the power structure says that it's bad, that your language is inferior. I simply think here that we're now making comparisons. It's very much like if I'm driving a Chevrolet and then I want to move to a Ford. It's just a different brand. But having Ebonics as a base, you are now able to show the children what is a different way of expressing themselves. It's like apples and bananas. I don't think an apple is superior to a banana. An apple has its own characteristics and a banana has its own characteristics, but both are fruits. Ebonics is a language and "Standard English" is a language and yet both are languages.

Yancy: Is there any relationship between cognitive functioning and language usage?

Williams: Cognitive means the recognition of certain phenomena in one's environment or becoming aware of that particular phenomena and understanding that phenomena. Now when you become aware of that, then the next step is to attach a label to that event or those objects. This is where language comes in. Language is the labeling of your cognitions. There is no difference in the cognitive development process of young children up to about age two. In other words, they become aware of up-ness, down-ness, out-ness, and all of these things. That is, they become aware of their environment. It is in the labeling process where there are differences. For example, one group of children might label the thing in the living room that they sit on as a sofa. The other children may label it a couch. So, there is this linguistic difference. Also, the way that sentences are put together to express oneself is different. One might say something in a sense that is characteristic of the broader society, "Standard English" form, whereas someone else might say something in the Ebonics form. Both have an understanding of the same events, but it's the kinds of labels that they attach to their environments.

Yancy: So, what is the source of the belief that to speak Ebonics is really to function "sub-cognitively"?

Williams: I think that the white power structure identifies our cognitive structure as deficient. For example, years ago, before I did the research, the superintendent of schools here in St. Louis, Missouri, said that Black children brought to school fewer than one-hundred words in their vocabulary and that they were cognitively deficient and linguistically deprived. What was happening there is that the children had the cognitive development, but the way that it was measured, through the psychological tests, didn't plug into the information that they had in their psychological structure. The questions that they used did not activate the language structure of the African-American child or the cognitive repertoire of the African-American child because they were asking questions in a code that the African-American child had not mastered. So, they were calling these children culturally deprived and academically deficient. So, we re-lexified the test. We put the test questions in the language that the children could understand and they were able to perform much better and much more able to understand the questions and to show that they were very bright children, who, otherwise, would have been labeled as mentally retarded and placed in special education.

Yancy: What are your thoughts on the relatively recent, 1996, Oakland School Board's positive acknowledgment of Ebonics?

Williams: I think that it's a bold, assertive, and correct way to go. I think that the resolutions have much broader implications than just Ebonics. Basically, they're dealing with the underachievement of African-American children and Oakland is not unique in this respect. That's a nationwide problem. But Oakland has taken a strong stance to develop methods that will educate our children in a better way and they're looking at language as being one of the most salient aspects in the educational process because it's the way that you communicate with the child. They're saying that many of their teachers have not connected with African-American children and therefore are not educating African-American children. So, I agree wholeheartedly with what they're doing, and I support them and give them all of the information that I possibly can. And I think other school districts around the country need to watch very closely what Oakland is doing and perhaps develop similar methods to help our children. When you have the reality that 71 percent of children in special education are

African-Americans then something is wrong with that and something needs to be done about it. I don't think all of those children need to be in special education.

Yancy: What do you see as positive coming from Oakland School Board's acknowledgment?

Williams: I think that it has brought the issue of Ebonics to national attention. As you know, recently we were in Washington, DC at a subcommittee hearing with Senator Arlen Specter of Pennsylvania. I think that now Ebonics and the whole issue of the underachievement of African-American children are in the public consciousness and people are raising questions. I've been traveling throughout the United States and everybody is interested in these issues. Before it was kind of dormant, there was no public debate or public discussion. And now we have that. We've put these issues on the table before the American people and I think that now some actions will be taken to resolve some of these critical issues regarding the education of our young African-American children. For example, in Oakland, California, they have sixty-one different languages that are spoken there and they have developed programs to help those children there to learn "Standard English" in reading. Out of the students in those programs only twenty-two are African-American, but they have about 10,000 students who are in these special programs for learning English as a second language. And I think it is horrible that they left those African-American children out. And even when you go around the country to other school systems you'll find similar situations where African-American children bring their home language to school, a language divergent from "Standard English," and are criticized and penalized rather than getting proper help.

Yancy: What is it about the Oakland School Board's decision that you see as problematic?

Williams: Well, one thing that I found problematic was that they used the term "genetically based" and I think that set off a furor of discussion because it was understood by the public as indicating something biological, as involving chromosomes and genes, but that's not what they intended. They were using the phrase "genetically based" in a linguistic way, that is, that one language develops out of another language. So, the genetic sense is used when we say that pidgin is developed and then Creole comes out of pidgin and then Ebonics out of that language. So, the term "genetic" here suggests a linguistic characteristic rather than a biological or a genetic characteristic. I think that there is also concern for the need of consultants and supporters. I don't know how many people were contacted, but I would certainly hope that they've contacted enough people to give them the expertise and kind of direction needed. I know that they did call me after the resolution was out and asked me to develop some evaluation tools. They're going to have to have methods which will need very, very close and adequate evaluation in order to present to the public and say that our methods are effective.

Yancy: What are some of the causes of academic, educational underachievement for African-Americans?

Williams: First, I think that it probably begins in the home in terms of the expectations of parents. I think there is a discontinuity between what's going on in the home and what's going on in the schools. There is no match. There needs to be a coming together of the school and the home in order to get the child on the same track so that the expectations can be the same. Second, I think that there are many teachers in the school system who do not really understand methods of teaching the African-American child and so that child is left behind. And they may not even be able to teach them. So, there needs to be a reformation of how African-American children are taught and the kind of teachers that they need. I think that what Detroit did with the all African-American male school was a forward step, though it was shut down by the court. There need to be specific models developed for educating the African-American child just as specific models were developed for teaching English as a second language to those immigrants and those people who had not mastered "Standard English."

Yancy: What impact has your work had on African-American culture?

Williams: I think the first impact that my work had was the Black intelligence test. It brought to national attention that Black people were not intellectually inferior to white folks, especially when you use a test that contains items from their cultural pool. That's what the Black intelligence test did. I did that back in the early 1970s and it created a storm of controversy just as Ebonics has done. I think that my work has led people to recognize that we have the same intellectual ability as all other people. My work with testing has been very, very influential. And Ebonics has helped to bring a dormant issue to the surface and to national attention. As Victor Hugo said, "Greater than the tread of mighty armies is an idea whose time has come." And this idea of Ebonics lay dormant for many years and now here it is facing us and we have to deal with it. It won't go away.

Chapter 21

Geneva Smitherman: The Social Ontology of African-American Language, the Power of *Nommo,* and the Dynamics of Resistance and Identity through Language

It is ABSURD to assume, as has been the tendency, among a great many Western anthropologists and sociologists, that all traces of Africa were erased from the Negro's mind because he learned English. The very nature of the English the Negro spoke and still speaks drops the lie on that idea.

—LeRoi Jones

Every dialect, every language, is a way of thinking. To speak means to assume a culture.

—Frantz Fanon

The spoken word is a gesture, and its meaning, a world.

—M. Merleau-Ponty

This chapter takes seriously Robert L. Williams' understanding of Ebonics or African-American English as anti-hegemonic vis-à-vis "Standard" English. It is an experimental chapter that delineates various aspects of the grammatical morphology of Ebonics or African-American English. Forming the conceptual framework of the chapter is the question: What might philosophy look like if spoken in Ebonics or African-American English? I leave it to those who do philosophy of language or those who critically engage Black vernacular speech, certainly more than I, to explore further what I've written here. With a cursory glance, what is clear is that some languages are marginalized within European and American philosophical discursive practices. Discussing the importance of Spanish and how it captures and communicates meaning, diversification, and enrichment within the context of American philosophy, José Medina writes, "Linguistic resistance is necessary in order to fight cultural hegemony: we cannot let the philosophical establishment (and the social and cultural powers that shape it) set the agenda for us and fix the language in which we must speak."[1] Within this context, Medina highlights what it means to be a *subject* of language. And discussing the importance of the spoken word, Charles R. Lawrence writes, "This is, for us, an especially important understanding of subjectivity, for the language we use to describe ourselves is both evidence of how we see ourselves and part of the means whereby our self-image is shaped."[2] Medina's and Lawrence's point fundamentally shapes the spirit of this chapter.

In order to illustrate the interconnection between *lived* experience, culture, discourse, and philosophy, I wrote a short and selective philosophical autobiography exploring my philosophical development.[3] In the chapter, I consciously decided to use the language of my *nurture* (Ebonics or African-American Language), the linguistic expressions of my life-world, that language which helped to capture the mood and cultural, aesthetic, and sonic texture of what it was like for me to live within the heart of North Philadelphia, one of America's Black urban spaces (what I'd call then, "ghettoes"). After all, what other linguistic medium could I use to articulate the rhythm, the fluidity, the angst, the aesthetics of coolness, and the beauty involved in traversing those dangerous, challenging, and inviting streets? These streets were sites where style mattered, where respect was key, where blood was shed, where families were poor and weary, where who you knew could save your life, and where one had to be bad, had to project that tough image, that badass persona, in order to survive. Writing about the background of this existential space of anguish and hope, a background within which my philosophical self evolved, was no easy task. However, writing *in* the language of my nurture not only helped me to remember much of what was "forgotten," but helped me to make "inroads against the established power-lines of speech."[4]

After having read my philosophical–autobiographical chapter, a white philosopher whom I admire came up to me at an American Philosophical Association conference and told me how he really enjoyed the piece and how he had not known so many intimate details about my life. He added: "I really enjoyed it, but why did you use *that language* [meaning African-American Language]. You write very well [meaning in 'Standard' American English]. You don't have to use that language to make your point." I listened in silence, realizing that he completely missed the point. Indeed, for him, African-American Language was not a viable language, not a legitimate semiotic medium through which my life-world could best be represented. Rather, in his view, the language that I chose to use was "slang," an "ersatz" form of communication that clearly should not have been used. By using

African-American English, I had somehow fallen from the "true heights" of academic professionalism and broken the norms of respectable philosophy-speak. Indeed, perhaps he thought that I was being "too Black" in my speech, not white enough, not "proper" enough. As Frantz Fanon observed, "Nothing is more astonishing than to hear a black man express himself properly, for then in truth he is putting on the white world."[5] Fanon's observations suggest deeper relationships that may exist between the function of language and a specifically *racialized* and racist philosophical anthropology. Again, Fanon observed:

> The Negro of the Antilles will be proportionately whiter—*that is, he will come closer to being a real human being*—in direct ratio to his mastery of the French language. I am not unaware that this is one of man's attitudes face to face with Being. A Man who has a language consequently possesses the world expressed and implied by that language. What we are getting at becomes plain: Mastery of language affords remarkable power.[6]

Fanon's observations also contain profound implications for the specifically racial, academic, and cultural dimensions of philosophy-speak. Indeed, perhaps in the United States it is philosophy-speak that is "too white," creating a kind of dislocation for many Black folk who find it necessary to speak African-American Language to communicate some subtle cultural experience or way of "seeing the world" philosophically. This does not mean that Anglo-American or European languages are inherently inadequate for expressing philosophical ideas per se; rather, the point is that these languages are presumed the normative media through which philosophy qua philosophy can best be engaged. It is the imperialist, and, of course, colonialist, tendency of these languages that is being rejected. Nevertheless, in my chapter, it was not I who failed philosophy, but it was "Standard" American English—that dominant, territorial, imperial medium of philosophical expression in the United States—that failed to convey the logic, the horror, the humanity, the existentially rank, the confluent, and the surreal realities embedded in my experiences in one of America's Black enclaves.

It is here that one might ask, Are Anglo-American and European philosophical forms of discourse inadequate for re-presenting the complexity of Black experiences? After all, not any form of discursivity will do. My experiences were in excess of what "Standard" American English could capture. Some forms of knowledge become substantially truncated and distorted, indeed, erased, if not expressed through the familiar linguistic media of those who have possession of such knowledge. In a passage rich with issues concerning the lack of power and effectiveness of "Standard" American English to capture the personal identity and personal experiences of a young Black boy, writer Robert H. DeCoy asks:

> How . . . my Nigger Son, can you ever hope to express what you are, who you are or your experiences with God, in a language so limited, conceived by a people who are quite helpless in explaining themselves? How can you, my Nigger Son, find your identity, articulate your experiences, in an order of words?[7]

Regarding white philosophers (or even Black ones) who simply fail or don't care to understand the importance of African-American Language as a rich cultural and philosophical site of expression, perhaps it is the duty of knowledgeable and responsible Black philosophers who take the issue of African-American English seriously vis-à-vis philosophy—at least for those who are willing to admit that they speak both the Language of Wider Communication (or LWC) and the powerful vernacular shaped by African retentions and African-American linguistic nuances—to invite them to enter African-American semiotic spaces of discursive difference and overlap. We should keep in mind that being Black or African-American in North America does not ipso facto mean that one is familiar with the subtle complexities and power of African-American Language. After all, there are Black philosophers from middle class (and lower class) backgrounds whose linguistic assimilation to "Standard" American English, a form of cultural capital ownership and privilege, functions both as a badge of white acceptance, and an antidote for reducing white anxiety and fear. The invitation, though, should not be a plea, but an honest gesture to explore the language on its own terms. This is why it was so very important that this present chapter be written unapologetically in the language of my *nurture*; the medium had to be the message. Keep in mind that an invitation is not a site of superimposition. This was the situation that Blacks of African descent faced; they were forced to learn the language of the colonizer, forced to split, to multiply in so many different cultural, psychological, linguistic, and spiritual directions against their will. The fact that this chapter appears in an authored philosophical text invites a certain level of cultural and linguistic splitting on the part of its readers, perhaps not very different from what is required when reading Kant or Heidegger, particularly given their penchant for neologism.

Let's be honest, articles and chapters that typically appear in philosophy journals and philosophy books have no doubt been written in "Standard" American English and by predominantly white male philosophers, philosophers who have been trained to engage in "proper" philosophical prose. I, too, can write in this language. To write in this language is to reproduce the professional culture of philosophy, to perpetuate lines of power, and to show that you have been "properly" educated and are worthy of hire. Moreover, to engage in this discourse is to *perform* linguistically before an audience of gatekeepers who probably fear too much "folk-cultural fat" in their discourse, too much play, too much signifying, too much indirection, too much ambiguity, too much vagueness, too much concrete, everyday reality. Like African-American Language within the larger context of "Standard" American Language, by appearing in this book this chapter also enters into a space of established norms of linguistic propriety, calling into question and perhaps rupturing the authority of "Standard" philosophical prose, that *unhip* discourse of professional philosophers. Of course, having this chapter published in this book could turn out to be a curse or a blessing. Realizing the degree to which "proper" philosophical discourse is required by philosophy texts and how such discourse in turn shapes and legitimates philosophy journals, and other sites of philosophical knowledge production, many readers of this book may read the chapter with contempt. Some may approach the chapter as a piece of exotica. Some may even view my use of African-American Language as a disgraceful "Stepin Fetchit" performance that does a disservice to Black philosophers who are all too eager to perform well in the presence of white power, to show the white world that *we be* real philosophers because we speak the language of Mister Charlie. Then, of course, there are some philosophers who are open to creative possibilities, differences, and alternatives to hegemonic linguistic territorialism, who believe in plural experiences and multiple discourses for articulating them. When the medium is the message, one has got to get wit da medium. It will take more than this chapter to impact significantly a certain linguistic–philosophical reference point that is buttressed by so much history and power that has historically structured philosophy-speak. To best articulate that Black existential space where the *real* world, the nonideal world (not that abstract possible world), is filled with pain, struggle, blood, tears, and laughter—where death follows a minute of joy, where so much is improvisatory and surreal, moving with the quickness, where the streets are hot, dangerous, and familial, where love is abundant and hate smiles in yo face, where melodic sounds fight to stay above the sounds of gunfire, where babies cry all night long, because mama done gone and hit the pipe, where a brotha gots to be down, where brothas be runnin game, talkin that talk, keepin it real, and showin much loyalty—requires fluency in the language which partly grows out of the nitty-gritty core of the epistemology and ontology of that space. I wonder how many Black professors quietly say to themselves when their Black students speak in class, "Oh, no! You're embarrassing me. There's no subject–verb agreement and you talk like you're from the hood. Hurry up and make your point! And please don't speak again."

It is my contention that African-American linguist Geneva Smitherman, the primary Black linguist whose work I pull from within this chapter, is working within the rich situated practices of Africana philosophy and should be acknowledged as such. She is self-consciously aware of the meta-reflective analysis that is necessary to make sense of what it means for Black people to have forged an identity through the muck and mire of white racism. After all, Black folk were deemed inherently inferior, cultureless, without *Geist*. Yet, Black agency survived the tortuous African bloodstained water of the Atlantic. Like Jazz (with its improvisatory structure and chromatic form), the Blues (with its ontology of lyrically holding at a survival distance incredible pain and sorrow), and rap music (with its beats, lyrical braggadocio, and in *yo* face street reality), African-American Language is a significant site of Black cultural innovation, syncretism, and survival, laden with situated epistemological insights. There is no other way to honor African-American English, to explore the "language-gaming" of everyday Black folk, without directly and unapologetically entering into the dynamic, rhythmic, ritual, and cognitive spaces of African-American linguistic expressiveness. In this regard, Smitherman's work is indispensable.

Hence, from the very giddayup, that is, befo I bees gittin into some really dope cultural, historical, philosophical, and linguistic analyses, let's engage in a lil bit of naming and claiming. Since coming to Atlanta or what some Black folk refer to as "Wakanda," I'll rephrase: I'm *finnin* to get into some deep cultural shit, but first Geneva. Word! The power of *Nommo*. I know that my twenty-first-century young fam will find my expressions wack, but, hey, we be in this marvelous discursive shit together.

Geneva Smitherman (aka Docta G) is an educational activist, a word warrior, a language rights fighter, a linguist-activist, and a linguistic democratizer. Can I get a witness? Yeah, that's right. She is the legitimizer[8] of African-American Language (AAL). The shonuff sista from the hood who is cognizant of what it means to be a New World African, to be linked to that shonuff Black space of talkin and testifyin, stylin, and profilin. AAL is the language of her nurture.[9] She was, after all, baptized "in the linguistic fire of Black Folk."[10] Believe me, for if I'm lyin, I'm flyin, she knows the source of those deleted copulas ("The coffee cold"), those post-vocalic -r sounds ("My feet be *tied*," not "tired"), redundant past tense marking ("I *likeded* her," not "liked"), few consonant pairs ("Those *tesses* was hard," not "tests"), stylizations, and rhetorical devices.

Docta G operates within that unique African-American space of performative "languaging," a space of agency, contestation, self-definition, poiesis, and hermeneutic combat. She is all up in the cultural sphere of ashy knees, nappy hair, and how we be actin so saddity. Ah, yes, and she knows about the hot comb as a cultural artifact of self-hatred, a form of hatred instilled through the power of colonial white aesthetics. She *member* where she come from. She got no desire to front. Docta G's medium *is* the message. She avoids what linguist-philosopher John L. Austin refers to as the "descriptive fallacy," which involves the assumption that the main function of language is to describe things. Through the incorporation of AAL *flava* in her written works (and no doubt in her lectures), Docta G is *doing something* with those words and phrases. Her writings, in short, are demonstrative enactments of the historical, stylistic, political, communicative, cognitive, and social ontological power of African-American Language. Docta G is the lion who has learned how to write, how to narrate a counter-historical narrative, and how to recognize and theorize a counter-language. A metalinguist, she is a cultural, ethical, and political theorist. If push comes to shove, she'll "choose goodness over grammar."[11] She knows that the politics of language policy is a larger question of the politics of reality construction, historical structuring of society, race, class, and Anglo-linguistic imperialism. As such, she moves between both the sociolinguists (who stress social and ethnic language) and the Cartesian or Chomskyan[12] linguists (who stress "ideally competent" language). She knows that the right to speak AAL is a question of linguistic freedom, agency, and justice. A Womanist, moving within that bold, self-assertive and *we-affirming* space of sistas like Sojourner Truth, Harriet Tubman, Rosa Parks, Claudette Colvin, Angela Davis, Alice Walker, Audre Lorde, bell hooks, Hortense Spillers, Patricia Hill Collins, Anita Allen, Joy James, Docta G is responsible, in charge, and serious. She's no prisoner of the academy; rather, she is existentially and politically committed to the Black community, its survival, and the continual actualization of its cultural generative force. Smitherman maintains that a womanist denotes an "African-American woman who is rooted in the Black community and committed to the development of herself and the entire community."[13] African-American women, empowered by their womanist consciousness, were well aware that white feminists had failed to critique, self-reflexively, the normativity of their own whiteness. Epistemologically, Black womanists occupied their own subject positions, positions that did not square with the theorizations of white middle-class women. You dig (Wolof: *dega*) what I'm sayin? Can I get an Amen?

Docta G, "daughter of the hood,"[14] raised in Brownsville, Tennessee, was culturally immersed in the rich locutionary acts of Black folk. Y'all wit me? I'm pointing to the significant links between Docta G's biographical *location* and how this influenced her later theorizations regarding AAL. Consistent with feminist, Womanist, social constructionist, and postmodernist insights, one's social location is a significant hermeneutic lens through which to understand one's theorizations. By emphasizing one's social location, one is able to avoid the obfuscating process of reification. As social constructionists Peter L. Berger and Thomas Luckmann maintain, "Reification is the apprehension of human phenomena as if they were things, that is, in non-human or possibly suprahuman terms."[15] In short, the lived-context, as existential phenomenology stresses, is always already presupposed in relationship to our epistemological claims. Props to Black women's standpoint epistemology.

Docta G, daughter of the Black ghetto, daughter of Reverend Napoleon, was an early witness to the illocutionary and perlocutionary acts within a linguistically rich Black family, a sharecropping community, and a Traditional Black Church. For example, she knows the power of tonal semantics, a significant feature of AAL that moves the listener through melodic structure and poignant rhetorical configuration. She relates that her father once expressed the following theme in one of his sermons: "I am nobody talking to Somebody Who can help anybody."[16] Geneva, monolingual and from the sociolinguistic margins, was well aware of what it meant to be deemed a problem, to endure the pain of being told that her speech was "pathological," "wrong," "inferior," "bad," and "derelict." Having gone North (or was it simply up South?) where she attended college, Geneva had to pass a test "in order to qualify for the teacher preparation program."[17] Given the then oppressive and racist language policy, a policy that stressed the importance of teachers being able to speak the language of those who "carry on the affairs of the English-speaking people,"[18] Geneva did not pass the speech test. Docta G explains:

> We found ourselves in a classroom with a speech therapist who wasn't sure what to do with us. Nobody was dyslexic. No one was aphasic. There was not even a stutterer among us. I mean here was this young white girl, a teaching assistant at the university, who was just trying to get her PhD, and she was presented with this perplexing problem of people who didn't have any of the communication disorders she had been trained to deal with.[19]

Although Geneva eventually passed the test by simply memorizing the pronunciation of particular sounds she needed to focus on, she came to interpret this experience as key to stimulating her politico-linguistic consciousness. She relates that "it aroused the fighting spirit in me, sent me off into critical linguistics and I eventually entered the lists of the language wars."[20] Clearly, this experience created in Geneva a powerful sense of agency and praxis. On the strength! You know it. Can't forget Bob Williams. Damn, he coined the term Ebonics. As Kenyan philosopher and literary figure Ngũgĩ wa Thiong'o argues, "There is no history which is purely and for all time that of actors and those always acted upon."[21] Uhm talkin bout a Womanist, Docta G. You know, the chief expert *witness* for the linguistic intelligence of Black children, the one who has made it her political project to challenge effectively the totalizing systems of Euro/Anglo-linguistic cultural normativity. You betta act like you know. She fightin against African-American *linguistic* erasure. Naw, even more so, she fightin *for* African-American hue-manity.

Docta G reveals that AAL is not some broken, ersatz sign system exclusively relegated to the confines of Black "ghetto" life; rather, AAL is the language of

Black America.[22] Docta G is up on it; she operates in that deeply deep space of African-American signs and symbols, a semiotic space where individual words and phrases carry the weight of an entire worldview. As Frantz Fanon asserts, "To speak a language is to take on a world, a culture."[23] I'm talkin bout an entire life-world where so many Black folk gotta live under conditions of much oppression, at the bottom, where Black bodies and souls constantly struggle to move within a compressing and collapsing social cosmos. Sendin out an SOS call. There appears to be a Blue Shift in the Black existential universe. But as we move to the center of it all, to the heart and soul of these historicizing, proud Black people, we notice a dynamic process of reconstitution, reinterpretation, being, and becoming. I'm also talkin bout love—Big Time! We be a praxis-oriented people who are defined by our communicative acts, our existential improvisatory modes of being, forms of world-making, and ways of re-narrating, over and over again, our historical and spiritual links to Africa and the Americas—a veritable *dispersion* of Black modes of being.

Toasts. Yo mamma! Some Baaaaad people we be. Coded language. Gangsta limp. Bloods and Crips. Lightin up that spliff. Yo, it's a Philly blunt! Catchin the spirit. Is it glossolalia or scatting? The Amen corner. Bench walkin preachers. "This ain no prayin church." "Naw, we a prayin church, Reb. Preach Brotha!" Call and response. Moans, shouts, and groans. All of these significations are capable of establishing a psycho-cognitive communal dynamic of shared cultural, religious, and intra-psychological meaningfulness.[24] In the fields, in the storefront church, or from the lips of the Godfather of Soul, it's all good. I can't forget even if I wanted to. I'll never forget those spaces; memories I refuse to erase. Just ask Lupe Fiasco. The sacred and secular always already organically fused. As Docta G notes, "It is, after all, only a short distance from 'sacred' Clara Ward's 'I'm climbin high mountains tryin to git Home' to 'secular' Curtis Mayfield's 'keep on pushin/can't stop me now/move up a little higher/someway or somehow.' "[25] Tarrying all night long. Those Black bodies, forming a deep and harmonious *Mitsein*, will move and groove until the break of dawn. These Bluesified, Jazzified, funkified, spiritualized, and aestheticized sites of existence.

Damn she slammin! She's a brick. Uhm talkin boodylicious. Shakin that jelly. Ask Destiny's Child. Movin those hips. You know it didn't start with Elvis. Boodylicious! Aesthetics? Erotica? It ain't for me to call. You tell me. The sistas got this one. I gots to come clean, though. Does the French naturalist Georges Cuvier fall within the same cipha with Sir Mix-A-Lot? Baby Got Back. Steatopygia? Cuvier came with all his racist porno-tropes, observing with that white hegemonic white gaze, those medical racist assumptions that saw a collage of "abnormal" buttocks and genitalia. Perhaps the song "Anaconda" grounds a Black woman's epistemic standpoint; a politics of the booty that she gets to articulate, express, *on her own terms*. Big ups to

Saartjie Baartmann. They called her "Hottentot Venus." Khoikhoi women in the house! Josephine Baker knew how to *work it*. Sistas know *Cosmo* ain representin. Big ups to the sistas who realize that aesthetics is political. The Sistas got some high standards, too. They ain no skeezers. You know you gotta show respect. Industry funded, paid for images got U hooked, Brotha. Believin all that hype, throwin all that chedda, tryin to bling bling yo way to a piece of that pie. Makin it rain. Do I see Cuvier behind yo gaze? Brotha gotta come real, his shit gotta be tight, no wack raps allowed. It ain all bout the benjamins! Is it Johnny Walker Red or a forty-ounce? Let's pour a lil bit for the brothas who ain heah. Singin doo-wop in some back ally. That's the way it usta be. Or rappin, freestylin, on some urban street corner. Even the Hawk, you know, Joe Chilly, don't stop these Brothas from talkin that talk. Yo, you gotta represent. The power of *Nommo* within these tight, fluctuatin, surreal, inviting and dangerous streets can save yo life. Ask Malcolm, not X, but Little. He was out there. You know, my man Detroit Red. He was tryin to make that chedda. The trickster. You've got to be improvisational on these chocolate city streets, constantly in existential negotiation, takin no shorts. In these streets, somethin always bout to kick off. It's summahtime and brothas be rollin tough, posse-style. Many, they be frontin, though. Whether duping Mister Charlie, Ole Massa, The Man, Po-Po, or 5–0. Black folk be flippin the script. The power of improvisatorial negotiation. Thelonious Monk, he is a child of the first twenty Africans to arrive. The Middle Passage. Negotiating. Creating. Makin somethin outta nothin. Learning how to play those microtones and enact those micro-disturbances of white hegemonic power. Black folk bees some BaddDDD people, all decked out in their marvelousness, their terribleness, contradictoriness, pains and pleasures. Ask DMX, he know WHO WE BE. From Africa to America, Black people bees tellin stories within stories. The African Griot. Field holler. A Blues song. A Jazz improvisation. Reb in the house! Revolutionary politico-poetics. Rap music. Big Momma's linguistic and paralinguistic style. And you know she got much Mother-wit. This is a complex, continuous, and contiguous historical cipher. The power of *Nommo* as both constant and constative. Sonia Sanchez shonuff knows this; Larry Neal and surrealist Ted Joans *still* knows it; and Amiri Baraka's vociferations tell it all. Yo, Docta G, kick the ballistics:

> The emergence of the Black Freedom Struggle marked a fundamental shift in linguistic consciousness as Black intellectuals, scholar–activists, and writer–artists deliberately and consciously engaged in an unprecedented search for a language to express Black identity and the Black condition.[26]

The entire cadre of the Black Arts Movement knew a change had to come. This ain just braggadocio, though we can do that, too. You smell me? Hips in motion with some serious attitude. Deconstructed linearity. Cakewalking, Swinging (just to stay alive), bopping, grooving, hip hopping, and Harlem shakin. Cool and hot expressiveness ever so fused. Talkin shit. Sometimes wino-style. Richard Pryor had a comedic–dramatic feel for all this *marvelous* Black everydayness; he was all up in the *Lebenswelt* of Black folk. Playin some craps. Heah come the PO-ice! Multiple sites of keepin it real: the Amen corner, barbershops, hair salons, the safe space of the kitchen, pool halls, clubs, street corners, and back allies. Cell phones and pagers in this postmodern urban space. Boody call. "It's my shorty, I gotta go. Shoot some hoops later. Peace out." "Damn, dog, I think you must be whupped." These are the speech acts of everydayness, the *lingua franca* of so many of my peeps. But not everything is linguistically permissible within this space. Within the framework of speech act theory, there are definite *felicity conditions*. Black people be movin in that rich semiotic space, suspended and immersed in webs of meaning, as Max Weber and Clifford Geertz would say. You might ask, why the delineation of these culturally thick, multiply semiotic, and intertextually rich streams? Answer: Docta G's work demands it! She writes:

> In my own work, I have very consciously sought to present the whole of Black Life, and the rich continuum of African American speech from the secular semantics of the street and the basketball court to the talkin and testifyin of the family reunion and the Black Church.[27]

This cultural space is thick, hyper-textual, protean, and diachronic. It is a cultural semiotic tale, a narrative force, told and lived by a people who, despite their horrendous experiences during the Middle Passage, the failures of Reconstruction, the presence of lynched Black bodies (or strange fruit), the water hoses, and "Nigger dogs" during the 1960s, see it as they duty to keep keepin on, keepin their "eye on the sparrow," and gittin ovuh. That's right: *AND STILL WE RISE!* Docta G knows that "niggers is more than deleted copulas."[28] To get a clear sense of the diachronic structure of AAL, it is important to understand the historicity and dynamic remaking of African folk in racist America; indeed, there is the need to be fully cognizant of what America bees puttin Black folk through. As I have suggested, Docta G is hip to the particular forms of life of so many African-Americans. She is all up in the epistemological, ontological, and cultural "language-gaming" of Black folk, from the pulpit, within the everyday urban and rural spaces of African-American linguistic performativity, to the complexity and aesthetics of talkin shit, to rapese. She recognizes that it is not simply an issue of getting at the lexical core of what makes AAL unique and legitimate, but it is an issue of "whose culture?" and "whose values?" and "whose identity?" Peep the insightful lines where she elaborates, "The moment is not which dialect, but which culture, not whose vocabulary but whose values, not *I* vs. *I be*, but

WHO DO I BE?"[29] It is a question of the axiological, linguistic, and cultural ontology of identity. But to get at "WHO DO I BE" involves moving beyond the discourse of pathology and what W. E. B. DuBois referred to as our being defined as *a problem* vis-à-vis white folk. Therefore, Docta G is engaged in a project that is fueled by de-pathologization, celebration, and reclamation of African-American humanity and identity. In sum, then, Ima have to continue writin a *responsible* chapter that captures the broad scope of what Docta G bees droppin.

At this juncture, I will briefly explore, in an expository, synthetic, and interpretive fashion, various aspects of Docta G's critical corpus: (1) the significance of the existentially terrifying journey from Africa, through the Middle Passage, and to the so-called New World, which will provide historical insight into the psycho-linguistic rupture, though not resulting in a complete cultural severance, caused by the malicious regime of white racism; (2) the significance of *Nommo* or the Word for Africans in America, and how *Nommo* is linked to the protean and resistant/resilient power of African/African-American identity; and (3) the structure of AAL in terms of significant lexical, phonological, stylistic, and semantic features, and what this means in terms of resisting/combating Euro/Anglo linguistic imperialism and hegemony.

Throughout Docta G's critical oeuvre she makes constant reference to 1619. For example, she notes:

The first cargo of African slaves to be deposited in what would become the United States of America arrived at Jamestown in 1619. From that point until the beginnings of the movement to abolish slavery in the nineteenth century, whites, by and large, perceived of America's African slave population as beasts of burden, exotic sexual objects, or curious primitives.[30]

In short, within the racist epistemological regime of white racism, these Africans were not *different*, but were deemed as constituting an *ontological deficiency*.[31] "We are trapped," according to Docta G, "in our own historical moment and wish to understand that."[32] In order to understand this historical moment, however, and Docta G is well aware of this, Black folk must understand their historical journey across space and time. It involves the narrative of Black folk's "unfinished business of what it means to be and talk like home."[33] Again, back to the connection between ontology, identity, and language. Docta G agrees with Fanon that white colonialism forces Black folk to question their sense of identity: "Who am I?"[34] After all, the institution of American and European slavery, with their disciplinary strategies and practices, was designed to instill in Africans a sense of inferiority and ontological servitude, to deracinate any sense of African pride, cultural identity, and home. This motif of "home" has been a rich trope for Black folk in North

America; for in their various stages of identity formation (African, Colored, Negro, Black, African-American) they have sought ways of negotiating a sense of themselves and a sense of *place* and *reality*. Docta G writes, "The societal complexity of the Black condition continues to necessitate a self-conscious construction of reality."[35]

Africans were taught to internalize negative images of themselves, to "know" themselves as chattel and property. This process was evident during the Middle Passage. During the voyage, precious Black bodies were subjected to tight forms of spatialization. The Middle Passage was itself part and parcel of a disciplinary practice to construct the Black body/self as a *thing*, to encourage Africans to begin thinking of themselves in subhuman terms. Black bodies were herded into suffocating spaces of confinement. Think here of the physically tight, economically impoverished, spaces of contemporary urban Black America. On the slave ship Pongas, for example, 250 women, many of whom were pregnant, were forced into a space of 16 by 18 feet. Feminist and cultural theorist bell hooks writes:

> The women who survived the initial stages of pregnancy gave birth aboard the ship with their bodies exposed to either the scorching sun or the freezing cold. The number of black women who died during childbirth or the number of stillborn children will never be known. Black women with children on board the slave ships were ridiculed, mocked, and treated contemptuously by the slaver crew. Often the slavers brutalized children to watch the anguish of their mothers.[36]

Molefi Asante captures the terror of the Middle Passage where he writes:

> Imagine crossing the ocean aboard a small ship made to hold 200 people but packed with 1,000 weeping and crying men, women, and children. Each African was forced to fit into a space no more than 55.9 centimeters (22 inches) high, roughly the height of a single gym locker, and 61 centimeters (24 inches) wide, scarcely an arm's length. There were no lights aboard the ships, little food, and no toilet facilities.[37]

The Middle Passage was a voyage of death, bodily objectification, humiliation, dehumanization, geographical and psychological dislocation. It was a process of cultural disruption, which involved a profound sense of religious, aesthetic, *linguistic*, teleological, and cosmological disorientation. In the "New World," we were sold from auction blocks; the Black body/self became a blood and flesh text upon which whites could project all of their fears, desires, fantasies, myths, and lies. They attempted to confiscate, permanently, our lives, our souls, and our bodies. Let's call this the "Sunken Place," that place so powerfully depicted in Jordan Peele's *Get Out*. For example, white fears and perversions created the myth of the so-called "Negro rapist." In 1903, Dr. William Lee Howard argued that Negro males attack innocent white women because of "racial instincts that are about as amenable to ethical culture as is the inherent odor of the race."[38] In 1900, Charles Carroll supported the pre-Adamite beliefs of Dr. Samuel Cartwright. The Negro was described as an ape and was said to be the actual "tempter of Eve."[39] The so-called sciences of physiognomy and phrenology, with their emphasis on the prognathous jaw of Negroes, were said to clearly support the "primitive" nature of African people. In short, the Black body/self, within the scientific discursive space of whiteness, which embodied a racist epistemology, was constructed as a mere object of the white racist gaze. Docta G is well aware of the historical existence of scientific racism where she notes:

> In the years just before the Civil War (roughly the 1840s and 1850s), scientific theories of racial superiority located social and behavioral differences between members of the human species in genetic factors, which became the basis of studies of black slaves.[40]

Through the powerful structuration of the white gaze, the Black body/self was codified and typified as a subhuman, savage beast devoid of culture. Dr. Paul B. Barringer drew from the Darwinian emphasis on heredity. According to the insights of historian George M. Frederickson, Barringer argued:

> The inborn characteristics of the Negro had been formed by natural selection during "ages of degradation" in Africa and his savage traits could not have been altered in any significant way by a mere two centuries of proximity to Caucasian civilization in America.[41]

The historian Joseph A. Tillinghast also theorized within the framework of Darwinian theory. For Tillinghast, "The Negro character had been formed in Africa, a region which supposedly showed an uninterrupted history of stagnation, inefficiency, ignorance, cannibalism, sexual license, and superstition."[42]

The idea was to "demonstrate" (though we know it was to rationalize white wicked deeds) that Africans had *no* language (perhaps a few words only), *no* history, *no* identity, and *no* peoplehood. But I/we must admit that them white boys was droppin some weak, mythical, indefensible, pseudoscientific, shit.

What is clear is that the newly arrived Africans found themselves in a hostile and dangerous world of anti-Blackness, a world that refused to recognize the complex cultural and subjective *here* from which Africans viewed the world and hated their captivity and oppression. "It was the practice of slavers to mix up Africans from different tribes."[43] Africans were forced into unfamiliar groupings so as to eliminate any sense of community, cultural, *linguistic*, or otherwise. The objective, despite, paradoxically, the racist belief that

Africans were devoid of any complex linguistic–communicative practices, was to prevent them from communicating, from gaining any sense of group identity, and, hence, suppressing any possibility of rebellion/overthrow. Consistent with Hume's belief that Africans spoke "a few words plainly," Docta G notes that in 1884, J. A. Harrison held that African-American speech was "based on African genetic inferiority."[44] For Harrison, much of Negro talk was "baby-talk."[45] Docta G concludes:

> Blinded by the science of biological determinism, early twentieth-century white linguistic scholars followed Harrison's lead, taking hold of his baby-talk theory of African American speech and widely disseminating it in academic discourse. The child language explanation of Black Language is linguistic racism that corresponds to the biological determinist assumption that blacks are lower forms of the human species whose evolution is incomplete.[46]

Such beliefs, however, were not limited to white racist "academics." As African-American linguist and anthropologist John Baugh correctly points out:

> The racist literature about blacks and black speech in particular should, of course, be dismissed in any serious analysis of the subject, but we must appreciate that the opinions expressed by white supremacists—while often absurd—reflected the feelings of a majority of white Americans.[47]

Finding themselves within this colonial context, a space of white supremacy (read: anti-Blackness), what were Africans to do? Torn from their own rich soil, and transplanted within this blood-soaked soil of North America, Africans, with their magnificent oral tradition, rich cultural modes of being, non-white constructions of reality, and their own conception of what it meant *to be*, had to make sense out of this imposed and absurd situation. *They had to survive* the existential horror and meaninglessness of white America. "But that is the essence of the Black experience: to make a way out of no way."[48] Keep in mind that North American slavery was also reinforced through the use of nondiscursive forms of brutality and oppression. It wasn't all about white racist abstract theory. Frederick Douglass knew all too well of the physical horrors of plantation life. He was torn from his mother at a very young age. The idea here was to eliminate any sense of biological and familial continuity, to attempt to break the spirit of oneness. In terms of sheer physical brutality, Douglass, who Docta G groups within the Black intellectual tradition of W. E. B. DuBois, Carter G. Woodson, and Lorenzo Turner, given his understanding of the rich oral/aural tradition of Black people, tells of the story of old Barney receiving thirty lashes on his Black flesh by Colonel Lloyd.[49] He tells of Demby who disobeyed an order given by Mr. Gore and was shot in the head as a result. Douglass says that "his mangled body sank out of sight, and blood and brains marked the water where he had stood."[50] Or, think of the young Black girl, Douglass' wife's cousin, who had fallen asleep while watching Mrs. Hick's baby. Mrs. Hick "jumped from her bed, seized an oak stick of wood by the fireplace, and with it broke the girl's nose and breast-bone, and thus ended her life."[51]

To be enslaved was to be subjected to terror. You had your teeth knocked out, were permanently separated from your family, burned to death, castrated, lynched; you watched your mother or sister raped, beaten, and shackled. This was an everyday reality and a constant live possibility for Africans bought to the "New World." But this is the historical space that must be explored, if only briefly, to understand the force of our *languaging*. Docta G is mindful of this: "I say . . . we can not talk about Black Idiom apart from Black culture and the Black experience."[52] Continuing with Douglass, Smitherman locates a significant aspect of our oral, aural, musical, and narrative motifs, viz., the use of song as a counter-hegemonic expression. These Black bodies, locked down, with very little space within which to move, must have had rich (Ghanaian, Dahomeyan, etc.) musical fire shut up in their bones. Memory. Retentions. Identity. Douglass dispels the false notion that enslaved Africans were "happy darkies" who sung their time away. Indeed, on the contrary, singing, which was a powerful semiotic marker of our enduring ability to create visions of counter-reality, solidarity, memory, and agency, was an illocutionary form of expression, communicating discontentment and protestation, which had a significant perlocutionary impact on the psychology of the enslaved. Douglass says:

> The songs of the slave represent the sorrows of his heart; and he is relieved by them, only as an aching heart is relieved by its tears . . . [the songs] told a tale of woe . . . they were tones loud, long, and deep; they breathed the prayer and complaint of souls boiling over with the bitterest anguish. Every tone was a testimony against slavery, and a prayer to God for deliverance from chains . . . To those songs I trace my first glimmering conception of the dehumanizing character of slavery . . . Those songs still follow me, to deepen my hatred of slavery, and quicken my sympathies for my brethren in bonds.[53]

Hence, even our "musicking" was a form of communication. But there were times when we had to code our language from the ofay. This is just one, though very important, semantic register of the Africans' creation of a counter-language.[54] Docta G points to an example of a stanza from an old Black folk song that includes the expression "not turn her." This was a brilliant coded way of referring to the revolutionary Black insurrectionist "Nat-Tur-ner." Docta G goes on to argue that many of the Negro spirituals were not speaking about other-worldly affairs, but about the historically concrete affairs of Black people, in the here and now of their servitude. Hence, though the lyrics (overheard by whites) suggested a *vertical* metaphysics that spoke to God, the lyrics contained a powerful social and political *horizontal* message that spoke to the urgency of escape. Docta G notes:

> The slaves used other-worldly lyrics, yes, but the spirituals had for them this-worldly meanings [What I be callin a "horizontal message."]. They moaned "steal away to Jesus" to mean stealing away FROM the plantation and TO freedom (that is, "Jesus"). They sang triumphantly "this train is bound for Glory," but the train they were really talking about was the "freedom train" that ran on the Underground Railroad. The symbolic Underground Railroad was actually a revolutionary network of escape routes and schemes devised to assist slaves fleeing to the "glory" of freedom in Canada and the North. "Go down, Moses, and tell Ole Pharaoh to let my people go." Moses—black freedom fighter Harriet Tubman, the "conductor" of the Underground Railroad, who in her lifetime assisted more than 300 slaves to escape. She would "go down" South and by her actions "tell" white slavers (Ole Pharaoh) to let her people go.[55]

This is one example of what I mean by the dynamics of linguistic resistance. Africans were able to use the language of white folk, curving it, warping it, and twisting it against them. This was/is a form of linguistic resistance/ combat and overthrow. In yo face style. Swish, two points! Docta G notes:

> When an enslaved African said, "Eve'body talkin bout Heaben ain goin dere," it was a double-voiced form of speech that *signified* on the slaveholders who professed Christianity but practiced slavery. This Africanized form of speaking became a code for Africans in America to talk about Black business, publicly or privately, and in the enslavement period, even to talk about "ole Massa" himself right in front of his face![56]

Of course, when the ofay caught on, Black folk had to change the word, expression. We talkin bout a dynamic process heah. Concerning the two-pronged dimensions of language, Ngũgĩ argues:

> Every language has two aspects. One aspect is its role as an agent that enables us to communicate with one another in our struggle to find the means for survival. The other is its role as a carrier of the history and the culture built into the process of that communication over time.[57]

Ngũgĩ sees these two aspects of language as forming a kind of dialectical unity.

Despite the long journey across the Middle Passage, one way that Africans were able to negotiate ways of surviving was through dynamic semiotic and linguistic modalities, to communicate with one another (in Pidgin and Creole) in a common struggle to stay alive. As Marlene Nourbese Philip notes:

> In the vortex of New World slavery, the African forged new and different words, developed strategies to impress her experience on the language. The formal standard language was subverted, turned upside down, inside out, and sometimes erased. Nouns became strangers to verbs and vice versa; tonal accentuation took the place of several words at a time; rhythms held sway.[58]

Africanized "Standard" American English also functioned as a medium of Black culture and reminded Black folk of the historicity of their African identity. Hence, the complete cultural rupture that was intended for enslaved Africans simply failed. "Using elements of the white man's speech, in combination with their own linguistic patterns and practices, enslaved Africans developed an oppositional way of speaking."[59] I see this as a dynamic process of sublation, which understands the African experience in America as a process of negation and preservation. No matter how much of WHO WE BE was negated, through a disruptive and colonialist "synthesis," we preserved significant and powerful elements of our rich historical past.

By God's grace! Yes, we got soul and we SUPER BAD! Soul, according to Docta G, involves "a world view that is not only God-centered, but includes the vision that Goodness and Justice is gon prevail."[60] She links soul with the dynamic philosophical category of style, which is rich with aesthetic, political, and ontological overtones. In other words, style is the dynamic expression or articulation of the motif of overcoming. She concludes: "If you got soul, yo style oughta reflect it."[61] But whassup wit all dis philosophical talk? Well, it's bout Black folk. Their linguistic preservation and combativeness constitute their style, which is deeply reflective of their souls. Yes, the souls of Black folk. DuBois be down wit it. Therefore, we need to move within that space of soul and style where our collective languaging is a commentary on both.

Contrary to the white colonialist view, Africans did not get off that Dutch ship in Jamestown without any sense of identity and culture as manifested in and structured through language. The many millions that were brought over in chains after 1619 also arrived with their nuanced cultural practices and religious worldviews as mediated through unique linguistic rules and styles. As *homo narrans* (creators of their own meaningful oral-narrative existence) and *homo significans* (creators of signs and symbols that ordered their reality), Africans already had their language and hence their own theory of reality. On this score, language is the medium through which reality is constructed. Language, then, shapes the contours of one's metaphysics. Africans had to feel a profound sense of cognitive and metaphysical dissonance within the white colonial order of things in America, with its strange language, and hence, its imposing and extraneous view of reality. As Docta G reminds us, "Language represents a society's theory of reality. It not only reflects that theory of reality, it explains, interprets, constructs, and reproduces that reality."[62] Although Docta G thinks that the Whorfians (followers of B. L. Whorf) overstate the importance of language vis-à-vis the construction of reality, she maintains:

> Reality is not merely *socially*, but *sociolinguistically* constructed. Real-world experience and phenomena do not exist in some raw, undifferentiated form. Rather, reality is always filtered, apprehended, encoded, codified, and conveyed via some linguistic shape.[63]

So as to clarify the sociolinguistic "determinist" implications of Docta G's position, it is important to note that she *does not* say that consciousness and ideology are supervenient upon sociolinguistic factors. She is careful to say that it is her "contention that ideology and consciousness are *largely* the products of what I call the 'sociolinguistic construction of reality.' "[64]

Attempting to understand this new colonial reality within the framework of their understanding of *Nommo*, the power of the word, Black folk had to feel a sense of double-consciousness or what Docta G refers to as the phenomenon of "linguistic push–pull."[65] Through the power of *Nommo*, Black folk *performatively* spoke (and continue to speak) a new reality and a new sense of identity into existence. Crossing the horror of the Middle Passage—which could take anywhere from thirty-five to ninety days, and having to contend with feces, lice, fleas, rats, disease, and dying Black bodies—failed to break the power of the African spirit; failed to silence the power of *Nommo*, which said "NO!" to white imperialism, "NO!" to white cultural hegemony, "NO!" to colonial brainwashing, and "NO!" to linguistic–cultural dispossession. There was a "deep structural" cultural awareness that the *word* can radically alter the *world*.[66] Docta G notes:

> The oral tradition, then, is part of the cultural baggage the African brought to America. The pre-slavery background was one in which the concept of Nommo, the magic power of the Word, was believed necessary to actualize life and give man mastery over things.[67]

She further notes:

> In traditional African culture, a newborn child is a mere thing until his father gives and speaks his name. No medicine, potion, or magic of any sort is considered effective without accompanying words. So strong is the African belief in the power and absolute necessity of Nommo that all craftsmanship must be accompanied by speech.[68]

Nommo is an essential ontological register of WHO WE BE. *Nommo* is capable of concretizing the Black spirit in the form of action, action that is necessary within the framework of a contentious and oppressive alien cultural environment. It was imperative that Diasporic Africans create *syncretistic constructions of reality* vis-à-vis "deep structural" linguistic–cultural (African) patterns and practices acting as the general framework through which new cultural elements were absorbed, synthesized, and reconfigured. This process is less like a Kuhnian paradigm-shift and more like a form of "adaptive fusion." It is a fusion (don't let the Jazz motif pass you by) that bespeaks the ability of Black folk to keep keepin on in the face of oppression and white terror. This process of fusion is indicative of the fact that Black folk live their lives within a *subjunctive* (indicative of our *possibilities*) ontological mode of ex-istence.[69] Docta G observes that African-American Language (or what she also refers to as Black English, Black Idiom, African-American English, African-American Vernacular English, Ebonics) "reflects the modal experiences of African-Americans and the continuing quest for freedom."[70] Given the aforementioned emphasis on the power of *Nommo* and the sheer protean and metastable force of African linguistic–cultural, psychological, and existential endurance, what then is African-American Language? The Docta is worth quoting in full:

> The Ebonics spoken in the U.S. is rooted in the Black American Oral Tradition, reflecting the combination of African languages (Niger–Congo) and Euro American English. It is a language forged in the crucible of enslavement, U.S.-style apartheid, and the struggle to survive and thrive in the face of domination. Ebonics is emphatically *not* "broken" English, nor "sloppy" speech. Nor is it merely "slang." Nor is it some bizarre form of language spoken by baggy-pants-wearing Black youth. Ebonics *is* a set of communication patterns and practices resulting from Africans' appropriation and transformation of a foreign tongue during the African Holocaust.[71]

From jump street, let's dispel certain assumptions. AAL ain no slang. "True, Black slang is Black Language, but all Black Language is not Black slang."[72] Also, we must not conflate AAL with nonstandard American English. As for the latter, examples are "the pronunciation of 'ask' as 'axe,' use of double negatives, as in 'They don't know nothing,' and the use of 'ain't.' Such features of American English are often *erroneously* characterized as Ebonics. They are not."[73] Keep in mind that Ebonics is known for its multiple negatives (this really frustrates the gatekeepers of European American Language), not simply the double negatives disapproved of by European American Language (EAL). Docta G provides an example of multiple negation from a member of the Traditional Black Church sometime during the 1960s: "Don't nobody don't know God can't tell me nothin!" And drawing from Lonne Elder's play, *Ceremonies in Dark Old Men*, Docta G provides another example: "Don't nobody pay no attention to no nigga that ain't crazy!" Multiple negation, in this example, signifies a form of linguistic, sociopsychological resistance. Docta G explains:

> Because "nigger" is a racialized epithet in EAL, AAL embraces its usage, encoding a variety of unique Black meanings. And "crazy niggas" are the rebellious ones, who resist racial supremacist domination and draw attention to their cause because they act in ways contrary to the inscribed role for Africans in America.[74]

Another point to keep in mind is that "U.S. Ebonics, aka African American Vernacular English, did not completely originate in British English, nor in other white-immigrant dialects from the seventeenth century."[75] For those who are proponents of Euro/Anglo linguistic hegemony, the state Anglicist ideologues, those who control the army, navy, major television stations, major news outlets, major publishing houses, curriculum planning, legal and corporate languaging, educational policy/policing, it's all bout the politics of erasure, rejecting Africanized linguistic–cultural legitimacy and the impact of the Africanist influence in America. In short, Euro/Anglo linguistic hegemony (*the* hegemonic tongue) is a form of colonialism and linguistic racism. As Docta G points out, however, there are syntactic patterns that are not to be found in older Anglicized syntax, but are found in West African languages. She gives as an example, "Me massa name Cunney Tomsee." The linguistic phenomenon of making a statement without the obligatory copula "is not a pattern of older British English dialects."[76] Docta G provides another example of a sentential construction without the use of the verb *to be*, which is required in English, given by an enslaved African who was located in the Dutch colony of Suriname in South America: "Me bella well" ("I am very well"). "He tall," "She my lady," and "She real phat" (no copulas) are also allowable forms of expression in West African languages.

Let's move to the aspectual verb. Docta G kicks it this way:

> This use of the verb "to be" [in AAL] derives from an aspectual verb system that is also found in many African languages, in Creole language forms of the Caribbean, in West African Pidgin English, and in the Gullah Creole spoken by blacks living on the Sea Island along the southeastern seaboard of the United States. Its use conveys the speaker's meaning with reference to qualitative character and distribution of an action over time.[77]

As an example, she provides, "He be hollin at us." This is the durative use of "to be"; it indicates iterativity or actions that are ongoing. "The sista be lookin fly" is also illustrative of iterativity. Docta G argues that the use of the verb system here demonstrates an "implied racial resistance," particularly in the light of the racist control of AAL by white America's linguistic rejection of such a verb system.[78] The "Standard English" verb system does not capture past, present, and future tense all at the same time. Consider the expression, "It bees dat way sometime." Here we have two African language features. First, "bees" is used as a habitual condition; and, second, "dat" is used instead of "that," because West African languages do not have a "th" sound; that is, the initial voiced *th* is realized as *d*. The reader will also note that in AAL the final *th* is realized as *f, t,* or *d* (e.g., "up souf" for "up south," and "wit" or "wid" for "with"). Wid regard to the expression "It bees dat way sometime," however, Docta G draws a very interesting distinction that has rich philosophical implications. She distinguishes between "language" and "style." In the previous example, language points to "bees" as an instance of iterativity. Style, however, points to a *Weltbild*, a way of picturing the world or a world picture. She argues that if we take the expression ("It bees dat way sometime") as "the total expression," then "the statement suggests a point of view, a way of looking at life, and a method of adapting to life's realities."[79] Her point here is well taken. When Nina Simone sings "It bees dat way sometime," there is the sense that life just ain fair. Docta G explains: "To live by the philosophy of 'It bees dat way sometime' is to come to grips with the changes that life bees puttin us through, and to accept the changes and bad times as a constant, ever-present reality."[80] I would only add that this expression is explosive with a surplus of significations. In this single locutionary act, we find a rich narrative of Black existence in America. It is not only descriptive, but prescriptive, suggesting how life ought to be approached. Implicit in its description is the power of the reality of existential fissure and fracture.

From what has been delineated previously, it is clear that as a people we are capable of living through and surviving white hatred, white brutality, white terror, improvising our way in and out of North American existential angst, and embracing and transcending our existential blues precisely by singing (languaging) them. The point here is that *Nommo* is operative here as a site of rupture. "It bees dat way sometime" expresses the power of the word to move Black folk toward a greater sense of community and collective hope and resistance. It's important that we recognize the symbolic weight of the locutionary act, for it speaks to the power of our ancestors to cope, endure, and survive. In other words, "It bees dat way sometime" points to the heteronomy of oppressive forces that attempt to subdue Black people, but the logic of the expression also sounds a clarion call for autonomy and is indicative of an existential transversal process that moves Black people closer to a sense of home. Docta G is all up in the deep epistemological implications of this African-American linguistic thang where she states:

What uhm runnin on you is bout a cognitive linguistic style whose semantics bees grounded not only in words but in the socio-psychological space between the words. In sum: a Black-based communications system derived from the oppressor's tongue—the words is Euro-American, the meanings, nuances and tone African American.[81]

It is precisely these meanings, nuances, and tone that are a threat to white America. For to control our own language is to control how we see ourselves, it is to some extent to explode the pathology of our double-consciousness.

Another important point regarding the verb system of AAL can be examined in relationship to Docta G's contention that we should refer to Black English as a "language" as opposed to a "dialect." The importance of this insight, and, hence, her re-conceptualization of Black English, is important in terms of African-American praxis. The reader will note that I have used African-American *Language* throughout the chapter, because I believe that this is the position that Docta G has come to embrace. However, in 1970, Docta G thought that the Black English sentential construction, "The coffee cold" was not very different from the white English version, "The coffee is cold." This was because Docta G relied upon the explanatory rules provided by the Transformational–Generative grammar framework whereby a deletion rule, permissible in English, "had been applied, so that the speaker went from 'The coffee is cold' to 'The coffee's cold,' to dropping the /'s/ in pronunciation, thereby producing 'The coffee cold.'"[82] Docta G realized that even the distinctiveness of Black English's rhetorical style and communication patterns failed to get at the distinction in meaning between "The coffee cold" and "The coffee be cold."[83] Later realizing the insights of linguist Sista Beryl Bailey, Docta G came to understand that

> There are indeed deep-structural linguistic differences, in addition to "deep" differences in rhetorical style and strategies of discourse. I began to speak of the "language," not the "dialect," of Black America. In time, I came to think of this linguistic phenomenon not only as a "language," but as a language that could be a vehicle for unifying America's outsiders and consequently as a tool for social transformation.[84]

Always with her eye on the larger political ramifications of language, Docta G insightfully notes:

> Since linguistics cannot offer the definitive word on language–dialect differentiation, it ultimately comes down to who has the power to define; or as Max Weinreich once put it, the difference between a language and a dialect is who's got the army.[85]

My sense is that when Docta G uses the expression "deep-structure," she should not be taken to mean that speakers of EAL and AAL are somehow constituted by *racially distinct* bioprograms. My sense is that, for Docta G,

AAL has a deep-structural component in that African-American languaging (as in the example, "The coffee be cold") should not be reduced to mere surface features of English, that is, that sentential constructions in AAL are merely surface representations of other sentential constructions in English. *Africanized* English is so deeply sedimented with African conceptions of the self, reality, time, and social norms of social interaction, and other modes of spiritual and cultural comportment, that there is something radically distinct— perhaps at the very psycho-linguistic (cultural) deep structural level—about AAL vis-à-vis EAL. Docta G, she postulating "that the two different speech communities employ differing thought patterns and conceptions of reality and that these differences are reflected in different styles of discourse."[86] Take for example the speech act, "What's happenin?" The expression is not simply indexed to the present moment. The question could refer to what happened already or what might be kickin off later. The point here is that the question "What's happenin?" assumes a culture, a fluid nexus of meanings, norms, and philosophical conceptions. Docta G advises that you got to get down wit the symbolic system at work here. She notes:

> See, in the Traditional African World View, time is cyclical, and verb structure is not concerned with tense, but modality or aspect. So "What's happenin?" could mean what happened in the past, what's happenin now, as well as what's gon happen in the future.[87]

Nevertheless, to refer to AAL as a *language*, to buttress this claim with solid historical and linguistic–cultural research, legal, and institutional support, is a danger to white America; for to use the term "language" is to suggest an entire cultural identity, a co-equal language (vis-à-vis EAL), and a legitimate mode of reality construction. (Whether its AAL or Gikuyu, it's all about the activity of self-empowerment and self-definition.) It is to put to rest the deficit model of African-American speech events, and, by implication, put to rest the deficit model that links AAL to inferior cognition, and, indeed, to call attention to the fact that we as a people constitute a NATION. Big Ups to our Nation Language advocates and theorists;[88] they deserve their *propers*. By the way, are you *down* with AAL as a Nation Language?

Let's talk a lil mow bout *AALanguagin*, some of its rhetorical devices. Take *call and response*. Here we have a powerful communication device utilized in both "secular" and "sacred" spheres of communication–interaction. In the latter case, in the Traditional Black Church, I recall my uncle, Reverend Matt, preachin: "Church, y'all don't heah me today!" The church folk would respond, "Preach!" Indeed, it was deemed a "dead" church if this dynamic of call and response, this *co-signing* and *co-narrating* of a shared communicative reality, failed to take place. There were even times when the music played by the pianist would seem to respond to his homiletic call. In the secular sphere (keeping in mind that the sacred and the secular constitute an organic unity in much of the African-American life-world) "the audience might manifest its response in giving skin (fives) when a really down verbal point is scored. Other approval responses include laughter and phrases like 'Oh, you mean, nigger,' 'Get back, nigger,' 'Git down baby,' etc."[89] Cognoscente of our Passage, our power to Africanize and reconfigure North American and European physical and cultural spaces, Docta G notes that call and response "is a basic organizing principle of Black American culture generally, for it enables traditional black folk to achieve the unified state of balance or harmony which is fundamental to the traditional African world view."[90] Indeed, call and response is symbolic of a profound level of intersubjectivity and linguistic–communal performativity that acknowledges the *ex-istence* (not locked in a private Cartesian sphere) of both speaker and listener. *Rhythmic pattern* is also a key feature of AAL. Again, let's return to Reverend Matt. After walking the benches (I mean, he be done got the spirit), and while the church folk up on they feet, he might say, rhythmically and melodically, in an almost "singing voice," "I-I-I-I-I-KNOOOOOW. YESSSSS-I-I-KNOOOOOW." The perlocutionary force of this form of languaging would set the church off. Half the church would git happy, deacons, members of the choir, even ushers would be dancin and shoutin in the aisles. And in a *proverbial* speech act, someone might shout, "My name is written on high," liquid joy flowin and streamin down they face. Docta G is on it: "The preacher will get a rhythm going, conveying his message through sound rather than depending on sheer semantic import."[91] The power of sound. System. Sound reasoning. Don't you go *soundin* on me. The power of an elongated *hum* can carry the pain and suffering of an entire people or signify a nod of epistemic approval.

Semantic inversion is similar in intent to the use of coded language. The idea here is to take familiar words from EAL and superimpose radically different meanings on them. For example, to be *down* with something is actually to be *up* with it, in support of it. To be *bad* is to be *good*. This linguistic practice is the same whether in Wolof, Mandingo, Ibo, or Yoruba. Docta G points out that it's the same linguistic process, but a different language.[92] She elaborates, "This linguistic reversal process, using negative terms with positive meanings, is present in a number of African languages—for example, the Mandingo *a ka nyi ko-jugu*, which literally means 'it is good badly,' that is, 'it is very good.' "[93] Again, here we have an instance of Black folk in America exercising linguistic resistance and agency, a practice of baffling and excluding the oppressive ofay.

Indirection is a linguistic species of coded language and semantic inversion. It thrives off of circumlocutory rhetoric. You know Black folk gotta move in nonlinear lines lest the evil spirits catch them. Docta G points to an example where Malcolm X gave a speech in which he opens by acknowledging his friends, sisters, brothers, and others, but goes on to acknowledge his enemies. "Not only is Malcolm neatly putting down his enemies in the audience without a direct frontal attack," according to Docta G, "he is also sending a hidden message (to those hip enough to dig it)."[94] Malcolm, in other words, is *signifyin* on those possible Black traitors ("Black Judases") sitting right there in his midst. But not only is circumlocutory rhetoric an important attribute of AAL, our language soars to the heights of *exaggeration*, another AAL discursive marker. Yo, we bees all up in the bombastic, grandiloquent, magniloquent, highfalutin, sonorous realm of talkin that talk. MLK, Jr., once referred to an issue as being "incandescently clear."[95] Docta G:

> Sometime the whole syntax of a sentence may be expressed in an elevated, formal manner, as in this invitation from a working-class black male: "My dear, would you care to dine with me tonight on some delectable red beans and rice?"[96]

And then there is that space of *braggadocio*. There are multiple signifiers within this space. "I'm the greatest!" Ali in the cultural mix. Stag-O-Lee. Jack Johnson. Rap ciphers where brothas be dropin some serious science, cultural codes, and philosophy. There are powerful tales of African folklores that narrate great escapes. Shine. Toasts. The Bad Nigga. Keepin Mista Charlie, Massa, or Miss Ann on they toes. Docta G: "Whether referring to physical badness, fighting ability, lovemanship, coolness (that is, 'grace under pressure'), the aim is to convey the image of an omnipotent fearless being, capable of doing the undoable."[97] The dynamic of *narrativizing* is also a salient feature of AAL discursivity. It involves explicating some event, some situation, in the style of the traditional African griot. The point here is that such existential events are constructed within a narrative structure, moving within a deep cultural semiotic space of familiarity. As contemporary philosophers begin to reassess the significance of the epistemological explanatory power of narrative, we been done engaged in this hermeneutic process.

Some still just don't want to recognize that rap is an ever growing, expansive linguistic space in our historical journey as masters of the Word. Rap ain no aberration. These complex brothas and sistas, engagin and pushin the discursive boundaries of what is said/sayable, articulating, through *Nommo*, what is beautiful, marvelous, mendacious, ugly, corrupt, fucked up, and surreal, are still moving Black folk in the direction of *home*. Docta G knows that rap and Hip Hop bees part of that *Nommo* continuum, that African sense of existential and communal balance. Those stylizations (linguistic, bodily, aesthetic, sonic, spiritual, metaphysical) coming out of those hood spaces/

places and hooded faces, they must be reflections of soul. And U know yo style oughta reflect it. Word! Docta G:

> Rap music is rooted in the Black Oral Tradition of tonal semantics, narrativizing, signification/signifyin, the Dozens/playin the Dozens, Africanized syntax, and other communicative practices. The Oral Tradition itself is rooted in the surviving African tradition of "Nommo" and the power of the word in human life.[98]

Let's rap/wrap it up. Docta G has shown that Black folk have always already been pushin the language envelope. Black folk have been fightin on all fronts, the physical, geopolitical, metaphysical, philosophical, aesthetic, religious, political, ideological, psychological, spiritual, symbolic, economic, hermeneutic, academic, linguistic, iconic, and more. It all points to the fact that *Black Lives Matter*. Through all of these wars, we have managed to maintain a sense of ethics, humanity, dignity, and sanity. Damn! We talkin bout folk who simply refuse to die. Don't even talk about givin up! What manner of people DO WE BE? Protean. Always already in struggle, always already beginning some new shit, conceptualizing some new order of things, some other/alternative/unheard of/unimagined/unexplored reality and mode of being. We bees doin da unthinkable. Must be *magical* and *real*. We always pushin. James Baldwin said that we've done the impossible. Whether its remaking and reconfiguring some superimposed language, creating musical instruments from some old found object, doctoring up a traditional instrument, because you know we gotta hear that twang and chromatic sound, or pushin the bounds of what it means to be human and democratic, we up on it, way out in front. Blusing. Bopping. Moving. Rapping. Hip Hopping. Historicizing. Morphing. Always in the process of red-shifting, even when we be down. And, yes, LANGUAGING. We are still in process. What next? Can't be sho. But I'll C U when WE get there. As Docta G says, stay tuned.

Chapter 22

Socially Grounded Ontology and Epistemological Agency: James G. Spady's Search for the Marvelous/ Imaginative within the Expansive and Expressive Domain of Rap Music and Hip Hop Self-Consciousness

Hip Hop is preeminently a cultural free space.

—James G. Spady

Hip Hop culture is not exclusionary. It encompasses a very wide range of black stylings. The lyrics come out of life histories, the everydayness of their experiences.

—James G. Spady

Hip Hop culture embodies privileged social knowledge communicated in its own language.

—James G. Spady

As with Docta G, James G. Spady is a scholar whose work privileges the culturally embedded and historically protean modes of being Black within the context of the quotidian, the everyday dynamic ways in which Black people make meaning. And as with Robert L. Williams, Spady takes very seriously the inventive sonic and structural dimensions of African-American discourse. Within the area of rap and Hip Hop cultural self-consciousness, Spady remains *unmatched* in methodological innovation and deep cultural and broad semiotic analysis. Indeed, to come to terms with Spady's work, it is requisite to deploy a hermeneutic lens that is capable of discerning culturally embedded signs and symbols, modes of ontological being and becoming, multifaceted epistemological ways of knowing and imagining, and broad historical trajectories that are always already protean and in process. In short, Spady's work demands a radical bracketing of assumptions that are antithetical to a dynamic social and historical ontology specific to the life-world of Black people and people of color.

Spady is a preeminent twenty-first-century cultural theorist and a cognoscente of the complex narrative and existential spaces of Hip Hop modes of being. His theoretical and epistemic point of embarkation vis-à-vis rap and Hip Hop self-consciousness demand our fullest attention and the best of our critical cognition. Moreover, Spady's work stipulates that it is our duty—assuming that we are genuinely and earnestly prepared to engage the *marvelous* world of rap and Hip Hop self-consciousness—to exercise fundamental respect for the interior/phenomenological and nuanced meaning-making and world-creating actualities and possibilities within rap and Hip Hop culture. For Spady, it is about both the ethics of knowledge production and the ethics of recognizing the integrity and imaginative agency of those Hip Hop beings who have created and continue to create rap and Hip Hop culture. Spady is unique in this regard. His approach to rap and Hip Hop culture militates against the superimposition of an extraneous explanatory framework that places under erasure the voices, perspectives, and subjectivities of those Hip Hop beings who are actively cognizing and creating their complex worlds on their own terms, within their own spaces. This makes his work especially difficult as it requires epistemic humility, the recognition of multiple geographies of cognition, the capacity to comprehend diverse and complex linguistic expressions and bodily articulations, the capacity to dwell within complex imaginative domains, and the cultural capital required to be respected within the *emic* spaces of Hip Hop beings. As such, Spady's work, in the areas of rap and Hip Hop culture, is methodologically innovative and rich in its theorization of the multiple complex cultural terrain and dynamics of rap and Hip Hop.

The triumvirate epigraphs at the beginning of this chapter constitute, though do not exhaust, essential philosophical struts that buttress Spady's culturally thick description and analysis of the highly expansive and expressive interlocking domains of rap music and Hip Hop self-consciousness. For Spady, rap music and Hip Hop self-consciousness are inextricably linked to a socially *grounded* ontology. As such, rap music and Hip Hop self-consciousness take their point of embarkation from the ground up. After all, to theorize the culturally complex sites of rap music and Hip Hop self-consciousness, one *must* be grounded analytically and synoptically. Indeed, one *must* be willing and able to traverse those highly activated streets where intelligibility itself gets negotiated. It is a mode of traversing that is not only physical, but conceptual. Indeed, for Spady, these modalities, the physical and the conceptual, do not constitute diametrically opposed poles, but are constantly in communication, intertextual and interpenetrative. In short, within this context, Spady rejects a strict and pure metaphysical dualism.

Regarding the former, the physical, there is the need to negotiate complex physical urban spaces that have their own situational, geographical histories and markers of meaning. One must be attentive to and cognizant of the differential spatial logics that operate within particular locations. One must be equipped *to be* in those spaces—where one's body schema is unstressed and one is indeed at home among the corporeal stylizations of a dignified people who know all too well when you're fakin' the funk. Regarding the latter, the conceptual, there is the necessity to understand how meaning is constructed and contested, how social worlds are constructed, understood and cognized—explicitly and implicitly. In short, to negotiate/traverse those spaces conceptually, it is important that one understands the *emic* dimensions embedded within those spaces, that is, how the social actors come to understand themselves and their world through symbol systems and folkways (the *lore* of it all) that are meaningful *to them*.

It is important, in other words, to comprehend how those who live within those spaces understand who they are, how they have become who they are, and what they make of the process of becoming who they are. One must also comprehend the complex tropes, mythologies, subtle paralinguistic gestures, *imaginings*, and narrative strategies that are deployed to frame who they have been/are/will be. In this way, epistemological respect is granted a priori. One must be prepared to keep abreast of those social worlds that are incredibly "fast-paced, urban, audacious, multivariant and highly auditory."[1] These fluid oral and aural spaces, as Spady suggests, "will not only enable you to come into contact with yourselves. [They] may even allow you to apprehend the flame of life within you."[2] In short, such spaces are not only self-revelatory, but have the capacity to engender deep levels of renewed existential vivacity.

One must be prepared to enter those heightened states of Hip Hop self-consciousness that will inevitably challenge one's sense of reality, one's place in the normative order of things, one's epistemic assumptions about what is known and what is knowable. And even if one shares, as Spady does, "the cultural, philosophical values embedded in Black life stylings,"[3] one must remain epistemologically humble and contextually flexible (again, as Spady does) and always already prepared to grasp new configurations of the "real" as experienced and expressed by diacritically Hip Hop conscious beings. It is about finding out "what members of the Hip Hop Nation think and do and why."[4] After all, "Daily, new words and even newer concepts spring forth from [these] urban enclave[s] of concrete and concepts."[5]

As Spady writes, "Only members of the Cognoscenti realize that Hip Hop embodied a modern, youthful developmental philosophy from the ground up—or more accurately—an African American philosophy from the streets up."[6] Notice the shift? Notice how Spady has moved the center, how he convinces us to relearn what we've learned. M. Merleau-Ponty reminds us that "true philosophy consists in relearning to look at the world."[7] If this is true, then Spady has effectively provided us with a paradigm shift, a way of seeing Black modes of being with greater depth, complexity, and respect. On this score, for Spady, the street is not only a site of Black *homo possibilitas*, but a site of Black *homo philosophicus*. In other words, human transcendence, growth, and learning need not be restricted to the academy; it is within the context of the streets that unique possibilities of self-transcendence, self-knowledge, and philosophical cognition are born. We should not underestimate the radical nature of this claim. These streets are not dominated by nihilism and pathology, but sites of *Bildung*. These streets are grounding; they are where folk dwell. The streets are ready-to-hand. Beanie Sigel is cognizant of the ontological and epistemic significance of street location, when he says, "in my music, I keep it street, to relate to them [the youth] 'cause that's where they at."[8]

For Spady, it is from within the context of this ontological grounded-ness that epistemological agency is activated, enacted, and shaped. Spady works with a conception of ontology that refuses to forget that *Black human existence* (*existere*, "to stand out") is dynamic, improvisational, multilayered, fluid, and an open horizon, one that constantly expands. Given the reality of this dynamic ontological grounding, the expressive possibilities within Black life and living are always already existentially penultimate. Black cultural *autopoiesis* or self-creation, while contextually and historically grounded, is always underway, resisting forms of fixity that oppress pregnant forms of expressivity. Germane here is the insight of the quintessential iconoclast of Western, white cultural models *and* idols, James T. Stewart. He argues that within the domain of the artifactual, we cannot "create *a* forever; but [we] can create forever."[9] Spady realizes that to superimpose an abstract ontology on the lived experiences of Black-people-in-motion is to misread and distort the unique and dynamic "universe of symbolic action"[10] within which they move and have their being; it is to misrepresent the rich and bold self-narrations and semiotic sites of meaning-making that they have crafted for themselves and the *pragmatics* that is specific to those sites; and, it is to misrepresent the axiological frames of reference that they deploy to make sense of their lives. For Spady, to comprehend these complex spaces of self-creation and self-understanding, it is important to respect such sites of indigeneity, sites where Black people continue to exercise levels of creative authority over their own bodies, voices, and geographic spaces.

Spady is concerned with uncovering what it is like for Hip Hop beings to feel deeply, to express emotions with joy, with celebration, and with tension, and what it means to revel in the mystery of Black life in the late twentieth and early twenty-first centuries. Yet, this hermeneutics of respect vis-à-vis the indigenous (and expansive) ontology, epistemology, and aesthetics of

Black people is not new to Spady, but has been a cardinal feature of his work for over forty years. *Indigené: An Anthropology of Future Black Arts* is a broad and complex text—one that called upon cultural workers in a variety of significant capacities—that attempts to capture and provide a feel for what it was like to be Black/hue-man within the context of the 1970s. For example, when framing the text, Spady wrote, "*Indigené*: is the anthology that gives us a feeling of what it is like to be Black—human—people of hue, people with ideas, people on the move."[11] My point here is that Spady's approach to complex Black cultural spaces has always been to understand and explicate the thick and rich cultural roots and grounded-ness of the people who inhabit the cultural cosmos of those cultural spaces. With tremendous integrity, Spady has, in the discourse of Black Arts Movement (BAM) theorist Larry Neal regarding the concept of culture, engaged "the values, the life styles and the feelings of the people as expressed in everyday life."[12] Indeed, in the powerful words that surrealist André Breton used to describe his friend and colleague, Negritude poet Aimé Césaire, I would argue that Spady "is one of the most demanding [cultural theorists] not only because he is probity itself, but because of the extent of his culture, [and] the quality and breadth of his knowledge."[13]

There is something kinetic and highly mobile within Black spaces of lived experience. Something is always about to kick off/jump off within these highly subjunctive, mundane spaces. One must look closely so one does not miss what *is* there, miss the complexity of Black bodies in motion, purposely moving through the streets, enacting and performing culturally rich speech acts, micro-social forms of transaction, and modes of being and being-together. One must be careful not to miss the complex epistemic claims that are made and contested within these spaces. Moreover, within such existentially rich spaces, narratives are woven, lives are storied, identities are created and deconstructed, and memories are made and cherished. Indeed, it is within such *remembered*, everyday cultural spaces that the quotidian takes on a dimension of the extraordinary, where detailed everyday modes of being fascinate and function as sharable and unforgettable lineaments of a life. For example, in Lupe Fiasco's "Never Forget You," he articulates with clarity memories that speak to questions of economics, like wearing second-hand clothes, and seeing prostitutes, and kids selling drugs, and drug needles where he and his friends would play catch.[14] And in Slick Rick's "Memories," he raps about Kool-Aid, and how he would slide notes in school, and chew Bazooka bubble gum and how within the package there would be Bazooka Joe cartoons.[15] And Will Smith's "Summertime" captures the sweltering heat on hot Philly streets, where Black boys and girls would turn on fire hydrants (or get adults to) in order to keep cool, and where Black boys would buy new sneakers and new gear to impress the girls on the neighborhood basketball courts.[16]

These quotidian forms of cultural engagement—communicated through rap—are rich in meaning and signify multiple layers of complexity that speak to the everydayness of modes of Black existence. Kool-Aid, Bozooka bubble gum, new sneaks, and running ball are significant markers of social identity. Like Neal's incredible versatility of discourse, rappers have this incredible verbal dexterity to "paint the smallest thing into something of absolute intense value."[17] Each bardic wordsmith discussed here describes a space that is *lived*; a secondary skin, as it were, that bears the ontological, epistemological, and corporeal signature of those Black bodies that are constantly and contiguously engaged. Yet, as *lived space*, Black bodies dwell within those spaces, and perform those cultural rituals, not as neoliberal atoms moving through a spatial void, but as profoundly social actors moving within a dramaturgical and normed space of *familiar* and *familial* places, faces, and cultural objects. One might say that Black bodies within these specific spaces are "potentialities already mobilized by the perception" of familiar street/grounded phenomena that "offer themselves to [Black people] as poles of action."[18] Yet, those Black bodies and those familiar street/grounded phenomena are always mutually communicative and transactional, constituting, as suggested previously, a "subject-*cum*-object" metaphysics that isn't stagnant, pure, and rigid. One might argue that those Black bodies and those familiar street/grounded phenomena constitute a network of transacting "actants." As such, Spady is not only cognizant of the genius of persons, but the "genius of place."[19] The two are symbiotic. To engage this place *and* space, it is necessary, as Spady might say, to take a *marvelous Black plunge* in search of meaning. My claim is that we can't really understand Spady's complex conceptual framing of rap and Hip Hop self-consciousness without having some understanding of his search for the marvelous and the plunge that is requisite.

In stream with Glifford Geertz and Max Weber, Black people are indeed suspended in webs of significance that they have spun themselves. Black culture, then, constitutes precisely these webs, and the analysis of these webs is "not an experimental science in search of law but an interpretive one in search of meaning."[20] Spady is well aware of the absolute significance of meaning, and the meaning *of meaning*. Yet, Spady explores instantiations of meaning, as Neal would say, where "the light is black (now, get that!) as are most of the meaningful tendencies in the world."[21] Hence, to understand Black culture requires a form of hermeneutics that is itself grounded within the stylizations and shared epistemic spaces of those Black people who inhabit those spaces; there is the importance of a shared familiarity, a shared social space of ontology—even as this shared space is always already in tension and under negotiation. This space is dynamic and metastable. To attempt to grasp the complexity of such lived spaces, it is necessary to immerse one's self into a cultural space of meaning-making that is highly charged, creative, and paradoxical; a cultural space where the "secular" and the "sacred" reside side by side; indeed, a space where the "secular" and the "sacred" are mutually implicative and where rigid disjunctions are interrogated. Indeed, this cultural space is tense and accommodating; it is a space where a "drunk" who can hardly walk and "crack fiend" in search of an everlasting high can still give *wise counsel*. It is a space where "Even thug niggahs pray"[22] and show each other love. Did you recoil? If so, then you've missed the complex existential hybridity and grounded density of Black life. Spady notes, "Among the most ancient of people, Blacks have never tried to dichotomize the sacred and secular."[23] Spady knows that "Diggers of the soil"[24] can see this marvelous cultural complex web of meaning, a web that leads off in so many directions, though not in linear directions—indeed, more rhizomic than arboric.

The webs of meaning within these cultural spaces constitute a veritable complex labyrinth that spirals, making links and references on the way toward some finite, though ever expanding, conceptual and consanguineal multiverse. What I have found (and continue to find) remarkable and formidable about Spady's writing style is that it *performs* (mimetically) the reality that it describes/explores. The words on the page are *doing something*, not simply conveying meaning. Yet, his writing also enriches and augments, without distorting, the reality that it engages/explores. It is a style of writing that is very demanding on its reader, especially as Spady deploys subtle and interlocking references that carry the trace of other complex fluid meanings, signs, and symbols. His writing style, in other words, enacts the same complex movement and density that is there being enacted within complex spaces of cultural existence. To enter into the space of his written texts is to enter into an interconnecting linguistic and metalinguistic space of multiple signifiers. It is to step into a universe of discourse that often requires a third and fourth reading. Spady has made that plunge; he is a digger of the soil.

Larry Neal was/is a digger as well. He knew and knows that "counter poised against this oppression [that Black people endure] is a fantastically dynamic culture."[25] Speaking of the blues, that existential form of being, becoming, and artistic creation that is capable of touching and yet transcending white forms of imposed degradation, Neal writes, "For the creation of the blues was a ritual act whose purpose was to make the race more able to survive."[26] Neal is speaking about the very heart of a people who refuse to die; who continue to self-create and resist the historical weight of white oppression. Yet, isn't this what it partially means to be in search of the marvelous, that which transcends a certain constructed reality? After all, Neal calls it a *fantastically* dynamic culture. Isn't the marvelous that which declares itself visible in the face of white hegemonic interpretive frameworks that can only, paradoxically, "see" invisibility? German philosopher Hegel failed to see it. He could only see the absence of *Geist*/Spirit. French philosopher Sartre

failed to see it. He could only see "Blackness" as a minor term of a larger dialectical progression, relegating the Négritude movement to laws outside of its
own self-determination. Yet, the very process of searching for the marvelous
rejects the insertion of "necessity into the foundation of [one's] freedom."[27]
Isn't the marvelous that which is always already in excess? Cheikh Anta Diop
notes, "To people whose history was arbitrarily reduced to a small number of
centuries by tendentious theorizers, the important factor is the restoration of
the feeling of historical continuity."[28] Isn't this feeling and fact of historical
continuity a site of the marvelous? As the extraordinary bard, word warrior, and magical realist Kamau Brathwaite notes, "African culture not only
crossed the Atlantic, it crossed, survived, and creatively adapted itself to its
new environment."[29] The continuity and survival of shared forms of worship,
bodily motility, linguistic and semiotic expression, and a rich sense of collective myth-making, storytelling, and urban *Toasting* speak to the existence of
the marvelous. As Spady notes, "A failure to link the two beings [our African
progenitors and contemporary Black people], result[s] in an estranged being
dangling between here and there. *Groundation is essential*."[30] Within this
context, Spady is aware of the dangers of an alienated Black consciousness,
a truncated historical and cultural existence.

Deploying the private mythology of Black America, I would argue that
Neal *is* Shine. And Neal refused/refuses to be defined, fragmented, and
tethered by white assumptions and white needs. So, Neal *swam on*, refusing
"to accept a truncated Negro history which cuts us off completely from our
African ancestry. To do so is to accept the very racist assumptions which we
abhor."[31] Spady knows that same deep river and he refuses to descend, refuses
to be conceptually limited by extraneous assumptions and constructs that do
epistemological violence to the integrity of the deep cultural links that extend
from Africa to Black America.

The fact that Black people were able (and are able) to nurture and voice
their past and contemporary visions speaks to the existence of the marvelous,
in spite of oppressive acts of white silencing through the use of the whip; in
spite of white attempts at rendering Black bodies docile and bestial; in spite
of Black bodies being packed into the hold of ships that permeated with the
stench of feces, urine, vomit, filth, and putrefaction; in spite of Black bodies that died in the darkness of Elmina Castle; in spite of Black bodies being
brutally silenced by iron muzzles forced around their mouths; in spite of
Black bodies being stopped, criminalized, and jailed by the establishment of
Black codes; in spite of Black bodies (many castrated) hanging from trees
in the form of strange fruit; in spite of Black bodies being policed by Jim
Crow laws; and, in spite of Black bodies being threatened and beaten as
they attempted to vote. Diop alludes to that site of the marvelous where he
exclaims, "We must rejoice!"[32] If Black culture was a site of Hegelian nullity,

then there would be no need to rejoice. If the "standard bearers with vested interest in the 'official culture' "[33] were allowed to define the reality of Black people, then there would be no need to rejoice. So, Black people must rejoice because they are able not only to "flip the script," but to rewrite the script, to reinvent who they are and to define their own realities. According to Spady, "Hip Hop culture mediates the corrosive discourse of the dominating society while at the same time functions as a subterranean subversion. Accommodating both internal tensions and dynamic ciphers, it establishes a counter discourse."[34] Theorizing the dynamism of Hip Hop, Spady also argues, "Its transformatory and emancipatory powers are evident each time you see a young blood locked to the music being transmitted through the earphone. They exist in a community of expressive rebellion, in states of always always, altering what has traditionally been the culture of the ruling class."[35]

Spady is theorizing at the very nucleus of the marvelous within the context of Hip Hop culture through the deployment of the term "subterranean subversion," a form of destabilization that comes from beneath, which is metaphorically linked to those who are diggers of the soil. His notion of "counter discourse" suggests the importance of a *disruptive* discursive performance that engages in its own counter-legitimating practices. Spady's conceptualization of transformatory and emancipatory spaces within Hip Hop speaks to the trans-phenomenal character of Hip Hop life and being. His notion of expressive rebellion theorizes the gesticulatory and articulatory domains of an embodied Black life-world that refuses to be silent and that insists upon exercising its muscular tensions and expressing its folk imaginative constructions. Spady's argument is that rap music and Hip Hop self-consciousness are sites of innovative creations that both reconfigure reality and redefine the meaning of reality. To inflect the words of Breton, Spady conceptualizes rap music and Hip Hop self-consciousness as sites which have the "character of extending, strangely, the limits of so-called reality."[36] For Spady, it is within the context of the everyday, the quotidian, that the real and the surreal are in creative tension. Many of us, unlike Spady, have missed the *fantastically* dynamic culture of Hip Hop Black youth who are willing to make that marvelous Black plunge and who are extending, strangely, the limits of so-called reality. Within these Hip Hop spaces, Spady is cognizant that many conceptual formulations and categories that grow out of these spaces are indeed *sur* ("beyond") *real*. According to Spady, categories which are foreign to the interior lived experiences of Black youth "don't always get at African world experiences. Those sharp dichotomies are much too rigid, too obfuscating for those modern knowers of reality and surreality."[37]

Perhaps we are asking the wrong questions, questions that elide the importance of an existential phenomenological approach that takes seriously what it means *to be* in the mode of Hip Hop. We have missed the fundamental necessity of executing a deep *social ontological* inquiry/analysis into the lives of Hip Hop beings. In other words, "what it meant [means] to *be* Hip Hop, to exist in a Hip Hop Culture-World, to possess a Hip Hop mode of being and way of viewing the world remains lost in obscure analyses, shit that don't even feel like Hip Hop."[38] Indeed, it is that shit that don't even feel like Hip Hop that obfuscates the marvelous. Like the Haitian born surrealist–activist Jacques Stephen Alexis, Spady understands the "intervention of the marvelous."[39] I would also argue that Spady understands how the forces of hegemonic Eurocentric ideologies function as "the terrible enemy of the Imagination"[40] of Black people. And like that of Ted Joans, a free and nomadic figure, another digger of the soil in quest for the marvelous, one preeminent function of Spady's wide ranging and prolific corpus serves to free us, to describe, conceptualize, and analyze the indomitable spirit of Black people. And where Alexis speaks of sites of power that devour fantasy, and the implied need to keep the imagination alive, it is Howard Thurman who speaks of the capacity of Black people to deploy laughter, which is a species joy, indeed, a weapon, capable of altering reality, to keep "their spirits from being eaten away by gloom and hopelessness."[41] Black laughter, in other words, can serve a *sur-real* function, altering, transforming, and transcending certain presumed manifestations of "reality," rendering dubious and questionable the taken for granted "real." Within this context, Black laughter and the deployment of the imagination function as powerful sites of embodied resistance, reconfiguration, and innovation.

The marvelous is the site of possibility. Spady is aware of how Neal embodied the marvelous: "Neal, the poet, came to understand that no matter how bleak things appeared to be at the moment, there were always possibilities."[42] For Neal, that sense of the marvelous, that search for the marvelous, was no doubt instilled in him, as Spady theorizes, "at an early age through 'normal' and 'paranormal' African-American experiences in North Philly."[43] Note the reference to the importance of *genius loci* (or genius of place) and the family resemblance between *para* ("above" or "beyond") normal, and *sur* in surreal. Malcolm X also knew of the power of the paranormal and the surreal; he knew of what it meant to have *visions* of possibility. Neal captures a moment in the life of Malcolm where extending, strangely, the limits of so-called reality was manifest. Prescient in his suggestiveness of a form of Jim Crowism vis-à-vis the prison–industrial complex, Neal writes, "America is the world's/greatest jailer,/and we all in jails/Black spirits contained like magnificent/birds of wonder/I now understand my father urged/on by the ghost of Garvey,/and see a small brown man standing in a corner. The/cell. cold. dank. The light around him vibrates. Am I crazy? But to understand is to submit to a more perfect will, a more perfect order. To understand is to surrender the imperfect self for a more perfect self."[44]

As argued at the beginning of this chapter, for Spady, rap music and Hip Hop self-consciousness are inextricably linked to a socially *grounded* ontology. However, as Spady and Neal might ask, "Now, can I lay this out, or will you take me through all kinds of changes?" Spady takes seriously the ways in which streets, corners, alleys, and other urban sites, function as part and parcel of wider social matrixes within which self-formation takes place. For example, in his insightful and consummate approach to understanding Neal, Spady writes, "His place of origin features strongly in his understanding of self and identity."[45] To "gain further insight into how belonging to this locality may have impacted Neal's formation of self,"[46] one must seek complex discursive and nondiscursive influences. And in his unprecedented exploration of the *Lebenswelt* of Georgie Woods, Spady writes, "In [the] attempt to locate the basis of Georgie Woods' reality we have to examine his life in the social environment that shared him. . . . It is there that we locate many of the fundamental societal elements that shaped his communication style as well as essence of his everydayness being."[47] Notice Spady's emphasis upon "communication style" and "everydayness being." Both of these phenomena are linked and essential to understanding Georgie Woods' reality. Extending these crucial assumptions to Hip Hop, the point here is that to understand the complexity of Hip Hop social actors, whether in the Bronx, Miami, Philly, Cali, Chi-town, Newark, Sydney, Dar Es Salaam, Japan, you name it, one must understand the *lived* world within which they are intimately engaged or *shared*, to use Spady's turn of phrase. And as Eve says in her own voice, a voice certain of who she is and how she became who she is: "Yeah! Just like I was saying, Philly made Eve. Everything that's in my rhymes. Everything that's in my style. Eve is from Philly, you know what I'm saying? It's not New York. It's nowhere else but Philly. Nobody else could sound like that! It's because I'm from Philly. Philly streets. They raised me good. They raised me right, obviously."[48] Notice her emphasis on "Philly streets." She is very specific about her genesis. She is well aware of how a specific social location impacts her being-in-style. There is no bad faith here, but a sense of honesty and gratitude.

Spady knows that to understand the situated *Erlebnis* of Hip Hop beings, which includes their vernacular reality, it is not just a question of deploying effective heuristics or achieving methodological accuracy, but it is a question of ethical obligation. In this regard, Spady's *oeuvre* is governed by both aesthetics and ethics. This approach is a species of *keeping it real*. After all, to understand Tupac's existence, for example, one must come to terms with understanding "the very life of a Hennessy-drenched, thug ethicized existence."[49] To understand that mode of thug existence is to come face to face with the everydayness of Black existence and its deep tensions, forms of tension that are not necessarily instances of contradictions or mutual exclusions.

Locating the lived space of Schooly D, Spady writes, "Philly is the logical space in which Schooly D exists. It is there that he both learns and ground[s] the validity of his speech acts, the lyrics of his highly charged story raps. To know Schooly is to have learned the extraordinary street wisdom, mores and ethics common to those growing up in Phillytown."[50] And while "the lyrics in segments of Hip Hop music represent different and often heightened dimensions of consciousness,"[51] for Spady, it is the social ontological ground/street that shapes this heightened consciousness. As Spady rightly asks, "What is text without context?"[52] Theorizing context (the site of street ontology) and text (the site of creative bards and other speech acts) within a larger framework, Spady writes, "No wonder they [Hip Hop bards] are so graphic, dynamic and allegorical. The imaginative locus of hip hop shifts in accordance with the course of racial history on the concrete streets of black America. The systemic character of this music reflects the here and now."[53] The "here and now," of course, does not deny that Hip Hop, along with its highly stylized discourse, is highly mobile and global. It has moved, after all, "from New York to New Zealand, from the Bay to Bei-rut."[54] Rather, the here and now suggests temporal and spatial localizations. On this score, "Localization forces us to contend with 'on-the-ground' realities, the specific ethnographic contexts, and the sociopolitical arrangement of the relations between language use, identities, and power."[55]

As stated, however, there is agency (epistemic and otherwise) on these streets. The relationship between one's social ontological grounding and one's agential force is symbiotic. One is marked by those spaces as one is also a marker of those spaces. As Philly's own Sha'dasious knows, "Putting your thing down means to leave your mark."[56] While Spady theorizes the reciprocal relationship between social grounding/social spaces and agential expressions and configurations of being/knowing/identity/self, he is also cognizant of how the streets can be dangerous, how they demand a specific tactical street knowledge. He knows about the importance of agile street comportment, "knowing how to move outside the range of a moving bullet, ducking in the alley, up the side streets."[57] Yet, there are different ways of confronting, marking, being on, dialoguing with, and talking back to those streets. Hip Hop, after all, can accommodate varied styles, multiple identities, heterogeneous selves, complex personas, excoriating satire, irony, embellished fantasy, and wide-ranging vernacular styles. And those multiple identities, they needn't be real, but can be just as rich and even edifying. I'm thinking here about Stag-O-Lee. The aesthetics of cool discourse or "cool talk" and what it means to "style and profile to the max"[58] can carry cultural capital that makes a difference in terms of how one negotiates those streets. This places us within that cultural terrain of braggadocio and swagger. Then again, that cultural/street terrain can be all-too-real. I'm thinking here about

Iceberg Slim. Spady writes, "He was master of the crazy side of the street, the up in your face, thrown down wherever you are, drinking, cursing, naming and profaning section of wherever you were. Yo! But he was Ice."[59] Yet, the street repertoire of Iceberg Slim is part of the everydayness of Black life— *one has to keep it real.*

Schooly D, cognoscente of the everydayness of street being and becoming, knows that "it is imperative to exhibit a rough exterior in order to exist"[60] in the midst of that everydayness. Capturing the everyday street dynamics of Black life, Spady writes, "Dancing and profiling. The streets remain the locus of the Hip Hop world. On the corners lessons are learned, reasoning done. You can dance to stop from freaking out. Not a lot of space here. So they run to the corner to get a cold beer. All while the *world* is closing in on them. Spinning, sinning and all the while defending."[61] Hip Hop pioneer Melle Mel knows about the importance of defending: "You gotta write your own ticket in this life because if you don't then somebody is definitely gonna write a ticket for you and you ain't gonna ride first class."[62]

Spady's critical work on rap music and Hip Hop culture takes readers on the *emic* cultural inside of the very dynamism of what it means to be a Hip Hop self-conscious being. In doing so, he is able to explore with great profundity and care the ways in which Black youth hermeneutically (and sometimes hermetically) engage their worlds. As H. Samy Alim, Samir Meghelli, and Spady write, "The hiphopography paradigm integrates the varied approaches of ethnography, biography, and social, cultural, and oral history to arrive at an emic view of Hip Hop Culture (what's really needed are *emic views of Hip Hop Cultures*)."[63] Notice the pluralizing. It is important in Hip Hop culture to valorize heteroglossia. Otherwise, as stated here, we will be left with shit that don't even feel like Hip Hop. As we know, Hip Hop voices can seriously challenge our aesthetic sensibilities, epistemological biases, and ethical frameworks. As Spady points out, however, there are Hip Hop lyricists who "have chosen to speak out of the private mythology of black street culture. It may be raw, rank and unnerving but it operates out of another side of the black stream."[64] The reader will note that Spady says "chosen." In short, Spady recognizes agency within the context of lyrical articulation, which implies that Hip Hop artists are able to name and claim their *own* realities, narrate who and what they are, and signify ways in which they prefer to be seen/understood. Yet, each unique standpoint is part of a larger complex cipha. This is why Spady is able to recognize the Hip Hop signature of the Fresh Prince. He writes, "No need to dis what was being done by other rappers. It was a cleaver, clearing of space for other dramaturgical African American experiences."[65] From the Geto Boys' "Mind is Playing Tricks on Me," Salt-N-Pepa's "Let's Talk About Sex," to Public Enemy's "Fight the Power," Lupe Fiasco's "Bitch Bad," and Jay-Z's "Empire State of Mind,"

Hip Hop is grounded in terms of heterogeneity and inextricably linked to, as Spady writes, "the tension of paradox, the presence of life tragedy, metaphors and similes [and], the profoundest, deepest sense of self-identification and self-actualization."[66] What we have here is the recognition that Hip Hop beings are *homo narrans* (agential storytellers) and *homo significans* (active symbol users). Spady also mentions "another side of the black stream." In other words, there are Black vernacular forms, metaphors, and similes that, while a part of another side of the Black stream, are nevertheless *within* the Black stream. This places us not only within the space of an organic, diverse, and web-like socially grounded ontology, but also within the space of epistemological agency and epistemological pluralism and the politics thereof.

As an example of Spady's engagement with the social ontology of place and space, conceptually and visually, his groundbreaking essay, "Grandmaster Caz and the HipHopography of the Bronx," helps to flesh out these concepts vis-à-vis the Hip Hop constituted and constituting being of Grandmaster Caz. The text also provides us with Spady's commitment to engaged dialogue and respect for the spatial locus of conversational dynamism, a space that functions to install mutual flourishing. What is effectively conveyed is the respect for the storied life of one's interlocutor and respect for the social space of his/her being and becoming. To disrespect the place is to disrespect the nurturing groundations of the interlocutor him/herself. There is nothing static about this process. This is made clear as Spady moves peripatetically with Grandmaster Caz through the Bronx, that "vast cityscape of multiple realities."[67] Spady is operating within a familiar space. Then again, anyone who has engaged face to face with Spady, as I have on *so many* occasions, has experienced the sheer range of urban sites/geographic spots where he is *at home*—conversationally. John Baugh enters the discourse cipha: "It is one thing to recognize the need to gather data from representative consultants, but it is another matter altogether to get the job done."[68] Yet, Spady gets the job done and does so with tremendous insight and cultural epistemic verve. Spady places great importance on conversational ethics where two or more are mutually present to one another. There is high regard for the voice of one's interlocutor, relational connectivity with one's interlocutor in terms of linguistic familiarity and the exercise of meaningful communicative body language that solicits and grounds a sense of mutual belonging or intersubjective solidarity, and there is a sense of shared respect for the historically and semiotically pregnant physical terrain. Spady provides us with an approach where the participant-observer is able "to temper individual confidence insensitive to the demands of story-laden content, persons, the historical situation, and new insights of revelation."[69]

As he moves through the cityscape of the Bronx, Spady is practicing nothing short of that perennial conversational style known as *philosophical engagement*, a dialogical space where *phronesis* (or practical wisdom exercised within situational contexts) and *elenchus* (or the critical emphasis upon conceptual and definitional clarity) are enacted. Spady is not only able to traverse the cityscape of the Bronx, thus dwelling near Caz within his milieu, but is able to speak the *nation language* that shapes Caz's worldview. This takes us back to Spady's emphasis upon communication style and everydayness of being. Not only does Spady speak nation language, with all of its specific contours and rhythms, but he shares "the cultural, philosophical values embedded in Black life stylings. HipHopography provides [a] unique means of assessing and accessing the word/world realities found therein."[70] Within HipHopography, there is also the deconstruction of hierarchical distancing approaches found in other works that explore the lives of Hip Hop beings. The de-hierarchical approach emphasizes a shared participatory space of mutual respect and equanimity. And it is with that mutual respect that Caz takes us through the Bronx—concernfully. Caz is ensconced within that space. Naming and claiming his reality, he knows the historical significance of early Hip Hop cultural sites such as the Hevalo, Sparkle, and the Roxy. He knows about the importance of early "graffiti" artists and Hip Hop progenitors such as Zulu Nation, Kool Herc, Afrika Bambaataa, and Melle Mel to the formation of Hip Hop culture. For Caz, moving through the space of the Bronx becomes mnemonic. He says, "Damn, I'm catching flashbacks already. This is where I used to live, and I haven't been back since I left New York. Yo, this is it. This is the [Disco] Fever, man you have to take a picture of this."[71] Notice his emphasis; he knows what needs to be documented and he is eager to finesse that space. Caz: "Come on, let's go to the next spot."[72]

Engaging Caz to reflect on what it was like to hear Kool Herc deejaying at the Hevalo, he says to Spady, "It was jumping off. . . . There were girls all over the place. I mean the music. They was breakdancing, the B-Boys were in there. I was like, *this is the shit*."[73] Check the rich discourse. Caz was aware of the aesthetic caliber of someone like Herc. The entire scene, the activated social space, was, as he says, *the shit*. Cognizant of his own place within Hop Hip and his own embodiment of mad skills, Caz narrates his own unmatched preeminence: "All the kids that be talking about 'old school this and old school that'—old my ass. I'll bust your ass right now, let's go. We don't even need a beat, let's go a cappella. Ain't nothing change but the weather."[74] One gets to witness Caz's self-knowledge and feel the daring and the challenge. He wants to set the record straight—*straight outta of the Bronx*. Within this conversational space, Spady engaged Caz on his own epistemic and social ontological turf. And Spady pays serious epistemic respect. Asking Caz to define what *he thinks* makes for an aesthetically dope cut, Caz says, "Being on time and being nice. Mixing was like disco. So being able to mix one record into another, that's cool. But you had to have the quickness

with your hands, and just how you throw the records in on people."[75] Having
battled Bambaataa in 1978, Caz gives props where they are due: "He blew
me out."[76] In his own parlance, Caz knew that Bam had the *juice*. Tracing
the origins of rap and Hip Hop, the Hip Hop cognoscente breaks it down: "It
began in the Bronx. It began in a club atmosphere with Kool Herc, who is like
the Godfather of Hip Hop in my and anybody else's opinion. Kool Herc is
West Indian and rap as we know it today originated from other forms of rap,
that just wasn't called rap, like The Last Poets and like toasting from Black
Americans and Jamaicans. Rap was just talking. That's what rap is. Now it's
just syncopated."[77]

What makes "Grandmaster Caz and the HipHopography of the Bronx"
such a powerful piece of writing is the felt movement of the piece, the powerful photographs (taken by Hip Hop photographer Leandre Jackson) that visually document the sites and sights, the bodies in motion as they shoot hoops
at Echo Park, and the shots of Caz as he takes us through a cultural semiotic
field rich with *wayblackmemories*, to deploy a powerful trope used by Spady.
What also makes the piece so important is that it provides an important
framework for scholars interested in doing serious HipHopographic field-
work. Spady does not superimpose a meta-narrative that places Caz's voice
under erasure; he does not import extraneous concepts a priori to make sense
of Caz's identity. Spady's HipHopographical approach militates against this
sort of ethnographic "solipsism" and arrogance. For Spady, alterity is greatly
valued within the context of engaging Hip Hop beings. As Sandra Harding
notes, "Listening carefully to different voices and attending thoughtfully to
others' values and interests can enlarge our vision and begin to correct for
inevitable ethnocentrisms."[78]

Philosophically engaging Caz's voice within the space of his own concrete
existential and generative cultural space, and dialoguing with him in terms
of his own authorial voice, Spady demonstrates key aspects of his HipHopographical framework. In short, for Spady, self-narration is a site of power and
epistemological agency. Alim, Meghelli, and Spady are clear on this point
where they argue, "Hip Hop is cultural practice embedded in the lived experience of Hip Hop-conscious beings existing in a home, street, hood, city,
state, country, continent, hemisphere near you. Too often in scholarship on
Hip Hop Culture, Hip Hop artists and practices are talked about but very sel-
dom are they themselves talking."[79] This is what is so incredibly important in
Spady's approach to Hip Hop culture and Hip Hop beings. Spady respects the
freedom and the knowledge that Hip Hop social actors bring to the dialogic
and dialectical encounter. In short, for Spady, the objective is to talk *with*
Hip Hop actors, to be attentive to their voices, visions, mythologies, panoply of discursive acts, cognitions, fantasies, and hyperboles. It is, in short,
to recognize their humanity and the epistemic agential force that they bring

to bear upon their lives and the lives of others. To be *talked about* within this context, however, implies that one is the *object* of a monologic voice, a voice that speaks alone; a voice that silences other voices and de-values other voices. In other words, to speak *about me* is to speak *for me*, which means to speak from an exterior space, a perspective, which does not honor my own self-understanding, my own first-person speech acts. It is to attempt to strip me of voice and subjectivity. We are back to iron muzzles referenced earlier, which is an act of violence.

The point here is that to ascertain the *lived* interiority of what it means to be a Hip Hop being, one must engage the Hip Hop social actor as a subject. To be treated as a subject involves the recognition that one has a perspective on the world and has an understanding of one's own sense of identity, one's values, and one's assumptions. To show respect toward the other, the other who is a subject, implies that one cedes, *ab initio*, some level of significance to what the subject says. It doesn't mean that one first *authorizes* what is to be said. Rather, one respects what is said within a larger space of shared intelligibility, where the voice of the interlocutor places an ethical demand on us to listen—even where one disagrees and does so vehemently. Respect does not, *ipso facto*, mean agreement. Spady doesn't "allow" Hip Hop beings to have a voice or *to voice*; rather, they speak with their own sense of authority—pure and simple. If "rap music is an externalization of highly charged inner feelings,"[80] as Spady writes, then how do we come to appreciate and respect those highly charged inner feelings as expressive of phenomenological richness and self-reflexive insight when we deem ourselves the "expert" storytellers/interpreters of *their* lives and feelings, where their linguistic alterity is occluded, and where their lived spaces (both physical and emotional) are judged nihilistic or pathological? And while it is true that all of us are embedded within a historical context, we are not simply the product of heteronomous forces. And while interpellation (or the process of "hailing") is certainly operative within the social spaces that we traverse as human beings, we are still able to resist the power of interpellation, and interrogate and intervene in those processes. Alim, Meghelli, and Spady make a very important link here. I agree with them where they critically observe, "Perhaps we should begin assessing the current body of rappers autobiographical narratives within the historical context of ex-slave narratives."[81] Take for example, as they suggest, Frederick Douglass. While Douglass was deemed a manipulatable "subhuman thing" within the context of white racist ideology and practice, he ontologically and epistemologically resisted those processes and provided the world with a powerful interior voice that can still be heard in the whirlwind. It was because he *spoke for himself* that his story is so rich and has such deep phenomenological value. So, too, Hip Hop beings speak for themselves in the spirit of Douglass' phenomenological self-disclosures. And, like Douglass, they theorize the meaning of those experiences. *In fact, they are the theorists.*

What Spady has done is to create an unprecedented critical body of work on rap/Hip Hop artists that is painstakingly attentive to the details of their lives as expressed in their voices. He has enabled us, as he says, "to move closer to the very protoplasm itself."[82] My sense is that rap/Hip Hop artists are often willing to engage aspects of the self that many of us are not prepared to do. Perhaps most of us are too dishonest to admit or disclose to ourselves who and what *we are*—too afraid of what we might see. To use DMX's metaphor of "doors," it is as if there are these doors that we refuse to open. In an engaging conversation with Spady, DMX says, "No. Damn right, I didn't wanna open them up, I don't know whether I wasn't ready to open them up or I figured I would never open them up. You know. At about five or six o'clock in the morning I would open those doors."[83] In opening those doors, DMX was able to see himself more fully; to be true to himself and express and experience a truer self. Similarly, when asked how one keeps Hip Hop real, E-Swift (from the Hip Hop group Tha Alkaholiks) says, "By just expressing your true self. What's inside you and not really listening to your label."[84] E-Swift touches on a deeply ethical issue, especially in the light of the seductive power of capitalism and market demand.

In stream with the idea of exploring the doors to the self and how difficult self-exploration can be, Eve, discussing her CD, *Let There Be Eve . . . Ruff Ryders' First Lady*, says, "I just started writing. It's just what I felt. My album is like a diary. You understand? So, it's a lot of difficult subjects because I went through a lot of difficult things. Females go through a lot of different things."[85] Eve marks the specific gendered aspects of her challenges. Perhaps this is why M. C. Lyte says, "I mostly rhyme about not being taken advantage of, not being a pushover."[86] These Black women know when and where they enter as they battle their way into an androcentric industry. They speak from a place of self-consciousness and agency, shaping their own narrative destinies and disrupting and reclaiming forms of discourse designed to distort and objectify. Manifesting the power to reclaim and rename, Trina embraces the appellation, "The BadddDDDest Bitch in Miami."[87] This is a powerful instance of self-claiming against the historical tide of male discourse. She says, "Don't just say bitch like you're saying any other bitch. I like to stand out. I'm very dominant. [I'm] very controlling, so I'm always gonna be on top of my game. So, therefore, bitch doesn't offend me at all. That's why I can use it so brazenly and so strongly."[88] Here is a case where Trina deploys a counter-discourse, a counter-semiotics that speaks to how she desires *to be known*. Note how to be the BadddDDDest is to reach the apex. Trina: "I mean, there's no extra extreme beyond what I am going to be for whatever I'm standing up for. Therefore, if this is gonna be my name, if this is gonna be the name of my album, then I'm going to represent it to the fullest, like let you know BAMMMMMM. It's in your face. That's that and it doesn't even matter how you feel about it."[89] Trina is bold and unapologetic. She asserts a moral imagination that cuts through various normative constraints that inhibit agency and the capacity to imagine otherwise. What and how *you* feel about how she re-presents to the fullest doesn't even enter the equation of her self-definitional praxis and discursive construction.

Trick Daddy is not only a witness to Trina's agency, but he drives home Eve's diary motif as he is ethically committed to *keeping it real*. He says, "Trina says what she means and she says what a lot of people want to say. You can listen to somebody and you can tell whether or not they really mean it. When you listen to my album and you listen to certain songs, and how it comes off, you like, 'Damn, this is real.' I don't do songs I've never experienced."[90] It is intriguing that Trick Daddy's definition of a thug is conceptually congruent with Trina's conception of what it means to be the BadddDDDest. Cutting through all of the preconceptions of what constitutes a "thug," especially as this identity is tied to certain negative representations of the "gangsta," Trick Daddy says, "A thug is someone who don't care how nobody else feels about him. He is going to do what he wanna do and what he got to do. He is going to respect his friends and know who to trust and who not to trust."[91]

What is clear in these sampled embodied voices is a full range of complex values. They attempt to remain true to their experiences, they speak to issues of strength of character, of being true to oneself, of self-determination (or *Kujichagulia*), of courageous speech (parrhesia), of discursive agency, and of modes of introspection and self-actualization. What is important here is that this is what is revealed when rap artists/Hip Hop beings *talk*.

One of the BadddDDDest artists who deploys the power of signification and reclamation vis-à-vis the meaning of her embodiment and identity is Lady Saw. As Spady would say, she is moving within that other side of the Black stream. Before Foxy Brown, Lil' Kim, and Rihanna, there was Lady Saw rapping/discoursing about her Pum Pum/Poonani. Then again, there are past discursive family resemblances in the aesthetics of Millie Jackson and Bessie Smith. Saw is critical of the hypocrisy that she experiences when she dares to lay claim to her body. Asked about what men, as opposed to women, can say within the context of Dancehall, she says, "I think it's a double standard, a downright double standard. I mean, why is it that a man can go onstage and talk about the vagina, incriminate a woman, and talk about how big she is and I go up there and I talk about *my vagina*, being proud of my vagina, telling ladies how to decorate the vagina and people going around saying, 'Oh she too lewd. She's too raunchy, she's nasty, she's X-rated?' But when a man says it, nobody complains, ya know."[92] Within the context of the sexist and racist imagery superimposed upon Black female bodies, specifically the myth of the hyper-sexual Jezebel figure, some might argue that Saw has already internalized and is already reinforcing those stereotypical images. Queen Latifah enters the cipha: "Can you relate to [a] sister dope enough to make you holler and scream?"[93] Linking this question to Latifah's pursuit of wholeness of self, Spady is correct: "Might be double messages in Latifah's Law."[94] After all, multiple entendre is standard within Black speech practices. Saw and Latifah are moving in that space of self-knowledge and governance, a form of knowledge and governance that is subversive. They are "blues women," as Angela Davis might argue, who are openly and self-consciously challenging various gender representations.[95] On my reading, *Saw is engaging a Black female epistemology of the Poonani*. Did I stutter? Latifah is talking about forms of pleasure that defy the space of male psychosexual hegemony, possession, and imagery. It's about Saw and Latifah—welcome to *their* erotic worlds! Both Black women are operating within a dynamic space of agency and with a hermeneutics of suspicion vis-à-vis various epistemic regimes regarding Black female sexuality. I would argue that Saw and Latifah are reclaiming their bodies within the context of the re-signified thug mentality/agency that Trick Daddy delineates here. Yet, isn't this what Frederick Douglass had to do as he fought the "slave-breaker," Covey? Isn't this what Harriet Jacobs had to do in her successful effort to combat Flint's white male sexual "authority" as he attempted to possess her sexually? Isn't this what Joseph Cinqué did as he led a revolt on the Amistad from the white body snatchers? Olaudah Equiano knew with all of his senses the horror of having his body confiscated and confined by white disciplinary orders that refused him corporeal autonomy. Each of these individuals had to be the BadddDDDest; they had to claim and take possession of what was rightfully theirs. They had to do "what [they] wanna do and what [they] got to do" in the name of liberation. We are in that space where autobiographical ex-slave narratives and the lives of contemporary Hip Hop beings converge, where ancestral tongues transmit at lower frequencies. Sonia Sanchez states: "Personally, one of the things that I believe is that we sometimes maintain the spirit of people who have gone before us—the Ancestors. Sometimes we manage to speak with their tongue or their energy. That kind of spirit-energy just does not dissipate in the universe."[96] Demanding and nominating. Saw and Latifah have taken charge; they are combating the discursive policing of the Black female body. It doesn't matter who the culprit happens to be. What matters is that Saw and Latifah must have it *their way*, on their own terms, in light of their own self-schemas. Indeed, undergirding their claims to their own bodies is a powerful question, one effectively and beautifully posed by Chyann L. Oliver: "Whose pussy is this?"[97] The question itself creates a powerful slippage and an interrogative performance of dispossession and ultimately possession by Saw and

Latifah. The question isn't "vulgar" or indicative of "hyper-sexuality," but part of a broader and complex narrative history of Black women defining and positioning themselves as epistemic subjects of their own multifaceted sexual embodiment. More generally, Hip Hop's cultural aesthetics, axiology, epistemology, and body semantics, whether in its global or localized expressions, is about freedom and the capacity to dwell in the world deliberately and to mark it, to change it, to disrupt it, with existential verve. Is this not what is explicitly posed in Oliver's question?

In sum, Hip Hop beings are at the forefront of creating the new, the innovative, and the imaginative. They continue to create an expanding global community. It is an expanding global community in which self-narration continues to usher in an array of differences and variances and where the interplay between social ontology and epistemological agency are philosophically central to understanding that expanding global community. Spady's work demands that we remain attentive to the everyday *lived* narrations, discursive strategies, and social practices of Hip Hop beings themselves. It is this demand that forces us to abandon ethnographic biases that privilege the perspective of the investigator and that distort the meanings, terms, and myths negotiated by Hip Hop beings within the framework of their own normative assumptions. For Spady, we are ethically obligated to explore the cultural world-making praxes of Hip Hop beings, to engage their hermeneutic horizons, their *emic* spaces, and to represent these as accurately as possible. Spady is at the very forefront of documenting, theorizing, and engaging important meta-philosophical questions regarding rap music and Hip Hop culture. He knows that rap music and Hip Hop culture involve "an inner need to express something new and exciting, outrageous, and engaging. Exuberant, bright, charismatic and endothermic . . . [they are] capable of both producing and absorbing heat. This is indicative of [their] dynamic power."[98] Ngũgĩ Wa Thiong'o writes, "Tyrants and their tyrannical systems are terrified at the sound of the wheels of history. History is subversive."[99] In stream with Ngũgĩ, Spady is more than aware that tyrants attempt to rewrite history and construct "official" history; he knows that the tyranny of this "official" history is another site that functions as the dreadful "enemy of the Imagination."[100] Through the deployment of philosophical engagement, where epistemic respectful conversation is valorized, and where the space and place of Hip Hop beings are not ethnographically truncated in their dynamic vivacity, funk, and *lived* integrity, Spady has documented (and continues to document) and *co-theorized* the ontologically protean character of the Hip Hop Nation across space and time.

Notes

CHAPTER 1

1. Posted by ECO. Soul. Intellectual, "A Nigger with a PhD," July 21, 2009, http://ecosoulintellectual.blogspot.com/2009/07/nigger-with-phd.html.

2. James Baldwin, *The Fire Next Time* (New York: Modern Library, 1962/1995), 94.

3. David Hume, "Of National Characters," in *The Philosophical Works of David Hume*, ed. T. H. Grose (Vol. 3) (London: Longman, Green, 1882), 224–44, 252n.

4. Frantz Fanon, *Black Skin, White Masks*, trans. Charles Lam Markmann (New York: Grove Press, Inc., 1967), 112.

5. David Levering Lewis (ed.), *W. E. B. DuBois: A Reader* (New York: Henry Holt and Company), 454.

6. bell hooks, *Killing Rage: Ending Racism* (New York: Henry Holt and Company), 46.

CHAPTER 2

1. Simone de Beauvoir, *The Ethics of Ambiguity* (New York: Citadel Press, 1976), 49–50.

2. James Baldwin, *The Fire Next Time* (New York: Modern Library, 1962/1995), 94.

3. Lottie L. Joiner, "Remembering Civil Rights Heroine Fannie Lou Hamer: 'I'm Sick and Tired of Being Sick and Tired,'" *Daily Beast*, September 2, 2014 (updated April 14, 2017), available at: https://www.thedailybeast.com/remembering-civil-rights-heroine-fannie-lou-hamer-im-sick-and-tired-of-being-sick-and-tired.

CHAPTER 3

1. James Baldwin, *Notes of a Native Son* (Vol. 39) (Boston: Beacon Press, 1984), 178.

2. James Baldwin, "White Man's Guilt," *Ebony*, Vol. 20, No. 10 (August 1965), 47–52, 47.

3. Joel Olson, *The Abolition of White Democracy* (Minneapolis: University of Minneapolis Press, 2004), 29–30.

4. Derrick A. Bell, Jr., "Racial Realism," in *Critical Race Theory: The Key Writings That Formed the Movement*, eds. Kimberlé Crenshaw, Neil Gotanda, Cary Peller, & Kendall Thomas (New York: The New Press, 1995), 302–12, 306.

CHAPTER 4

1. Barack Obama, *Remarks by the President on Trayvon Martin* [transcript], The White House, Office of the Press Secretary, July 19, 2013, available at: https://obamawhitehouse.archives.gov/the-press-office/2013/07/19/remarks-president-trayvon-martin.

2. Ibid.

3. David Hume, "Of National Characters," in *The Philosophical Works of David Hume*, ed. T. H. Grose (Vol. 3) (London: Longman, Green, 1882), 224–44, 252n.

4. Immanuel Kant, *Observations on the Feeling of the Beautiful and Sublime*, trans. John T. Goldthwait (Berkeley: University of California Press, 1960), 113.

5. Earl Conrad, *The Invention of the Negro* (New York: Paul S. Eriksson, Inc., 1966), 74.

6. Ralph Ellison, *Invisible Man* (1947; reprint, New York: Vintage Books, 1995), 3.

7. https://www.youtube.com/watch?v=L04Vh4do6bY.

8. William David Hart, "Dead Black Man, Just Walking," in *Pursuing Trayvon Martin: Historical Contexts and Contemporary Manifestations of Racial Dynamics*, eds. George Yancy & Janine Jones (Lanham, MD: Lexington Books, 2013), 91–102, 91.

9. João Costa Vargas and Joy A. James, "Refusing Blackness-as-Victimization: Trayvon Martin and the Black Cyborgs," in *Pursuing Trayvon Martin: Historical Contexts and Contemporary Manifestations of Racial Dynamics*, eds. George Yancy & Janine Jones (Lanham, MD: Lexington Books, 2013), 193–203, 195.

10. W. E. B. DuBois, *The Souls of Black Folk* (1903; reprint, New York: New American Library, 1982), 231.

CHAPTER 5

1. James Baldwin, *The Fire Next Time* (New York: Modern Library, 1962/1995), 5.

2. Toni Morrison, *Beloved* (1987; reprint, New York: Vintage Books, 2004), 101.

CHAPTER 6

1. Richard Wright, *Black Boy*, with an introduction by Jerry W. Ward, Jr. (New York: First Perennial Classics, 1998), 272.

2. Mary Elizabeth Hobgood, *Dismantling Privilege: An Ethics of Accountability* (Cleveland, OH: The Pilgrim Press, 2009), 51.

3. Kwame Anthony Appiah and Henry Louis Gates, eds., *Africana: The Encyclopedia of the African and African-American Experience* (Philadelphia, PA: Running Press Book Publishers, 2003), 633.

4. Ronald L. Jackson, II, *Scripting the Black Masculine Body: Identity, Discourse, and Racial Politics in Popular Media* (Albany: State University of New York Press, 2006), 24.

5. Peggy McIntosh, "White Privilege and Male Privilege: A Personal Account of Coming to See Correspondences through Work in Women's Studies," in *Critical Whiteness Studies: Looking Behind the Mirror*, ed. Richard Delgado and Jean Stefancic (Philadelphia, PA: Temple University Press, 1997), 291–99, 293.

6. Vincent Woodard, Dwight McBride, and Justin A. Joyce, eds., *The Delectable Negro: Human Consumption and Homoeroticism within US Slave Culture* (New York: NYU Press, 2006), 18.

7. Richard Dyer, *White* (New York: Routledge, 1997), 51.

8. Joe R. Feagin and Hernán Vera, *White Racism* (New York: Routledge, 1995), xii.

9. Christy Mag Uidhir, "What's So Bad about Blackface?," in *Race, Philosophy, and Film*, eds. Mary K. Bloodsworth-Lugo and Dan Flory (New York: Routledge, 2013), 51–68, 51.

10. Hernán Vera and Andrew M. Gordon, *Screen Saviors: Hollywood Fictions of Whiteness* (Lanham, MD: Rowman & Littlefield, 2003), 119.

11. Feagin and Vera, *White Racism*, xii.

12. Grace Elizabeth Hale, *Making Whiteness: The Culture of Segregation in the South, 1890–1940* (New York: Vintage Books, 1999), 153.

13. Kennedy Warne, "Organization Man: Carl Linnaeus, Born 300 Years Ago, Brought Order to Nature's Blooming, Buzzing Confusion," *Smithsonian Magazine*, May 2007, available at: https://www.smithsonianmag.com/science-nature/organization-man-151908042/.

14. Jackson, *Scripting the Black Masculine Body*, 24.

15. Joe R. Feagin and Kimberley Ducey, *Racist America: Roots, Current Realities, and Future Reparations* (4th ed.) (New York: Routledge, 2019), 100.

CHAPTER 7

1. Lillian Smith, *Killers of the Dream* (1949; reprint, New York: W. W. Norton & Company, 1994), 28.

2. Ibid., 29.

3. Frederick Douglass, *Narrative of the Life of Frederick Douglass, An American Slave: Written by Himself*, ed. and with an introduction by David W. Blight (1845; reprint, New York: Bedford/St. Martin's Press, 1993), 105.

4. Ibid., 142.

5. Leigh Beeson, "Freedom Breakfast Speaker Calls for Unity and Love," *UGA Today*, January 18, 2019, available at: https://news.uga.edu/freedom-breakfast-2019/.

6. Martin Luther King, Jr., *A Testament of Hope: The Essential Writings and Speeches of Martin Luther King, Jr.*, ed. James M. Washington (New York: Harper-San Francisco, 1991), 295.

7. Judith Butler, *Precarious Life: The Powers of Mourning and Violence* (New York: Verso, 2006), 23.

8. Judith Butler, *Giving an Account of Oneself* (New York: Fordham University Press, 2015), 103.

CHAPTER 8

1. Martin Luther King, Jr., *A Testament of Hope: The Essential Writings and Speeches of Martin Luther King, Jr.*, ed. James M. Washington (New York: Harper-San Francisco, 1991), 25.

2. Cornel West, ed., *The Radical King: Martin Luther King, Jr.* (New York: Beacon Press, 2015), 201.

3. Immanuel Kant, "On the Different Races of Man," in *Race and the Enlightenment: A Reader*, ed. E. C. Eze (Malden, MA: Blackwell Publishing, 1997), 38–64, 48.

4. Tom LoBianco and Ashley Killough, "Trump Pitches Black Voters: 'What the Hell Do You Have to Lose?,'" *CNN Politics*, August 20, 2016, available at: https://edition.cnn.com/2016/08/19/politics/donald-trump-african-american-voters/index.html.

5. Joel Kovel, *White Racism: A Psychohistory* (New York: Columbia University Press, 1984), 83.

6. Ibid., 84.

7. Ibid., 82.

8. Kant, "On the Different Races of Man," 46.

9. Jan Nederveen Pieterse, *White on Black: Images of Africa and Blacks in Western Popular Culture* (New Haven, CT: Yale University Press, 1992), 196.

10. Stefan Kühl, *The Nazi Connection: Eugenics, American Racism, and German National Socialism* (New York: Oxford University Press, 1994), 99.

11. Jon Swaine, "Trump Renews Racist Attack on Squad: 'They're Not Capable of Loving the US,'" *The Guardian*, July 21, 2019, available at: https://www.theguardian.com/us-news/2019/jul/21/trump-racist-squad-democrats-omar-ocasio-cortez-tlaib-pressley.

12. Kühl, *The Nazi Connection*, 25–26.

13. Ibid., 26.

14. Veronica Stracqualursi, "Trump Attacks Another African American Lawmaker, and Calls Baltimore a 'Disgusting, Rat and Rodent Infested Mess,'" *CNN*

Politics, July 28, 2019, available at: https://www.cnn.com/2019/07/27/politics/elijah-cummings-trump-baltimore/index.html.

15. Ibid.

16. Jane Coaston, "Trump's New Defense of His Charlottesville Comments Is Incredibly False," *Vox*, April 26, 2019, available at: https://www.vox.com/2019/4/26/18517980/trump-unite-the-right-racism-defense-charlotte sville.

CHAPTER 9

1. Hans Küng, *Does God Exist? An Answer for Today* (New York: Vintage Books, 1981), 57.

2. Friedrich Nietzsche, *Twilight of the Idols and the Anti-Christ*, trans. R. J. Hollingdale (New York: Penguin Books, 1990), 163.

3. Susannah Heschel, ed., *Abraham Joshua Heschel: Essential Writings* (Maryknoll, NY: Orbis Books, 2011), 69.

4. Elisabeth T. Vasko, *Beyond Apathy: A Theology for Bystanders* (Minneapolis, MN: Fortress Press, 2015), 220.

5. Heschel, *Abraham Joshua Heschel*, 17.

6. Ibid., 66.

7. James Baldwin, *The Fire Next Time* (New York: Modern Library, 1962/1995), 56.

8. Jerome Loving, *Mark Twain: The Adventures of Samuel L. Clemens* (Oakland: University of California Press, 2010).

9. Martin Luther King, Jr., *A Testament of Hope: The Essential Writings and Speeches of Martin Luther King, Jr.*, ed. James M. Washington (New York: HarperSan Francisco, 1991), 290.

10. Heschel, *Abraham Joshua Heschel*, 85.

11. Ibid., 177.

12. Ibid.

13. Abraham Joshua Heschel, *Man Is Not Alone: A Philosophy of Religion* (New York: Farrar, Straus, Giroux, 1976), 152.

14. Heschel, *Abraham Joshua Heschel*, 74.

15. Ibid., 65.

16. Ibid., 176.

17. Ibid., 63.

18. Vasko, *Beyond Apathy*, 132.

19. Heschel, *Abraham Joshua Heschel*, 68.

20. Ibid., 178.

21. Ibid., 17.

22. Ibid., 62.

23. Ibid., 83.

24. Ibid.

CHAPTER 10

1. George Orwell, *1984* (New York: Harcourt Brace Jovanovich, Inc., 1949), 247.

2. Toni Morrison, *The Bluest Eye* (New York: A Plume Book, 1970), 50.

3. Audre Lorde, *Sister Outsider: Essays and Speeches*, with a new foreword by Cheryl Clarke (Berkeley, CA: Crossing Press, 1984), 57.

4. Frantz Fanon, *Black Skin, White Masks*, trans. Charles Lam Markmann (New York: Grove Press, Inc., 1967), 116.

5. Friedrich Nietzsche, *Twilight of the Idols and the Anti-Christ*, trans. R. J. Hollingdale (New York: Penguin Books, 1990), 45.

6. Martin Luther King, Jr., *A Testament of Hope: The Essential Writings and Speeches of Martin Luther King, Jr.*, ed. James M. Washington (New York: Harper-San Francisco, 1991), 216.

7. Plato, *Five Dialogues: Euthyphro, Apology, Crito, Meno, Phaedo*, trans. G. M. A. Grube (Indianapolis, IN: Hackett Publishing Company, Inc., 2002), 29d.

CHAPTER 11

1. H. A. Nethery would like to thank Taine Duncan for her helpful assistance and feedback during the process of creating these questions, especially in regard to the second and third questions. Her advice on phrasing was invaluable.

2. James Baldwin, *The Fire Next Time* (New York: Modern Library, 1962/1995), 94.

3. James Baldwin, "White Man's Guilt," *Ebony*, Vol. 20, No. 10 (August 1965), 47–52, 47.

4. Cornel West with David Ritz, *Brother West: Living and Loving Out Loud, A Memoir* (New York: SmileyBooks, 2009), 4–5.

5. Charles W. Mills, *Blackness Visible: Essays on Philosophy and Race* (Ithaca: Cornell University Press, 1998), 11.

6. Martin Luther King, Jr., *A Testament of Hope: The Essential Writings and Speeches of Martin Luther King, Jr.*, ed. James M. Washington (New York: Harper-San Francisco, 1991), 291.

7. Ibid.

8. Ibid., 286.

9. Judith Butler, *Precarious Life: The Powers of Mourning and Violence* (New York: Verso, 2006), 22.

10. John Donne, "No Man Is an Island," available at: https://www.scottishpoetryli brary.org.uk/poem/no-man-is-an-island/.

11. Frantz Fanon, *Black Skin, White Masks*, trans. Charles Lam Markmann (New York: Grove Press, Inc., 1967), 110.

12. Sara Ahmed, "A Phenomenology of Whiteness," *Feminist Theory*, Vol. 8, No. 2 (2007), 149–68, 165.

13. Lottie L. Joiner, "Remembering Civil Rights Heroine Fannie Lou Hamer: 'I'm Sick and Tired of Being Sick and Tired,'" *Daily Beast*, September 2, 2014 (updated April 14, 2017), available at: https://www.thedailybeast.com/remembering-civil-rights-heroine-fannie-lou-hamer-im-sick-and-tired-of-being-sick-and-tired.

14. Adrienne Rich, "Notes toward a Politics of Location," in *Blood, Bread, and Poetry: Selected Prose 1979–1985* (New York: W. W. Norton, 1949), 210–31, 213–14.

15. Charles R. Lawrence, "The Id, the Ego, and Equal Protection: Reckoning With Unconscious Racism," in *Critical Race Theory: The Key Writings That Formed the Movement*, eds. Kimberlé Crenshaw, Neil Gotanda, Cary Peller, & Kendall Thomas (New York: The New Press, 1995), 235–56, 238.

16. Charles R. Lawrence, "The Word and the River: Pedagogy as Scholarship as Struggle," in *Critical Race Theory: The Key Writings That Formed the Movement*, eds. Kimberlé Crenshaw, Neil Gotanda, Cary Peller, & Kendall Thomas (New York: The New Press, 1995), 350.

CHAPTER 12

1. This article appears as chapter 10 in this book, though expanded and retitled.

2. This article appears as chapter 9 in this book, though expanded and retitled.

3. See "Is Your God Dead," June 24, 2017, available at: https://www.youtube.com/results?search_query=Yancy%2C+Is+your+God+dead%3F.

4. Maya Angelou, "Still I Rise," available at: https://poets.org/poem/still-i-rise.

CHAPTER 13

1. Frantz Fanon, *Black Skin, White Masks*, trans. Charles Lam Markmann (New York: Grove Press, Inc., 1967), 192.

2. Kenneth M. Stampp, *The Peculiar Institution: Slavery in the Ante-Bellum South* (New York: Vintage Books, 1956), 109.

3. Cornel West with David Ritz, *Brother West: Living and Loving Out Loud, A Memoir* (New York: SmileyBooks, 2009), 28–29.

4. https://www.youtube.com/watch?v=5V_ruIM_KTw.

5. Just think here about the tragic deaths in El Paso, Texas, in 2019.

PART 3

1. Desirée H. Melton, "Are You My People?: The Surprising Places This Black Woman Philosopher Did Not Find Community," in the Special Issue on the Role of Black Philosophy (ed. George Yancy), in *The Black Scholar*, Vol. 43, No. 4 (Winter 2013), 80–85, 84.

CHAPTER 14

1. The reader will note that while I use the terms Black and African-American interchangeably, it is my position that "Black," as a marker of identity, is broader than the term African-American, especially given the fact that "Black" includes people who are not African-American.

2. George Yancy, ed., "Robert E. Birt," in *African-American Philosophers, 17 Conversations* (New York: Routledge, 1998), 343–58, 351.

3. George Yancy, ed., "Cornel West," in *African-American Philosophers, 17 Conversations* (New York: Routledge, 1998), 31–48, 38.

4. Charles W. Mills, *Blackness Visible: Essays on Philosophy and Race* (Ithaca: Cornell University Press, 1998), 10 (my emphasis).

5. And while it is true that white women were excluded from this normative philosophical community, they were nevertheless literally part of the monochromatic family.

6. Molefi Kete Asante, *African American History: A Journey of Liberation* (New Jersey: The People's Publishing Group, Inc., 1995), 37.

7. Nelson Maldonado-Torres, *Against War: Views form the Underground of Modernity* (Durham and London: Duke University Press, 2008), 3.

8. Mills, *Blackness Visible*, 8.

9. Ibid.

10. René Descartes, *Discourse on Method and Meditations on First Philosophy*, trans. Donald A. Cress (Indianapolis: Hackett Publishing Company, 1637, 1641, 1998), sec 25.

11. Ibid., sec 34.

12. Mills, *Blackness Visible*, 8.

13. George Yancy, ed., "Leonard Harris," in *African-American Philosophers, 17 Conversations* (New York: Routledge, 1998), 207–27, 214.

14. Norm R. Allen, Jr., ed., "Leonard Harris on the Life and Work of Alain Locke," in *African-American Humanism: An Anthology* (Amherst: Prometheus Books, 1991), 273.

15. Yancy, "Leonard Harris," 218–19.

16. Ibid., 219.

17. James H. Cone, *A Black Theology of Liberation* (New York: Orbis Books, 1986, 1990), 86.

18. Fred Lee Hord (Mzee Lasana Okpara) and Jonathan Scott Lee, eds., "'I Am Because We Are': An Introduction to Black Philosophy," in *I Am Because We Are: Reading in Black Philosophy* (Amherst: University of Massachusetts Press, 1995), 1–16, 7.

19. The anterior "they are" also points to the vulnerability of the self, its dependence, its fragility. The "they are" vis-à-vis the self, then, does not prima facie signify a relationship of in-authenticity, or a loss of self. Rather, the "they are" speaks to the ways in which the self is inextricably linked to others, signifying a connectivity that constitutes human reality. It is through this connectivity that the clarity of the self

might be found, not obscured or hidden. I would like to thank Cynthia Willett for the general spirit of this claim.

20. Maurice Natanson, *The Journeying Self: A Study in Philosophy and Social Role* (Reading, MA: Addison-Wesley Publishing Company, 1970), 47.

21. Ibid.

22. Cornel West, "The Black Underclass and Black Philosophers," in *I Am Because We Are: Reading in Black Philosophy*, eds. Fred Lee Hord (Mzee Lasana Okpara) and Jonathan Scott Lee (Amherst: University of Massachusetts Press, 1995), 356–66, 356.

23. Lucius Outlaw, *On Race and Philosophy* (New York: Routledge, 1996), 23.

24. African-American philosopher John McClendon's article, "The Afro-American Philosopher and the Philosophy of the Black Experience: A Bibliographic Essay on a Neglected Topic in Both Philosophy and Black Studies," in *Sage Race Relations Abstracts*, Vol. 7, No. 4 (November 1982), in my opinion, is the first serious and thorough research piece written on early professional African-American philosophers and philosophy of the Black experience. It was published in 1983, a year before Harris' important text. McClendon holds a seminal place in the history of efforts to document and theorize African-American philosophy and philosophy of the Black experience.

25. West, "The Black Underclass and Black Philosophers," 357.

26. Cornel West, "Philosophy and the Afro-American Experience," in *A Companion to African-American Philosophy*, eds. Tommy L. Lott and John P. Pittman (Malden, MA: Blackwell Publishing, 2005), 7–32, 8.

27. Ibid.

28. Ibid.

29. Cornel West's prophetic pragmatism shares this anti-Cartesian approach to philosophy. Not only does his prophetic pragmatism reject a form of epistemological foundationalism, but it highlights the importance of history, the tragic and the hopeful; it "affirms the Niebuhrian strenuous mood, never giving up on new possibilities for human agency—both individual and collective." See Cornel West, *The American Evasion of Philosophy: A Genealogy of Pragmatism* (Madison, WI: The University of Wisconsin Press, 1989), 28.

30. There is no attempt to obfuscate the fact that there are many African-American philosophers who, while they see themselves as doing African-American philosophy, conceptualize the dynamics of struggle differently. Keeping abreast of this avoids eliding the political differences (Marxist-Leninist, liberal, conservative, etc.) that differentiate African-American philosophers along significant ideological lines. Philosopher Stephen Ferguson is thanked for emphasizing this point in a personal correspondence.

31. Mills, *Blackness Visible*, 6.

32. Ralph Ellison, *Invisible Man* (1947; reprint, New York: Vintage Books, 1995), 3.

33. Outlaw has suggested that Black people were bombarded with such overwhelming racist absurdity that the issue for some Blacks became: "Should I continue or should I commit suicide?" Under the weight of white racism, the disjunction, for some, became a very live option.

34. Frantz Fanon, *The Wretched of the Earth* (New York: Grove Press, Inc., 1963), 47.

35. Ibid.

36. Friedrich Nietzsche, *Beyond Good and Evil*, trans. Walter Kaufmann (New York: Vintage Books, 1966), 5.

37. See Jacqueline Scott and Todd Franklin, eds., *Critical Affinities: Nietzsche and African American Thought* (Albany: State University of New York Press, 2006).

38. Friedrich Nietzsche, *On the Genealogy of Morals*, trans. Walter Kaufmann and R. J. Hollingdale (New York: Vintage Books, 1989), 68.

39. West, "The Black Underclass and Black Philosophers," 357.

40. George Yancy, ed., "Angela Y. Davis," in *African-American Philosophers, 17 Conversations* (New York: Routledge, 1998), 13–30, 23.

41. Ibid.

42. Outlaw, *On Race and Philosophy*, 25 (my emphasis).

43. George Yancy, ed., "Lewis R. Gordon," in *African-American Philosophers, 17 Conversations* (New York: Routledge, 1998), 95–118, 112.

44. Ibid.

45. George Yancy, ed., "Laurence Thomas," in *African-American Philosophers, 17 Conversations* (New York: Routledge, 1998), 287–305, 293. I would also note here that my interview with Thomas was over twenty years ago. I say this because he may have shifted his position since that time.

46. Leonard Harris, ed., "Introduction," in *Philosophy Born of Struggle: Afro-American Philosophy from 1917* (Dubuque, IA: Kendall/Hunt, 1983), ix.

47. Yancy, "Lewis R. Gordon," 112.

48. George Yancy, ed., "Anita L. Allen," in *African-American Philosophers, 17 Conversations* (New York: Routledge, 1998), 163–85, 172.

49. Mills, *Blackness Visible*, 10.

50. Yancy, "Anita L. Allen," 168.

51. George Yancy, ed., "Albert Mosely," in *African-American Philosophers, 17 Conversations* (New York: Routledge, 1998), 139–62, 145–55.

52. See Bernard Boxill, *Blacks and Social Justice* (rev. ed.) (Lanham, MD: Rowman & Littlefield, 1992).

53. Yancy, "Cornel West," 38.

54. Linda Furgerson Selzer, *Charles Johnson in Context* (Amherst: University of Massachusetts Press, 2009), 27.

55. Mills, *Blackness Visible*, 9.

56. W. E. B. DuBois, *The Souls of Black Folk* (1903; reprint, New York: New American Library, 1982), 45–46.

57. Frantz Fanon, *Black Skin, White Masks*, trans. Charles Lam Markmann (New York: Grove Press, Inc., 1967), 115.

58. George Yancy, "Situated Black Women's Voices in/on the Profession of Philosophy," in *Hypatia: A Journal of Feminist Philosophy*, Vol. 23, No. 2 (2008), 155–59, 155.

59. T. Denean Sharpley-Whiting, "Thanatic Pornography, Interracial Rape, and the Ku Klux Klan," in *A Companion to African-American Philosophy*, ed. Tommy L. Lott and John P. Pittman (Malden, MA: Blackwell Publishing, 2005), 407–12, 410.

60. Dorothy Roberts, *Killing the Black Body: Race, Reproduction, and the Meaning of Liberty* (New York: Vintage Books, 1997, 1999), 11.

61. George Yancy, *African-American Philosophers, 17 Conversations* (New York: Routledge, 1998), 49–71, 59.

62. Fanon, *The Wretched of the Earth*, 250.

63. Fanon, *Black Skin, White Masks*, 112.

64. Outlaw, *On Race and Philosophy*, 29–30.

65. I would like to thank philosopher Clarence S. Johnson for suggesting that the negative/positive distinction that I draw here be made more explicit.

66. Mills, *Blackness Visible*, 9.

67. Yancy, "Cornel West," 39.

68. Yancy, "Leonard Harris," 216.

69. Yancy, "Laurence Thomas," 291.

70. Ibid., 291, 292.

71. George Yancy, ed., "Michelle M. Moody-Adams," in *African-American Philosophers, 17 Conversations* (New York: Routledge, 1998), 119–37, 126.

72. Yancy, "Robert E. Birt," 352.

73. Paget Henry, "Afro-American Studies and the Rise of African-American Philosophy," in *A Companion to African-American Studies*, eds. Lewis R. Gordon and Jane Anna Gordon (Malden, MA: Blackwell Publishing, 2006), 223–45, 238.

74. Lewis R. Gordon, *An Introduction to Africana Philosophy* (Cambridge: Cambridge University Press, 2008), 111.

75. The reader will note that within the context of the history of African-American philosophy, Charles Johnson and Tom Slaughter wrote seminal pieces deploying a phenomenological approach to the Black body. These were two early and formative pieces in the tradition of what is now termed Africana philosophy of existence. Johnson's article, "A Phenomenology of the Black Body," was written as early as 1975, and was subsequently published in the Winter 1976 issue of *Ju-Ju: Research Papers in Afro-American Studies*. Johnson's article appears prior to Thomas F. Slaughter, Jr.'s "Epidermalizing the World: A Basic Mode of Being Black," which was included as a chapter in Leonard Harris' *Philosophy Born of Struggle*. For the first edited text to engage Africana philosophy of existence, see *Existence in Black: An Anthology of Black Existential Philosophy*, ed. Lewis R. Gordon (New York: Routledge, 1997). Describing two features that run throughout the chapters within that text, Gordon notes, "The interesting thing about all of the essays is that all of them featured arguments (1) rejecting essence as a feature of human being and (2) supporting the importance of recognizing the sociohistorical context in which we theorize." See Yancy, *African-American Philosophers, 17 Conversations*, 105. It is important to note the conceptual family resemblance between the meta-philosophical features that I have identified within this chapter regarding African-American philosophy and the two salient lines of argument that Gordon identifies within his text.

76. Philosopher Clarence S. Johnson is thanked for this point.

77. Kuklick appears to restrict DuBois to the role of a public intellectual.

78. John H. McClendon, "The African American Philosopher and Academic Philosophy: On the Problem of Historical Interpretation," in *The APA Newsletter on Philosophy and the Black Experience*, Vol. 4, No. 1 (Fall 2004), 1–9, 8.

79. Ibid., 7. See also https://aaregistry.org/story/a-legal-and-political-advisor-richard-greener/.

80. I would like to thank John McClendon for me informing about the work of Francis Monroe Hammond.

81. Yale University was the first American university to grant the PhD in philosophy in 1866.

82. For an exploration of the life and work of Baker, see chapter 15 in this book.

83. For an examination of the life and work of Jones, see chapter 16 in this book.

84. I have had the great privilege and honor of being Cook's colleague and friend. In chapter 17 of this book, I provide the first extensive examination of her life and work.

85. William Jones, "Crisis in Philosophy: The Black Presence," in *Radical Philosophers' News Journal* (August 1974), 40–45, 40.

86. George Yancy, "Howard McGary, Jr.," in *African American Philosophers, 17 Conversations*, ed. George Yancy, (New York: Routledge, 1998), 73–93, 85.

87. George Yancy, "Tommy L. Lott," in *African American Philosophers, 17 Conversations*, ed. George Yancy, (New York: Routledge, 1998), 187–206, 195.

88. This information was obtained through a personal correspondence. During this time, Green was influenced by Roy D. Morrison after taking his course on Søren Kierkegaard. Morrison taught at Wesley seminary in Washington, DC, where he explored issues regarding Black philosophy of culture and religion. At the time, Green was at Howard University, where he was in the process of obtaining an MA in religion and a doctorate in divinity.

89. Yancy, "Cornel West," 46.

90. Yancy, "Cornel West," 46 (my emphasis).

91. Yancy, "Howard McGary, Jr.," 84.

92. It was sponsored by the Johnson Foundation: Wingspread Conference Center in Racine, Wisconsin.

93. Within this historical context, Outlaw mentions Howard McGary, Jr., Leonard Harris, Joyce Mitchell Cook, Bernard Boxill, William Jones, Robert C. Williams (now deceased), Ifeanyi Menkiti, Robert Chemooke, Albert Mosley, John Murungi, Tom Slaughter, Laurence Thomas, Cornel West, Bill Lawson, George Garrison, and Johnny Washington. See Outlaw, *On Race and Philosophy*, xxix. The reader will note that Charles Johnson, the prominent philosopher-literary figure, was a student of Tom Slaughter at Southern Illinois University. In her groundbreaking text, *Charles Johnson in Context* (Amherst: University of Massachusetts Press, 2009), Linda Selzer notes, "But in 1974 both Slaughter and Johnson entered the Ph.D. program in philosophy together at SUNY Stony Brook." Within this remarkable text, Selzer does an excellent and insightful job of situating Johnson within the historical context of African American philosophy.

94. Outlaw, *On Race and Philosophy*, xxix.

95. George Yancy, "Adrian M.S. Piper," 61.

96. Adrian M. S. Piper, "Xenophobia and Kantian Rationalism," in *African-American Perspectives and Philosophical Traditions*, ed. John P. Pittman (New York: Routledge, 1997), 188–232, 189.

97. Piper, "Xenophobia and Kantian Rationalism," 189.

CHAPTER 15

1. Leonard Harris, "The Horror of Tradition or How to Burn Babylon and Build Benin While Reading A Preface to a Twenty-Volume Suicide Note," in *Philosophical Forum*, Vol. 24, No. 1–3 (1993), 94–118, 106.

2. I thank Fred Evans for the unique ways in which he has theorized oracle voices.

3. William R. Jones, "The Legitimacy and Necessity of Black Philosophy: Some Preliminary Considerations," in *Philosophical Forum*, Vol. 9, No. 2 (1977), 149–60, 157.

4. Harry Washington Greene, *Holders of Doctorates among American Negroes: An Educational and Social Study of Negroes Who Have Earned Doctoral Degrees in Course, 1876–1943* (Newton, MA: Crofton Publishing Corporation, 1974), 202.

5. Amritjit Singh, *The Novels of the Harlem Renaissance: Twelve Black Writers 1923–1933* (University Park: Pennsylvania State University Press, 1976), 16.

6. "Rev. T Nelson Baker Is Honored by Parishioners," from an untitled Pittsfield, MA, newspaper (August 29, 1927). See Baker file at Hampton University Archives, no page numbers.

7. Thomas Nelson Baker, "The Ethical Significance of the Connection between Mind and Body," unpublished doctoral dissertation (New Haven, CT: Yale University, 1903), 27.

8. Frederick Douglass, *Narrative of the Life of Frederick Douglass, An American Slave: Written by Himself*, ed. and with an introduction by David W. Blight (1845; reprint, New York: Bedford/St. Martin's Press, 1993), 136.

9. Kennell Jackson, *America Is Me* (New York: Harper Perennial, 1996), 248.

10. "Commencement Honors: They Fall to Mr. T. N. Baker, a Colored Youth, and Miss A. I. Henry of Boston University," from an untitled newspaper. See Baker file at Hampton University Archives under "Items of Interest," no page numbers.

11. Ibid.

12. Ibid.

13. Ibid.

14. See Baker file at Hampton University Archives under "Items of Interest," referenced as S. L., December 1886.

15. Personal letter from Baker dated May 31, 1898. I thank the archivist at Northfield Mount Hermon for providing this important document.

16. See Baker's obituary record at Yale University Alumni Records, 1940–1941, published in 1942.

17. I thank Newman Taylor Baker for this information, which he graciously shared in a personal correspondence on May 24, 2019.

18. "Rev. Dr. Baker Dies in His Sleep in His Home: Former Pastor Started Life as a Slave Boy," *The Berkshire Eagle*, Vol. 49, No. 207 (no date found), 1. See Baker file at Hampton University Archives.

19. In an earlier version of this article, I stated that Baker died on February 25, 1940, as this is the information that was made available to me at that time. Since then I have found that there are conflicting reports regarding his date of death. His headstone at Pittsfield Cemetery records his date of birth as August 1, 1860, and his date

of death as February 23, 1941. However, *The Berkshire Evening Eagle* (February 24, 1941, 1) reported Baker's death as February 22, 1941. Thanks to Robert G. Anderson for this information (personal communication, June 3, 2019).

20. "Commencement Honors."

21. Thomas N. Baker, "Not Pity But Respect," *Alexander's Magazine*, Vol. 2 (May 1906), 111.

22. "Rev. Dr. T. Nelson Baker Says Hampton Institute Is Doing a Miraculous Work," *The Berkshire Eagle* (October 30, 1919). See Baker file at Hampton University Archives, no page numbers.

23. Baker, "Not Pity but Respect," 111.

24. Ibid., 112.

25. Ibid.

26. Thomas N. Baker, "Ideals" (part 1), *Alexander's Magazine*, Vol. 2 (September 1906), 28.

27. See Baker file at Hampton University Archives under "Items of Interest," *Southern Workman* (April 1908).

28. Thomas N. Baker, "Ideals" (part 2), *Alexander's Magazine*, Vol. 2 (October 1906), 40.

29. Baker, "Ideals" (part 1), 23.

30. Charles W. Mills, *Blackness Visible: Essays on Philosophy and Race* (Ithaca: Cornell University Press, 1998), 112.

31. Baker, "Ideals" (part 1), 26.

32. For a productive discussion related to the problematic claims that Baker made regarding Black women, see Robert G. Anderson, "Not Pity but Respect: Thomas Nelson Baker," *The Monday Evening Club*, January 25, 2013, available at: http://mondayeveningclub.blogspot.com/2013/01/not-pity-but-respect.html.

33. Thomas N. Baker, "The Negro Woman," *Alexander's Magazine*, Vol. 3 (December 1906), 74.

34. Baker, "Not Pity but Respect," 111.

35. Baker, "Ideals" (part 2), 40–41.

36. Addison Gayle, Jr., *The Black Aesthetic* (New York: Doubleday, 1971), 272.

37. "Rev. Dr. T. Nelson Baker Says Hampton Institute Is Doing a Miraculous Work" (my emphasis).

38. Mills, *Blackness Visible*, 112.

39. Baker, "Ideals" (part 1), 26.

40. "Rev. Dr. T. Nelson Baker Says Hampton Institute Is Doing a Miraculous Work."

41. Baker, "The Ethical Significance," 238.

42. Ibid., 247.

43. Ibid., 299.

44. "An Example of What Motherhood Can Do," *The Berkshire Eagle* (July 13, 1908), no page numbers. See Baker file at Hampton University Archives.

45. From a personal phone interview with Mr. Willie Singleton on May 5, 2001.

46. Herbert Aptheker, ed., *The Correspondence of W. E. B. DuBois*, Vol. 1, Selections, 1877–1934 (Amherst: University of Massachusetts Press, 1973), 117.

47. For a more detailed examination of one of the critical points of difference between Baker and DuBois, see Anderson, "Not Pity but Respect: Thomas Nelson Baker."

CHAPTER 16

1. See Jones' file at Wilberforce University's Archives and Special Collection at Rembert E. Stokes LRC Library under "*A Message to the Class of '39.*" Copied from Wilberforce University's yearbook class of 1939.

2. Ibid.

3. Ibid.

4. See *History of Greene County*, Ohio, Broadstone, Vol. 2, R. 977.174, 953ff or see *Who's Who in Colored America*, 1933 to 1937, ARC. E 185.96 W6, 297 (received photocopy from Wilberforce University's Archives and Special Collection at Rembert E. Stokes LRC Library, hereafter ASC).

5. *History of Greene County*, 53.

6. William M. Banks, *Black Intellectuals: Race and Responsibility in American Life* (New York: W. W. Norton & Company), 243.

7. Ibid., 45.

8. *History of Greene County*, 954.

9. F. A. McGinnis, *A History and an Interpretation of Wilberforce University*, 72 (copy from ASC).

10. Ibid.

11. *History of Greene Country*, 954.

12. See *Journal of the Twenty-Ninth Quadrennial Session, General Conference, of the AME Church* (May 2–16, 1932, Cleveland, Ohio), 382.

13. Ibid., 382–83.

14. Ibid., 382.

15. Ibid.

16. Ibid., 181.

17. Ibid., 383.

18. Ibid., 384.

19. I appreciate John McClendon for bringing Hill to my attention and providing me with this personal account. McClendon believes, as do I, in the importance of documenting the early path created by African-American philosophers. It is within such a historical framework, one that is true to the philosophical reflections and social, cultural, and political lived context of the philosopher that we can better understand our current historical moment as contemporary African-American philosophers.

20. "Dr. Gilbert Haven Jones Has Rejoined Wilberforce University Faculty," in *The Gazette*, Xenia, Ohio (June 1950).

21. To date, I have not come across any of the other articles.

22. Robert Munro also has the distinction of writing his dissertation on Jones. It is entitled *Historical Considerations in African American Philosophy: The Intellectual*

Career of Gilbert Haven Jones (East Lansing: Michigan State University, 2013). We are indebted to Munro.

23. See copy at ASC or *Who's Who*, 297.

24. Simon Blackbum, *The Oxford Dictionary of Philosophy* (New York: Oxford University Press, 1994), 225.

25. Robert V. Guthrie, *Even the Rat was White: A Historical View of Psychology* (New York: Harper & Row Publishers, 1976), 123.

26. Peter T. Manicus, *A History and Philosophy of the Social Sciences* (New York: Basil Blackwell, 1987), 181–82.

27. Gilbert H. Jones, *Education in Theory and Practice* (Boston: The Gorham Press, 1919), 14 (my emphasis).

28. Ibid., 14–15.

29. Ibid., 25.

30. Ibid., 48.

31. Ibid.

32. Ibid., 24. John McClendon also recognizes the "dialectical" dimensions of Jones' conception of mental life. McClendon sees Jones as advancing a "materialist" thesis given Jones' emphasis upon the significance and necessity of human adjustment to nature as fundamental and as having priority over mental life. Of course, McClendon also recognizes the critical class analysis vis-à-vis education and power offered by Jones. Telescoping Jones' class analysis, McClendon notes, "Jones was critical of the Social Darwinist notion that wealth was the result of individual achievement and educational attainment. He repudiated theories of genetic superiority and upheld the democratic demand for equal opportunity. However, he recognized that "some" of those in possession of power and influence sought to hinder the aim 'to equalize opportunity of all.' Thus, the social implication of Jones' educational philosophy was the explicit affirmation of the necessity of social change with a materialist recognition of the actual prohibitive nature of class society." For more on Jones, and other early significant African-American philosophers and philosophy of the Black experience, see further McClendon's article "The Afro-American Philosopher and the Philosophy of the Black Experience: A Bibliographic Essay on a Neglected Topic in Both Philosophy and Black Studies," in *Sage Race Relations Abstracts*, Vol. 7, No. 4 (November 1982), 1–53. The above quoted material on Jones is taken from pp. 30–31 of this article.

33. Ibid., 38.

34. Ibid., 49.

35. Ibid., 39.

36. Ibid., 251.

37. Ibid., 39.

38. Ibid., 35.

39. Ibid., 38.

40. Ibid.

41. Ibid., 216.

42. See Jones' file at Wilberforce University's Archives and Special Collection at Rembert E. Stokes LRC Library under "*A Message to the Class of '47*." Copied from Wilberforce University's yearbook class of 1939.

43. Ibid.

44. Jones, *Education*, 247.

CHAPTER 17

1. I have always thought highly of Adrian; she is a stellar philosopher and conceptual artist. Yes, she is brilliant at both. Although now in Berlin with no intention of returning to the United States, her impact here in the United States is still felt and greatly appreciated. It is shameful that certain academic institutions and professional philosophers failed to show the courage and honor of fighting to keep Adrian here. See Piper's memoir, *Escape to Berlin: A Travel Memoir* (Berlin: APRA Foundation Berlin, 2018).

2. Conversation with author, 1997.

3. Ibid.

4. Ibid.

5. Cook's niece, Gail Y. Mitchell, is a wonderful human being. Not only does she look like Joyce, but her voice, especially over the phone, reminds me of Joyce's voice. I am so thankful to Gail for all of her efforts to make sure that Joyce's wishes were honored. Her love of Joyce is palpable. I'm indebted to Gail and also to George Jones who helped with the legal logistics regarding the execution of Joyce's wishes. I am so incredibly thankful.

6. George Yancy, "Thomas Nelson Baker: The First African-American to Receive the PhD in Philosophy," in *The Western Journal of Black Studies*, Vol. 21, No. 4 (1997), 253–60.

7. Thanks to John H. McClendon III for this information.

8. George Yancy, ed., *African-American Philosophers, 17 Conversations* (New York: Routledge, 1998), 225.

9. Unpublished interview, 1997.

10. Ibid.

11. Ibid.

12. Ibid.

13. Ibid.

14. See Joyce Mitchell Cook, "Abstract," in *A Critical Examination of Stephen C. Pepper's Theory of Value*, dissertation (New Haven: Yale University, 1965).

15. See J. W. Walters, "Letter to the Editor," *Satyagraha*, Vol. 53, No. 25 (March 10, 1970), 2. A huge thanks to archivist Rose Oliveira, who is the Linda Lear Special Collections Librarian at Connecticut College, for her invaluable assistance with accessing and making available to me this letter and Cook's response.

16. See Joyce Mitchell Cook, "Letter to the Editor," *Satyagraha*, Vol. 53, No. 26 (March 17, 1970), 2.

17. Unpublished interview, 1997.

18. Ibid.

19. Ibid.

20. Joyce Mitchell Cook, "The Examined Life," *Bryn Mawr College Alumnae Bulletin* (October 1973), 8–9, 8.

21. The reader should note that Cook was also a participant in the historic 1968 Connecticut College Black Womanhood Conference that was designed to get prominent Black women (e.g., professors, lawyers, biologists, political figures, famous dancers) to visit Connecticut College and share their stories. I have not been able, as of this writing, to obtain a copy of Cook's talk. Again, thanks to archivist Rose Oliveira.

22. See Yancy, *17 Conversations*.

23. Unpublished interview, 1997.

24. Cook, "The Examined Life," 9.

25. Ibid.

26. While a published article, the copy I have has neither a date nor the source where it originally appeared.

27. Joyce Mitchell Cook, "Values: Black/White," an unpublished address delivered at Morgan State College Conference on Philosophy and the Black Experience (April 1972), 18.

28. Cook was an avid pianist and loved the work of Frederic Chopin.

29. Cook, "The Examined Life," 9.

30. Unpublished interview, 1997.

31. Ibid. (my emphasis).

32. Yancy, *17 Conversations*, 59.

33. George Yancy, "Situated Black Women's Voices in/on the Profession of Philosophy," in *Hypatia: A Journal of Feminist Philosophy*, Vol. 23, No. 2 (2008), 155–59, 155.

34. The reader should note that this was my impression. Perhaps there were others who spoke with Cook and think differently about this.

35. Unpublished interview, 1997.

36. Yancy, *17 Conversations*, 59.

37. According to John H. McClendon III, a very explicit form of male chauvinism structured Howard's philosophy beginning with Alain Locke's chair of the department.

38. Unpublished interview, 1997.

39. The source is an unpublished, undated, and untitled paper, 5.

40. Unpublished interview, 1997.

41. Ibid.

42. Ibid.

43. Ibid (my emphasis).

44. Ibid.

45. Ibid.

46. Ibid.

47. Ibid.

48. Ibid.

49. Ibid.

50. Ibid.

51. Ibid.

52. Cook, "Values," 2.

53. Joyce Mitchell Cook, unpublished address entitled "The Search for Personal Identity," 6.

54. Ibid.
55. Unpublished interview, 1997.
56. Ibid.
57. Ibid.
58. Ibid.
59. Ibid.
60. Ibid.
61. Ibid.
62. Ibid.
63. Ibid.
64. Ibid.

CHAPTER 18

1. George Yancy, ed., *African-American Philosophers, 17 Conversations* (New York: Routledge, 1998), 59.
2. Martin Luther King, Jr., *A Testament of Hope: The Essential Writings and Speeches of Martin Luther King, Jr.*, ed. James M. Washington (New York: Harper-San Francisco, 1991), 290.

CHAPTER 19

1. Frantz Fanon, *Black Skin, White Masks*, trans. Charles Lam Markmann (New York: Grove Press, Inc., 1967), 232.

CHAPTER 20

1. I would like to thank Dr. John Baugh, who works in the areas of anthropology, ethnology, linguistics, and sociology, for this important background information in a personal correspondence, September 29, 2010.
2. Ngũgĩ Wa Thiong'o, *Moving the Centre: The Struggle for Cultural Freedoms* (Portsmouth, New Hampshire: Heinemann Educational Books, Inc., 1993), 30.
3. Frantz Fanon, *Black Skin, White Masks*, trans. Charles Lam Markmann (New York: Grove Press, Inc., 1967), 17–18.

CHAPTER 21

1. José Medina, "Linguistic Hegemony and Linguistic Resistance: English, Spanish, and American Philosophy," in *Reframing the Practice of Philosophy: Bodies of Color, Bodies of Knowledge*, ed. George Yancy (Albany: State University of New York Press, 2012), 341–62, 358–59.

2. Charles R. Lawrence, "The Id, the Ego, and Equal Protection: Reckoning with Unconscious Racism," in *Critical Race Theory: The Key Writings That Formed the Movement*, eds. Kimberlé Crenshaw, Neil Gotanda, Cary Peller, & Kendall Thomas (New York: The New Press, 1995), 235–56, 340.

3. George Yancy, ed., "Between Facticity and Possibility," in *The Philosophical I: Personal Reflections on Life in Philosophy* (Lanham, MD: Rowman & Littlefield, 2002), 129–53.

4. Russell A. Potter, *Spectacular Vernaculars: Hip-Hop and the Politics of Postmodernism* (Albany: State University of New York Press, 1995), 58.

5. Frantz Fanon, *Black Skin, White Masks*, trans. Charles Lam Markmann (New York: Grove Press, Inc., 1967), 36.

6. Ibid., 18 (my emphasis).

7. Robert H. DeCoy, *The Nigger Bible* (Los Angeles, CA: Holloway House Publishing Co., 1967), 21–26, 24.

8. Geneva Smitherman, *Talkin That Talk: Language, Culture and Education in African America* (London and New York: Routledge, 2001), 347.

9. Ibid., 343.

10. Geneva Smitherman, *Talkin and Testifyin: The Language of Black America* (Detroit: Wayne State University Press, 1977), 242.

11. Smitherman, *Talkin That Talk*, 349.

12. Props to my man, Noam!

13. Geneva Smitherman, "A Womanist Looks at the Million Man March," in *The Womanist Reader*, ed. Layli Phillips (New York: Routledge, 2006), 207–12, 207.

14. Geneva Smitherman, *Black Talk: Words and Phrases from the Hood to the Amen Corner* (rev. updated ed.) (Boston and New York: Houghton Mifflin, 2000), xiii.

15. Peter L. Berger and Thomas Luckmann, "The Dehumanized World," in *The Truth About the Truth: De-Confusing and Re-Constructing the Postmodern World*, ed. Walter T. Anderson (New York: A Jeremy P. Tarcher/Putnam Book, 1995), 36–39, 36.

16. Smitherman, *Talkin That Talk*, 222.

17. Ibid., 1.

18. Ibid., 2.

19. Ibid.

20. Ibid., 3.

21. Ngũgĩ wa Thiong'o, *Moving the Centre: The Struggle for Cultural Freedoms* (Portsmouth, New Hampshire: Heinemann Educational Books, Inc., 1993), 131.

22. Smitherman, *Talkin That Talk*, 350.

23. Fanon, *Black Skin, White Masks*, 38.

24. Smitherman, *Talkin That Talk*, 222.

25. Smitherman, *Talkin and Testifyin*, 56.

26. Smitherman, *Black Talk*, 4.

27. Smitherman, *Talkin That Talk*, 8.

28. Ibid., 58.

29. Ibid., 66.

30. Ibid., 70.

31. Ibid., 71.

32. Ibid., 113.

33. Smitherman, *Black Talk*, 38.

34. Smitherman, *Talkin That Talk*, 317.

35. Ibid., 43.

36. bell hooks, *Ain't I A Woman: Black Women and Feminism* (Boston: South End Press, 1981), 18–19.

37. Ibid., 59.

38. George M. Frederickson, *The Black Image in the White Mind: The Debate on Afro-America Character and Destiny, 1817–1914* (Hanover, NH: Wesleyan University Press., 1971), 279.

39. Ibid., 277.

40. Smitherman, *Talkin That Talk*, 71.

41. Frederickson, *The Black Image in the White Mind*, 253.

42. Ibid.

43. Smitherman, *Talkin and Testifyin*, 7.

44. Smitherman, *Talkin That Talk*, 72.

45. Ibid.

46. Ibid., 73.

47. John Baugh, *Black Street Speech: It's History, Structure and Survival* (Austin: University of Texas Press, 1983), 14.

48. Smitherman, *Talkin That Talk*, 240.

49. Frederick Douglass, *Narrative of the Life of Frederick Douglass, An American Slave: Written by Himself*, ed. and with an introduction by David W. Blight (1845; reprint, New York: Bedford/St. Martin's Press, 1993), 49.

50. Ibid., 52.

51. Ibid., 53.

52. Smitherman, *Talkin That Talk*, 57.

53. Smitherman, *Talkin and Testifyin*, 48–49.

54. Smitherman, *Talkin That Talk*, 19.

55. Smitherman, *Talkin and Testifyin*, 48.

56. Smitherman, *Talkin That Talk*, 19.

57. Thiong'o, *Moving the Centre*, 30.

58. Potter, *Spectacular Vernaculars*, 57.

59. Smitherman, *Talkin That Talk*, 19.

60. Ibid., 344.

61. Ibid.

62. Ibid., 99.

63. Ibid., 43.

64. Ibid., 96 (my emphasis).

65. Ibid., 146.

66. Ibid., 54.

67. Ibid., 203.

68. Ibid.

69. In other words, existence, etymologically, means to *ex* (out) and *sistere* (take a stand). Hence, ex-istence, interpreted dynamically, means "to standout," which is linked to ecstasy or "standing outside oneself."

70. Smitherman, *Talkin That Talk*, 101.

71. Ibid., 19.

72. Smitherman, *Black Talk*, 2.

73. Smitherman, *Talkin That Talk*, 20.

74. Ibid., 272.

75. Ibid., 20.

76. Ibid., 31.

77. Ibid., 136–37.

78. Ibid., 272.

79. Smitherman, *Talkin and Testifyin*, 3.

80. Ibid.

81. Smitherman, *Talkin That Talk*, 351.

82. Ibid., 15.

83. Ibid.

84. Ibid., 16.

85. Ibid., 139.

86. Ibid., 140.

87. Ibid., 358.

88. For example, see Kamau Brathwaite, *History of the Voice: The Development of Nation Language in Anglophone Caribbean Poetry* (London: New Beacon Books, 1984).

89. Smitherman, *Talkin That Talk*, 64.

90. Smitherman, *Talkin and Testifyin*, 104.

91. Smitherman, *Talkin That Talk*, 64.

92. Smitherman, *Talkin and Testifyin*, 44.

93. Ibid.

94. Smitherman, *Talkin That Talk*, 220.

95. Ibid., 217.

96. Ibid.

97. Ibid., 219.

98. Ibid., 269.

CHAPTER 22

1. James G. Spady, "'Ima Put My Thing Down': Afro-American Expressive Culture and the Hip Hop Community," in *TYANABA Revue de la Societe d'Anthropologie*, Vol. 20, No. 2 (1993), 93–98, 93.

2. James G. Spady, Stephan Dupree, and Charles G. Lee, *Twisted Tales: In the Hip Hop Streets of Philly* (Philadelphia, PA: Black History Museum UMUM/LOH Publishers, 1995), ll.

3. Joseph Eure and James G. Spady, *Nation Conscious Rap* (New York: PC International Press, 1991), vii.

4. James G. Spady, H. Samy Alim, and Samir Meghelli, *Tha Global Cipha: Hip Hop Culture and Consciousness* (Philadelphia, PA: Black History Museum UMUM/ LOH Publishers, 2006), 35.

5. Spady, "Ima Put My Thing Down," 93.

6. James G. Spady, "Living in America Where the Brother Got to Get Esoterica: The Philly Language and Philosophy of Schooly D," in *Fourth Dimension*, Vol. 4, No. 1, (1994), 26–27, 27.

7. Maurice Jean Jacques Merleau-Ponty, *Phenomenology of Perception*, trans. C. Smith (New York: Routledge, 1962), xx.

8. Spady, Alim, and Meghelli, *Tha Global Cipha*, 54.

9. Leroy Jones and Larry Neal, *Black Fire: An Anthology of Afro-American Writing* (New York: William Morrow and Company, Inc., 1968), 4.

10. Glifford Geertz, *The Interpretation of Cultures* (New York: Basic Books, Inc., 1973), 24.

11. James G. Spady, "Introduction," in *Indigené: An Anthropology of Future Black Arts*, ed. B. H. Committee (Philadelphia, PA: Black History Museum UMUM/LOH Publishers, 1978), 1–4, 1.

12. James G. Spady, *Larry Neal: Liberated Black Philly Poet with a Blues Streak of Mellow Wisdom* (Philadelphia, PA: PC International Press and Black History Museum UMUM/LOH Publishers, 1989), 2.

13. Aime Césaire, *Notebook of a Return to the Native Land*, ed. and trans. C. Eschelman and A. Smith (Middletown, CT: Wesleyan University Press, 2001), xiv.

14. Lupe Fiasco (performer), "Never Forgot You," on *Lasers* (Atlantic Records, 2011).

15. Slick Rick (performer), "Memories," on *The Art of Storytelling* (Def Jam Records, Inc., 1999).

16. Will Smith (performer), "Summertime," on *Homebase* (Jive, 1991).

17. James G. Spady, *Marcus Garvey: Jazz, Reggae, Hip Hop and The African Diaspora* (Philadelphia, PA: Marcus Garvey Foundation Publishers, 2011), 134.

18. Merleau-Ponty, *Phenomenology of Perception*, 106.

19. Spady, *Larry Neal*, 1.

20. Geertz, *The Interpretation of Cultures*, 5.

21. Jones and Neal, *Black Fire*, 652.

22. James G. Spady, "Tupac's Exile: The Black Night Longs for the Moon," *Philadelphia New Observer* (1996), 15.

23. James G. Spady, "Surrealism and the Marvelous Black Plunge in Search of Yemanga and the Human Condition," *Cultural Correspondence*, Nos. 12–14 (Summer 1981), 92–95, 92.

24. Ibid.

25. Spady, *Larry Neal*, 1.

26. Ibid.

27. Frantz Fanon, *Black Skin, White Masks*, trans. Charles Lam Markmann (New York: Grove Press, Inc., 1967), 135.

28. James G. Spady, "Dr. Cheikh Anta Diop and The African Origins of Civilization," in *Cheikh Anta Diop: Poem for the Living*, M. S. Okantah (Philadelphia, PA: Black History Museum UMUM/LOH Publishers, 1997), 22–26, 24.

29. Kamau Brathwaite, *Roots* (Ann Arbor: The University of Michigan Press, 1993), 192.

30. Spady, "Dr. Cheikh Anta Diop and The African Origins of Civilization," 23.

31. Jones and Neal, *Black Fire*, 639.

32. Spady, "Dr. Cheikh Anta Diop and The African Origins of Civilization," 25.

33. Spady, "Ima Put My Thing Down," 94.

34. Ibid.

35. Ibid., 95.

36. Spady, "Surrealism and the Marvelous Black Plunge in Search of Yemanga and the Human Condition," 92.

37. Spady, "Ima Put My Thing Down," 94.

38. Spady, Alim, and Meghelli, *Tha Global Cipha*, 29.

39. Spady, "Surrealism and the Marvelous Black Plunge in Search of Yemanga and the Human Condition," 93.

40. Ibid.

41. Spady, Alim, and Meghelli, *Tha Global Cipha*, 26.

42. Spady, *Marcus Garvey*, 136.

43. Ibid., 123.

44. Jones and Neal, *Black Fire*, 316.

45. Ibid., 127.

46. Spady, *Marcus Garvey*, 127.

47. James G. Spady, *Georgie Woods: I'm Only a Man!—The Life Story of a Mass Communicator* (Philadelphia, PA: Snack-Pac Book Division, 1992), Word section.

48. James G. Spady, "Eve's Holding It down for P-H-I-L-A Period: Rapping, Blacktalking, Allegory and Allusion Philly Style," *Philadelphia New Observer* (1999), 27–28.

49. Spady, "Tupac's Exile," 15.

50. Spady, "Living in America Where the Brother Got to Get Esoterica," 26.

51. James G. Spady, "Rap Lyrics Express Elements of Black Like," *Philadelphia New Observer* (1991), 18.

52. James G. Spady, "Black Youth Culture Impacts the World and Art," *Philadelphia New Observer* (1995), 20.

53. Spady, "Ima Put My Thing Down," 94.

54. Spady, Alim, and Meghelli, *Tha Global Cipha*, 8.

55. Ibid., 9.

56. Spady, "Ima Put My Thing Down," 93.

57. Ibid., 96.

58. Geneva Smitherman, *Talkin and Testifyin: The Language of Black America* (Detroit: Wayne State University Press, 1977), 52.

59. Spady, "Ima Put My Thing Down," 96.

60. Spady, "Living in America Where the Brother Got to Get Esoterica," 27.

61. Eure and Spady, *Nation Conscious Rap*, 406–7.

62. Spady, "Ima Put My Thing Down," 96.

63. Spady, Alim, and Meghelli, *Tha Global Cipha*, 28.

64. Eure and Spady, *Nation Conscious Rap*, 149.

65. Ibid., 408–9.

66. Spady, "Ima Put My Thing Down," 93.

67. Eure and Spady, *Nation Conscious Rap*, xi.

68. John Baugh, *Black Street Speech: Its History, Structure, and Survival* (Austin: University of Texas Press, 1983), 36.

69. Ronald C. Arnett, *Dialogic Confession: Bonhoeffer's Rhetoric of Responsibility* (Carbondale: Southern Illinois University Press, 2005), 84.

70. Eure and Spady, *Nation Conscious Rap*, vii.

71. Ibid., xxi.

72. Ibid., xxii.

73. Ibid., xvii.

74. Ibid., xxiii.

75. Ibid., xix.

76. Ibid.

77. Ibid., xiii.

78. Sandra Harding, "Strong Objectivity and Socially Situated Knowledge," in *The Feminist Reader*, eds. Alison Bailey and Cris Cuomo (New York: McGraw Hill, 2007), 741–56, 749.

79. Spady, Alim, and Meghelli, *Tha Global Cipha*, 29.

80. Eure and Spady, *Nation Conscious Rap*, 401.

81. Spady, Alim, and Meghelli, *Tha Global Cipha*, 26–27.

82. Spady, Dupree, and Lee, *Twisted Tales*, ii.

83. Spady, Alim, and Meghelli, *Tha Global Cipha*, 423.

84. Spady, Dupree, and Lee, *Twisted Tales*, 112.

85. Spady, "Eve's Holding It down for P-H-I-L-A Period," 22.

86. Spady, "Rap Lyrics Express Elements of Black Like," 18.

87. Spady, Alim, and Meghelli, *Tha Global Cipha*, 486.

88. Ibid.

89. Ibid., 487.

90. Ibid., 484.

91. Ibid., 483.

92. Ibid., 546.

93. Eure and Spady, *Nation Conscious Rap*, 148.

94. Ibid.

95. Angela Davis, *Blues Legacies and Black Feminism: Gertrude "MA" Rainey, Bessie Smith, and Billie Holiday* (New York: Random House, 1998), 41.

96. James G. Spady, "Black Jazz Daughter When She Is Singing: The Historical Blues Journey of a Sonia Sanchez (-X)," in *The Sonia Sanchez Literary Review*, Vol. 2, No. 1, 1–43, 15.

97. Chyann L. Oliver, "Whose Pussy Is This?," in *Home Girls Make Some Noise!: Hip Hop Feminism Anthology*, eds. Gwendolyn D. Pough, Elaine Richardson, Aisha Durham, and Rachel Raimist (Mira Loma, CA: Parker Publishing, 2007), 167–69, 167.

98. Eure and Spady, *Nation Conscious Rap*, 401.

99. Ngũgĩ wa Thiong'o, *Moving the Centre: The Struggle for Cultural Freedoms* (Portsmouth, New Hampshire: Heinemann Educational Books, Inc., 1993), 96.

100. Spady, "Surrealism and the Marvelous Black Plunge in Search of Yemanga and the Human Condition," 93.

Index

About the Author

George Yancy is the Samuel Candler Dobbs Professor of Philosophy at Emory University and a Montgomery Fellow at Dartmouth College. He is also the University of Pennsylvania's inaugural fellow in the Provost's Distinguished Faculty Fellowship Program (spring semester of 2020 academic year). He received his BA in philosophy from the University of Pittsburgh (with honors). His first MA in philosophy is from Yale University, and he obtained his second MA from New York University in Africana Studies, where he received the distinguished Henry M. MacCracken Fellowship. He received his PhD from Duquesne University (with distinction) and was the first graduate student to receive the McAnulty Fellowship in the Department of Philosophy. He is also the first Black professor of philosophy to receive tenure at Duquesne University. He is the author, editor, and co-editor of over twenty books, numerous scholarly articles and chapters ranging from issues within critical philosophy of race, critical whiteness studies, critical phenomenology, and philosophy of the Black experience. Three of his books were named *CHOICE* Outstanding Academic Titles. His book *Black Bodies, White Gazes* received an Honorable Mention from the Gustavus Myers Center for the Study of Bigotry and Human Rights. His co-edited book *Our Black Sons Matter* was listed by *Booklist* as a Top Ten Diverse Nonfiction Book. Yancy is well known for his influential essays and interviews in *The New York Times* philosophy Column, "The Stone." He has twice won the American Philosophical Committee on Public Philosophy's Op-Ed Contest. Yancy's five most recent books are the second (and expanded) edition of his authored book *Black Bodies, White Gazes* (Rowman & Littlefield, 2017) and *On Race: 34 Conversations in a Time of Crisis* (Oxford University Press, 2017); his authored book *Backlash: What Happens When We Talk Honestly* *about Racism in America* (Rowman & Littlefield, 2018); his edited book *Educating for Critical Consciousness* (Routledge, 2019); and his coedited book *Buddhism and Whiteness: Critical Reflections* (Lexington Books, 2019). Yancy is Philosophy of Race book series editor at Lexington Books.